269

To

Robert W. Greaves

in appreciation

of many kindnesses

from

William H. McLoughlin Jr.

October, 1965

Billy Sunday
Was His Real Name

Billy Sunday
Was His Real Name

By

William G. McLoughlin, Jr.

THE UNIVERSITY OF CHICAGO PRESS

Sunday, William Ashley

Library of Congress Catalog Number: 55-5138

THE UNIVERSITY OF CHICAGO PRESS, CHICAGO 37
Cambridge University Press, London, N.W. 1, England
The University of Toronto Press, Toronto 5, Canada

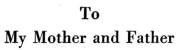

To
My Mother and Father

PREFACE

This book is about Billy Sunday, but it is also about the revival tradition in which he worked and the era in which he lived. It is necessary at the outset to distinguish between these three elements—the man, the tradition, and the temper of the times—in order to give each its proper weight and position in the picture. Billy Sunday's revivals were not simply the sensational machinations of an itinerant evangelist who, by studied manipulation of mob psychology, was able to induce waves of mass hysteria whenever he preached. If this had been so, Sunday would have been uniformly successful throughout his forty-year career, instead of reaching a peak of success in the years 1908–18 which he never again equaled. Furthermore, such an explanation of revivalism fails to account for the fact that religious movements of such broad scope as Sunday's do not occur more than once in every forty or fifty years. There are always skilful evangelists, but there are not always crowds ready to hear and to be moved by them.

The view that all revivals are merely outbreaks of mob hysteria or mass hypnotism, like the corollary view that all conversions are psychological readjustments by immature or neurotic individuals, is useful only within narrow limits. This view belies the complexity of human life and of the manifold cultural forces which provide the context in which revivals flourish. It is true that during the nineteenth century every small town in the nation had annual revivals in which some itinerant evangelist tried to arouse the churchgoers and to convert their adolescent children by his fervent preaching, and it is also true that Billy Sunday's revivals had their roots in these modifications of the frontier camp meetings; nevertheless, his work cannot be dismissed merely as large-scale imitations of them. To say that the human mechanism, under certain given conditions, will react in a highly emotional and irrational way or to point out that any clever orator may temporarily arouse a fairly homogeneous crowd to a high pitch of excitement obscures the more fundamental questions about revivalism. It does not explain why, at certain periods throughout history, whole nations have been caught up in spontaneous waves of religious enthusiasm.

vii

Another misleading attitude toward revivalism, and one which tends to play down the difference between traditional local revivals in small American towns and more extensive eruptions of religious excitement, is the view taken by those historians of religion who lump together such widely different movements as the Crusades, the Reformation, the rise of Puritanism, and a host of other historical events on the assumption that all of them were supernatural in origin and were sustained throughout simply by the inspired spiritual fervor of their participants. To these historians the hand of providence is perceptible in all revivals, great or small, and hence they argue that there is no difference between them except as to degree. They maintain that it is possible for any small-scale revival, even in one church or one prayer meeting, to start a spark that will "spread like a prairie fire" across a nation or the world. Certain learned theologians have given support to this view by declaring that the inner spiritual meaning of every religious movement is the eternal conflict between the powers of good and the powers of evil for dominion over the souls of men and that all conversions, whether individual or en masse, are part of the same perpetual attempt at *rapprochement* between natural, sinful man and his divine Creator. Like the oversimplified psychological or sociological explanations of revivalism, this approach ignores the historical context which makes every widespread religious awakening a unique reaction to unique events.

And, finally, there is the confusion that arises from sheer lack of adequate historical information about revivalism. For the most part, the scholarly secular historian has, until very recently, grossly neglected this aspect of American history. Those who have touched upon it either have generally presented revivals as curious bits of social history or else have treated them solely in terms of abstract reinterpretations of Calvinism, Arminianism, theistic evolutionism, or neo-orthodoxy. The vital interrelations between the tangibles and the intangibles of history are minimized. Apart from theology, religion is considered of importance to most historians only in so far as its influence can be measured in terms of the legislation regarding the separation of church and state or the institutional activities of missions and welfare work or the comparative statistical growth of various denominations.

It is the purpose of this book to show that Billy Sunday's career, considered as a whole, represents a significant religious movement in America which cannot be measured in terms either of mob psychology or of declension and growth in church membership. Furthermore, this book tries to demonstrate that this religious movement was essentially different from the other major revival movements in our history because it represented an emotional upheaval growing out of special circumstances peculiar to Sunday's day and age. This is not to ignore the debt that Sunday owed to the evangelical tradition and to his predecessors in itinerant evangelism, but it is to place his revivalism in the wider context of an era. It is not, in other words, to see his work solely in terms of the institutional structure of American Protestantism but to see it in terms of a critical reorientation in the ideological structure of American life.

Superficially, the difference between this awakening and its predecessors might seem to lie in the character or personality of Sunday himself. But this is to assume that he made the movement in his image rather than vice versa. To understand Billy Sunday, it is necessary to understand something of the multifarious aspects of American social, political, economic, and intellectual history. Or, conversely—and this is the real starting point from which the book evolved—to understand Sunday's revivalism is to understand better the era in which he lived.

WILLIAM G. McLOUGHLIN, JR.

PROVIDENCE, RHODE ISLAND
March 19, 1955

ACKNOWLEDGMENTS

I would like to give my special thanks to Mrs. Helen A. Sunday, whose permission to study and to quote from the sermons and other materials connected with her husband's career and whose kindness in answering my many questions made this book possible. I would also like to express my thanks to all the friends and acquaintances of Billy Sunday who through personal interviews or letters have greatly enriched my knowledge of his character and career.

Harvard University granted a generous traveling fellowship to help me in collecting materials in towns and cities throughout the nation, and a host of competent and co-operative librarians rendered my task immeasurably simpler. Howard Mumford Jones and Sidney E. Mead read my manuscript and offered helpful suggestions which I have used, I hope, to good advantage. I owe a particularly large debt to Oscar Handlin, whose sympathy, friendship, and wisdom have been unfailing sources of guidance and inspiration from the inception of this book to its completion.

My parents have played a direct as well as an indirect role in the production of this book by their considerable help in reading, proofreading, and commenting on it. My wife, Virginia Ward McLoughlin, has, throughout, shared the burdens of preparing and editing the manuscript and has provided enlightening criticism, unfailing patience, and heartening encouragement when they were needed most.

TABLE OF CONTENTS

LIST OF ILLUSTRATIONS

Prologue

At five o'clock on Saturday afternoon, April 7, 1917, the day after
the United States had declared war on the Kaiser's Germany, a
crowd of three thousand enthusiastic New Yorkers jammed Pennsylvania Station to welcome Billy Sunday, the famous "baseball
evangelist," to New York City for a ten-week religious revival. He
had been invited by 399 ministers and twice that number of laymen, who had been preparing for his arrival for more than a year.
At the corner of Broadway and 168th Street a sprawling wooden
tabernacle had been built—the "largest structure for public meetings ever erected in New York." It could comfortably seat 16,000,
with standing room for 4,000 more, and it had cost over $65,000. A
week earlier, on April 1, this tabernacle had been filled for an impressive dedication ceremony in which the governor of the state
and dozens of other leading citizens had taken part.

For Billy Sunday the storming of New York, the modern Babylon,
the capital of Satan, was the apex of a career in evangelism that
began in 1896 and ended only with his death in 1935. The one-
hundred-and-fifty-odd revivals that he had conducted prior to 1917
were merely a preparation for this. From the first day of his first
campaign in a little whistle-stop town in Iowa, his great purpose had
been to lead the assault against the wicked cities which were, in
his words, "polluting the countryside around them" and endanger-
ing the whole spiritual and cultural fiber of America.

For twenty years Sunday had thrown every ounce of his tremendous energy and oratorical talent into the effort to perfect himself
in his calling. By 1917 he was considered by many the greatest
revivalist in American history, perhaps the greatest since the days of
the apostles. And now he was staking his fame and his genius on
the attempt to reform the city known as "the graveyard of evangelists." Billy Sunday has crossed his Rubicon, said one national
magazine of his decision to come to New York.

The crowd broke into a cheer of welcome as the dapper Mr. Sunday, his wife, and two of his sons appeared at the door of the station waiting-room. The band struck up "Brighten the Corner," and the crowd took up the song. Sunday beamed, said something to his wife, waved his hand to the throng, and began shaking hands with the members of his campaign committee, who rushed forward to greet him. A cordon of policemen made a path through the crowd as Sunday was led to a waiting sedan. He paused briefly on the sidewalk to pose for a dozen photographers, then stepped into the car, and was driven off with a police escort in front and a cavalcade of fourteen automobiles trailing behind.

The motor procession sped northward to a twenty-two-room red-brick house on the corner of 182d Street and Northern Avenue, which was to be Sunday's home for the next ten weeks. His oldest son, George, who had been in New York for six months as business manager for the Sunday team, had arranged an informal reception for his father, and on his arrival Sunday found the press and the members of the Billy Sunday Evangelistic Committee of New York waiting for him. Among the local committee members was John D. Rockefeller, Jr., who had gone to the station to meet Sunday but had missed him in the crowd. Catching sight of him at the reception, Sunday bounded over, calling, "Hello, old chap!" and threw an arm around his shoulder.

The members of the New York press, many of whom had reported Sunday's sensational revivals in Philadelphia and Paterson, noted that he was as "nervously active as usual and seemed to be full of eagerness and enthusiasm" for the job ahead. Despite his fifty-five years, he looked as healthy, slim, and bouncy as a twenty-year-old. The tension and energy packed into his slim five feet eight inches made him seem bigger than he was. He wore an immaculately tailored conservative single-breasted gray business suit with a sharp crease in the trousers and had a dazzling shine on his black patent leather shoes.

Sunday would make no statement on the prospects of the campaign; but, when asked whether he planned to help in the war effort, he said, "Help the government? Yes, sir! Anything I can do to help the government in any way I am going to do. No doubt about that." The reception soon broke up, and, after a brief conference with his staff, Sunday and his family ate the supper prepared by Mrs. Rose M. Foutts, the special housekeeper who accompanied him in every campaign. Then the evangelist retired to his room to study his sermon notes. After repeating to himself the two sermons he was to give the next day, he prayed aloud to the Lord for help and victory and went to bed.

The tabernacle was packed to capacity long before 2:00 P.M. the next afternoon. Sunday's choir leader and master of ceremonies, Homer A. Rodeheaver, led the crowd in singing "Come Thou Almighty King." Rodeheaver was described by the New York Times as "a fat, dark man in a frock coat" but "one of the most expert masters of crowd psychology in the country." He played his trombone, sang a solo, told a few funny stories, and directed the massive two-thousand-voice choir in "Onward, Christian Soldiers," while his assistants, George A. Brewster and Robert Matthews, accompanied by "thumping on two grand pianos with the fury and noise of steam hammers pounding rivets."

A cheer went up in the middle of the hymn, as the crowd caught sight of Sunday slipping into his seat at the rear of the platform. The collection was taken, a few preliminary announcements and introductions were made, and then Sunday walked to the center of the stage under the huge sounding board which was his only aid for addressing the vast throng of twenty thousand. He grasped the edges of the pulpit with both hands and smiled his "wistful, boyish, good-humored smile" as he waited for the applause to die down.

"I notice," he began casually, "you're the same warm-hearted, enthusiastic bunch you used to be when you sat in the grandstand and bleachers when I played at the old Polo Grounds. It didn't matter if a fellow was on the other side or not. If he made a good play he got the glad hand rather than the marble heart." They applauded again. He could see that the crowd was neither hostile nor cold. Without further comment he launched into the sermon which opened every campaign: "Have Ye Received the Holy Spirit?" "Paul, that stoop-shouldered, dim-eyed, wrinkle-browed, white-haired gospel veteran, was full of the Holy Spirit. He was on the firing line for years, and never dipped his colors. . . . But an angel from heaven couldn't come down to New York and stay here two weeks and trim with the crowd some of you trim with, that call them[selves] good, and go back to heaven without a bath of lysol, carbolic, and formaldehyde. . . . Now I don't believe in the universal Fatherhood of God and the universal brotherhood of man. You're a *creature* of God. So is a hog eating slop out of a trough. You've got to be a *child* of God." And only conversion by the Holy Spirit can make men children of God.

"Joshua was full of the Holy Spirit. Joshua said, 'Lord, it's taking me longer than I figured out to clean up on this gang, if you'll keep the sun in the skies, I can whip the bunch to a frazzle, and I'll send your name ringing down through the ages.' And God reached up there and grabbed the sun and said: 'Stay there; don't move till my servant, Joshua, gives you the highball!' "

Sunday threw his whole body into action while he spoke. As the *Times* reporter said, "He raced up and down the green-carpeted platform . . . waving his hands, kicking up one knee now and again, like a park-walking horse, brandishing a chair, standing with one foot on the chair and another on the pulpit, bending over backwards like a springy sword blade, bobbing back and forth and waving a handkerchief between his legs as he reeled off one of his amazing long lists of vituperative epithets and displaying as much energy, determination, and virtuous enthusiasm as Douglas Fairbanks."

The crowd watched every move, ready to laugh, cheer, or applaud at the slightest sign of a pause in the torrential rush of his oratory. They particularly enjoyed his attack on the "damnable, hellish, vile, corrupt, iniquitous liquor business," which he delivered standing with one foot on a chair and one on the pulpit: "This God-forsaken whisky gang is the worst this side of hell. They offered money to the editor of one of the biggest papers in New York to print their dirty lies about me, and he told them to go to hell. He's a church member, too." The church members in the audience cheered. "They've raised, I understand, $500,000 to get me. I say to them, 'Come on, you God-forsaken, weasel-eyed, white-livered, black-hearted, gang of thugs. Come on. I defy you.' I've put them out of two hundred million dollars worth of business. I ask no quarter and I give none." He leaned forward and dropped his voice to a venomous, defiant whisper: "None. Absolutely none. None whatever. None."

When Sunday ended his sermon, the cheering spectators burst into the "Battle Hymn of the Republic." There was no doubt that Sunday had won the first round in his battle. But the most telling stroke in this opening sermon was a digression, an interpolation concerning the money people said he was going to make out of this campaign. It was rumored that the voluntary contributions which were to be collected from the audiences at the conclusion of this revival in order to recompense the evangelist would probably reach a total of $100,000. He had received over $53,000 for ten weeks' work in Philadelphia and more than that in Boston; as New York was more than twice as large as either of these, it was expected to give him twice as much.

Sunday consequently caused a sensation in the midst of this first sermon when he stopped to remark that he had often been called "a grafter" for the money he made but that the entire amount of the offering to be given him at the end of this campagin was going to be donated by him to the Red Cross and to the war work of the YMCA. The applause and cheers were deafening.

But it was the evening sermon, rather than the afternoon one, which was the real start of the campaign. It was for the evening crowd that Sunday saved his big guns, and it was this sermon which gained him the headlines in the papers on Monday morning. As in the afternoon, he began casually: "From what I heard, I thought that New York would be cold and critical, that they kind of look at you out of the corner of the eye. I've been preaching for twenty years, and I never saw a town with so much vim, ginger, tabasco, and pepperino as little old New York." And, as in the afternoon, the crowd applauded for itself. Then he lashed out at Germany in a sermon called "God's Grenadiers" which he had rewritten specially for this occasion.

"The German people have been blindly led," he said. "They have had the doctrine that might makes right and that the end justifies the means inoculated into them for generations. It was the salvation of the German people that led us to enter into this great conflict. What we want is to see them set free from militarism that has enslaved them for generations. . . .

"Ghastly, hideous, infernal Prussian militarism, stand up and look at the women and children you have murdered as they climb up the coral reefs from the haven of lost ships, weeping, holding out their hands toward the Stars and Stripes crying, 'Help, help! Help us!'

"Look at the millions of poor, tortured Belgium as she turns her weeping eyes over three thousand miles of ocean, her bleeding hands outstretched toward the Stars and Stripes for help.

"Look at the millions of poor, tortured, outraged, murdered women and children of Armenia with their hands outstretched toward the Stars and Stripes crying for help.

"If it were not for the brave men under the flag of Italy, under the tricolor of France, under the Union Jack of Great Britain, the Germans would be pounding at our doors. If it were not for the British fleet under Admiral Jellicoe and Admiral Beatty, New York would now be a heap of ruins and you'd be paying the price. Now German militarism is doomed and the guns of the United States will help dig its grave. We will destroy it or it will destroy the world."

Sunday concluded, "Our flag has never been unfurled for conquest, and we're not unfurling it for conquest now. We don't want an acre of German land or a cent of German money. We're unfurling the flag for the liberty of the world!"

As the headlines pointed out the next day, this sermon was a medley of "war and religion mixed" in equal proportions. At the conclusion of it, Sunday was standing on top of his pulpit waving an enormous American flag as the crowd again broke out into the "Battle Hymn of the Republic" and sang "America" for good measure. His greatest campaign was off to a successful start.

Monday was Sunday's day of rest. But, although he gave no sermons at the tabernacle on Mondays, he was never inactive. This first Monday he had lunch at the home of John D. Rockefeller, Jr. The other guests included Major General Leonard Wood and Colonel Theodore Roosevelt. None of them would tell the reporters who waited outside the door what had been said at the meeting, but from some of Sunday's remarks later in the day it was apparent that the philanthropist, the general, and the former President were worried about the small number of voluntary enlistments which had occurred since war had been declared. Later that day Sunday said that only seventy men had been recruited in New York in the preceding twenty-four hours: "At that rate the Emperor William could have whiskers down to his knees and the war would be over before they had 100,000." If there had not already been a recruiting station at the Armory across the street from the tabernacle, it is certain that Sunday would have had one installed there.

That Sunday intended to do something about enlistment at his meetings was evident, but only his quick wit saved him from an embarrassing situation later in the campaign, when he called to his audience from the platform, "How many of you registered today? Stand up." Only one or two persons stood up, and Sunday seemed to be impugning the crowd's patriotism. But, before the chill could settle, he quickly added, "How many would like to have registered but couldn't? Stand up." And virtually the entire audience jumped to its feet.

After dining with Rockefeller and Roosevelt, Sunday met with the ministers representing the numerous churches co-operating in the campaign. He introduced his staff of twenty experts and explained, "We expect you to help us just as we shall help you. I want you to lay aside your preconceived notions as to how this work ought to be done. . . . All the suggestions we have to offer about the conduct of an evangelistic campaign have been forged on the anvil of experience." He then announced that 6,313 homes in New York were currently holding prayer meetings for the campaign and that 79,717 persons had so far attended such cottage prayer meetings. Other statistics showed that approximately 50,000 persons were actively working in the revival in one capacity or another—6,000 were in the three choirs which sang on alternate nights at the tabernacle.

The opening night of the revival crowned a year of preparation and was therefore something of a climax, but the meetings which followed were no less successful. Twice every day Billy Sunday spoke to the crowds in the tabernacle, and the sermons of the first two weeks of the campaign were among the most colorful, vitriolic, and explosive in his repertoire. Reporters never lacked a headline or a lead paragraph, whether the sermon attacked the somnolent churches, the sinful citizenry, the demon rum, or any one of a dozen other evils which Sunday so magniloquently exposed to his blistering attacks.

Sunday became so prominent a figure in New York that headlines were given even to those who attacked him. And the attacks were numerous. Rabbi Stephen S. Wise twice filled Carnegie Hall before Sunday's arrival, for meetings in which he denounced him as a symbol of the intellectually moribund and theologically standpat position of the Christian churches. Wise said that during one campaign in Pennsylvania Sunday's supporters actually drove a young rabbi out of town for criticizing the evangelist, and he described with horror Sunday's reference to the current tension between the United States and Mexico: "God tells America to wipe Mexico off the face of the earth." The well-known Unitarian John Haynes Holmes, the Baptist leader John Herman Randall, the Episcopalian K. S. Guthrie, all denounced Sunday from their New York pulpits during the revival, calling him a preacher of antiquated theology and of "department store religion." And a Jesuit priest wrote in *The Catholic Mind* on the eve of the revival that Sunday was a blasphemous heretic whom it would be sinful for Roman Catholics to hear.

Labor unions attacked the revival committee for not employing union labor at the tabernacle cafeteria. The managing director of the Labor Forum stated that Sunday's willingness to collaborate with robber barons like John D. Rockefeller, Jr., nullified any good his preaching might do. The outspoken Socialist Jacob Alsofrom threatened to lead an invasion of 1,500 workingmen to the tabernacle one afternoon, carrying signs asking, "Is it moral to be rich?" because Sunday had borne false witness against the Socialists. The policemen on duty at the tabernacle were constantly driving away cranks who peddled "exposés" of Sunday's methods. Even two such clashing personalities as the Princess Troubetzkoy and Isadora Duncan, the exotic exponent of modern dancing, were agreed in their dislike for Sunday. The princess declared his preaching blasphemous sacrilege, and the dancer denounced him for proclaiming that Aeschylus and Walt Whitman were roasting in hell for their pernicious writings.

But Sunday's defenders in New York were more numerous, more prominent, and just as varied. Praise came from Warren S. Stone, Lyman Abbott, Elbert H. Gary, Ambassador James W. Gerard, and Cardinal Gibbons, not to mention such pillars among his campaign supporters as George W. Perkins, Henry W. Jessup, Bishop Luther B. Wilson, and James M. Speers. The names of his New York committee read like a page out of the social register or from the list of the two hundred families controlling the American economy. Sunday could well afford to ignore critics whose carping sounded so much like sour grapes; their attacks merely served to keep the revival in the news.

More than any other factor serving to keep Sunday's name before the public was the breathless anticipation of his first call for converts. Unlike other successful evangelists who preceded him, Sunday did not try for conversions on the opening night of his revival or on any night for the first ten days or two weeks. He kept the public, the reporters, and even his own staff in the dark as to exactly when the first call would come. Here was the acid test of his preaching: Would it produce conversions? Would it change sinners into saints? Would it make sophisticated New Yorkers come to the altar and give their souls to Christ?

The night Sunday chose was April 19, the twelfth day of the campaign. He gave no hint or warning. His sermon described the revival which Elijah had produced in Israel: "He repaired the altars of the Lord that were broken down," was the text. Like all his sermons, it was highly dramatic, and toward the end of it he mounted a chair on the platform and shouted: "Do you want God's blessing on you, your home, your church, your nation, on New York? If you do, raise your hands." A "forest of hands" went up, and cries of "Yes!" "Yes!" were heard throughout the building. "How many of you men and women will jump to your feet and come down and say, 'Bill, here's my hand for God, for home, for my native land, to live and conquer for Christ?'" He paused for half a second; then, "Come on!" he shouted; "Come on; come on!"

Rodeheaver knew his cue; he signaled to the choir, and it burst into "Onward, Christian Soldiers." Men and women began to crowd down the aisles of the tabernacle toward the pulpit. As they reached the platform, carefully trained ushers directed them into two lines past the point where Sunday leaned forward to shake the upstretched hand of each individual. "Thank you," "God bless you," "Thank you," he murmured as they gripped his hand and passed on.

The ministers and dignitaries at the back of the platform left their seats and excitedly moved forward to watch the astounding spectacle. As far up the long aisles as they could see, solid lines of men and women moved steadily and quietly forward. The choir changed from "Onward, Christian Soldiers" to the more plaintive, "Just as I Am, without One Plea." The local committee members looked at one another in amazement, in wonder, and in unspeakable happiness. This exceeded their fondest hopes. They turned toward Sunday and watched him with fascination as he bent forward over the edge of the platform, absorbed in his work, looking each convert in the eye, giving each a warm handclasp, a word of encouragement, and showing by his earnest concentration the seriousness with which he performed this aspect of his calling.

The reporters tried desperately to keep track of the number of people who pressed forward but had to give it up; they came too fast to be counted. Five minutes, ten minutes, fifteen minutes passed, and still they came. Some were in tears, some smiling, some serious. The choir continued to sing, repeating the verses over and over. Slowly the lines thinned out; a few last stragglers walked down. Sunday straightened up. The first call for converts was over. The estimate, the closest any reporter could make, was that over 2,000 persons had "hit the trail"—one person out of every ten in that audience of 20,000. It was unbelievable, a miracle, gasped the awe-stricken clergy.

Sunday delivered a brief prayer to the converts assembled before the platform and closed the meeting. Carefully trained religious workers stayed to talk with the newly regenerated and to take their names and addresses for future follow-up. From that night forward

Sunday called for converts at every meeting, and the newspapers began to print a daily box score of the totals: 1,814 in the afternoon; 1,792 in the evening; total to date, 5,623. Day after day the total mounted by more than 2,000 at a time. On Sundays there were three sermons, and the figures jumped most rapidly over the week ends.

Statistics were also kept on the attendance record and on the more crucial matter of the collections taken to defray the $200,000 spent for the campaign. Some of this had been raised in advance, but the daily tabernacle collections were expected to raise the major part of it. It was Sunday's boast that his campaigns were entirely self-supporting, that they paid for themselves and no debts were ever left behind. Still, no campaign had ever been as expensive as this, and many doubted whether Sunday could live up to his boast.

The excitement of this daily tabulation was not the only thing that kept public attention on the revival. Sunday was constantly making headlines by pungent references to contemporary events or personalities and by engaging in activities outside the tabernacle which were news in themselves. He delivered special talks at the homes of John D. Rockefeller, Jr., George W. Perkins, and Stephen Baker; he spoke at the annual fund-raising drive for the New York newsboys; he addressed the prisoners in the Tombs; he spoke at a "Wake Up, America" rally with Will Rogers; he helped Daniel Frohman raise money for the actors' relief fund; he prayed for the salvation of Wall Street; he attacked the "slackers" and draft-dodgers; he demanded that Congress send Theodore Roosevelt to France at the head of an army of volunteers; and he denounced the government for censoring the press. He commended the jailing of those who criticized Wilson; he taught the children at a special Saturday-afternoon meeting at the tabernacle to hiss the German flag; he turned down an offer of $200,000 to make a movie; he praised the leaders of the Russian revolution and the Provisional Government; and he delivered a special group of highly controversial sermons to men only and to women only. He even offered the government a slogan to launch a drive to sell one-dollar war bonds: "A Bond for a Bone."

Two items of publicity came to Sunday without asking. One was an invitation from Theodore Roosevelt to spend a day at Sagamore Hill, Oyster Bay. The other was Mrs. Sunday's sudden attack of appendicitis, for which she was operated on by Dr. Howard A. Kelly of Johns Hopkins, the most famous surgeon in America and a personal friend of the Sundays.

During the ten weeks Sunday was in New York, America's part in the war was so small that the newspapers were never forced to put him out of sight. He remained news, often front-page news in the tabloids, from the first day to the last. And the last day was, if anything, an even greater triumph than the first.

The campaign closed on Sunday, June 17, after seventy-one days. On that day the tabernacle was filled for the 7:30 meeting by 6:00 P.M. Sunday appeared on the platform at 6:45, wearing a white suit, a white shirt, white shoes, and a white belt. He took off his coat at once and invited the men in the audience to take off theirs. He looked tired and worn, and his voice seemed too hoarse to be heard beyond the third row; but as he began his sermon, he appeared to be galvanized from within. His voice returned, and his body was as lithe and active as it had been on the first day.

The sermon was called, "And He Said, 'Tomorrow' ": " 'Now' means victory in heaven; 'tomorrow' means defeat in hell. The whole world can be divided into two classes; those who do it now, and those who are going to do it tomorrow. But Time has been chasing tomorrow since the beginning of time, and never has overtaken it. So what chance have you got?" He concluded with a prayer and a farewell: "And now I must say my goodbye. . . . I hope, New Yorkers, that we'll all go tramping together up the hill toward Zion when Gabriel blows his trumpet. Goodbye newspaper boys and girls. You've been great. Goodbye preachers; if I've said anything that hurt your feelings, well, maybe you deserved it. Goodbye choir, you've been wonderful. . . . Goodbye everybody. And now, come and give me your hand—for the last time. Do it now, for there won't be any tomorrow."

There was a rush for the platform, and for a moment it looked as though the whole audience was coming forward. The aisles were choked with a steady throng as Sunday continued for a full half-hour to shake hands. This time an official count was made, and the total exceeded all previous records, even that of the Day of Pentecost. With this last sermon in New York, Billy Sunday converted 3,326 persons. The total for the last day was 7,238 for the three meetings.

With tears in his eyes, Sunday stood on the New York tabernacle platform for the last time. Every man, woman, and child in the audience was waving a handkerchief and shouting "Goodbye" and "God bless you." Surrounded by his staff and committee members, Sunday stretched his arms out over the crowd. "I don't want to go. I don't want to go," he said, shaking his head slowly. The crowd became silent for a moment to hear his last words. Choking with emotion, he could only manage to call, "Goodbye, New York!" and he swung out his arms in a gesture of thanks and farewell.

The next morning at eleven Sunday and his family caught a train to take them home to Winona Lake, Indiana. The station was even more crowded than at his arrival. The crowd cheered and shouted and sang hymns. Sunday looked utterly worn out but happy. He had a three-month vacation before him, most of which he would spend at his ranch in Hood River, Oregon, prior to starting out on next season's revival campaigns already scheduled in Los Angeles, Atlanta, Washington, D.C., Chicago, and Duluth.

As Sunday's train pulled out of the station, New Yorkers were reading in their morning papers the final statistical report on his greatest campaign. The collection for expenses had ceased on June 6, and the committee declared that all expenses had been met. During the final week thousands of dollars rolled in as Sunday's gift to the Red Cross and the YMCA. The total figure reached $120,490, of which the Red Cross and the YMCA each received $32,382; the YWCA (by special arrangement), $55,300; $426 was set aside for a load of baseball uniforms for the Army and the Navy. The attendance figures were impressive: the grand total, including the Sunday-morning meetings, was 1,443,000. The conversion total showed that 98,264 persons had come forward to answer Sunday's invitation over the ten-week period.

In a special interview on the day of Sunday's departure, John D. Rockefeller, Jr., declared, "Billy Sunday's campaign in New York City has been tremendously successful—exceeding the most enthusiastic expectations of those who invited him here. . . . So far as the awakening of the city to religious things is concerned, the campaign is scarcely beginning. Think of the vast number of men and women who have been led by Billy to take an interest in cleaner living. . . . I am very glad that I had a part in bringing this great religious force to New York." Governor Charles S. Whitman sent Sunday a telegram before he left the city: "The people of New York City and State recognize and appreciate this great service you have rendered." There seemed little doubt in the minds of those who had worked in the revival that Billy Sunday had made good. Now it was up to the local ministers to make the most of the opportunity he had created for them.

But there were those who were skeptical of the whole affair. To a nation that believed in statistics Sunday's achievements were impressive, but to a nation that was becoming slightly cynical about success stories there was something superficial about the newspaper reports of Sunday's meetings. Whether Sunday was as great as his statistical record implied depended largely on the story behind the headlines.

The answers to the questions raised by Billy Sunday's revivals were not simple. His career could not be dismissed with a laugh or a sneer, yet there was need for a closer examination of the framework of big-city revivalism. The twentieth century was not so willing as the nineteenth century to explain such events in terms of the outpouring of the Holy Spirit. But Americans still had a lot to learn about religious revivals. In spite of the tremendous publicity given to Sunday, in spite of his two authorized biographies—one of which had sold 350,000 copies by 1917—the public had never been given a real glimpse behind the scenes. Sunday himself was largely a myth —a myth created partly by blind admiration, partly out of spiteful malice, and partly out of sheer ignorance of the man and his methods. Almost everyone saw Sunday in terms of religious revivalism; few saw the deeper significance of his career as the product and expression of the era in which he lived.

1

"A RUBE OF THE RUBES"

Billy Sunday was his real name. He was born on November 19, 1862. His father, William Sunday, was the son of German immigrants whose name had been Sonntag in the old country but became Americanized, as they themselves had, in Chambersburg, Pennsylvania, in the early part of the nineteenth century.[1]

No one knows why William Sunday wanted his son christened William Ashley. He made the request to his wife in one of the last letters she received from him. At the time, he was a private in the Union Army; he died of pneumonia on December 23, 1862, without ever having seen the son who was to make his name a household word in America. The widowed mother and her three children were in desperate straits. Her husband had left his little farm near Ames, Iowa, to enlist on August 14, 1862. Whether it was patriotism or his lack of ability as a farmer that prompted him to go is not clear, but the three boys, Albert (age four), Edward (age two), and Willie, would have been a heavy burden for the young mother even had her husband lived to complete his three-year enlistment.

With the help of a government pension and assistance from her parents (named Corey) who lived near by, the widow struggled on alone for six years and then married a man named Heizer. Two more children were born, and then, in 1874, at the height of a disastrous depression, Heizer disappeared and was never heard from again. The harassed woman and her five children had no choice but to fall back upon her parents completely. She left the two-room cabin of roughly hewn logs in which Willie had been born and moved into the more spacious home of the Coreys.

Martin Corey, known in the vicinity of Story County, Iowa, as "Squire" Corey, had come to Iowa in 1848, two years after it achieved statehood. His father fought in the American Revolution, as had the father of his wife, whom he had met and married in Kosciusko County, Indiana. Squire Corey, a second cousin and boyhood playmate of Ulysses S. Grant, was a man of some importance in

1

Ames, Iowa. As one of the early settlers, he had helped to found the Iowa Agricultural College, now Iowa State College, and had given part of his land for it. On the remaining land he built a sawmill, a grainmill, and a sugar-cane mill. In later years Sunday spoke of his grandfather as "the most versatile man I have ever known!" Despite frequent tiffs with the old man, Sunday admired and loved him. He, and not Heizer, took the place of the boy's father.

Like all frontier farmers, Squire Corey was a Jack-of-all-trades. "He made wagons, the wheels and all parts of them," said Sunday. "He could build houses and lay stone walls. He made a turning lathe and made bedposts, spindles for banisters, made bureaus, water wheels, and many other things. He had a blacksmith shop and made horseshoes and wedges with which to split wood. He could dress a millstone on which to grind corn and wheat. . . . He made a loom upon which grandmother spun and made cloth."

It had probably been a blow to the Squire when his daughter married William Sunday, a ne'er-do-well bricklayer from Pennsylvania, but he stood ready to help her when she needed him. His grandchildren led the usual rough, laborious life of an Iowa farm. Sunday's brief "Autobiography," written in 1933 for the *Ladies' Home Journal,* told of his milking ten cows "night and morning," making sorghum molasses at midnight in a steaming sugar-mill, plowing, reaping, and binding day after day in the hot Iowa wheat- and cornfields. His schooling, what there was of it, came during the winter months and was more laborious to the young plowboy than the farm chores. "I was a dunce in arithmetic and grammar was not my long-suit either," he wrote. "At the end of the term of school it was customary for the teachers to give us little cards with a hand in one corner holding a scroll and in that scroll was a place to write the name 'Willie Sunday, good boy.' Willie Sunday never got hump-backed lugging them home, I can tell you."

Sunday's heritage as a country boy, which in his early years as a preacher he tried to overcome, later was flaunted as a prime attribute. He came to see himself as a young Lochinvar from the West and proudly boasted of his association with the common people. "I am a rube of the rubes," he told his audiences. "I am a graduate of the University of Poverty. I have blacked my boots with stove-blacking, greased my hair with goose grease. I never knew what an undergarment or a nightdress was until I was eighteen years old. I have dried my face and wiped my proboscis on a flour sack towel. I

2

have helped grub stumps that stood in the way of the plowshare of advancing civilization."[2]

As an infant Sunday was delicate and sickly. His mother carried him around on a pillow until he was two, and at the age of three he could scarcely walk. Then one day an itinerant "doctor" prescribed a syrup made of mulberry and elderberry leaves and various other herbs and roots. The homemade remedy cured the ailing child completely, and Sunday always claimed that nature had made an herb or plant to cure every human ill if only man were intelligent enough to find and utilize it.

When his mother married Heizer, young Willie, who did not get along with his stepfather, moved into his grandfather's house. He developed a strong attachment for his grandmother Corey, and when she died, he stole out to the newly filled grave and lay on it weeping through most of a wintry night, until his grandfather found him and carried him home. In 1874 Willie Sunday and his brother Edward were sent to the Soldiers' Orphan Home at Glenwood (later at Davenport), Iowa—some reports say it was at the demand of Heizer, and some say it was the result of the financial hardship following Heizer's disappearance. Two other tragedies had preceded this: Albert Sunday was kicked in the head by a horse and had to be sent to a home for the feeble-minded, where he remained until his death in 1893, and Elizabeth (Libbie) Heizer, Sunday's half-sister, was burned to death when her dress caught fire while she was tending a bonfire. After 1874 only little Leroy Heizer was left to the mother.

Life at the orphan home was rigorously disciplined but not entirely unpleasant. The worst punishment was that for running away. Any boy caught doing this was made to walk around a cinder track in front of the administration building eight hours a day for a week, with time off only for meals; during that time no one was allowed to speak to him. Still, the boys preferred this or the whippings of the superintendent to the prayers, tears, and entreaties of his wife, whose weepy affection was unbearable. A strict merit system regulated their privileges, and too many demerits for untidiness or tardiness meant the loss of the coveted Saturday trips to town. The habits of neatness and cleanliness which Sunday acquired stayed with him throughout his life. But his religious and educational training at the orphanage did not have so pronounced an effect. He received enough education to complete the equivalent of grammar school, but the religious training, which consisted principally of memorizing Bible verses, did not take effect for many years. Sunday acquired a wider renown at the home for his prowess at running and fighting than for his religiosity.

The age limit for orphans was sixteen, and when his brother Ed had to leave in 1876, Willie insisted on going with him. They returned to their grandfather's farm at Ames and, together with their half-brother "Roy," helped the old man to operate his many enterprises. But not for long. Willie was as quick-tempered as his grandfather, and one day, when the old man cursed him for some minor mishap, the fourteen-year-old borrowed a horse from a friend and rode eight miles away to the town of Nevada, Iowa. Here he got a job as a hotel errand boy and never again went home to live.

Willie did go home once to visit his mother, several months later, but after two days he returned to Nevada. The hotel proprietor fired him for overstaying his twenty-four-hour "vacation," and Sunday had to get another job. He went to work as a stableboy and errand-runner for Colonel John Scott, once lieutenant-governor of Iowa. Scott and his wife grew so fond of him that they took him into their home and helped send him to high school in Nevada. For four years he attended classes, during the last two years acting as school janitor as well as doing the daily chores for the Scotts. The Scotts paid him eight dollars a month plus room and board. The janitorship paid for his schoolbooks.

Sunday's first fame came as a runner; several victories in local Fourth of July races and his talent as an athlete eventually caused him to miss graduation from high school. The fire brigade of Marshalltown, Iowa, needed a fast man to help them in their annual fire-fighting tournament, which fell that year on Sunday's graduation day. Since belonging to a fire brigade was a considerable honor, Sunday accepted their offer and skipped the graduation ceremony.

Helping the fire brigade was not a full-time job; so Sunday took a position as an undertaker's assistant and worked in the undertaker's furniture store in Marshalltown at $3.00 a week. This left him sufficient time not only for firemen's tournaments but also to play baseball on the Marshalltown team. His team won the state championship in 1883, and Sunday's playing brought him to the attention of A. C. ("Pop") Anson, the manager of the Chicago Whitestockings, a big-league professional team owned by A. G. Spalding. Anson persuaded Sunday, without too much difficulty, to exchange his undertaking career for one as a professional baseball player at $60.00 a month. Sunday arrived in Chicago wearing a six-dollar sage-green suit, with one dollar in his pocket. He overcame the jibes of "hick" and "hayseed" leveled by his teammates when he agreed to race the fastest man on the team and, in his bare feet, beat him by fifteen feet in a hundred-yard race.

Sunday's baseball career lasted eight years, from 1883 to 1891. During that time he claimed to have made two baseball records which stood for many years: he rounded the bases from a standing start in fourteen seconds and stole 95 bases in one season. The latter record, he said, was not beaten until 1915 when Ty Cobb stole 96 bases in one season. Sunday once batted .359 for a season, but his lifetime average was only .259, and according to Anson he was generally a poor batter—he struck out his first thirteen times at bat.

Sunday's favorite story of his baseball career, and one which he regularly told in his sermons, had to do with his fielding ability. It was the last half of the ninth inning in a crucial game with Detroit. Chicago was leading, but Detroit had the tying and winning runs on base. Two men were out, the count was two and three, and the batter slammed the ball high toward Sunday out in right field. "As I saw the ball rise in the air I knew it was going clear over my head into the crowd that overflowed the field," said Sunday. "I turned my back to the ball and ran. The field was crowded with people and as I ran I yelled, 'Get out of the way!' and that crowd opened like the Red Sea for the rod of Moses. I ran on, and as I ran I made a prayer; it wasn't theological either, I tell you that. I said 'God, if you ever helped mortal man, help me to get that ball!' I ran and jumped over the bench when I thought I was under it, and stopped. I looked back and saw it going over my head, and I jumped and shoved out my left hand, and the ball hit it and stuck! At the rate I was going the momentum carried me on and I fell under the feet of a team of horses. But I held on to it and jumped up with the ball in my hand. My how they yelled! Tom Johnson, who used to be mayor of Cleveland—dead now—rushed up to me and poked a ten dollar bill in my hand. 'Here, Bill,' he cried to me, 'Greatest thing I ever saw! Buy yourself the best hat in Chicago. That catch won me $1500.'"

This sign of divine approbation occurred after Sunday's religious conversion, but even before that, Sunday had been noted for his honesty and uprightness. Not that he did not try to drink and fight and chase the girls with the rest of his teammates in those days before baseball became respectable. Even back in Nevada, Iowa, the mayor reported that Sunday had been "no angel," that he "liked the girls" and "would fight at the drop of a hat." But his innate country ingenuousness and his fastidious orphanage training made him somewhat less obstreperous than his teammates. Anson considered him sufficiently reliable to make him business manager of the team, and Sunday never betrayed his trust.

The Whitestockings had their headquarters in Chicago, and it was here that Sunday met Helen A. Thompson. Born in 1868, she was the daughter of a Chicago dairyman and ice-cream manufacturer. The family were staunch Scotch Presbyterians, and Helen ("Nell") was converted to salvation at the age of fourteen. Sunday met her in 1885. Her younger brother, William Thompson, Jr., was the mascot and bat boy for the Chicago team. Although his mother was a Methodist, Sunday began to attend the Jefferson Park Presbyterian Church, where Nell was a devout worker for the Christian Endeavor Society. But Nell's father did not take kindly to the idea of his daughter's being courted by a professional baseball player who worked as a locomotive fireman in the wintertime. It was almost three years before the father was won over, and even this persistence would not have succeeded had Sunday not shown evidence by his conversion during this period that he was not following the wicked path of his unregenerate teammates.

The conversion took place in 1886. "It was Sunday afternoon and we got tanked up and then went and sat down on a corner," said Sunday describing the event. Outside the saloon he and his team-mates stopped to listen to an evangelistic group from the Pacific Garden Mission, "singing the gospel hymns that I used to hear my mother sing back in the log cabin in Iowa." Harry Monroe, the leader of the evangelistic group, invited the ballplayers to come to the mission "to hear the story of men who used to be dips, yeggs, burglars, second story workers, drunkards . . . and of women who used to sell their womanhood to whoever would buy."

"I went to the mission," said Sunday, "and liked what I heard. I went back again and again," and, finally, through the motherly per-suasion of Mrs. Clark, wife of the founder of the mission, "one night I went forward and publicly accepted Christ as my Saviour." Shortly after this, he said, "I went over to the west side of Chicago where I was keeping company with a girl now my wife. She was a Presby-terian, so I am a Presbyterian. If she had been a Catholic, I would have been a Catholic—because I was hot on the trail of Nell."[3] He was at once admitted as a member of the Jefferson Park Presbyterian Church, but it was two more years before Nell and her father con-sented to the marriage. Even after his marriage, on September 5, 1888, Sunday continued to play baseball. He was shortly transferred

6

to the Pittsburgh team and later to Philadelphia. Sometimes he took his wife with him on the circuit, but more often he left her at home in Chicago.

Sunday's conversion was not without its effect. He gave up drinking, swearing, gambling, and going to theaters, and he refused to play baseball on Sundays. Instead, he gave talks to boys at the YMCA in whatever city the team was playing. The boys came to hear about baseball, but Sunday insisted on telling them of his conversion and lecturing on "Earnestness in Christian Life." It was at this time that he began to get his first press notices as a purveyor of religion. "As a public speaker," said a Pittsburgh newspaper, "William A. Sunday, more familiarly known on the diamond as 'Billy,' can compare favorably with a majority of young clergymen in the city pulpits. He is not an ordained minister, but a member of the Pittsburgh baseball team with Christian principles."[4] The newspaper descriptions of his talks indicated that the young convert had not yet adopted the sensational slanginess of expression which later made his preaching so popular: "When speaking, his delivery is pleasant and grammatical. He has a ready command of the English language and uses many poetic phrases. His knowledge of human nature and the Scriptures were clearly evident in the half-hour address at the YMCA yesterday afternoon. He made no reference to the baseball profession and instead of using slang, his words were well chosen. He spoke earnestly, but at first seemed somewhat nervous."

The urge for self-improvement, fostered partly by his desire to establish himself in the eyes of Nell's parents and partly from the inbred American ethic of "getting ahead" in the world, led Sunday to seek some higher education during the winter months. Nell had gone to business college, and Sunday decided that he would get some college training at Northwestern. He was not able to matriculate as a fully accredited student, but he made an agreement with the university whereby he coached the college baseball team and in return was permitted to enrol as a special student at Evanston Academy, which was run by the university as a preparatory school. This arrangement lasted only one winter, 1887–88, but he always recalled with gratitude his course in rhetoric under Dean Cumnock of the school of oratory. Here he learned the proper enunciation and rhetorical flourishes to be used in reciting such epics as "The Charge of the Light Brigade," "Curfew Shall Not Ring Tonight," and "Spartacus to the Gladiators."[5]

The next winter, Sunday began to take courses in Bible study at the Chicago YMCA. He was so zealous that the director urged him to work for them permanently. Sunday was hesitant and put off acceptance of the offer for the time being. In the winter of 1890–91 he again worked at the YMCA. The desire to show others the way to righteousness became stronger. "I felt I was definitely called to enter Christian work." But he had just signed a three-year contract to play for the Philadelphia team. They were not willing to release him, and he was "greatly troubled" over the problem. As he had learned from his religious study, the problem must be taken to God. Some sign from heaven was needed to show the way. "I made it a matter of most earnest prayer," he said, "and even went so far as to make a proposition saying, 'Lord, if I don't get my release by March 25th, I will take that as assurance you want me to continue to play ball; if I get it before that date I will accept that as evidence you want me to quit playing ball and go into Christian work.'"

The release for which Sunday had asked was granted on March 17, but almost immediately another problem came up. The Cincinnati team, hearing of his release, offered him $500 a month to play for them for the seven-month season. His job at the YMCA would bring him only $83.33 a month. His mother had remarried for the third time, but he now had a one-year-old daughter, Helen, and his invalid brother Albert was dependent on him for support; was it fair to them and to his wife to give up this new offer? He asked his friends Cyrus McCormick, president of the YMCA, and J. V. Farwell, a wealthy trustee of the association, what to do. But the matter was settled when his wife said to him, "There is nothing to consider; you promised God to quit."

At the YMCA Sunday became assistant secretary of the religious department and worked six days a week from 8 A.M. to 10 P.M. To save money, he walked to work and back every day, went without lunch, wore a celluloid collar, and had his old clothes made over and dyed to look new. His work consisted of distributing tracts in saloons, giving talks on street corners, providing speakers for association meetings at Farwell Hall, leading prayer meetings, and helping "down-and-outers" to find salvation and jobs. "We never had a man on our staff who was more consecrated, more deeply spiritual, more self-sacrificing," said L. W. Messer, the general secretary. "He was especially strong in his personal effort among men who were strongly tempted and among those who had fallen by the way."

Sunday liked his work. His salary was raised to $1,200 the second

8

year and to $1,500 the third. But the depression of 1893 seriously curtailed the donations on which the YMCA subsisted, and Sunday's salary often fell sadly in arrears. Just as the depression was at its worst, Sunday received an offer to assist the well-known evangelist J. Wilbur Chapman in conducting revival meetings throughout the country. Sunday was recommended to Chapman by the gospel singer and hymn-writer P. P. Bilhorn, who knew of his work at the Chicago YMCA. Chapman offered Sunday $40.00 a week to act as his assistant, and, since there was no question of the worthiness of Dr. Chapman's religious endeavors, Sunday was easily persuaded to leave his difficult work among the downtrodden in Chicago's slums and take up the work of spreading the gospel in wider and greener fields.

J. Wilbur Chapman later became the most famous and successful professional evangelist of the first decade of the twentieth century. Their work together in the 1890's made him Sunday's closest personal friend, and Chapman was instrumental in starting Sunday on his own career as an evangelist. In 1895 Chapman was described by Dwight L. Moody as "the greatest evangelist in the country."[6] There was no doubt of his talent as a preacher and evangelistic organizer, though in the history of American urban revivalism it was Moody and Sankey who deserved the most credit for establishing the trend which Sunday eventually brought to its peak.

Working with Chapman in the years 1893–95, Sunday became what was known in the evangelistic profession as "the advance man." He went to communities in advance of Chapman's revivals to see that all was in readiness. He made certain that sufficient money was contributed to cover the initial expenses of renting a hall and paying for advertisements. With the help of the ministers and volunteer church workers, he organized and directed the activities of the necessary committees: the choir, the ushers' committee, the prayer-meeting committee, the publicity committee, the finance committee, and the personal workers' committee, whose members dealt with anxious or awakened sinners in the inquiry rooms after each sermon.

For two or more weeks Sunday trained these committee members in their duties and completed the arrangements for awakening the town to its need for religion. If he did his work properly, by the time Chapman and his gospel-singing assistant, P. P. Bilhorn, arrived, the success of the revival was all but assured. Chapman had only to preach effectively, and conversions would be inevitable. During the revival Sunday acted as general factotum; he was the head usher, he sometimes led prayer meetings, he arranged for space for overflow meetings in case the crowds could not fit into the hall where Chapman was speaking, he helped to take up the collections, and he undertook personal work. In general, he saw to it that all the technical details of the revival ran smoothly. Always on the alert to enhance the revival, he one night spotted former President Benjamin Harrison in the audience and deftly persuaded him to take a seat on the platform in order to display publicly his sympathy with revivalism.

Chapman had not yet invented the "simultaneous" evangelistic technique which was to win him nation-wide fame in the years 1906–11; in the two and a half years when Sunday worked with him, his revivals were puny affairs compared to those conducted by B. Fay Mills and D. L. Moody. The services of the latter were sought after by the largest cities in the country; Chapman was invited principally to small midwestern cities like Paris, Ottawa, and Peoria, Illinois, or Terre Haute, Evansville, and Fort Wayne, Indiana. On several occasions in these years Chapman was invited by groups of ministers in places like Indianapolis, Brooklyn, and Boston, but these were only neighborhood revivals whose influence did not reach beyond a few square blocks; no attempt was made to arouse these cities as a whole to join in the movement, as they did when Mills or Moody came to town. Once or twice when Chapman had no revival scheduled, Sunday aided a less-well-known evangelist named Milan B. Williams, who did most of his work in small towns in Iowa. But for the most part the years 1893–95 were spent by Sunday in aiding and learning from Chapman.

In late December of 1895, without any forewarning to Sunday, Chapman suddenly decided to give up revivalism, temporarily, at least, and settle down as pastor of John Wanamaker's Bethany Church in Philadelphia. Sunday, now the father of two children, was spending the holidays with his family in Chicago when he received Chapman's telegram. He had little money saved and no other job in prospect. "We worried and prayed what to do and discussed if I should go back to play baseball," Sunday said. A few days later a letter arrived from some ministers in the town of Garner, Iowa, asking Sunday to conduct a revival campaign for them. "We knew it was a direct answer to our prayers," wrote Sunday.

It was not an easy decision for Sunday to make. He had never conducted a revival by himself. He had no gospel singer and no advance man; no preparations had been made; he did not even have any sermons written, except his old talk on "Earnestness in Christian

Life." That the ministers in Garner had thought of writing to him at all was surprising, but it was later discovered that Chapman had asked them to do so. Chapman had tried to train Sunday in evangelistic techniques and had encouraged him to take part in the revivals. He reported, however, that when he asked Sunday to speak to the congregation during a meeting in Urbana, Ohio, "he seemed greatly frightened, said he could not speak and that he was not the man for the place." Chapman said, "I suggested to him that he ought to go to a number of places and stay for a week's meetings. When he told me that he did not have sermons I asked him to make use of anything that he had heard me say."[7] Finally forced to sink or swim, Sunday took Chapman's advice. He also took seven outlines of Chapman's sermons.

Garner was located in the north-central part of Iowa and had a population of about 1,000. It had four churches, one of them Roman Catholic. The three Protestant churches which were co-operating to promote Sunday's revival had raised enough money to rent the local opera house for a week, and they did what they could to advertise the coming event, which was to start on January 9, 1896. "The Garner papers," said the *Hancock Signal,* "announced that union evangelistic services, to be conducted by W. A. Sunday will be held in the opera house in our neighboring town commencing Friday evening of this week. This must be 'Billy' Sunday who used to play ball for Anson with the Chicago Whitestockings. 'Billy' is as true a Christian gentleman as he was a rattling ball player, and that is saying a good deal."

A choir of twenty was recruited from the Garner churches. Sunday himself led the singing, "although," he later admitted, "I did not know a note from a horsefly." He preached each evening at 7:30 and held a special sunrise service at 7:00 A.M. on Sunday. On the last night of the week of meetings a special "thank-offering" was taken up for the evangelist, which was his only remuneration; it amounted to $68.00. A short notice on the third page of the local paper on January 15 reported that "the union meetings which have been conducted by W. A. Sunday closed today at 10:30 A.M. These meetings have been well-attended and much good has been accomplished. We understand there has [sic] been nearly 100 conversions during the meetings."[8]

Even before he arrived in Garner, Sunday had received another invitation to come to Sigourney, Iowa, for a week's revival, and when he left Garner, he took the train for this small town of 1,800 persons in the southeast corner of the state. For two preceding weeks the *Sigourney News* had carried a large advertisement paid for by the four local churches: "You are cordially invited to attend all of the special union meetings of the Baptist, Christian, Methodist, and Presbyterian churches conducted by the Rev. William Sunday. Meetings begin Friday, January 17th. Place will be announced later." Sunday was not entitled to be called "Reverend," but the local ministers apparently did not know this when they invited him. The *Sigourney News* printed several testimonials in Sunday's behalf written obviously in answer to inquiries by the ministers. One testimonial stated that "it is enough to say of Mr. Sunday that Dr. J. W. Chapman has chosen him as his forerunner." An engraving of Sunday which appeared in the *News* showed him wearing a bow tie and wing collar. He parted his hair in the center to cover the receding hairline which belied his thirty-four years. So far as possible, he tried to assume the dignity befitting a man who had been Chapman's "forerunner."

Evidently word had reached the ministers concerning Sunday's difficulties as a choir leader, for they hired a "songster" named Joseph E. Van Winkle from Keota, Iowa, to lead the singing. The services were held in the various co-operating churches, except for the Sunday-afternoon meetings, which were held in the courthouse. "Mr. Sunday was somewhat surprised to see such a large audience," said the newspaper report of the first meeting. "He has had larger audiences than any minister that ever visited our city," the report went on. "Men go to these meetings that are seldom seen in churches. One great trouble is there is no house in the city large enough to hold the crowds. . . . A great many are in from the country every night."[9] One reason for the crowds at the evening meetings was readily explained: "The business houses close at 7:30 and Mr. Sunday thanks them, for it adds greatly to the meetings and shows a kindly spirit and interest." The more important reason was Sunday's personal charm and the earnestness of his preaching. "He talks good sound sense and has a way about him that people admire." The greatest possible compliment was paid to the young evangelist when the editor stated, "His sermons are similar to those of Mr. Moody."

Sunday, like Chapman, had printed up a supply of "decision cards," which he asked those converted at the meetings to sign. "Mr. Sunday uses the same kind of card that Dr. Chapman uses: [It reads:] 'I have an honest desire henceforth to live a Christian life. I am willing to follow any light God may give me. I ask the people of God to pray for me. Name.......... Residence........ Church or pastor preferred............ Usher's name............'" After every meeting "quite a number decided to live Christian lives." And, said the *News*, "no one can say they signed while under excitement for Mr. Sunday appeals to their good sense and judgment only." When Sunday finished his ten days of meetings, "the people of Sigourney were loth to let him go," said the paper. "There was an unanimous vote of the large congregation [at the last meeting] for him to remain a few days longer, but he could not do it." The amount of the "thank-offering" was not reported, but the following week it was announced that forty-nine persons had already joined the churches as a result of the revival, and "a great many others will unite [with the churches] in the course of a few weeks."

From Sigourney, Sunday went to Pawnee City, Nebraska. "I went to five towns, one after the other before I went home," Sunday recalled, and never again in his life was he without more calls for his services than he could accept. The Pawnee City campaign was similar to that in Sigourney, except for a remarkable occurrence which Sunday loved to retell to his audiences: "When I went to Pawnee City, Nebraska, I was entertained in the home of a hardware merchant named Harrington. An infidel in that section came into his store and was abusing and cursing me and denouncing him for having me as a guest in his home. He said he did not believe in a God and if there was a God let him strike him dead. He dropped to the floor and before a doctor arrived he was dead."[10] There is no confirmation of this incident in existence, but for most of Sunday's hearers no confirmation was necessary.

The Garner and Sigourney revivals were typical of the sixty-odd campaigns which Sunday held in small towns of the Midwest in the next five years. In these towns the yearly revival meetings were sacred and solemn occasions, and Sunday was careful to follow the accepted traditions of itinerant evangelists as they had been practiced since the days of Charles Finney's frontier camp meetings. Invited to help the local ministers of two or three evangelical churches to conduct their services, he felt honored and diffident and was eager to co-operate with them in every way. He usually preached in the churches and gave the ministers a primary position in conducting the meetings. "Mr. Sunday did not preach Sunday morning," reported a local paper in 1896, "but advised the different ministers to fill their own pulpits."[11] The young evangelist made no attempt to exalt himself at the expense of the regular pastors.

When the meetings were held in an opera house, collections were taken to pay the rent, but no pressure was exerted for contributions. No charges of commercialism arose, and nothing was on sale at the meetings. In these years Sunday had no staff of his own, and if one of the local pastors could not lead the singing, then a "songster" in the vicinity was hired for the job. The free-will or "thank-offerings" by which Sunday was paid were genuinely spontaneous and were solely the product of the collections taken at the last day of the revival. Sometimes they were heartbreakingly small recompense for the amount of time and energy involved. "I have worked in towns and received in my free-will offering scarcely enough to pay my way home," he recalled somewhat bitterly. "I worked in one whiskey-soaked, gambling-cursed, jay-rube town out in the short-grass country on the kerosene circuit for two weeks and had one hundred and twenty-seven people accept Christ as their Saviour. They gave me thirty-three dollars." Traveling costs were not considered part of the legitimate revival expenses and therefore came out of his own pocket. But his living expenses during his stay were met by local hospitality.

Sunday's wing collar, bow tie, and white waistcoat symbolized his attempt to assume the dignity of the cloth, and he made a sincere effort to perfect his faulty grammar. He said of the minister in whose home he stayed in Sigourney, "He was a brilliant man; he never got an adjective, noun, or pronoun out of joint; he took great interest in me and my manner of speech. He taught me the proper use of such words as 'did it,' 'done it,' 'came,' 'come,' 'seen,' 'saw,' and the like. . . . I also used to say 'I was born and raised in Ames, Iowa.' He taught me to say, 'Born and reared in Ames, Iowa.'"

Although Sunday's irrepressible energy and enthusiasm could not be entirely subdued, he tried to conduct his meetings in the serious and dignified style of his idol, Dr. Chapman. And, like Chapman, he held the usual prayer meetings, meetings for young folks, meetings for men only and meetings for women only, children's meetings, and old folks' meetings. After each sermon, in these first years, he held an afterservice, or altar service, during which those who had shown by raising their hands or by standing that they were anxious about their souls gathered in the front seats after the rest of the congregation had been dismissed. Sunday briefly exhorted these "awakened" or "anxious" persons to confess their sins and accept Christ as their Savior and then asked them to sign a decision card. After a short prayer they were dismissed.

Unlike Chapman and Moody, Sunday never made use of inquiry rooms. The personal work which took place in these rooms after the sermons—the arguing, praying, and quoting scripture on bended knees (a practice at which the aggressive and domineering Moody was a past master) did not appeal to the young preacher, who was still unsure of himself. He left this type of work to the local pastors, to whom he turned over the decision cards so that they might track down the converts and "follow up" the general appeal of the sermon with a pressing, personal appeal.

As an evangelist Sunday was a success from the start. Newspaper reports indicated that, despite the lack of advance preparations which sometimes found him preaching to half-filled churches on the first few days, his meetings were soon crowded to overflowing night after night. The Elliott, Iowa, paper said that "his preaching is stirring the country for miles around us. His congregations are sometimes larger than the population of the town." Another Iowa town, with a population of 2,000, reported that "the capacity of the church was overtaxed again last night. People began pouring in at five-thirty [for the seven-thirty service] and at six-thirty standing room was at a premium. Many who came in the afternoon remained to be sure of seats at the night meetings."[12] Farmers and their families flocked into town each evening to hear him. Even when he extended his stay from ten days to two or three weeks and, finally, by the year 1900, to four weeks, his audiences did not fall away. Only the shortage of his sermon material and the importunate invitations from other towns forced him to move on. After his visits, local bards wrote poems in his praise. The following appeared in the *Semi-weekly Telegraph* of Atlantic, Iowa:

> Four weeks he's been here preaching,
>   I tell you it was grand;
> They say that more than twenty score
>   On the Lord's side took their stand.[13]

By 1898 Sunday was holding his meetings in a large tent wherever possible. Tents had occasionally been used by revivalists since the early 1800's. Charles G. Finney held annual revivals in a tent at Oberlin in the 1830's, and Sunday had helped Chapman put up tents for his meetings. Big-city evangelists had the advantage of large auditoriums or armories, but in the little "jay-rube" towns in Iowa the local churches and opera houses seldom had a capacity of over a few hundred. A tent provided not only more seats but also the attractive connotations of a circus, chautauqua, or county fair. The churches rented the tents, but Sunday had to erect them. "I used to put up my own tents and care for them. When a rainstorm would come up in the night I would get up and light a lantern that I kept in my room and go down to loosen the ropes, for rain contracts canvas and rope and the tent would become like a drumhead and pull the stakes and down would come the tent. I have sat up all night watching the tent."

With his increasing popularity and prosperity, Sunday decided in 1900 to hire a gospel singer who would travel with him permanently and be paid, at least in part, out of his own pocket—just as Moody had paid Ira Sankey. He chose as his partner Fred Fischer, a cousin of Chapman's singer, P. P. Bilhorn. Fischer first sang with Sunday in Bedford, Iowa, in 1900. He remained with Sunday for ten years. A large handsome man, with a walrus moustache and wavy hair, Fischer always wore a high, stiff collar and pince-nez. He sang the familiar hymns like "In the Sweet Bye and Bye," "When the Roll Is Called up Yonder, I'll Be There," "We'll Gather by the River," and the old Sankey favorites. He had no training as a singer or choir leader, nor did he write or publish gospel hymns. But he was always referred to by Sunday as "Mr. Fischer," and the local press usually spoke of his "musical direction" as "a grand success."

Sunday also began to receive assistance from his wife in organizing revivals. "Dad hated managing finances," said Mrs. Sunday; "but I love figures, and Dad let me handle all the business details of his meetings." Though two more children were born to them in 1901 and 1907, Mrs. Sunday spent every moment she could helping her husband. She not only acted as business manager but also led prayer meetings, conducted Bible classes, spoke at women's meetings, and even helped lead the singing. The children were left home with their grandparents and later sent to boarding schools.

Prior to 1904 his wife and gospel singer were Sunday's only assistants. His popularity took him to towns in Illinois, Indiana, Minnesota, Nebraska, Wisconsin, and Missouri, but over 50 per cent of his one hundred revivals in the years 1896–1906 took place in Iowa. His itinerary in this state seemed to follow the course of the railroad tracks, with a revival campaign at every stop. Throughout the first decade of his preaching he spoke outside the area of the corn belt only once or twice.

The fact that he needed and could pay for the help of Fischer and for his wife's expenses, however, was proof of Sunday's growing popularity. His popularity not only gave him greater self-assurance, which affected his style of preaching, but it also altered his revival methods. He began to be less concerned with his grammar and pulpit dignity after 1900 and more eager to attract a crowd. In order to assure himself of these crowds, he began to make more demands upon the ministers who invited him. His new approach did not please the more conservative pastors, but they were outnumbered by those who preferred crowded meetings to clerical dignity. As Moody had pointedly remarked in 1875, "Some ministers think it undignified to advertise their services; it is a good deal more undignified to preach to empty pews, I think."[14]

Murmurs of disapproval in regard to Sunday's revivals began to be heard shortly after the turn of the century. In Audubon, Iowa, in 1902, the newspapers reported that opposition had been voiced at the meeting of the local ministerial association when it was decided to bring Sunday to that town: "Some dislike his methods and some things he says in the pulpit," the editor remarked. Particularly distasteful to many was his growing tendency to berate the local ministers who criticized him. "Infidelity is rampant and rank unbelief is preached from many a pulpit," he told the people of Jefferson, Iowa, in 1903, and the implication was clear that he and his supporters were the only true preachers of Christianity. He denounced the "hireling ministry" and the "fashionable church." "We don't need new church members half so much as we need the old ones made over. . . . Some people can knock better than they can boost. . . . We as preachers must be something more than walking theological mummies with isms, schism, and ologies." Whenever he made such remarks, he said, "some salaried quack cries out 'he's stabbing the church.'" To many conservative preachers Sunday's remarks seemed like overly harsh condemnation of their hard and earnest work in the vineyard.

Instead of deferentially advising the local ministers to fill their own pulpits on Sunday mornings, as he had done in his first years as an evangelist, Sunday began to demand that no preaching whatsoever be done by local ministers while he was in town. All church services were to be discontinued and all church doors closed during the revival, so that his tent would be the center of all religious activity and his sermons the sole source of spiritual nourishment.[15]

Another aspect of Sunday's revivals after 1900 which drew adverse comment was the tendency of his meetings to take on the aspect of entertainment. It was true that Moody had been the first to feature a handsome gospel singer and that he frankly advertised

17

his revivals in the entertainment columns of the newspapers, but
Moody was an exceptional man of proved devotion to his sacred
profession. Besides, Sankey had always prefaced his solos with a
prayer, for the express purpose of showing that he was not singing
merely to entertain. Fred Fischer was not known to do this, nor was
the "lady singer," Miss Mamie Lorimer, whom Sunday hired on several occasions to assist Fischer. Sankey had used a small church
organ on which to accompany himself. Fischer had a piano accom-
panist and encouraged local trombone and cornet players to come
on the platform to accompany the hymns. In Jefferson, Iowa, a
twelve-piece orchestra was on hand the first night. And the decorum
of the religious service could hardly be maintained when Fischer
urged the audience to whistle one verse of a hymn or asked the men
to compete with the women to see which could sing more loudly.
Fischer, of course, was merely using some of the tricks of the graduates of the singing courses at the Moody Bible Institute—tricks
currently coming into use with men like Charles Alexander, who
was Reuben A. Torrey's and later Chapman's "chorister." The idea
of turning revival meetings into a community songfest was far less
acceptable in the conservative farming communities of Iowa than it
was in the big cities where Torrey and Alexander conducted their
meetings in the early 1900's. But the attitude toward revivalism was
subtly changing in these years, and the rural areas did their best to
keep up with the cities.

If Sunday did not please all the ministers, he did succeed in pleasing most of the lay members of the churches—especially those merchants and businessmen who admired the aggressive, enterprising,
up-to-date approach which they associated with business enterprise.
They felt that, if louder, more daring, more "modern" methods of
getting ahead were profitable in business, there was no reason why
they should not be used in the churches. Certainly even the most
conservative minister had to admit that Sunday drew thousands of
people into revival meetings who had never come before. Maybe a
more enterprising attitude on the part of the clergy was just what
the church needed to meet the problems of the twentieth century.
The newspapers enjoyed and praised the novelty of Sunday's revivals. "He is an up-to-date man. . . . He is in no old rut," said the
Audubon Republican in 1902. And there was no end of comment to
the effect that "he gets results." It was not surprising, therefore,
that almost every town reported of his revivals, "Many of the best
businessmen of the town have united their efforts with the cause."

One of the most far-reaching changes in Sunday's methods after 1900 was his decision to require a wooden tabernacle rather than a tent for his meetings. He defended this on the grounds of necessity. Tents were satisfactory enough in warm weather, but in the winter, the usual season for revivals, they had distinct disadvantages. The sad proof of this took place in a campaign in Salida, Colorado, in October, 1905. On the last day of the campaign a heavy snowstorm started. Sunday told the story: "I had ten men with long poles with boards nailed on the end to push and pull the snow from the top of the tent. The snow fell so fast it piled three feet deep on the tent and broke the center poles and the side poles and tore the tent into ribbons. We went into the opera house for the closing services."

If tents were dangerous and opera houses too small, tabernacles seemed the only alternative. Moody had used tabernacles very successfully in his major campaigns in 1875–78. Sam Jones and M. B. Williams had occasionally used them in the 1880's and 1890's. Sunday had his first tabernacle specially built for his revival in Perry, Iowa, in 1901. It proved to be a turning point not only in his career, but in the whole profession of revivalism.

Perry had a population of about 4,000. The tabernacle was built to hold 1,000. Made entirely of wood and looking like a squat basilica, it was completely functional in design, with no decoration other than the banners posted outside announcing the meetings. The wooden roof was covered with tar paper; the walls were made of half-inch-thick pine boards which were fastened by only two nails, so that in case of fire or panic the crowd could push them off the upright support posts. Double barn doors were placed at the end of each aisle and cross-aisle.

The interior was lined with pine benches without backs and had a platform about five feet high and twenty feet long. Space was provided for the piano and choir at the rear of the platform; a small lectern was placed in the center. The wooden floor of this first tabernacle was so noisy that Sunday insisted on covering it with sawdust, shavings, or tanbark. When firemen questioned the safety of heating such a building with potbelly stoves, Sunday took a shovel and strewed red-hot coals over the floor to show them that the sawdust would not ignite. The tabernacle cost $750, which was partly reimbursed to the church members who had contributed it by reselling the lumber after the building was torn down.

This tabernacle was the prototype for those used in all Sunday's later campaigns. It proved so successful that he required tabernacles with increasing frequency, and after the Salida tent debacle he insisted on having a special tabernacle built even in towns or cities which had large auditoriums or armories. Naturally, the larger the town the larger the tabernacle. The one for Keokuk, Iowa, in 1904 held 3,000 persons and cost $2,000; during the course of Sunday's thirty-one-day revival in that city he held seventy-three meetings in this building and had a total attendance of 130,000. The tabernacle in Burlington, Iowa, in 1905 held 4,000.

The principal problem in tabernacle evangelism, as Moody had discovered, was the large expense. Sunday always justified this by pointing to the added publicity, the increased attendance, and the better functional design for revival purposes as compared to any other type of structure. The ministers of Perry, Iowa, were well content with the cost in view of the results; their whole revival cost only $1,300, and, said the local paper, "in consideration of the great good accomplished it has been money well invested. In no other way could so small a sum have done so much for the community."[16]

But in larger towns the expenses were considerably greater, and some pastors expressed grave doubts regarding the tendencies of this type of revivalism. The necessity of raising large sums of money eliminated the possibility of spontaneity in revivalism and detracted from its solemnity. There was no longer any attempt to pretend that revivals were unpredictable acts of God. Money for building the tabernacle had to be raised in advance of the meetings, and, since the backers of Sunday's revivals in these small towns and cities were not able, as Moody's wealthy backers had been, to donate this money without thought of return, it was expected that collections at the meetings would repay the loans of the churches and their people, who could ill afford to lose the money.

Often the loans met only part of the expenses, and the revival proceeded on a credit basis. As the bills for lumber, sawdust, coal, and labor mounted, there was constant fear lest the collections would not be sufficient to cover the costs. In Atlantic, Iowa, in 1902, for example, anxious reports were printed during the revival that $500 more was needed to meet the $1,100 expenses. This was the first of many such notices—often frantic in their appeal—which were to accompany Sunday's revivals in subsequent years.

Under such conditions success could not be left to the chance descent of the Holy Spirit, whose presence would quicken the sinners into conversion and hence generosity. To most midwesterners, being in debt was the first step to sin, if not sin itself; it became a sacred duty to use every possible form of organizational and crowd-winning technique which would assure financial solvency. In the process, religious decorum and traditions were flouted with increasing regularity, and the old-time revival which was "prayed down, not worked up" disappeared.

Sunday's increasing prominence as an evangelist stemmed as much from his ability to meet his campaign expenses as from his ability to convert sinners. The problems of raising the expenses for even such a small town as Jefferson, Iowa, with a population of 2,601 in 1903, became too much for the local ministers, and Sunday had to take charge of increasing the collections. When, after three weeks of this four-week revival, $600 of the $2,200 expenses was still unraised, he devoted the first part of his Sunday-morning and Sunday-afternoon meetings to a high-pressure fund-raising campaign. According to the local newspaper, "He proved himself a past-master in the art of getting people to give. . . . In twenty minutes' time the evangelist got pledges for $500 and in the afternoon $100 more."[17] During the next week another $150 in expenses was run up, and this, too, Sunday raised. It became an accepted part of his campaigns in these years to devote the next-to-last Sunday to "special efforts" to meet the expenses.

The ministers were expected to reciprocate in kind when it came time to collect the free-will offering to remunerate Sunday. A week before the revival ended in Jefferson, the Rev. Mr. Corkey spoke from the platform to call attention to the fact that "next Sunday this offering will be received. Everybody recognizes Mr. Sunday's ability. He has been offered $100 to go on the lecture platform. His expenses are very high, keeping up a home in Chicago while he travels over the country. It costs him over $200 a month. This is an honest debt we owe to Mr. Sunday." On the final day in Jefferson, "Judge" Church presided over the collection for the free-will offering before the morning service. "Secretaries and solicitors were stationed throughout the audience to take names and amounts of subscriptions." Twelve hundred dollars was raised at that service and $200 more at the afternoon service.

Sunday was discreetly absent during this process. The following morning he told a reporter, "I shall always carry the most pleasant recollections of my stay in Jefferson. Her people have won my heart. This has been one of the easiest towns to raise money for current expenses that I have visited in years." He concluded his farewell message to new converts: "Keep your account straight so when the

Great Bookkeeper calls for a statement, your account will show a balance in your favor."[18] The executive committee presented an audited account of the revival to the public, and the *Jefferson Bee,* in a front-page box, reported, "Jefferson's total investment . . . $2,350. Jefferson's Dividend on Investment: The conversion of more than half the population outside the churches."

From 1896 to 1902 Sunday's free-will offerings ranged from $33 to $1,536. The latter sum he received in Audubon in 1902, and it was the largest he had received up to that time. But during the next four years his offerings averaged over $2,000 per campaign, and by 1906 they reached four and five thousand dollars for four weeks of preaching. Since local ministers often worked all year for only $600 or $800, friction frequently developed—especially in view of the fact that Sunday, unlike Moody, did not donate his earnings to charitable or religious institutions, though he did tithe his income.

Sunday continued to perfect his technique, and his consistent success brought invitations from larger towns. In Keokuk, in 1904, he inaugurated a system which was to cause much bad publicity in future years. Before the revival started he demanded that the ministers obtain contribution pledges of $2,000 from their church members in order to cover all the expected expenses of the revival; these pledges were only to be enforced if the collections and his fund-raising technique during the revival failed to produce the necessary sum. This wise move to guarantee that Sunday would not have to leave a town with the debts from his revival unpaid was later pointed to by critics as an unjustifiable demand from an evangelist—largely because of a misunderstanding of the procedure. Fortunately, in Keokuk, as in 99 per cent of all Sunday's campaigns, the expenses were raised from the collections, and none of the guarantee pledges had to be made good.

That same year, 1904, Sunday added two additional members to his staff to aid in the heavier work involved in organizing revivals in these larger towns. His schedule was so tightly packed that he had invitations for more than a year in advance, and consequently he decided that he needed an advance man. He hired the Rev. I. E. Honeywell to take over this task; Honeywell also acted as Sunday's assistant during the revivals, just as Sunday had done for Chapman. One of the most time-consuming jobs connected with the revivals was the care of the tabernacle, and it was for this work that Sunday hired Fred Seibert. Seibert, a graduate of the Moody Bible Institute, had been conducting revivals himself under the title of "the Cowboy Evangelist." His new job evidently provided steadier employment. He was required, as caretaker of the tabernacle, to sleep in the building every night in order to protect it from fire and vandalism.

The exact salaries of these men are unknown, but at one time Honeywell and Fischer between them received $300 per month. Sunday paid one-third of this out of his own pocket. The rest was paid by the local clergy as part of the regular revival expenses. The additional help not only made his revivals function more smoothly but also left Sunday more time for preparing new sermons. During his month in Keokuk he preached sixty-three different sermons at his seventy-three meetings.

Other measures inaugurated about this time to increase interest in the revivals were the increased size of the choirs (which by 1904 reached three hundred), the instituting of "cottage prayer meetings" at various homes throughout the city both prior to and during the campaign, and the encouraging of delegations of ministers and converts from other towns to visit campaigns. This delegation system was later to become the mainstay of revivalism, but in the early years it was merely the product of an enthusiastic and sentimental interest in Sunday which led those who had previously worked with him or had been converted by him to come to hear him again when he was in a near-by town. Sunday willingly arranged reservations of seats for those delegates who cared to travel to his meetings at their own expense.

The larger towns which he visited after 1904 also provided a more enterprising and co-operative press coverage for his meetings. Daily papers, especially competing dailies, gave much more space to his meetings than the weekly or semiweekly papers of towns like Garner and Sigourney. Reporters were assigned to cover his meetings from start to finish, and special press boxes were arranged in the tabernacles. By 1906 local publicity had reached the point where daily box scores of converts and collection totals were printed on the front pages. The program of sermons, prayer meetings, and Bible classes was printed for a week in advance. Some papers listed the name and address of every citizen in whose home a semiweekly cottage prayer meeting was held—a figure sometimes reaching several dozen. The local ministers who co-operated in the movement were frequently rewarded by having their pictures and brief biographies printed in the news.

Sunday provided the press with posed publicity stills showing him in various dramatic stances which he assumed during his sermons. No photographers were permitted in the tabernacle during the meetings for fear that they might distract the attention of the crowd by the flash and noise. Larger city papers got around this by having staff cartoonists make sketches of Sunday in action. Occasionally Sunday released advance copies of his sermons to the press so that the reporters would not have to take down his rapid delivery. Collections of epigrams from his sermons, commonly under the heading of "Sundayisms," began to appear each day in the papers and were obviously provided for the press by Sunday or Honeywell.

In the publicity photographs of 1906 Sunday was shown wearing the formal regalia of earlier years: wing collar, white waistcoat, bow tie, and cutaway coat—"I am an old-fashioned preacher of the old-time religion," he told his audiences; but on the platform he no longer dressed in the stereotyped pattern of the old-fashioned preacher. The Keokuk paper, the *Daily Gate City*, stated that Sunday looked "like a businessman" and "in a meeting of a board of trade might be taken for a successful broker. He looks like a prosperous man, dressed well, quietly, and in good taste, in a business suit." Other papers described him as "natty." The rigid taboo against wearing jewelry and other accouterments of luxurious wastefulness which had played so large a part in the revival preaching of men like Charles Finney had apparently been relaxed, for it was noted in Keokuk that Sunday "does not disdain to wear a diamond stud and another diamond in a ring."[19]

All these changes in Sunday's revivalism did not come suddenly but were gradually developed by trial and error, from necessity, or by chance in the first ten years of his career. His advance to larger and larger cities was responsible for most of the innovations in his system, and yet, of the one hundred revivals which he conducted in the decade from 1896 to 1906, more than half were in towns of under 2,500. An account of his revival in Marshall, Minnesota, in 1903 by a resident of that city gives a good picture of this early phase of his career and its effect upon such small communities.[20]

Marshall was a typical prairie town of about 2,000 persons. Its residents, including those of the surrounding farms, were mostly "of old American stock," either born in the state or emigrants from Ohio, New York, Pennsylvania, or near-by western states. There was "a sprinkling" of foreign-born from Canada, England, Ireland, Scandinavia. The town had two railroads, a flourmill, a federal land office, and six churches. Diversional entertainments were mostly "of the home made variety," such as husking bees, house-raisings, weddings, christenings, and funerals. Various social events were put on by the lodges, the grange, and the churches. "A fair-sized second floor 'town hall'" was available for imported theatrical and musical performances, but these were few and far between. Occasionally there were visiting lecturers who talked about Iceland, Greenland, China, or some other "romantic spot," with lantern slides. The first demonstration of the phonograph and the motion picture were local events of great importance around the turn of the century. Almost equally sensational was the visit of a versatile hypnotist named "Doctor" Ewen. There were, of course, no automobiles, and the first public telephone exchange did not reach Marshall until after 1900.

In the dull winter months the local evangelical churches continued their nineteenth-century custom of holding annual revival meetings. These were usually small but exciting affairs conducted "by some outside specialist." When Billy Sunday was invited for the winter of 1903, it caused a "tremendous stir" because of the tabernacle and the special sensationalism of his publicity and sermon performances. "He drew hearers not only from among the townspeople, but also from the countryside all around. About 600 people were said to have been converted—among them the town's allegedly most clever and worldly-wise lawyer, a man past middle age." At his departure Sunday received an offering of $2,100.

This was characteristic of Sunday's meetings. The area in which he preached in this decade was virtually equivalent to the great midwestern corn belt—an area in which the general tenor of existence and the traditions and types of people were very much alike. Though Sunday spoke in towns as far apart as western Iowa and eastern Indiana, the fact that they were farming communities interested primarily in the prices of corn and wheat on weekdays and in churchgoing on Sundays made them react similarly to his preaching.

Sunday's popularity in the small towns of this region gave him the self-assurance to dispense with the imitative sermon style which he had used at first and to speak and act in a manner more consonant with his own ebullient personality. Not only was Chapman's style alien to his nature, but it was not the most useful in arousing the simple, uneducated farmers and townspeople of the corn belt. By the same methods of trial and error which led to the perfection of the technical aspects of his revivalism, Sunday gradually developed a style of preaching which was as popular as it was sensational. He began by imitating those idols of midwestern oratory, William Jennings Bryan and Robert G. Ingersoll, both of whom he had heard in Chicago. He even went so far as to paraphrase the agnostic Ingersoll in one of his sermons, in order to prove to his audiences that a man who believed in the orthodox Protestant faith could be just as eloquent as one who flouted it. He also took some humorous anecdotes from the sensational sermons of his fellow-evangelists M. B. Williams and Sam Jones. And for doctrinal exegesis with force, wit, and pathos he borrowed freely from the sermons of D. L. Moody and T. DeWitt Talmage.

The conglomeration of different sources tended for a time to bury Sunday's own personality, but the results enraptured his audiences. In 1901 his words were described as those of "a ripe scholar . . . wit and humor coupled with his flights of oratory . . . interesting and entertaining and instructive . . . rhetorically correct." "The sermon that has done the most to make Mr. Sunday famous," said a report in 1904, was "The Inspiration of the Bible." It was made up of "prose poems and pictures . . . rhetorical gems . . . sparkling, parti-colored, pulsing, vivid description of Eden with Adam and Eve— a wonderful picture painted with riotous voluptuousness of color in words—a poem equal to any of Ossian in strength and the only prose poem ever heard equal to the finest passages of Robert G. Ingersoll."[21]

Another aspect of Sunday's style which attracted enthusiastic response (except from the more conservative clergy) was his "power of ridicule and denunciation," which was "developed to perfection with a fearlessness and bravery seldom equalled." Typical of his slangy humor was his opening-night expression: "Exercise good country cow sense and we'll get along all right. There'll be in my sermons good fodder and rock salt, barbed wire and dynamite." After this first sermon the headlines in one town read, "Sunday a Whirlwind," "Preacher Sets Town Afire." It seemed quite appropriate in the days of the Russo-Japanese War to compare the rapidity and accuracy of his delivery to "a battery of Japanese light artillery" sending "shrapnel at sin."[22]

The *Jefferson Bee* claimed quite correctly: "He is not conventional. . . . He is not namby-pamby. . . . He does not mince words. . . . He is not dull. . . . He is not afraid to wave his hands and shout. . . . He is not in favor of higher culture and higher criticism." In delivering his little speech about being "a rube of the rubes," he conveniently forgot that his home was in Chicago and that he had lived there for almost twenty years. He instinctively knew that to

please his audience he must attack the city and its highbrow pretensions to culture. Like Bryan, he let no occasion pass without
making it clear that the farmer could live without the city dweller
but the city dweller would perish without the farmer. He gleefully
satirized the pseudo-sophistication of those young men whose fathers
sent them away to college:

> I'm a dandy, I'm a swell,
> Just from college, can't you tell,
> I'm the beau of every belle,
> I'm the swellest of the swell.
>
> I'm the king of all the balls,
> I'm a Prince in banquet halls,
> My Daddy's rich, they know it well,
> I'm the swellest of the swell.[23]

Ministers and reporters noted with surprise that "there are more
smiles than tears in the faces of the converts." But it was approving-
ly stated that "Mr. Sunday is a hearty, healthy, and happy Christian.
. . . He likes to see people happy." Sunday himself pointed out that
"God wants people to be happy." After each sermon, Sunday asked
those willing to take their stand for Christ and the Christian way
of life to come forward and shake his hand. "His manner is magnetic and his smile so winsome," said one journal, "that the heart
of a misanthrope would go out toward him. When he reaches out
to shake hands, and give that firm, hearty grip, it is time to surrender."[24] It was not noted that the surrender was more likely to be
a surrender to Sunday's charm than to Christ.

Not only was Sunday's sermon style becoming more sensational,
but his delivery began to resemble that of a vaudeville monologist.
"Those who went to hear him last night to be entertained," said the
Centerville Daily Citizen in 1904, "got the worth of their money."
His sermons were compared to "a series of moving pictures in
the pulpit." One headline stated: "Evangelist Does Great Vaudeville Stunts in Tabernacle Pulpit. . . . One of the Most Unique
and Entertaining Addresses Ever Heard in Burlington." The article
continued: "Sunday has imitated nearly everybody and everything
in the whole gamut of stage acting, even in diving off the stage and
coming up blowing water out of his lungs in imitation of a man
diving after a pearl." He acted out with sound effects a locomotive
race which took ten full minutes to portray. Reports of his meetings
resembled theater reviews: "There is an accuracy in his mimicry
that is seldom seen since Clara Morris left the stage."[25] Perhaps the

most sensational and undignified of his actions was a growing tendency to shed his coat and vest in the heat of his performances. "Sunday grew so lurid that he shed first his collar, then his coat, and as he closed his sermon proceeded to put on his raiment with the nonchalance of a man talking to an intimate friend in his boudoir," said the *Centerville Daily Citizen.*

The net result of this flamboyant pulpit oratory was that the whole temper of religious revivalism was gradually transformed from one of intense but reverent excitement into the superficially contrived enthusiasm and strident heartiness of a political convention. By the third night of one of Sunday's revivals the audience realized that their old-fashioned ideas of the solemn sanctity of evangelistic services was out of date. Sunday had brought something new to revivalism, something which Moody, Mills, Chapman, Williams, and Jones had only hinted at in the last quarter of the nineteenth century. Involuntarily ejaculated hallelujahs were being replaced by artfully elicited applause. But instead of being shocked, the audiences were, on the whole, vastly pleased with the novelty of Sunday's technique. "Hitherto the audience showed its satisfaction in a sort of repressed churchy way," said the *Daily Gate City* on the fourth day of Sunday's revival in Keokuk, "but last night it was carried out of that idea and broke out in loud hand-clapping several times."

As Sunday departed further and further from the strictly religious aspect of evangelism, in order to give his revivals the broad appeal necessary to fill his large tabernacles week after week, he began to advertise them as a means to civic improvement. By reviving people's interest in religion, Sunday said, a town would undergo not only spiritual refreshening but also moral improvement. "The gospel rightly understood and faithfully preached interferes with every form of iniquitous business," he said. This meant principally the iniquitous business of the saloons and their allied evils, gambling, dancing, cardplaying, and prostitution. Not only did this appeal to civic pride attract many nonchurchgoers and occasional churchgoers who otherwise would never have darkened the door of a revival tabernacle, but it appealed especially to the businessmen, who, while already good church members for the most part, were eager to improve their community so that decent and substantial citizens would settle there, raise real estate prices, and increase business.

Some ministers were displeased at this departure from the strictly religious purpose of revivalism. They wanted to fill the churches and not to engage in what Sunday called "cleaning up the town."

The ministers of Audubon, Iowa, though they voted to invite Sunday to their city, placed a notice in their local paper to try to make their stand on this clear. "The churches interested [in sponsoring Sunday] are not starting any reform. It is no crusade against existing evils other than sin. It is to be for the good of the town and community, hoping to give society a moral uplift, a strong public sentiment for purity, and sobriety, and an ingathering of the unsaved."[26] A certain ambiguity in this statement, however, made it seem to imply that the moral uplift of the community was of primary importance and the "ingathering of the unsaved" secondary.

The ingenuity of Sunday in injecting this civic reform spirit into his revivals and the justifiable fears of the local clergy that such a tendency might seriously involve the churches in complicated political activities were clearly indicated in Sunday's revival in Burlington, Iowa, in 1905. To what extent Sunday was aware of the explosive forces with which he was toying in this revival and to what extent he became the naïve tool of certain clever politicians can best be surmised from an intimate relation of some of the curious events surrounding the whole campaign.

In 1905 Burlington was a city of about 25,000. It was the largest city that had yet invited Sunday, and the expenses were expected to be almost double those of his Keokuk campaign, his largest up to that time. The figure was estimated at over $4,000. This was a large investment for the churches of the community, and the ministers needed to be certain that they would receive substantial support in the undertaking from their laymen. They obtained, with Sunday's help, letters from bankers and businessmen of other towns where he had campaigned, giving complete indorsement of the project. Then they called a conference to consider extending the invitation to Sunday. At this conference it was carefully specified that "each church shall be represented by the pastor and two lay members, and an additional lay member for each one hundred members of the church."[27] It was evident that Sunday's revivals were now business enterprises and that, being in the majority, the laymen and not the ministers would call the tune in the policy decisions concerning the methods and procedure.

The letters which were read at the conference of the Burlington pastors and laymen indorsed Sunday's work in glowing terms; they were particularly enthusiastic about the moral improvement and the increase in civic virtue and civic reform sentiment which grew out of his revivals. Not only had souls been saved, but alcoholic consumption had decreased, swearing had virtually disappeared, and cards, dancing, and gambling had been almost eliminated.

The ministers and laymen of Burlington were particularly sensitive to this aspect of Sunday's revivalism for a very definite reason. More than a year before, a committee of respectable citizens, including most of the members of the ministerial association, had approached the mayor of Burlington to ask why he did not enforce the law regarding the regulation of saloons in the city. This law, the Martin Liquor Tax Statute, had been passed by the state legislature in 1894 largely as the result of agitation by the rural areas of the state, which were caught up in the post–Civil War temperance movement. The urban areas were opposed to temperance, but their representatives were outnumbered in the legislature. After a fierce battle the Martin law was passed as a compromise measure.

This statute prohibited the sale of alcohol throughout the state, but it permitted referendums in any town or city on the issue. In order to prevent wholesale nullification of the law by these referendums, the statute prescribed certain strict regulations which were to govern saloons in any city which voted to license them. In the first place, it posed a very large license fee—so large that the statute became known colloquially as "the Mulct Law" because of its attempt to mulct the saloonkeeper of any possible profit. In addition, all saloons were to be closed at 10:00 P.M. daily and all day Sunday, no gambling was to be permitted in the saloons, and no cardplaying or dancing.

Enforcement was left up to the city authorities. And this was the rub. For in cities like Burlington, which, soon after the law passed, voted to permit saloons, no mayor or police chief was so foolish as to try to enforce the ten o'clock closing or any of the other restrictions imposed by the rural Prohibitionists. The enforcement in Burlington was so lax that the *Burlington Hawkeye* rightly asserted that "that class of citizens from the rural areas feel that they have been 'buncoed' in a deal in which the liquor traffic was again legalized under certain conditions. The dealers gained the benefit of the legalization without meeting the conditions." When the citizens' committee visited Mayor J. S. Caster in 1904 to ask him to do his duty in enforcing the law, he calmly told them that it was impossible for him to do so. The majority of the people, he said, would not stand for it. He was not going to oppose the popular will just to please a few sticklers for the letter of the law. "Public sentiment must be worked up to support a movement of this kind before it can be done successfully," he told the committee.[28]

There was no doubt that this state of affairs motivated many of those at the conference which voted to invite and support a Billy Sunday revival in Burlington. What was not so obvious was what the mayor and those interested in the liquor business and its allied fields planned to do about the revival. Sunday arrived in Burlington on November 10, 1905. "One of his earliest acts was to examine municipal conditions, as is his practice when he goes to a new field of evangelistic work," wrote the *Hawkeye*'s reporter. As usual, Sunday also took the time and trouble to introduce himself to the various local officials, and after a conference with Mayor Caster he publicly announced that the mayor was a fine man who was doing the best job he could under the circumstances.

Throughout the revival, Sunday vigorously advocated Prohibition and attacked the liquor interests. Since 1902, when he first began to take an interest in civic reform, he had been working on a special sermon devoted to Prohibition, and by 1905 it had replaced his sermon on "The Inspiration of the Bible" as his most famous piece of oratory. He called the sermon "Booze, or Get on the Water Wagon," but it was popularly known simply as "The Booze Sermon." The climactic meeting of the Burlington revival took place on December 17, when, to a tabernacle audience composed of 4,000 cheering men, he delivered this "Booze Sermon." As he concluded, he called out, "How many of you men would stand by Mayor Caster if he would put the lid on and close up the saloons tight on Sunday and put the gamblers out of business?" The entire audience sprang to its feet with a roar of approval.

Two days later, after Sunday had departed with a free-will offering of $4,000 and a total of 2,500 conversions, the *Hawkeye* said, "There has been a veritable revolution in public opinion. . . . There can be no doubt about it. It is the splendid fruitage of the great religious awakening in Burlington under the masterful leadership of William A. Sunday." That same Tuesday morning Mayor Caster issued a proclamation which began, "Whereas, at a men's meeting held in the tabernacle on Sunday, December 17th, 1905, a resolution asking for the closing of saloons on Sunday was adopted by over 4,000 votes . . . every person caught selling intoxicating liquors on Sunday within the corporate limits of the city of Burlington, Iowa, will be prosecuted." The headline of the *Hawkeye* read, "MAYOR CASTER PUTS THE LID ON: The Result of Sunday's Work."

The mayor's proclamation had not come spontaneously. On Monday, December 16, after Sunday had left the city with the parting remark, "Farewell, fellow sinners; I'm free of your blood," a mass meeting was called by the leaders of the revival. It was held in the tabernacle, and the mayor himself was present. The ministers and laymen announced that a Civic Federation had been formed and that it had called the meeting of the townspeople in order to make certain demands upon the mayor. After a stormy session, in which the mayor was again charged with malfeasance for his failure to enforce the "Mulct Law," he acceded to the popular pressure and agreed to prosecute violators. His proclamation followed.

The church people were proud of their achievement, and they gave Sunday due credit for helping them. The heightened emotion of the revival had not only saved 2,500 souls but had infused new moral fervor into the people of the community. Not only had personal reformations been produced, but civic reformation was under way. "Burlington now enters upon a new era of municipal reform," said the newspaper. "The mayor not only has public sentiment behind him, but he will have the help of the Civic Federation which will deal not only with moral but economic problems, all tending to improvement of municipal administration in all departments."

But some people were skeptical. They wondered if the ministerial association was not patting itself on the back too heartily and too soon. These doubting Thomases had their fears confirmed ten days later, when a letter from the Rev. Carl Eklund was published in the papers which gave some hint of the true significance of the revival. Eklund, pastor of the Swedish Methodist Episcopal Church in Burlington, was one of the leaders in the revival and in forming the Civic Federation. Instead of being pleased with the mayor's proclamation and the publicity given to the campaign by the *Burlington Hawkeye,* he accused the mayor of pusillanimity, if not outright corruption, and claimed that the *Hawkeye* was in collusion with the very forces of evil which the revival was trying to overthrow. The *Hawkeye,* he said, had outraged "the feelings of all Christian sentiment when it tried to make political capital out of Mr. Sunday and the meetings from the first day to the last." This was not Sunday's fault. "Mr. Sunday was a stranger, no blame is on him. He was honest." But the men who controlled the *Hawkeye* and the party which had elected Mayor Caster were not honest.

"Why?" asked Eklund, did the *Hawkeye* "try to uphold an administration that had delighted in flaunting in the face of ministers and people its indefensible policy? . . . When other people were praying and working for the regeneration of Burlington these ill-smelling political rags were flaunted everywhere." At the Monday-night meeting of the Civic Federation the mayor had continued to defend his policy of nonenforcement of the law even in the face of aroused public sentiment. "If the mayor wants to show his good faith why doesn't he go after the slot machines and order down curtains, close up the back doors and shut up basement saloons?" he asked, instead of issuing "his little, defective, half-way order?"

Eklund was embarrassingly close to the truth. The mayor's proclamation had said nothing whatsoever about closing the saloons at 10:00 P.M. on weekdays, nothing about gambling or cardplaying; and it was clear that his proclamation was not being enforced, even in its diluted form. The Liquor Dealers Protective Union of Burlington, to which most of the more respectable saloon-owners belonged, had voluntarily voted to close their saloons on Sundays, but the other saloons, the worst dens in the city, were neither closed nor prosecuted. "It is a pity that the prosecuting power in both the county and the city lies in so irresponsible hands as the case is," said Eklund. The Swedish pastor was fighting mad, and he withered his rivals with scorn: "The Christian men of Burlington," he said, "will elect a clean outfit next spring." "How in the world can we trust a man who tries to please all sides in order to reach some political plum?" he demanded. "If that is politics, then to hell with politics!"

But Eklund's wrath was lost in the jovial mood of self-congratulation in which the excited citizens wallowed after Sunday had titillated their sense of righteousness. Eklund's letter was buried on the back pages of the papers. The headlines of the preceding week had succeeded in promulgating the feeling that the revival and the Civic Federation had been a success, that Mayor Caster had at last manfully stood up against the forces of evil, and that Billy Sunday had started a new era of civic reform in Burlington. This attitude spread far beyond the town limits. The whole state of Iowa was reporting the glorious reformation. A banner headline in Des Moines announced the news of "BURLINGTON'S SPIRITUAL UPHEAVAL." And a Dubuque newspaper reported, "BURLINGTON IS DRY. Billy Sunday Has Made Graveyard Out of Once Fast Town."

Sunday's apprenticeship was almost over. He was ready to leave the small "jay-rube" towns of his home state and to go into the big cities, bringing his combined program of personal and municipal reform. He was going to represent the people of the rural areas who felt that they had been "buncoed" by the corrupt forces of the cities during the preceding twenty or thirty years; he was going to voice their protest against the new and unpleasant political and economic system of the twentieth century. A wave of reform was growing mountain-high in these years, and Billy Sunday was prepared to ride the crest of it.

2

" 'BIG BUSINESS' FOR THE LORD"

Billy Sunday's crusade in Burlington, Iowa, in 1905 set a pattern for his later revivals. It proved that he could be as effective in the city as in the rural towns. It indicated the type of planning needed to unite a whole city and the type of preaching that would arouse it to fever pitch. Sunday still had much to learn as a professional revivalist, and his technique needed more careful organization, but the path to nation-wide fame and fortune now lay open. He had only to continue to give vehement and colorful expression to the prevailing mood to achieve nation-wide fame and success.

For Sunday this was easy. He had a natural bent for sensationalism in speech and action and a forceful, magnetic personality which captivated his audience and gave his words the ring of burning conviction. Sunday believed what he said, and he said what he believed. Once he had overcome his innate shyness, he found it the most natural thing in the world to tell thousands of people what was needed to solve the country's problems, and the solution he offered was one which appealed to almost everyone: simple, familiar, and apparently sure-fire, this solution was based upon the traditional American thought patterns, buttressed by a sentimental longing for "the good old days," and expressed in terms of "that old-time religion."

In effect, Sunday offered Americans of the twentieth century the ideology of the nineteenth century. He hold them that the problems with which they struggled in an industrial society were based on the same evil tendencies inherent in human nature since Adam's fall. Panics and depressions, strikes and riots, political corruption and economic monopoly, were all merely the outgrowths of man's sinful propensities. The nation was crying out for reform, and Sunday cried with it; but he offered an old-fashioned diagnosis and an overly facile remedy for disturbingly new and complex problems.

Sunday was, however, sufficiently in tune with his times to phrase his diagnosis in contemporary terms. Like Theodore Roosevelt, he denounced "the malefactors of great wealth"; like William Jennings Bryan, he trumpeted against the "money-changers" of Wall Street; like the muckrakers, he excoriated "bossism" and "the shame of the cities." He was not only willing to designate human wickedness by its new manifestations, but he also called his remedy by a new name. Since "progressivism" was the rallying cry of the opening years of the twentieth century, he stood up to proclaim himself the champion of "progressive Christianity" or, as he more often phrased it, "progressive orthodoxy."

"Progressive orthodoxy" had just the right flavor to attract those interested in reforming the current state of affairs without making any basic changes in the national institutions. And, of all the nation's institutions, the Protestant churches were perhaps the most torn between the old and the new, between an agrarian society and an urban industrial society, between the nineteenth century and the twentieth. Their theological structure was tottering from the onslaught of Darwin and the higher critics of the Bible; their role in the life of the nation was being altered by the advocates of the Social Gospel; their financial structure was suffering from the migration of communicants from the country to the city and from the city to the suburbs; and their membership problem was staggering under the impact of millions of immigrants of other faiths, or no faith, who crowded the middle-class Protestant church members out of the downtown district of city after city.

At the heart of the emotional upheaval which found expression in the cry for reform was the cultural change which the nation had undergone since the Civil War. Small towns and cities which had for years been only sleepy crossroads communities changed within the course of a decade or two into moiling industrial centers; thousands of strangers streamed in to man the factories and establish homes, leaving the older residents resentful and insecure as they watched their traditional way of life being destroyed by the inexorable new system. The rural economy of the last century had evoked an ideology based on a romantic and optimistic view of men's relationship to nature, to God, and to each other. In an industrial, urban society this ideology was no longer valid; it still existed in church sermons and Fourth of July orations, but it had no relationship to the hard facts of life. The workingman wanted the collective action of unionism, not the rugged individualism of the frontiersman; the white-collar worker, the small businessman, and the independent farmer needed the regulatory action of state and national legislation, not the self-reliance of laissez faire capitalism; even the big businessmen, the more farsighted of them, preferred co-operative amalgamation to cutthroat competition.

And yet no group in America, no group which had grown up there in the nineteenth century—except for a handful of radical intellectuals—wanted to abandon the traditional pattern of the American free-enterprise system. What most people wanted was one or two legislative restraints upon excessive abuses of the system. Some thought this could be done simply by antitrust laws to break up monopolies, pure food and drug acts to prevent unhygienic packing processes, civil service laws to curtail "politics" in government, and interstate commerce commissions to prohibit unfair or discriminatory practices not covered by state laws.

Others, of whom Sunday became the leading spokesman, thought that the personal reformation of wicked individuals, the moral regeneration or spiritual refreshening of the collective national conscience, a return to the old-fashioned, God-fearing, Christian morality of "our fathers," were all that was needed. After all, these people said, the only way to have good government was to have good men in it, and the only way to get good men elected was to have an honest and upright electorate; without individual integrity all the legislative controls in the world would be ineffective in controlling abuses of the great American system.

There was only one matter on which this latter group was willing to see some merit in legislative reform, and that was "the liquor question." It was necessary, they said, to prevent the manufacture and sale of alcohol just as it was to make laws against murder and robbery, since liquor dealers were, in fact, nothing less than murderers and robbers. Or, put another way, it was right and proper for the government to remove the temptation to sin from those weak-willed, unregenerate mortals unable to restrain themselves.

The Prohibition movement quite logically reached its triumphant climax in this era of progressive reform because it provided such a simple, concrete panacea for all the national ills and because at this particular stage in their history the American people were ready to depart, however slightly, from their traditional attitude of laissez faire. Dwight L. Moody, the father of modern revivalism, despite his ardent devotion to temperance, was a lifelong opponent of legislative Prohibition, and it was not until after his death in 1899 that the Anti-Saloon League was successful in dealing the deathblow to the temperance pledge approach to "the liquor question" and launching instead the nation-wide program for Constitutional Prohibition.

Billy Sunday thus came on the scene at a crucial turning point in American thinking, and he shared the new outlook—to a degree. But he would never have attained the pre-eminent position which he had by 1915 if he had not been as "orthodox" as he was "progressive." He kept the evangelical theology of the nineteenth century intact throughout his career, and, despite his tendency to use certain Social Gospel expressions, his preaching was based on the same theology that evangelist Charles G. Finney formulated in the 1820's. What was more important, Sunday represented the last wave of the great tide of evangelical revivalism which had begun shortly after the United States adopted its Constitution and which swept to ever increasing heights in sporadic swells throughout the nineteenth century. Finney's preaching marked the climax of the first phase of this recurrent revival; Moody's campaigns marked the climax of the second phase; and Sunday, though he did not realize it, was to climax the final, culminating phase.

Finney congealed the frontier revival message of the early 1800's into a firmly fixed theology in which Wesleyan Arminianism, or the ability of the sinner to change his own heart, replaced the Calvinistic determinism of predestined sainthood or damnation; he gave professional evangelism its characteristic undenominational aspect by his "union meetings," in which he was supported by all the ministers in town; he developed the techniques of controlled and directed mass psychological manipulation which replaced the spontaneous individual and mass hysteria of the camp-meeting orgies; and in his doctrine of "Perfectionism" he integrated religious reform with the multifarious social reforms prevalent in the 1830's and 1840's. His unwillingness, however, to integrate revivalism with the most important of all these reform movements, antislavery, served temporarily to check the flow of revivalism. The pre–Civil War decades represented a momentary ebb in the great evangelical tidal wave, while the slavery question pushed revivalism into the background.[1]

But, when the Civil War was over, D. L. Moody took up where Finney had left off, and the tide surged forward again. Moody carefully kept social reform out of his revivalism, making it at most a by-product of individual reform; his preaching was primarily a glorification of the status quo. His success was due to his striking adaptation of Finney's evangelistic technique to the large new industrial centers. The great migration of American youth from the rural communities to the cities in post–Civil War decades produced a new problem for urban Protestantism, and Moody successfully showed the churches how to evangelize this particular portion of the cities' masses. He was welcomed with open arms as the preserver of Protestantism in an industrial society, for he created almost singlehanded the vital new profession of urban evangelism and thus laid the groundwork for all future big-city revivalists.

The technique which Moody evolved was complex and expensive. It needed wealthy backers, co-operative church workers, and talented leadership. He demanded, and received, almost unanimous support from the evangelical ministers of Brooklyn, Philadelphia, New York, Chicago, and Boston for his city-wide revivals in 1875–78. Ministers as diverse in personality as Phillips Brooks, T. DeWitt Talmage, Henry Ward Beecher, and Theodore Cuyler sat on his platforms and offered their prayers for his success. He demanded and received financial support for the building and maintenance of his huge, specially constructed tabernacles from the wealthiest and most influential business leaders of his day; men like J. P. Morgan, W. E. Dodge, R. K. Remington, Morris K. Jesup, Joseph Story, Amos Lawrence, Cyrus McCormick, Louis Swift, J. V. Farwell, Philip Armour, A. J. Drexel, Jay Cooke, George Childs, and John Wanamaker acted on his committees and gave thousands of dollars not only to promote the revivals but as gifts to the YMCA's, seminaries, and Bible schools which Moody helped to found.

Itinerant revivalists had, of course, been prevalent since before Finney's day, but their efforts were largely confined to reviving church life in country towns; few of them invaded the cities, and none succeeded in winning the united support of the urban clergy and laity as Moody did. The methods he perfected of arousing an audience to stream down the aisles and seek conversion in his inquiry rooms were totally unlike those used by rural evangelists and considerably shocked some conservative ministers, but the effectiveness of these methods in producing converts silenced all argument. The gospel hymns written and sung by his co-worker, Ira D. Sankey, inaugurated a new era in religious music and formed a vital part in bringing religion to "the masses." The organization of thousands of church workers as ushers, choir singers, doormen, personal workers, prayer-meeting leaders, and "flying squadrons" of home-visiting soul-winners reinvigorated the church life in the cities. But the whole procedure required a masterly administrative ability such as few captains of industry and fewer ministers possessed.

The number of converts in Moody's "preaching missions," as he called his revivals, numbered in the thousands in each city; the cost of his biggest revivals averaged $45,000 each, or approximately $5,000 per week; the contributions to his enterprises numbered in the tens and hundreds of thousands of dollars; the number of persons who heard him speak was in the millions. Moody made city revivalism not only a profession but a big-business enterprise. For the capable evangelist who adopted Moody's system there were sizable rewards, a fact which helped to attract the necessary talent for the difficult task. Moody himself was not interested in amassing a fortune, and when the royalties from the hymnbooks owned jointly by himself and Sankey became embarrassingly large, he set up a trust fund administered by three businessmen friends who used it as Moody directed. Most of the money went to the Moody Bible Institute, founded in 1886, and to the nondenominational Northfield and Mount Hermon seminaries in Northfield, Massachusetts, which Moody started in 1879 and 1881. Here he trained men and women to save souls according to his methods rather than according to those taught in the old and conservative denominational seminaries, which were more interested in producing cultured theologians than in promoting revivals.

Either through training in these schools or by association with Moody's revivals or by indirect imitation of Moody's methods, a host of professional evangelists arose in the late nineteenth century who, on a lesser scale, attempted to undertake revivals in the cities. Most of these men were soon forgotten, but three of them stood out as direct contributors to the history and methods of the revivalism which eventually produced Billy Sunday. They were B. Fay Mills, Reuben A. Torrey, and J. Wilbur Chapman. These three men altered Moody's techniques by new experiments, won the respect and admiration of the clergy, and helped make city-wide mass evangelism an accepted part of the Protestant churches' institutional structure. It was largely on the strength of the tradition they established that Sunday won recognition in the churches. He drew heavily on their experiments, and without a knowledge of their work it would be impossible to account for Sunday's amazing success.

The innovations of B. Fay Mills came in the early 1890's, when Moody had largely given up his earlier system of tabernacle evangelism and was devoting his time to his schools and to evangelistic conferences. Mills invented what he called the "District Combination Plan of Evangelism," which sought to avoid the expense of building huge tabernacles by reviving cities piecemeal. He divided each city to which he was invited into eight or ten districts and had the co-operating ministers rent a hall or auditorium for him in each district. After preparations had been carefully made according to a special booklet which Mills wrote for the guidance of the local clergy, he and his singer held a ten-day revival in each district, one after the other, and concluded with a two-week finale in the center of the city in the largest meeting place available. He also put into general use the decision-card system, so that local ministers could undertake more systematic "follow-up work" and make certain that those awakened at the revival meetings would join a church. Decision cards introduced a less praiseworthy aspect into evangelism, however, because revivalists inevitably began to use them as a statistical measurement of success. When Mills turned Unitarian in 1896, he renounced evangelism, and his district combination plan went out of fashion.

Reuben A. Torrey, who was superintendent of the Moody Bible Institute from 1889 to 1905, took it upon himself to become Moody's successor. He organized the first world-wide evangelistic campaign in 1901–5, visiting cities in Japan, China, Tasmania, New Zealand, Australia, India, the British Isles, and Canada. Sometimes he used tabernacles, but more often he and his soloist–choir leader, Charles Alexander, conducted their meetings much along the lines of Moody's meetings, in large auditoriums or armories.

"Charlie" Alexander was himself a vital contributor to the new techniques of city evangelism. He abandoned the church organ, which Sankey and other evangelistic singers had used to accompany themselves and the choirs, and he substituted instead a piano or horn accompaniment—sometimes both. He was the first of a long line of "choristers" produced by the Moody Bible Institute who combined the ingratiating personality of a master of ceremonies with the vivacious inspirationalism of the leader of a community songfest. He added a new element of hilarious entertainment and conviviality to revival meetings; his jocular methods of "warming up" an audience made them feel that they had an active and important part in the meetings and brought back something of the social significance of religious life which had played such a large part in frontier camp meetings. This was of prime importance in bringing religion to the lonely city dwellers who felt lost and overwhelmed by the complexity and anonymity of urban life. Billy Sunday's choristers modeled themselves upon Alexander and not on Sankey.

Because of his cold, humorless personality and his extremely domineering style of preaching, Reuben Torrey's career in the United States was short-lived, and after 1907, when Alexander left him to join Chapman, Torrey seldom undertook revival meetings. Chapman, who had been working as an evangelist since the 1880's, evolved a new technique after 1906 which he called the "Simultaneous Evangelistic Campaign." Like Mills, he divided a city into districts, but instead of preaching in each of these himself, he enlisted a band of evangelistic co-workers and assigned two to a district—one to do the preaching, the other the singing. In some cities he had as many as twenty-seven pairs of revivalists and singers working for him. For two or three weeks all the districts engaged in revivalism simultaneously, with Chapman himself speaking in the largest centrally located church in the city. This was considered a sensational innovation in 1906; "an advance in Evangelistic prophecy," it was called, though it had been tried before by Moody in Chicago in 1893 and by Chapman himself in Philadelphia in 1896. From 1906 to 1911 Chapman successfully used this simultaneous system in cities throughout the United States. "It is the opinion of our city leaders," said a New Haven minister after Chapman's revival there in 1908, "that this 'interdenominational simultaneous movement' is destined to be the most potent form of extensive evangelism in the next decade." But the prophecy was overoptimistic.

By 1911 the fad of simultaneous evangelism had palled, largely because many of Chapman's co-workers lacked the ability or sincerity to give satisfaction to the outlying districts. Chapman and Alexander always had packed, enthusiastic meetings, but the lesser-known evangelistic pairs often preached to half-empty churches. In 1911 Chapman and Alexander went on a world-wide evangelistic tour following in Torrey's footsteps. The two were never again the popular leaders of revivalism in the United States, for by 1912 Billy Sunday had come forward with a new technique—or rather, a reworking of Moody's technique—which established him as the current idol of the Protestant clergy.

Sunday had a solid tradition on which to build, but despite the general acceptance of professional evangelism, it was no easy task to win personal recognition. Mass evangelism was sensational; the churches were essentially conservative. Each new evangelist had to undergo a long apprenticeship before he won the recognition and esteem without which it was impossible to unite a large city of fifty thousand or more behind a revival campaign. Urban revivals needed the co-operation of most, if not all, of the evangelical churches of every denomination if they were to have any chance of success. Moody had to establish his ability by successful campaigns in the British Isles before he was accepted by the American clergy; Chapman, Mills, and Torrey served long apprenticeships as pastors before becoming evangelists.

The churches had good reason to be cautious. Mass evangelism was a hazardous undertaking. The fanatical Alexander Dowie had made a laughingstock of himself in a series of revival meetings in New York's Madison Square Garden in 1905, and, while none of the orthodox clergy had supported him, the cause of religion had suffered from his dismal spectacle. Too many evangelists were not much better than Dowie; they lacked the talent and sincerity of a Moody or a Chapman and seriously harmed the professional standing of legitimate revivalism by oversensational and basically unethical methods. Ministers in many cities had their fingers burned by too hastily supporting new schemes of evangelism invented by self-seeking or foolish revivalists who succeeded only in leaving debt and dissension in their wake by their unsound manipulations of the highly explosive, emotional material of revivals.

Even such stable and conservative evangelists as Torrey and Chapman had difficulty in this regard. Torrey wrote confidentially to a friend in 1904, "Many of the evangelists are being ruined by commercialism that has entered in evangelistic work. A good deal of commercialism has been creeping into our work and more and more machinery, and I fear, less dependence upon God. I am going to have a talk with Alexander about it."[2] A year later certain American ministers were accusing Torrey of using "machine-like methods" and decrying his "brass band work, big choir work, big 'statistics,' and everything on the score of bigness." Chapman was subject to the same accusations by conservative ministers who continued to think of evangelism in terms of the "outpouring of the Holy Spirit" rather than in terms of the efficient results of well-planned human activity: "Some of us were fairly frightened at the complexity of the machinery and its man-made look," said a New Haven minister of Chapman's revival there in 1908.[3]

When such notably "safe and sane" evangelists were thus suspect, it was not surprising that Billy Sunday should have had such a long uphill fight for recognition. His phenomenal success in Burlington had aroused new interest in his work, it was true, but it had by no means brought him the seal of approval of the clergy even in the Midwest. There was a distinct suspicion that his sensationalism might be as dangerous as it was powerful. But Sunday had at least established the fact, by 1906, that he was ready to leave the minor league of small-town evangelism for a tryout in the major league of the big cities. If Chapman was the most valuable player of the year in evangelistic circles in 1906, Sunday was certainly the most promising rookie of the year. Torrey, past the prime of his evangelistic career in 1907, expressed his conservative view of the rising young evangelist in a letter to Moody's son-in-law, A. P. Fitt, who was considering inviting Sunday to speak at a conference on evangelism at the Moody Bible Institute; he told Fitt that he did not think Sunday should be invited to the conference because his sermons and revival methods were far too sensational to be encouraged.

In order to allay the hostility of conservatives without modifying his methods to the point where he was no longer able to fill his tabernacles, pay his expenses, and win record convert totals and publicity, Sunday decided early in his career to seek ordination as a Presbyterian minister. Evangelism, being a profession distinct from the ministry, did not require ordination, and Moody had, in fact, set an example against it by declining ordination; but Sunday realized that for him, as indeed for most professional evangelists since Moody, ordination was essential. He needed it to help overcome his baseball background and to prove his dedication to the church. He needed it to give him dignity and standing with the ministers with whom he daily came in contact. In addition, the title of "Reverend" would be a prime asset in gaining the respect of the laity and in adding weight to his gospel interpretations. A lifelong feeling of intellectual inferiority harassed his peace of mind, and there was undoubtedly some security in the fact that his work would be approved by a powerful and ancient denomination.

Sunday evidently had little doubt of passing the examination which took place before a board of ministers of the Chicago Presbytery in 1903. To most of its theological and historical questions he replied, "That's too deep for me," or "I'll have to pass that up," but after a few minutes of questioning one of the members who was a friend of his moved that the remainder of the examination be waived on the grounds that "God has used him to win more souls to Christ than all of us combined and must have ordained him long before we ever thought of it." The board agreed, and Sunday was passed.[4] J. Wilbur Chapman preached his ordination sermon in the Jefferson Park Presbyterian Church.

Ordination did not stop Sunday from calling himself "Billy" rather than "the Reverend Mr. Sunday," nor did it stop his playing a game of baseball now and then to stir up publicity for his campaigns. But, in spite of his sensationalism, there was no criticism of Sunday's sincerity and honesty in the years prior to 1906. Whatever the financial rewards, it was not an easy life. He saw his children and even his wife only intermittently, for it was not until after their fourth and last child was born in 1907 that Mrs. Sunday regularly took part in his revivals.

Sunday worked to the utmost limits of his physical endurance. Newspapers reported time and again that at the close of a sermon he would lean wearily upon his pulpit, his voice hoarse, his clothes dripping wet, "almost exhausted physically" and hardly able to speak. He stated that the nervous excitement frequently prevented sleep: "The blood in my brain works like a trip hammer. When I lie down I go over every sermon I preach. I preach it all over. I see the faces in front of me." With complete conviction he told his audiences, "I never expect to be an old man . . . I am burning up to do you good and keep you out of hell."[5] As early as 1908, and throughout his life thereafter, he was frequently told by doctors that he would not live another ten years if he kept on at the pace he was going, but he never slowed down; he did not know how and would not have if he could.

Nevertheless, though he could not stop, Sunday was not anxious to proceed too fast. Several times before 1906 he had held revivals in large cities with poor results. In 1898 he visited the city of Lincoln, Nebraska, which had a population of 40,000, and made virtually no impression on it. In 1900 he held a revival in Elgin, Illinois, a city of 22,433 persons, and was a dismal failure. Although he made 800 converts there, he usually had that many in towns of 2,500. Other early campaigns in Dubuque, Iowa, and Rockford, Illinois, both over 25,000, were equally unsuccessful. Because he still lacked confidence in himself, and in his evangelistic system, he moved slowly in his assault upon the big city. In the years 1906–10 he preached in only nine cities that were larger than Burlington, and most of these were midwestern cities like Bloomington, Decatur, and Danville, Illinois, and Cedar Rapids and Waterloo, Iowa.

The average population of the six cities in which he spoke in 1907 was 10,000; in 1908 the average was 20,000.[6]

In 1909 Sunday accepted an invitation to Spokane, Washington, his first revival in a city of over 100,000 persons. A Prohibition movement there helped to stimulate interest and was influential in his decision to try such a large city. But his convert total reached only 5,666, just slightly more than double the Burlington figure, or about 5 per cent of the population. In 1911 he campaigned in Toledo, Ohio, with its 168,000 population, and converted only about 4 per cent of them. Since his average campaign prior to 1908 had resulted in the conversion of about 20 per cent of each town's population, he and his wife were convinced that cities of 30,000 were the maximum which could be efficiently moved by a city-wide revival. "When they're larger than that," said Mrs. Sunday, "it is impossible to reach everybody."

Nevertheless, in 1912 Sunday accepted an invitation to visit Columbus, Ohio, and here 18,419 of the 182,000 inhabitants signed decision cards. This was two and one-half times the Toledo figure and more than triple the conversions in Spokane. It was evident that his technique was improving. The ministers and laymen of Columbus were well pleased that even 10 per cent of the population made professions of faith. Emboldened by this success and spurred by the fame it engendered, Sunday went on in the next five years to reach the climax of his career and hold campaigns in the largest cities of the nation.

The average population of the cities Sunday visited in 1913 was 76,000; in 1914 it reached 171,000; in 1915, 528,000; in 1916, 584,000; and in 1917, the year he came to New York City, the average amounted to nearly 1,750,000. In the years 1906–18 he held city-wide revivals in ten of the fifteen largest cities in the United States and in more than one-third of the cities which had over 100,000 inhabitants. The increased scope of his activity in this period can be measured by comparing it to his 1896–1906 period, when ninety of the one hundred revivals he held were in towns of under 10,000. From 1906 to 1918 only six of his sixty-five revivals were in cities of under 10,000; twenty-five were in cities of 10,000–50,000; eleven were in cities of 50,000–100,000; and twenty-three were in cities of over 100,000. Of the last twenty-three, nine were in cities of over 500,000—four of them over 1,000,000.

The geographical range of Sunday's activity increased as radically. Through the year 1911 he remained essentially in the corn-belt area, though in 1908 he held a campaign in Pennsylvania, in 1909 he went to Washington State, and in 1910 and 1911 he added Ohio and Kansas to his list. Then, from 1912 to 1918, he held campaigns in twenty-one different states in the following order of frequency: Pennsylvania, seven; Ohio, four; New York, three; New Jersey, two; West Virginia, two; Colorado, two; and once each in Massachusetts, Rhode Island, Washington, D.C., Georgia, Maryland, Michigan, Iowa, Illinois, Kansas, Indiana, North Dakota, Nebraska, California, Minnesota, and Texas. The over-all trend of his activity was toward the "wicked and godless East." The climactic years 1912–18 took him, among other places, into Pittsburgh, Philadelphia, Baltimore, Atlanta, Boston, Los Angeles, Dallas, Detroit, and Washington, D.C. He reached the peak of success in 1917, when he preached to the largest city in the country, New York, with its six million inhabitants. The story behind this path to glory from Garner, Iowa, to New York was as complex as it was spectacular. It involved not only the climax of the tradition of revivalism but also the personality of Sunday and the details of the technique he evolved.

In the course of his climb to success, Sunday came to believe that he had a divine mission in life—a mission to lead America in a crusade against the forces of evil. Like most native-born, rural-bred Americans, he firmly believed that the big cities were the citadels of sin from which emanated all the evil and destructive forces which were threatening the "good old ways," "the American way," and "the old-time religion." "If America has the sins of Babylon," he said, "she will have the punishment of Babylon."[7] In accepting the leadership of the assault upon Babylon, Sunday was, however, pushed as much by outside forces as by his own inner compulsions. For one thing, his wife and the members of his staff were eager to push on to greater triumphs and rewards. For another, he was running out of cities to conquer in the Midwest. But most compelling of all was the power of his own fame and the crying needs of the urban clergy in search of a leader. Though the more conservative of them, particularly in the large eastern cities, were not convinced until after the Columbus revival that Sunday was the leader they sought, his reputation for safe, sane, and, above all, efficient results spread rapidly after 1906.

The earliest reports of Sunday's work that reached the big cities beyond the corn belt were in the freethinker magazines, such as Brann's *Iconoclast* (Chicago), the *Melting Pot* (St. Louis), and the *Truth Seeker* (New York). They were hardly complimentary. In

1906 the *Truth Seeker* listed Sunday's free-will offerings as totaling $16,900 for four campaigns and remarked sardonically, "Reports from the West show that 'Billy' Sunday, formerly a baseball player with the Chicago National League team, has bettered himself by turning revivalist." An editorial two years later in the same paper said, "We can imagine the kind of people caught up by [his] preaching. They are the kind who would applaud a noisy-mouthed hoodlum on the coaching line where Sunday doubtless earned his fame as a ball player." The circulation of these magazines was small, but their notice of him was significant.

In September, 1907, Sunday achieved his first nation-wide publicity when the *American Magazine* printed a feature story about his revival in Fairfield, Iowa, that spring. The illustrated article, by Lindsay Denison, was entitled "The Reverend Billy Sunday and His War on the Devil." Denison wrote with an eye for the more sensational aspects of the revival, and the illustrations played this up. But instead of making Sunday an object of laughter and ridicule, the article had the opposite effect upon most evangelical ministers and laymen. It aroused curiosity, wonder, and genuine admiration.

Denison stated, without attempting to analyze the figures, that Sunday had made 100,000 converts in the course of his career and that 75,000 of these had joined some church. Answers to letters written by Fairfield ministers to eleven towns in which Sunday had held revivals stated that the number of backsliders was "negligible." The article quoted enthusiastic comments by the Fairfield clergy and emphasized that over 20 per cent of the population was converted at a cost of only $3,200 (excluding the $3,660 that Sunday received as a free-will offering). Fairfield had a population of less than 5,000, but some ministers seemed to think that Sunday could do just as well in a city of 500,000. In Boston the *Watchman-Examiner* ("A National Baptist Paper") quoted large parts of this article. The editor called it "extremely significant" and was impressed by the fact that "he gets results." Henceforth the *Watchman* gave more attention to reports from Baptist ministers in the Midwest telling of their fruitful experience with Sunday's campaigns. Other religious journals in the East and West did the same.

In 1908 the *Nation* brought Sunday to the attention of another segment of the public when it roundly denounced him in an article called "Making Religion Yellow." And that same year a volume of Sunday's sermons appeared in a pirated edition; it was at once repudiated by Sunday for its inaccuracies, and soon after that he began to copyright his sermon material. Some years later he bought the plates of this volume and destroyed them.[8] By 1911 Sunday was considered sufficiently well known both as a preacher and as a former baseball star to be asked by *Collier's* to name the All-American professional baseball team for the season. In 1912 he was asked to come to Wilkes-Barre, Pennsylvania for a campaign, his first revival east of the Alleghenies.

In 1913 Sunday's first biography appeared. Written by a man named T. T. Frankenberg, it was called "a fraud" by Sunday, despite the fact that he had collaborated with Frankenberg on it in the early stages.[9] The quarrel with Frankenberg was apparently engendered by the latter's insistence on stating that Sunday's conversion took place after he met Mrs. Sunday, thus spoiling the story which Sunday always told that he had met his wife-to-be at a prayer meeting after he had joined the Jefferson Park Presbyterian Church. Sunday at once commissioned an "authorized" biography and paid his former assistant, Elijah Brown, to put into readable form the mass of clippings which had been accumulated over the years. This volume, called *The Real Billy Sunday*, appeared in 1914 and was sold for one dollar a copy at all meetings.

That same year the John T. Winston Publishing Company in Philadelphia asked for, and received, Sunday's permission to print another authorized biography by William T. Ellis, a free-lance writer on religious subjects. Eighty per cent of Ellis' book, which was entitled *Billy Sunday: The Man and His Message,* consisted of quotations from his sermons and little that was not in Brown's book. Needless to say, neither book contained any derogatory, or even mildly critical, material, since both were plainly intended to be eulogistic campaign biographies. Their circulation greatly enhanced Sunday's reputation, and in the next three years these biographies were among the best-selling religious books of the year.

In a poll of its readers conducted by the *American Magazine* in 1914 on the question, "Who is the greatest man in the United States?" Billy Sunday appeared in eighth place. He was tied in this position with Andrew Carnegie and Judge Ben Lindsey. The only other minister named in the voting was Bishop John H. Vincent, of chautauqua fame. Perhaps the symbolic proof that Sunday had achieved national recognition came on February 23, 1914, when the *New York Times* first considered a story about him as part of "the news that's fit to print." The article, on page sixteen, stated that Sunday was expected to receive $35,000 as a free-will offering from his current revival in Pittsburgh. A year later, even this symbolic act was climaxed when he was received at the White House by President Woodrow Wilson, who was quoted as having said, "God bless you and your work."[10]

But more valuable than all this publicity in the years after 1906 was the information that spread by word of mouth. In denominational conferences, Sunday-school and YMCA conventions, and Prohibition rallies, those who had personal experience with Sunday's work met those whose curiosity had been whetted by news stories and magazine articles. At such gatherings church and lay workers were eager to learn of new evangelistic methods and new leaders who might help their cause. This type of interpersonal propagandizing did more than anything else to establish Sunday as the churches' man of the hour, the man who "gets results."

During the years 1906–12, while the press and the public were becoming more closely acquainted with Sunday's results and while the evangelical ministers were convincing themselves that he was the leader they sought, Sunday was carefully perfecting his technique. As he adapted it to bigger and bigger cities, he gradually abandoned his earlier criterion of success—the conversion of approximately 20 per cent of a town's population—and assumed that if a city met certain basic stipulations regarding the support he wanted for a revival, he could produce a sufficient number of converts to satisfy his backers, even though it was only a relatively small percentage of the total population.

But obtaining the required backing after 1912 was a tremendous problem, for Sunday's stipulations were such that they transferred the major burdens of the revival to those who wished his help. There were three major requirements which had to be met by those who wanted him to revive their city. First, any invitation to him had to represent the "united support" of all the evangelical ministers of the city. Second, those who invited him had to build a wooden tabernacle under the supervision of Sunday's personal tabernacle architect, at a central location in the city suitable to Sunday. And, finally, his sponsors had to provide a financial guarantee in advance—in pledges or in cash—which would cover all, or at least a large part, of the estimated expenses of the revival. Unless these stipulations were met to his complete satisfaction, Sunday declared, no invita-

tion, no matter what city or what individuals stood behind it, would
be considered.

Undoubtedly the first stipulation, the demand for "united support," was the most difficult requirement to meet, though it was one
which Moody had declared essential for successful city-wide mass
evangelism. Sunday sometimes referred to this as "unanimous support," but he never went so far as to hold strictly to this. In large
cities with four or five hundred ministers and scores of different denominations it was impossible to get them all to agree to support
him. Sunday never expected the Roman Catholic churches or the
Episcopalians, Lutherans, Unitarians, Universalists, Christian Scientists, or Jews to support him. What he wanted was the united
support of the so-called "evangelical" Protestant churches—the
churches which followed the general tenets of the Arminian-Cal-
vinist compromise so ably spelled out by Charles Finney in the
1830's. In effect, he sought and generally obtained his support from
the major Protestant denominations—the Presbyterians, Methodists,
Baptists, Congregationalists, Christians, and Disciples and their
manifold offshoots. These were the churches which called themselves "evangelical" (as opposed to "liturgical") and which contained the great bulk of Protestant church members in the nation. If
he had their united support, he had all he could ask and more than
enough to successfully conduct his campaign.

However, professional evangelism was not welcomed by all the
ministers of these denominations, and even if Sunday had not been
so controversial a figure, the growing split between liberals and
Fundamentalists in the churches would have made unanimous support for his work impossible. In the end, therefore, Sunday left it
up to his advance man and business agent to estimate the amount
of support which any given invitation represented. Usually he expected to have at least a majority vote of the city's ministerial association, or majority votes of the ministers of each evangelical denomination in the city. The advance man had to uncover the nature
and extent of the opposition and inform Sunday of its possible del-
eterious effect on the campaign.

Often Sunday's decision seemed arbitrary on this point. For example, he twice turned down delegations from Brooklyn on the
ground that they lacked sufficient unity of support—on the first
occasion it was reported that the belief that N. D. Hillis and S.
Parkes Cadman opposed him had brought this rejection; on the
second, when these two ministers made it clear that they did not

object, he turned down the invitation of four hundred Brooklyn pastors largely because he had made up his mind to campaign in New York City and felt that Brooklyn was too near by. In 1915 he declined an invitation from Cleveland brought to him by the Rev. George Bustard, pastor of John D. Rockefeller, Sr.'s, church, because four Presbyterian churches and one Congregational church opposed him. And it was stated that the opposition of the influential Washington Gladden was sufficient to keep him from accepting an invitation to come to Indianapolis, although Sunday had recently held a campaign in Columbus, where Gladden's church refused to co-operate.[11]

Sometimes a particular layman's approval was more important to Sunday than church unity—and ministerial associations were wise to have their leading laymen join in the invitation to Sunday. He turned down the first invitation from Syracuse, New York, because the petition did not include the name of the chancellor of the University of Syracuse, James R. Day, whose patron was John D. Archbold, of Standard Oil. When Day's approval was obtained, Sunday changed his mind.[12] The tremendous amount of pressure which often was exerted by influential ministers and laymen upon their fellows in order to get them to sign an invitation to Sunday was seldom noted in the press. It usually took place in secret meetings, and quite often rather unprincipaled means were used to extort cooperation from opponents. The difficulties in such large cities as Boston, New York, and Washington, D.C., were particularly apparent and could not entirely be hidden from the public eye.

It was in February of 1915 that the movement to invite Sunday to Boston was begun by several influential clergymen.[13] Under the leadership of Cortland Myers, pastor of Tremont Temple (Baptist), and A. Z. Conrad, pastor of Park Street Church (Congregationalist), one hundred ministers of the Evangelical Alliance in that city voted at their monthly meeting to extend an invitation to Sunday to revive the backslidden and unregenerate populace of Boston. Since there were over five hundred evangelical ministers within the metropolitan area of Boston, Myers and Conrad realized that Sunday would not even look at an invitation with only one hundred names on it. So they sent out letters to every church within twenty miles, asking them to join in supporting Sunday.

The opposition began at once. The editor of *Zion's Herald* (Methodist Episcopal, Boston) stated that he considered that Sunday's coming would be "a calamity," and he printed a supposedly objective symposium on the subject in which three ministers who supported Sunday were answered by three who opposed him. The next day the *Watchman-Examiner* (Baptist, Boston) stated that the Baptists and Presbyterians of the city were unanimously behind the movement, regardless of the Methodists. The editor also reported that 186 ministers and laymen had signed a petition asking Sunday to set a date for Boston.

Six days after this, Myers and Conrad led a delegation of seventy-five ministers and laymen to Philadelphia, where they presented a long petition of names to Sunday and asked him to accept their invitation. Myers reportedly made some unkind remarks about the Unitarians and about Harvard College's being in need of Sunday's preaching. According to the editor of the *Congregationalist* (Boston), who strongly opposed Sunday, Myers said, "We want you to come to Boston and give some of the opposition, as you say, the devil." The *Congregationalist* also reported that only 184 out of 500 evangelical churches in the vicinity of Boston had taken favorable action in answer to the Myers-Conrad invitation to join in inviting Sunday; out of 100 Congregational churches, only 35 had been among this 184. The Methodist journal noted that only six of the seventy-five members of the delegation which went to see Sunday in Philadelphia were Methodists. It was clear not only that there was strong opposition to Sunday but that in spite of it Sunday was going to accept the invitation to revive the city.

A glimpse behind the scenes of this hectic situation was given by a Methodist minister of Everett, Massachusetts, who stated that "covert and steamroller methods" had been used to railroad through the meeting of the Evangelical Alliance the vote asking Sunday to come; the leaders of the movement had accused pastors who opposed the invitation of "fighting against God" and had made outright threats to see that those who did not co-operate would lose their pulpits. He said that the petition given to Sunday "was a tissue of misrepresentation," that 40 per cent of the ministers on the list did not even know that their names had been included. One of those whose name was on the list "was browbeaten over the telephone" until he permitted his name to be added. "It was also stated to Mr. Sunday," said the Everett pastor, "that letters had been sent and replies received from all the Baptist, Presbyterian, and Methodist churches, all in favor of his coming. That was a falsehood also."

But Sunday was wiser than this minister realized—or else better informed by his advance man than was realized. Soon after he accepted the Boston invitation, both the editor of *Zion's Herald* and the *Congregationalist* changed their minds and decided to back the campaign. By the time Sunday arrived in Boston, on November 12, 1916, it was announced that four hundred evangelical pastors had gotten on the band wagon.

The New York City invitation to Sunday followed an even more devious and tortuous path, stretching over more than a year of wrangling among the eight hundred or so ministers in and around the city.[14] The first step was taken by the New York Evangelistic Committee, whose principal activity was the management of the summer tent meetings for religious services in the city. This group asked Sunday to make a benefit appearance for them at Carnegie Hall, the proceeds to go to their tenth annual open-air and shop-meeting campaign. The fact that Stephen Baker, the chairman of the committee (and also the president of the Bank of Manhattan and the Bank of the Metropolis), later became a member of the executive committee which supported Sunday's campaign indicated an ulterior purpose.

On March 9, 1914, Sunday came down from his campaign in Scranton to make a one-night appearance in New York City. The crowd at Carnegie Hall was so large that Andrew Carnegie and his wife were unable to get into the meeting. Stephen Baker presided, and Bishop Luther B. Wilson (Methodist) delivered the opening prayer. In introducing Sunday to the audience, the Rev. J. K. McClurkin, of Pittsburgh, compared him to John the Baptist and told of the 26,600 conversions resulting from Sunday's Pittsburgh revival. Sunday's chorister led the audience in a few hymns, and then Sunday gave his famous sermon on "The Need for Revival," in which he stated that evil days had fallen upon the church, which was reduced to a social club and an amusement bureau. The sermon was loudly applauded, but the collection netted Baker's Evangelistic Committee only $389.20 plus several hundred dollars in pledges.

A week later at a meeting of the Methodist ministers of New York someone brought up the question of inviting Sunday to the city for a revival. The suggestion produced violent arguments and some denunciations, and after a heated debate the question was temporarily dropped. On April 2 the annual meeting of the Methodist Episcopal Conference of New York took place, and Dr. C. A. Boswell, the secretary for home missions and church extension, took the occasion to make a speech praising Sunday. When he closed by declaring that "he can deliver the goods," Dr. Boswell was greeted with loud applause.

Ten days after this, a group of evangelical leaders called a special meeting of the ministers of the city in order to discuss certain misrepresentations about Sunday which they said had been spreading. Three speakers had been obtained: Dr. Maitland Alexander, of Pittsburgh, who told how Sunday added 419 members to his Presbyterian church; W. H. Donner, president of the Cambria Steel Company of Johnstown, Pennsylvania, who described how thousands of his steelworkers, "led by officers of the company," attended Sunday's revival in that city; and Thomas Atherton, a leading attorney of Wilkes-Barre, who related the story of the conversion of a gentleman's poker club in that city into a Bible class after a Sunday campaign. These effective speakers gave new life to the movement to unite New York for an invitation. But it was nine months before the forces of righteousness had sufficient strength to come to a showdown.

At a secret meeting on January 18, 1915, the Methodist ministers of the city voted to invite Sunday, but not without loud opposition from a vigorous minority. The *New York Times* reported the next day that the Baptist, Presbyterian, and Reformed church ministers had also voted to ask him to come. For another week pressure was brought against the opponents of the invitation, and then, by special invitation, 400 of those ministers who were in favor of the movement met at the Marble Collegiate Church in order to pass a unanimous resolution which could be presented to Sunday. At the last minute the pastor of the People's Baptist Church changed his mind and voted against the measure, but the other 399 ministers voted for it, and 300 of these made a trip to Philadelphia on January 28 to hear Sunday speak and to present their petition. During the course of the sermon Sunday stated for their benefit, "I would not fear failure in New York."

The petition of the New York pastors read: "We, the undersigned, deeply interested in the religious life of our city, unite in extending to the Rev. William A. Sunday an invitation to conduct an Evangelistic Campaign in New York early in the year 1916." But Sunday's advance agent evidently reported to him that the opposition was still strong, and on April 12, when Sunday was asked at a dinner of the New York Press Club whether or not he had accepted the invitation, he said that he had not yet committed himself.

At the next meeting of the New York ministers' conference some clergymen who had evidently not been invited to the special meeting at the Marble Collegiate Church rose to say that they were upset by the fact that certain ministers had extended an invitation to Sunday in the name of the ministers of New York when obviously many did not want him to come. Others arose to say that they were in favor of the invitation but had not been given a change to indorse the movement. Since it was apparent that the opposition was in the minority, Dr. Charles L. Goodell (Methodist), who was presiding at the meeting, decided to appoint a new delegation of ministers to present a second plea to Sunday. Goodell and one hundred clergymen went to Paterson on May 21 and presented New York's final offer, which Sunday accepted. The case of the second delegation had been greatly improved by the fact that John D. Rockefeller, Jr., had added his support to the invitation.

However, there was no doubt that Sunday compromised his stipulation regarding "united" or "unanimous" support of the evangelical clergy when he agreed to come to New York. He was more optimistic about his chances of success there than was his friend John Wanamaker, who wrote to him on June 23, 1915: "The Lord's people are very peculiar people, not only in Philadelphia and Paterson, but in New York where only half the people wanted you, and in some other places where they did not want you at all." Although the latter reference was not clear in Wanamaker's letter, it probably concerned the invitation which Sunday had recently received from Washington, D.C. The story behind this invitation was revealed by one of the lay members of Sunday's executive committee there, who gave it as an example of the extent to which Sunday and his advance agent were themselves responsible for implementing a movement for an invitation in cities which on their own initiative were unwilling to undertake one.[15] At the time, of course, Sunday made it seem to the public that he had absolutely nothing to do with soliciting any of the invitations which he received. As he told a reporter who asked him why he had held six revivals in Pennsylvania within a two-year period, "I didn't plan it that way. God planned it. I just go where I'm called."[16] And his calls, he claimed, were the results solely of local lay and clerical desire for his services.

The Washington, D.C., ministers had, as a matter of fact, considered inviting Sunday late in 1914, but after much debate on the question it "was not voted upon because the difference of opinion was so great that it was feared a vote might not be wholesome." When this news reached Sunday's advance man, who at that time was the Rev. J. W. Welch, he immediately went to Washington to see if something could not be done to bring about a change of heart. Welch went first to see William K. Cooper, general secretary of the Washington YMCA. He explained the merits of a Sunday revival and persuaded him to talk to certain influential laymen on Sunday's behalf. Cooper approached John C. Letts, the grocery chain-store millionaire, who was a devoted benefactor of the YMCA and an equally devout Baptist. Letts was convinced that a Sunday campaign would be good for Washington. He and Cooper then went to Merrit O. Chance, the city postmaster, and to several prominent ministers and heads of civic groups. About fifteen of these formed a citizens' committee to promote an invitation to Sunday. They made a trip to Philadelphia to hear Sunday and made arrangements with Welch to have Sunday speak for one night in Washington in order to stir up enthusiasm and allay misapprehensions.

On January 18, 1915, Sunday made his first trip to Washington, D.C. He was received by President Wilson at the White House, had lunch with Secretary of State William Jennings Bryan, had dinner with the citizens' committee, and then spoke to a specially selected audience of celebrities and ministers at Convention Hall. He was introduced by Champ Clark, Speaker of the House of Representatives, and in a sermon noticeably free of slang and acrobatics he discussed the question, "If Christ Came to Washington." After he had gone, the citizens' committee formally made its decision to invite him and appointed an executive committee of seven men (including Cooper, Letts, and Chance) to complete the arrangements. They organized a general committee of one hundred ministers and laymen, who eventually presented an invitation to Sunday which stated that sixty churches in Washington were eager to have him come. He accepted.

Leonard W. DeGast, who later succeeded Cooper as general secretary of the YMCA, worked with Cooper on the executive committee as treasurer of the campaign, and, in telling this story of the inner workings of the invitation, he stated that the pressure of the laymen upon the ministers had been the deciding factor in reversing the original decision not to invite Sunday. This view was confirmed by a statement made by the Rev. A. Z. Conrad, of Boston, who was trying to overcome ministerial opposition there at the same time that Cooper and Letts were doing similar work in Washington. Conrad told the Boston ministers that the laymen of Boston were going to take a lesson from the laymen of Washington: "The laymen of Boston," he threatened, "will secure Billy Sunday no matter what the attitude of the ministers, just as in the city of Washington they served notice on the ministers they would do. The laymen of America have arisen in their determination that the church shall not be strangled with interrogation points nor sent to its death sleep by subtle theological sophisms."[17]

While the part played by Sunday and his agents in gaining invitations was not publicly known, the part played by wealthy laymen in promoting these revivals was a generally accepted fact. The newspapers helped to promote the view that certain wealthy and influential men were behind a Sunday revival; they did so because better headlines resulted from secularizing the otherwise limited appeal of a religious movement. Certain laymen took it upon themselves to boast about their influence in supporting revivalism: George B. Arnold, the millionaire silk manufacturer of Paterson, stated publicly that he was responsible for bringing Sunday to that city. John D. Rockefeller, Jr., implied that he was instrumental in persuading Sunday to accept New York's invitation. John Wanamaker; Cyrus Curtis; John C. Winston, the publisher; and Alba B. Johnson, president of the Baldwin Locomotive Works, were given credit for making the Philadelphia campaign possible. Mrs. Sunday stated that Allan C. Emery, of the Boston Wool Trade Association, brought Billy Sunday to Boston.

Among the noted laymen mentioned as prime movers in Sunday's campaigns were John M. Studebaker, W. H. Donner, S. S. Kresge, B. A. Walker, Joshua Levering, Daniel Baker, H. J. Heinz, and Henry Leland. Countless other leading laymen had their names linked with Sunday's in these years because they either served on his committees, sat on his platform, or invited him to their homes. Among them were Theodore Roosevelt, Elbert H. Gary, William Jennings Bryan, Henry Clay Frick, John Archbold, George W. Perkins, George Wharton Pepper, Finley J. Shepard, Victor Lawson, Louis F. Swift, H. P. Crowell, E. T. Stotesbury, A. J. Drexel-Biddle, J. Ogden Armour, Henry A. Stimson, William Lyon Phelps, Henry W. Jessup, David Whitney, and Arthur Brisbane.

The pressure of laymen not only could compel the ministers of a city to invite Sunday; it could also prevent a revival. In Louisville, Kentucky, in 1914, when the Commercial Club in that city, made up principally of bourbon distillers, decided that a Sunday campaign would help the Prohibition cause, its members exerted sufficient pressure upon the ministers of the city to make them withdraw their decision to invite Sunday after they had already voted to do so. A religious journal commented sadly, "The opposition of the Commercial Club was due to the evangelist's effective method of fighting the whiskey traffic. We are sorry that the churches allowed the Commercial Club to interfere with their plans, but probably leaders in the Commercial Club are leaders in the churches, and so it goes."[18] But in most cities the lay influence was heavily in the other direction.

Obtaining at least a measure of outward church and lay support was merely the first step in preparing for a successful revival. The next step was fixing the date for the revival, and after that came the remaining stipulations regarding the erection of the tabernacle and the raising of the expense fund. Generally a revival was scheduled at the first available date on Sunday's calendar. The committees which had won the battles for the invitation were anxious to capitalize upon their success as soon as possible. Unfortunately for them, however, Sunday's schedule was fixed far in advance, and it was frequently with amazement and shock that committees learned that the closest available date for their city was two or three years away. Many cities, like Worcester, Massachusetts, and New Haven and Bridgeport, Connecticut, were unable to find a date suitable both to themselves and to Sunday, and their hoped-for revival never took place. But the demand for his services was so great that Sunday could afford to treat his offers cavalierly in these years. While he was in Boston in 1916, it was reported that seventeen different cities in New England alone had asked him to visit them.

The New York invitation stated that a date "early in the year 1916" was preferred, but Sunday put them off until April, 1917. He cared enough about coming to New York, however, to use all his powers of persuasion to force the Chicago committee to yield its campaign date to New York, or else New York would have had to wait even longer. Chicago then had the unpleasant experience of being put off until March, 1918, despite the fact that its invitation had been signed by 55,000 persons representing 500 churches. When Sunday tried to get Trenton, New Jersey, to trade places with Chicago (a contingency upon which he had counted in persuading Chicago to yield to New York), he was disappointed to find that the Trenton clergy absolutely refused. The ultimate failure of the Chicago campaign was blamed by many persons on the shabby treatment which the city had received at Sunday's hands in this regard.

Almost as much difficulty was involved in meeting the second requirement, concerning the location and erection of the special wooden tabernacle. Most cities had building or fire ordinances which prohibited the erection of a temporary structure in the downtown area, but Sunday nonetheless insisted. This meant that pressure had to be brought upon local authorities to obtain a temporary revocation of the ordinances. In Boston a special act of the state legislature was required to waive the building ordinance. Many legislators balked at this, and it was only when a telegram from Sunday was published, saying that without a wooden tabernacle he could not preach effectively, that the bill was passed. Then Governor McCall vetoed the bill. He pointed out that the legislature had recently passed an act forbidding the use of wooden stables in the city, and he thought human beings deserved as much consideration as horses. All the arguments of Sunday's tabernacle architect regarding the complete safety of the proposed structure could not make the legislators pass the bill over the governor's veto, and so it was necessary to build the tabernacle of terra cotta and steel; the expenses of the campaign were almost doubled as a result.

In most cases the influential supporters of the revival were able to obtain the waiver of such ordinances. Opposition to the measure was always charged to enemies of righteousness—such as the liquor interests. In Boston many ministers agreed with the editor of the *Watchman-Examiner* that the opposition came from the Unitarians, Episcopalians, and the Roman Catholic hierarchy (the governor was an Episcopalian) or, as the editor put it, from "the unevangelical elements."[19] In Johnstown, Pennsylvania, it was necessary to have the city council break the will of the city's founder, in order that the tabernacle might be built in a public park which the will specifically stated was to be kept entirely for the use of the city's children. It took two years of pressure to force the council to do this.

Sunday was frequently asked to consider using available auditoriums, convention halls, and other permanent buildings in order to save the trouble and expense of a special tabernacle. He consistently refused to do so. In Pittsburgh, when an injunction was demanded by opponents of the revival to prevent the tabernacle's being built in a zone where wooden buildings were prohibited, Sunday was asked why he could not use Exposition Hall. The local committee pointed out that the well-known evangelist "Gypsy"

Smith had held a successful revival there some years previously. The efficiency-minded Sunday answered that the $20,000 asked for rent, heat, and light for Exposition Hall was "exorbitant." Besides, he reminded them, "excursions will be coming into Pittsburgh all the time which will net money for Pittsburgh," and the equipment for the tabernacle would be purchased from local merchants and would thus aid business. Furthermore, the hall held only 4,000 persons, while at that moment he was speaking nightly in Johnstown in a tabernacle for 8,000. "Why be satisfied in Pittsburgh with 4,000?" he asked. In conclusion, he threatened to go on to Scranton, the next town on his schedule, if Pittsburgh did not have a tabernacle built by the time his revival ended in Johnstown.[20] The Pittsburgh committee fought off the injunction by getting a bill through the city council waiving the fire ordinance. When Joseph Spiece, Sunday's tabernacle architect, built a tabernacle (on land donated free of charge by Henry Clay Frick) which held 15,000 persons at a cost of only $18,000, Sunday's efficiency was demonstrated. As Mrs. Sunday told reporters, "You know you cannot keep the Gospel out if God wants it in a city."

The New York committee had such difficulty in locating a suitable site for a tabernacle that they offered to rent Madison Square Garden. Again Sunday refused. They then tried to make arrangements for the use of one of the city's playgrounds. Mayor Mitchel agreed, but a hue and cry went up in the local press, and the committee and the mayor changed their minds. The only available lots in New York were far from the city's center or else off the main bus and subway lines. At one time it was reported that Sunday had given up hope of finding a suitable site and would not come. Neither the advance man nor the business agent (who at that time was Sunday's son George) nor Sunday himself could decide upon a place. Finally, Mrs. Sunday made a special trip to New York to look at the last three possibilities. She stated that one of them had no available space for parking cars, while the second was located in a Negro district where people would not, she claimed, feel safe in leaving their cars. She was compelled to accept the third place, a vacant lot at 168th Street and Broadway, where the subway station was 116 feet below the ground and had only one small elevator to the surface.[21] The Fifth Avenue Bus Company was granted a special franchise to change its route to accommodate the crowds.

Once the site was obtained and the building permit granted, the tabernacle expert arrived in the city to supervise the construction.

The size of the tabernacles had increased steadily, from the tabernacle for 1,000 in Perry, Iowa, to the New York tabernacle, with a capacity of 20,000. But the basic design of the buildings remained much the same. The basilica-like nave of the early tabernacles gradually flattened out until the roof came to be described as "turtle-backed." To save electricity, dozens of dormer windows gave light for the afternoon meetings. The bare plank walls, the double barn doors, and the long rows of pine benches continued unchanged, except that the interior was sometimes given a coat of whitewash and back rests were put on the benches.

The platform grew higher and longer from year to year. In 1914 Joseph Spiece constructed a trap door in the platform at the front edge near the pulpit which opened into a waist-high well in the floor. Here Sunday stood after the sermon when he shook hands with the converts; the recess made it considerably easier for him to reach the upstretched hands of those standing on the floor ten feet below. The pulpit itself was built as part of the platform and was constructed to permit Sunday to stand on it without danger of its collapsing or tipping. The platform was covered with a carpet to deaden the sound of Sunday's prancing feet. At each end of the platform were the press tables. These tables were on the same level as the floor of the platform and were often merely extensions of it. The reporters sat facing the audience and literally wrote on the platform itself. Occasionally they had to remove their notes and hands in order to avoid being trampled on by Sunday.

Behind the platform (or off to one side) another lower platform held the two pianos. Directly in back of the pianos tiers of seats sloped up toward the roof in a semicircle. These seats accommodated 1,000–2,000 persons, the lower rows being reserved for local clergymen, prominent committee members, and visiting dignitaries; the upper rows held the thousand- or two-thousand-voice choir. Hundreds of bare electric-light bulbs were strung across the rafters to provide a brilliant, glaring light. In the winter, heat was provided by iron stoves for which special stokers were hired. (The Philadelphia tabernacle, which held 18,000 persons, had thirty stoves.) The floor sloped slightly forward and was usually the ground itself. On it were scattered tons of sawdust or shavings, which often were bought up after the campaign and sifted for the coins which were lost in them during the course of the collection-taking over the weeks.

The front of the building carried a banner saying "Billy Sunday

Tabernacle," and the interior walls had texts or mottoes, such as "Get Right with God," "Saved for Service," or "Now Is the Appointed Time" written on them. The platform was usually draped with bright-colored bunting, and the pulpit with the American flag. Above the platform was a banner containing the name of the city in the phrase "——— for Christ." In Paterson two electric signs carried the slogans "New Jersey for Christ" and "Christ for New Jersey."

The seating capacity of the tabernacles varied in proportion to the size of the city. For cities of under 200,000 the tabernacle was built to hold 10 per cent of the population. Larger cities were limited to buildings for 18,000 to 20,000, partly because it would have been difficult to fill a larger tabernacle twice a day for eight or ten weeks and partly because, in an era before the invention of electrical loud-speaking apparatus, Sunday's voice could not stand the strain. Even with the help of a sounding board called an "Acousticon," specially designed by Spiece, Sunday could not make himself heard by people in the back rows, which were sometimes the length of a football field away. "You people probably think sometimes I'm a crank about all these little noises," Sunday told a crowded tabernacle in Wichita, Kansas, which he had admonished for the third time, "but if you had to make your bread and butter by preaching the word of God, you'd be careful, too, that people didn't make you strain your voice."[22]

The cost of the tabernacles varied with size and place. Sunday claimed that he always used union labor in constructing them, though some sources denied this. Despite every effort to minimize costs, the tabernacle remained the principal expense of each campaign. The Denver tabernacle for 10,000 persons cost $8,000—over 40 per cent of the total expenses. A tabernacle the same size in Columbus cost $10,200—over 50 per cent of the expenses. In Paterson a tabernacle for only 8,000 persons cost $14,000—about 50 per cent of the total. On the average, Sunday could count on a cost of a dollar to a dollar and a half per seat for the tabernacles.

The terra cotta and steel structure which was forced upon Sunday in Boston cost $45,000 for 18,000 persons. But the most expensive of all tabernacles was that in New York, holding 20,000, which, though largely of wood, cost $65,000, including the grading of the land, furnishings, and repairs. By way of comparison, the tabernacle for 18,000 in Philadelphia cost only $24,000. One reason for the high cost of the New York tabernacle was its elaborate facilities. A description of the work involved, published by the New York committee, showed that 400 workmen had taken two months to complete the building, that it was 344 by 247 feet, that 400,000 feet of lumber and 250 barrels of nails were used; four carloads of shavings covered the floor, and there were 38 doors, 2,000 seats back of the platform, 16,000 on the main floor. "The seats on the main floor were divided into forty-eight sections with three wide aisles running across and ten aisles running lengthwise." In addition to the main meeting-room, this tabernacle contained "a post office, a hospital, rooms for the personal workers, ushers, members of the press, the custodian, and the doorkeepers; also book rooms, and a retiring room for the evangelist."

Police and fire protection for the tabernacle was a factor in running up the expenses. Some towns provided this protection at the taxpayers' expense, but others demanded that the revival committee pay for the extra duty. The police were usually most active in driving away or arresting vendors of anti-Sunday magazines or leaflets and in ejecting hecklers from the tabernacle, but they were also needed to handle the traffic and the crowds. In addition, they were given the job of protecting Sunday from possible attacks by cranks and fanatics, who often sent him threatening letters. "In the old saloon days," Sunday wrote in his "Autobiography," "the city officials always assigned men to guard me and the house where I stayed day and night." And sometimes they had to guard the men who backed Sunday, like George Arnold, as well.

However, on the two occasions when Sunday was actually assailed by fanatics, there were no policemen on hand to protect him. The first and more sensational assault came in Springfield, Illinois, in 1909 on the opening night of the revival. He had just stood up to start his sermon when a dark, burly man leaped out of the front bench and began flailing at him with a horsewhip, shouting, "I have a commission from God to horsewhip you." He struck Sunday twice, and then Sunday leaped down at him from the platform yelling, "Well, I have a commission from God to knock the tar out of you, you lobster." Sunday wrote later, "I jumped from the platform and rushed at him with my fist doubled. . . . I gave him a [blow to the] solar plexus and a left hook to the jaw." But according to the newspaper accounts of the day, Sunday never caught up with the man, who was stopped running up the aisle by one of Sunday's assistants. Sunday sprained his ankle in jumping from the platform and had to deliver his sermons for the rest of the campaign on crutches, but he did not prosecute his assailant, a man named Sherman Potts, who, it turned out, had formerly been an inmate of the state insane asylum.[23] The second assault on Sunday was made in Atlanta, Georgia, during World War I, when an irate German-American attacked him with a whip for his denunciations of the Kaiser.

With or without policemen, however, the expense of running a Sunday revival placed a tremendous burden upon the churches. Even with the support of wealthy laymen, the stipulation that sufficient cash or pledges to pay all the expenses be on hand prior to the campaign was difficult to meet. Admittedly, the tabernacle had to be paid for in advance, but the demand that the money to meet the running expenses of the campaign also must be on hand seemed unnecessarily stringent to Sunday's backers. Nevertheless, he was as insistent on this requirement as on the others.

It was unfortunate for Sunday that he called the sum which he required each city to raise in advance a "guarantee fund." He meant by this only that it guaranteed the revival against deficits—a matter which some unscrupulous or inefficient evangelists failed to provide for, much to the distress of their sponsors. Sunday claimed that never in his career had the collections taken at the meetings failed to meet all the expenses and thereby pay back the loans or pledges made for the guarantee. Sunday's enemies, or those whose acquaintance with his work was obtained by a cursory glance at the headlines, construed the term "guarantee fund" to mean that this large sum of money was specified in advance by Sunday as the minimum payment for his services. No amount of denials could persuade such critics that Sunday's sole reward was the free-will offering donated voluntarily at the end of the campaign.

There was another reason why Sunday insisted upon a guarantee fund, and that was to arouse interest in the campaign. Not only did it provide publicity, but it made certain that there was a serious intention on the part of those who invited him to back him to the limit. As Sunday put it, "Where a man's treasure is, there is his heart also." The sum fixed for the guarantee was decided upon by Sunday after consultation with his advance man, business agent, and the local committee. Sometimes he demanded that it be large enough to cover only a percentage of the estimated total expenses, sometimes that it cover the total expenses. And sometimes he demanded a guarantee which was obviously more than the expenses could possibly be.

The local committee in Pittsburgh, for example, complained that the guarantee of $150,000 which Sunday had set for them was out of all proportion to the expenses. He told reporters, "But they won't have to pay anything like that. I know the expenses of that campaign in Pittsburgh, everything included, will not go over $25,000." His exaggerated demand evidently came from the belief that $150,-000 in pledges often dwindled to less than $50,000 when it came time to provide the cash, but he added, "Whatever the campaign costs, it is the church people who are paying, and they are paying willingly."[24]

In Denver, Colorado, in 1914 the advance man, A. P. Gill, quoted a much more reasonable price to the local ministers when they were considering inviting Sunday. "The campaign will cost you $25,000," he said. "For $25,000 you can give the devil a good run for his money." The ministers agreed without complaint to raise this guarantee.[25]

The method of raising the guarantee fund varied from city to city. In Philadelphia John Wanamaker offered to underwrite the whole campaign himself, but Sunday refused, saying that he would rather have a million people pledge one dollar than have one man pledge a million. In Philadelphia, as elsewhere, it was the business-men who put the bulk of the $50,000 in pledges. The Rev. George H. Bickley, vice-chairman of the committee there, told how the pledges were converted into cash to pay for the labor and equipment of the tabernacle: "We took the pledges to the banks as collateral and borrowed cash to float the enterprise." This was the method followed in most cities.

The Syracuse guarantee of $20,000 was raised not only by gifts from the churches and from individuals but also by donations from certain corporations which viewed the revival as a legitimate investment for their business. In New York it was agreed that the guarantee fund should amount to only one-half the estimated $150,-000 expenses. This $75,000 was raised partly by "a canvass of the churches" but more largely from "persons interested in the evangelization of New York City."

In the Columbus, Wilkes-Barre, and Johnstown campaigns in 1912–13, the years when Sunday's invasion of the large cities first raised his revivals to a big-business enterprise, the local ministers and businessmen who sponsored the movement had themselves incorporated under the state laws as the William A. Sunday Evangelistic Association, Inc. They then printed stock certificates for their enterprise, which sold at a dollar a share. At the close of the cam-

THE JEFFERSON BEE.

JEFFERSON, IOWA, THURSDAY, JANUARY 7 1904.

516 TURN TO CHRIST

RESULTS OF THE UNION MEETINGS

Conversions during meetings	516
Voluntary offering Sunday	$1,400
Number present Sunday night	2,600
Conversions on Sunday	107
Men present Sunday afternoon	1,500
Men converted Sunday afternoon	60
Collection Sunday morning	$1,200
Current expense collection	$ 950
Jefferson's total investment	$2,350

Jefferson's Dividends on Investment

The conversion of more than half of the population outside the churches.

Classes Professing Conversion

Business men, city officials, farmers, county officers, young men, old men, aged women and girls, the high and low, the rich and poor.

SUNDAY ⚊ AND ⚊ HIS WORK

SUNDAY A GREAT DAY.

THE UNION REVIVAL CLOSED.

From the front page of the *Jefferson Bee* at the conclusion of Sunday's revival in Jefferson, Iowa, in January, 1904. The converts were listed by name in the right-hand column.

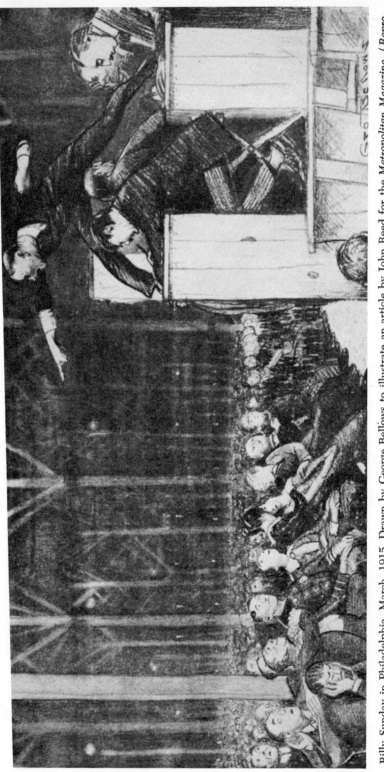

Billy Sunday in Philadelphia, March, 1915. Drawn by George Bellows to illustrate an article by John Reed for the *Metropolitan Magazine*. (*Reproduced courtesy of Mrs. George Bellows.*)

paign these shares were redeemable at face value from the money collected at the tabernacle. Though few cities adopted such a colorful method of raising money, virtually all Sunday's committees after 1912 took the precaution of incorporating themselves.

Cash was always preferable to pledges, even when banks were willing to accept pledges as collateral. In Washington, D.C., the pledges passed out by the ministers in the churches were actually promissory notes to pay cash at a certain date or on a series of dates. The $75,000 guarantee there was started by $2,500 in cash from Letts and $1,000 each from five other members of the committee. This money was used to rent an office, where the campaign's treasurer and two assistants kept accounts of all the pledges and the dates when cash was due on each. As the money was mailed to this office in fulfilment of the pledges, it was deposited at the bank and drawn upon for the expenses. Most of the pledges, according to the treasurer, were in amounts of from five to thirty dollars. Here, as elsewhere, the donors received their money back after the campaign from the funds collected at the services.

There is no record of Sunday's ever having canceled a meeting because the full amount set for the guarantee fund was not raised, though many places, including Denver, Pittsburgh, Washington, D.C., and New York did not raise it. An antagonistic minister in Boston remarked that, while Sunday had originally demanded "unanimous" support from the ministers, "it now appears that 'unanimous support' means enough to get the money." If Sunday was convinced that sufficient money was on hand and that the backers were wholeheartedly behind him, he did not press for the full amount of the guarantee any more than he did for unanimous support.

Once the basic problems of the invitation, starting date, tabernacle, and guarantee fund were under control, the advance man made his appearance publicly to instruct the local committee in regard to the preparatory work. Eight months before the campaign was to start in Boston, the advance man, Welch, told the cooperating ministers that he would need a total of 20,000 volunteer workers, some of them doing more than one job, to lay the groundwork of the revival. He demanded 8,000 to sing in the choir; 2,000 ushers; 700 "secretaries" to be trained to help the converts fill out decision cards; 200 doorkeepers; 7,000 homes in which "cottage prayer meetings" could be held; 7,000 prayer-meeting leaders; 5,000 personal workers; 1,000 women to help organize the city's businesswomen; 1,000 women to help hold meetings in factories, hospitals, hotels, etc.; 300 automobiles with drivers; 500 women to organize the noonday lunches and devotional meetings; and 500 women to care for children under four who were not permitted in the tabernacle but were kept at "the nursery" in a near-by church while their parents went to the service. In reporting these demands, the enthusiastic *Watchman-Examiner* chortled editorially, "This is 'Big Business' for the Lord."[26]

In order to obtain volunteers, the ministers were instructed to pass out "work cards" at their church services which were to be filled out and returned, indicating which of the multifarious revival committees the church member wished to serve on and how much time he could give to them each week. It was estimated that 35,000 persons were actively engaged in promoting the revival in Boston and 50,000 in New York.

The number and size of the committees varied, but the following were usually considered essential: executive, music, prayer-meeting, building, finance, businessmen's work, businesswomen's work, nursery, personal work, ushers', secretaries', shopwork, extension, printing, publicity, students' work, boys' and girls' work, young people's work, entertainment, and transportation; these twenty committees, filled by volunteers from the churches, corresponded to the various specialists on Sunday's staff. The advance man acquainted the local chairmen of each committee with what was expected of him, so that all would be ready when the staff specialists arrived to take command at the start of the revival.

In addition to volunteer labor, certain paid workers were required. In New York a suite of twelve rooms was rented in the Metropolitan Building a year in advance of the revival and staffed with seventy-five clerks and stenographers to handle the correspondence and other details of the preparation. In order to train the personal workers who were to help save souls at the tabernacle, the advance man usually persuaded the local committee to hire the Rev. Howard A. Johnston, who went from city to city training those who volunteered for this work in Sunday's campaigns. Another associate expert whom the advance agent recommended for hire was the Rev. George Dowey, a specialist in building up the number and size of the Bible classes, particularly men's Bible classes. In New York Dowey was given credit for increasing the number of men's Bible classes from thirty-four to ninety-one, and in Philadelphia it was reported that "more than 50,000 men were organized in Bible classes" during the revival.

The cottage-prayer-meeting system which the advance man organized provided astronomical figures to demonstrate the interest in the revival. Every city was divided into districts, containing from forty to one hundred families. One home was selected in each district, in which a volunteer agreed to hold prayer meetings twice weekly. These meetings began months before the revival and continued throughout it. Boston reported 79,784 prayer meetings during the course of its campaign. In Baltimore there were 1,200 districts where biweekly meetings attended by, on the average, fifteen persons continued for sixteen weeks—this meant that nearly 500,000 prayers were said for Baltimore's regeneration. If it is assumed that an average of fifteen persons had attended each of the Boston prayer meetings, it meant 1,200,000 prayers were said there. How many of these were the same prayer repeated twice a week by the same person was a different matter.

It was also part of the advance man's work to see that the wealthy members of the community were aroused. Prominent businessmen, lawyers, doctors, and clergymen who had co-operated in previous campaigns in other cities were brought to the city to speak at the churches, fraternal lodges, Rotary Club, the chamber of commerce, and at special banquets. Albert J. Saunders, a wholesale produce merchant who was referred to in the press as a Scranton "businessman," was converted at one of Sunday's meetings in Scranton in 1914 and for several years made a career of speaking to such groups. He called himself "Billy Sunday's most famous convert," and Sunday's committees in cities across the country paid him to speak at promotional functions. He was considered particularly adept at reaching the society and business groups. In New York he spoke at the home of Mrs. John D. Rockefeller, Jr., to a group of two hundred leading society women. Prominent personalities like the Rev. Maitland Alexander, a moderator of the Presbyterian General Assembly; Dr. Howard Kelly, of Johns Hopkins; and the Rev. Charles R. Erdman, of Princeton Seminary, were also instrumental in stimulating the interest among the wealthy and influential. They of course received no pay for this but spoke out of their own conviction of Sunday's importance, and they were the more convincing for that reason.

Leading citizens, particularly those holding political office, were persuaded by the prominent backers of the campaign to appear at dinners and meetings given to promote the revival. In Boston Mayor James M. Curley and twelve mayors of the Boston suburbs acted as a committee to greet eight distinguished out-of-town speakers at a revival promotion luncheon attended by four hundred Boston businessmen at the Boston City Club. Curley, a Roman Catholic, told the group, which paid two dollars apiece for the privilege of attending, that he wished Mr. Sunday success: "Mr. Sunday makes men think of the hereafter, and anyone who does this is doing a worthy work regardless of his race or creed."[27]

The audited expense account of the New York campaign contained an item of $2,937.16 for "public luncheons and dinner meetings" and specifically stated that "these meetings were held for the promotion of the campaign and included large meetings at the Hotels Astor, Savoy, etc." In the local press they were referred to as "millionaires' lunches" because of the number of wealthy men who attended them.[28]

In order to give a well-rounded sampling of Sunday's work, speakers were invited from the less prominent walks of life. Converted saloonkeepers, drunkards, ex-convicts, streetcar conductors, and clerks gave their testimony to the power of Sunday's preaching. They spoke in churches, prayer meetings, and YMCA's. One thousand such men were brought to New York one Sunday before the revival at the committee's expense to speak in all the co-operating churches. Philadelphia imported eight hundred converts from Scranton and Wilkes-Barre to describe "in [a] simple but effective way the change which had been wrought in their lives by the work of Mr. Sunday."

The advance man also took charge of obtaining publicity for the campaign. No paper could ignore the movement, and most assigned reporters and photographers to cover it from start to finish, but the advance man had to see that these reporters got the most useful information and got it at carefully spaced intervals in order to keep the story alive. Some newspapers manufactured their own news stories, like the *Philadelphia North American,* which sent a special train with seven hundred Philadelphia ministers to hear Sunday in Scranton prior to the Philadelphia campaign. The Rev. George Bickley, of the Philadelphia committee, told the New York ministers that press co-operation had been obtained in his city by giving the owners of the newspapers prominent positions in the revival organization. This, he asserted, resulted in the suppression of unfavorable news of the campaign.[29]

In addition to the newspaper coverage, posters, placards, and handbills were distributed around the city. Co-operating churches placed large signs in front of their doors saying, "This Church Is Co-operating in the Sunday Revival." The New York committee obtained from Rockefeller the services of one of the nation's top publicity experts, Ivy Lee, to act as chairman of the publicity committee. He spent $5,732.29 for the publication of a four-page precampaign bulletin which was issued four times prior to the meetings, announcing all the preparatory activities.[30] Lee's principal contribution was undoubtedly of a more subtle kind in influencing the local press.

One of the high lights of the preparation was the dedication of the tabernacle. The building of the tabernacle attracted a great deal of publicity for months prior to the campaign, and its completion was a moment of great rejoicing. The dedication ceremony was timed to precede Sunday's arrival by about a week, and though it was not, as in Moody's revivals, primarily a fund-raising meeting, admission was by ticket only, and the audience was carefully picked. Political figures were given prominence as speakers, and the outstanding local clergymen, preferably bishops, led the prayers. Sunday's advance representative, tabernacle architect, and business manager, as well as prominent campaign backers, were featured.

Chancellor Day dedicated the Syracuse tabernacle after an enormous parade took place through the city. At the Philadelphia dedication Governor-elect Brumbaugh, Mayor Blankenberg, the Rev. Maitland Alexander, and Bishop Joseph Berry (Methodist) were among the speakers. At New York's ceremony Governor Charles S. Whitman and Bishop Luther B. Wilson (Methodist) took part, as well as Stephen Baker of the Evangelistic Committee. Whitman stated that he was "not much concerned with the theology of Mr. Sunday," but he asked rhetorically, "Are we a Christian nation?" And did not Sunday aid Christianity?

Another preliminary flurry of excitement preceding the opening day of the campaign was Sunday's arrival in the city. The revival always began on a Sunday, and the evangelist usually arrived on Friday evening. He was met at the station by a welcoming committee, brass bands, marching choirs, and a large, hymn-singing crowd. Then a parade marched through the streets of the city as Sunday waved from the back of an open sedan. He was triumphantly escorted by mounted police to the home which he and his staff were to occupy for the campaign. There he was given a reception, introduced to the local dignitaries, and interviewed by the press. On Saturday morning he held a closed meeting of the co-operating ministers and committee chairmen at which he introduced his staff and outlined the plans for the campaign. "You brought me here," he told them. "I did not ask to come. This is not my campaign, but yours." He made it clear that he would give the orders and that they were to obey without question. "There are a lot of things you won't understand," he said, "but theory has got to go into the scrap heap when it comes to experience." There was to be no criticism and no attempt to alter his system. "You must do what you are told, or the organization will be smashed." They had hired a specialist, an efficiency expert, and they were obliged to follow his prescription. He concluded his preliminary talk with the warning, "You'll get out of this campaign just what you put into it."[31]

If some ministers were startled by this dictatorial attitude, it was too late now for them to back out. Thousands of souls, thousands of dollars, tens of thousands of hours of preparation, and the whole reputation of Protestant evangelism were at stake. Usually the advance man, the associate experts, and the committee chairmen had organized the preliminary work so smoothly and diffused their publicity so widely that there was little likelihood that any were ready to forsake the movement. On the contrary, enthusiasm was generally at such a fever pitch by the opening day that nothing Sunday could have said or done would have dampened it. Churches which had hesitated, or even opposed the invitation to Sunday, often were caught up in the last-minute excitement and threw themselves wholeheartedly into the crusade for Christianity, for civic improvement, for Prohibition, for decency and morality and respectability. The ministers and volunteer workers were only too glad to turn over the burden of responsibility to Sunday and his experts and to follow wherever they led.

3

"TWO DOLLARS A SOUL"

Efficiency was Sunday's trademark. The organization which he evolved to get the efficient results he so confidently promised was ranked by one professor of economics among the top five most successful businesses in the country, along with the Standard Oil Company, United States Steel, and National Cash Register.[1]

Sunday sometimes called himself a general in the army of the Lord, but he more often referred to his revivals as a business enterprise. To most Americans the business corporation, not the army, was the symbol of efficiency, and Sunday caught the mood of the era when he described his revivals as sales campaigns rather than battle campaigns. Moody spoke of "taking the city by storm," but "Sunday and his helpers," said the *New York Times*, "made it clear that they were going after souls as a successful commercial corporation goes after sales."[2] Speaking as an efficiency expert, Sunday told those who backed him, "You want to use good methods in religion; if you used such methods in business as you do in the work of the church the sheriff's sale flag would soon be hanging outside your door."[3] In his sermon for businessmen he wrote, "I am not only a preacher, but [a] businessman; I endeavor [to] bring: 1. System—Organization; 2. Business principles; 3. Common sense" into the work of the church.[4]

The central factor in Sunday's organization was his staff of experts, whom he called "the Sunday party." At his closed meeting with the local ministers the day before each campaign started, he introduced the members of this staff with the remark: "You can't conduct business as you did twenty-five years ago, neither can you religion. This is a day of specialists." Beginning with his first singing assistant in 1900, Sunday steadily added to his staff new specialists, each of whom dealt with one particular phase of the revivals and assumed the responsibility for it. Although all ultimate responsibility and authority rested in Sunday, he recognized the necessity for a board of directors or, more accurately, of executive vice-presidents to whom he could delegate the manifold tasks of his complex undertakings.

Sunday discovered first, as most evangelists had, that he could not preach and handle the singing, so he acquired Fred Fischer. He could not be an advance man and at the same time conduct his campaigns, so he hired Honeywell. He could not take care of the tabernacle and still have time to work on his sermons, so he hired Seibert. He had no head for business, so he permitted his wife to act as his business manager. But even these assistants were not sufficient for organizing a city of 500,000 people.

In the years 1900–1918 the Sunday party grew from three to twenty-three members. Each specialist directed the enthusiasm and good intentions of local volunteers in one particular aspect of revival work, which was systematically co-ordinated with every other aspect of the campaign. Chapman, whose biggest revivals were nothing more than a dozen small revivals all taking place at once, called Sunday's highly centralized technique "the very opposite of my own."

In addition to Fischer and Seibert, Sunday hired Elijah ("Ram's Horn") Brown in 1906 to be his special assistant. Brown had edited a magazine of evangelical comment entitled the Ram's Horn for which he wrote several columns of humorous aphorisms and pithy Bible talks. Sunday hired him for the express purpose of collecting, writing, and outlining material for his sermons, and much of the matter from Brown's columns found its way into Sunday's work. Also in 1906, Miss Frances Miller joined the party. She acted as a specialist in Bible teaching, conducted Bible classes during the campaign, and organized Bible study groups for the churches on a permanent basis so that the interest stimulated by the revival could be carried on by the churches afterward. She later became a specialist in organizing "businesswomen" (shopgirls, stenographers, clerks, telephone operators, maids) into prayer-meeting groups which met daily in their places of business during the revival.

By 1907 the musical aspect of the revival had become too large for Fischer to handle by himself, and Charles Butler was hired to act as his assistant. Butler was replaced in 1908 by Charles P. Pledger. These men not only assisted in training and leading the choirs (which by 1908 sometimes numbered seven or eight hundred), but they also played the piano, sang solos, and joined Fischer in duets. In 1907 Sunday also hired Bentley D. Ackley as his "confidential secretary." Ackley, a former newspaper reporter, was for eight years a key member of the party. When "Ram's Horn" Brown left the party, Ackley took his place in organizing Sunday's sermon material. He also played the piano and wrote numerous popular hymns, among them "I Walk with the King" and "If Your Heart Keeps Right." But the most important part of his work, apart from handling Sunday's correspondence, was managing the press and public relations. He saw to it that the publicity built up to a grand climax on the opening day and provided advance photos of Sunday and the party, together with lists of Sunday's records of converts and offerings. He saw to it that the newspapers received not only feature material but advance copies of the sermons and announcements of the revival activities.

In order to see that the tabernacles were properly constructed, Sunday hired A. P. Gill as "tabernacle architect" in 1908. Gill preceded Sunday from city to city with the blueprints of the tabernacle and directed the carpenters hired by the local committees, so that the expenses were kept to a minimum and the seating capacity at a maximum. Gill held this position until 1912, when he was replaced by Joseph Spiece.

Perhaps the most notable addition to the party was Homer Alvin Rodeheaver, who replaced Fred Fischer as chorister in 1910. The jovial, suave, and self-assured Rodeheaver was far better suited than the old-fashioned Fischer, with his stiff collar and pince-nez, to "warm up" a big-city crowd. He remained with Sunday for twenty years and made the half-hour "inspirational" song services which preceded each meeting a memorable part of the revival procedure.

At least a dozen other specialists were hired in the ensuing years: Mr. and Mrs. William Asher, who had been a sensation in Chapman's revivals with their impromptu meetings in saloons and on street corners, joined the party in 1911; Miss Rae Muirhead came to assist Miss Miller with women's work; Miss Grace Saxe took over as director of Bible study; Miss Alice Gamlin became director of boys' and girls' work; and Miss Florence Kinney specialized in working with students of high-school and college age. In fact, there was soon a specialist for every age group and every segment of the population of a big city, and most of the specialists had assistants. The Sunday party as of 1917 contained the following chief specialists, headed by the Sundays' eldest son, George, who, at the age of twenty-five, became the business manager of the party:

Rev. James E. Walker......................Advance representative
Rev. I. E. Honeywell......................Assistant to Mr. Sunday

Homer Rodeheaver....................................Chorister
Robert Matthews.....................Pianist and private secretary
Rev. Isaac Ward.........................Director of men's work
A. B. MacDonald...........................Men's work assistant
George Ashley Brewster.........................Pianist and soloist
Miss Frances Miller...............Director of businesswomen's work
Mrs. William Asher.....................Director of extension work
Miss Grace Saxe.........................Director of Bible study
Miss Alice M. Gamlin...............Director of boys' and girls' work
Miss Florence Kinney...................Director of students' work
Miss Jean Lamont.........................Assistant Bible teacher
Joseph Spiece............................Tabernacle builder
Albert Peterson...........................Custodian of tabernacle
Miss Florence K. Whitbeck...................Reservation secretary

And this did not include Sunday's personal masseur, Jack Cardiff, who had been a contender for the welterweight boxing title when he was converted and joined Sunday in 1912; he left the party in 1917 to become pastor of a church in Anthony, Kansas, and Peterson took over his duties.

Although George Sunday was officially listed as business manager, Mrs. Sunday still handled the major decisions in this regard. She was instrumental in the hiring and firing of personnel and was consulted on every aspect of the organization. "While supreme in his own province of preaching," said Mrs. Sunday of her husband after his death, "he was otherwise dependent upon me. He fretted if I was not near. He seemed helpless without me. I was his business manager and no decision was ever made without me."[5] This was a slight exaggeration. Sunday did get along without her on several occasions when she was ill or at home with the children; Sunday's private secretary remarked of his ability as an executive, "He is the quickest man I ever saw [at making decisions] and I never knew him to make a tactical error or a diplomatic mistake."[6]

But Sunday's nature was mercurial and undependable. The nervous tension of the campaign often brought on sudden fits of temper, and an imagined insult sent him sulking to his room. On these occasions Mrs. Sunday was the only person who could manage him. "My job," she used to tell the co-operating ministers, "is to sit on the safety valve." She prevented Sunday from being intruded upon in his rest hours and made amends when his quick temper brought on quarrels within the group or with important outside people. In his jovial moods Sunday was apt to be so overgenerous with his time and money that his wife was more often needed to

76

curb his good will than to make amends for his lack of it. In spite of her best efforts to conserve his strength, he frequently accepted offers to speak (free of charge) at dozens of outside meetings during each campaign.

Sunday's staff was so large by 1908 that in order to direct its activities he began to ask the local committees to provide a private house with sufficient rooms for him and his entire party to live in during the campaign. The expenses of evangelists and their helpers had always been paid by the local committees, but prior to 1900 this had been easily taken care of through the hospitality of several of the more well-to-do pastors or laymen at whose homes the evangelist and his co-worker were guests for the duration of the revival. Now the housing expenses became greatly increased, especially when cooks, chambermaids, and butlers had to be provided to run the party's temporary home. In this home the party lived and ate as a family unit, so that all could be in touch with one another and all could be available to Sunday. Each meal, according to one person who worked on the staff, became like a meeting of a board of directors. Sunday and his wife sat at the head of the table and listened to reports from each specialist. Then they gave their orders and set the policy for the new tasks ahead.

For the most part the working relationship among the members of the party was friendly and co-operative. All of them were publicly professed, "born-again" Christians and believed, as did Sunday, in the divine guidance and righteousness of their work. Still, it was a business organization in which they all recognized the need for careful, as well as "prayerful," planning and co-ordination among themselves. They believed that God worked through human agents, and it seemed clear that Billy Sunday was one of those agents. The party members all referred to him as "the Boss" and obeyed his orders explicitly. Sunday was well liked by those who worked for him. He was friendly, easygoing, and generous, with a boyish sense of humor and love of practical jokes; he lost his temper quickly, but he was quick to forgive and forget when the anger of the moment had passed.

Mrs. Sunday, on the other hand, was obeyed more from fear or respect than from love. She was hardheaded and hard-working, and she demanded as much from every member of the party as she gave herself. She could always be counted on to help out in any task, and she expected unquestioned obedience to her orders when she required some help. Though some of the group called her, as Sunday himself did, "Ma," more of them kept the respectful title of "Mrs. Sunday." They were all glad that she kept a more business-like eye on the complex enterprise than her husband, but, while they gave obedience to her, they gave their affection to him.

As the profession went, they were all well paid. Their salaries averaged thirty to fifty dollars a week, and they received their room and board free. Although Rodeheaver was paid $200 a week at one time, Ackley, the next most important member of the party, never received over $40 a week. But they were all frequently given gifts of considerable value by grateful converts or members of the local committees with whom they worked. In addition, Rodeheaver and Ackley made money writing hymns and publishing the Billy Sunday hymnbook, *Songs for Service*. Seibert was given the concession of selling photo postcards of Sunday and various religious pamphlets. Unlike other evangelists, Sunday did not demand a percentage of these concessions, but neither did he share his free-will offering with them.

Although individual salaries were not large, the total aggregate of the wages for the Sunday party soon assumed astounding proportions. In 1909 their wages totaled $2,700 for one campaign; by 1916 this had increased to $12,000; and at the time of the New York revival the salaries and traveling expenses of the party reached the peak of $21,163.65 for a ten-week period. At first Sunday paid these wages completely out of his own pocket, as Moody and Chapman had paid their assistants. But shortly after 1906 he began to stipulate that at least a portion of their salaries should be included among the expenses to be paid by the local committees. In Spokane he paid $1,000 of the salaries, and the committee paid $1,678. Later he began to split the amount fifty-fifty, as, for example, in Boston, where he and the committee each paid $6,000 of the payroll.[7] Although some cities offered to include all the wages of the staff as part of the legitimate expenses, Sunday insisted upon paying at least one-third and thereby kept the authority over his workers vested in himself.

As the party increased, the technique of evangelism became more complex; and as more and more cities demanded Sunday's services, he was in a position to make greater demands upon them. In addition to his three major stipulations regarding the united support, the tabernacle, and the guarantee fund, there were three minor ones which often caused some difficulty. First, he insisted on conducting his campaigns according tʊ his set pattern and would make no alterations in it to suit anyone. Not even John Wanamaker, who tried to persuade him to conduct three separate campaigns in three separate parts of Philadelphia rather than to try to revive that huge city all at once, could persuade him to alter his highly centralized system. "I don't believe in it," Sunday said. "I want to grip the city with a single great campaign. That's the only way to reach any city."[8]

Sunday also refused to conduct a revival in any city which had recently employed another evangelist. He had no hesitation in campaigning in large cities six or eight years after Torrey or Chapman had been there, but if the city was under fifty thousand population and if it had hired some minor evangelist to hold a city-wide campaign within the past year or two, he would categorically refuse an invitation. He was so adamant in this rule that when the city of Washington, Pennsylvania, to which he had agreed to come in 1915, held a revival a year before he was scheduled to arrive, he broke his engagement, saying that he would not follow in anyone's footsteps.[9]

And, finally, a rule which Sunday had tentatively adopted in 1902 became a fixed part of his procedure: this was that no church co-operating in the revival was to hold any services during his campaign. "The tabernacle is the center of interest and everything should be concentrated there," he told the ministers. "Don't have any meetings in your churches during the campaign except Sunday School and the evening services, if you must have them, but it would be better if they were cut out."[10] This was quite the opposite from Moody's practice of so integrating his revival with the regular work of the churches that no revival meetings were scheduled at an hour which might in any way conflict with established church services. But it was B. Fay Mills and not Sunday who had originally departed from this co-operative attitude, and all professional evangelists since the early 1890's had seen the necessity of channeling the regular churchgoers into the revival meetings in order to obtain maximum attendance and support.

Those who had questioned the "man-made look" of the revivals of Mills, Torrey, and Chapman, as manifested by such regulations, were utterly overwhelmed when confronted with the greatly increased mechanical aspects of a Billy Sunday revival. But whenever some of the older brethren offered querulous complaints, Sunday borrowed a sentence from Finney's "Defense of Revivals" to silence them: "God Almighty may use any method or means or individual that he pleases in order to promote a revival"; and he added, "Don't growl if I use some things that you don't like."[11]

By bitter experience Sunday discovered that the success of a revival depended largely on carefully organized mechanics, and particularly upon the effective transition from the mechanics of the preparation to the mechanics of the campaign proper. Inadequate preliminary organization had sometimes proved embarrassing. For example, in Fairfield, Iowa, in 1907 so little interest had been stimulated by the advance man and local committees that during the first week's meetings the tabernacle was half-empty. Sunday remedied this by visiting all the local shopkeepers and organizing them into two baseball teams—the northwest corner of the town square against the southwest. A game was scheduled at which Sunday and his wife arrived in a wagon hauled by the only yoke of oxen in the county and driven by the oldest white man born in the county. Sunday donned his professional baseball uniform and played for both teams.

That same year in his Knoxville, Iowa, campaign Sunday went to the extent of hiring a former Barnum and Bailey circus "Giant" to act as an usher for the revival meetings in order to attract attention to them.[12] Such publicity stunts filled Sunday's tabernacles within a few days after the campaigns opened, but precious time was lost. If Fairfield and Knoxville had not been small towns with relatively homogeneous populations, the initial disinterest might have meant serious financial and conversion losses. In a large city the result of such inadequate mechanics would have been complete failure.

During the climactic years after 1912 Sunday's experts, with their advance preparation and publicity, provided a completely different atmosphere for the first meeting of a campaign. Public interest was aroused to such a point that crowds appeared at the tabernacle six, eight, and ten hours before the doors opened for the first meeting. Police riot squads had to be called out. Traffic was snarled for blocks. Twenty minutes after the doors were opened in Philadelphia, the tabernacle's 18,000 seats were filled. The police and firemen tried in vain to hold back the people who jammed into the aisles and vestibules and climbed into the rafters. Men crawled up on the tabernacle roof to peek through the dormer windows. Although overflow meetings had been arranged in near-by churches, the crowd grew steadily larger outside the tabernacle. A police escort had to force a path through the crowd for Sunday and his wife. Throughout his sermon Sunday was interrupted by the shouts and poundings at the doors and the noise of policemen chasing spectators off the roof.

The first meeting usually took place at 10:30 A.M. Sunday morning. Two more meetings were scheduled that day, at 3:00 P.M. and 7:00 P.M. No sooner had the first sermon ended and the audience moved out than the newcomers took their places. In many cities those who came for the first meeting brought their lunches and dinners and sat in the tabernacle all day. Seventy thousand persons heard Sunday the first day in Philadelphia, and a crowd of 35,000 was turned away in the evening. This scene was repeated in city after city. Throughout the campaign Sunday spoke daily at 2:00 P.M. and 7:00 P.M.; on Sunday he preached at 11:00 A.M., 3:00 P.M., and 7:00 P.M. No regular meetings were scheduled on Mondays. Afternoon meetings were not as crowded as in the evening, but with amazing regularity the newspapers reported that the tabernacle, whether its capacity was 12,000, 15,000, or 20,000, was filled day after day. On the last day of the revival, after two months or more of preaching, the crowds were even larger than on the opening day. The total attendance for New York was estimated at more than a million and a quarter; for Boston, a million and a half; and for Philadelphia, where the revival lasted a week longer than at either of these, two million.

The elaborate publicity and preparation explained in large part the reason for the opening-day crowds, but the continued attendance was due to the expertly directed mechanics of the Sunday system during the campaign. Sunday's personal genius as an orator and actor was the central factor around which all else was built, but his talent as an administrator, plus the combined talents of his staff, also contributed heavily to make his revivals the spectacular climax to the profession of evangelism. The friendly community spirit generated by the gospel singing at the tabernacle, the jovial warmth promoted by the delegation system, and the whole atmosphere of excitement, gaiety, and entertainment made Sunday's tabernacle a prime attraction for city dwellers and out-of-town visitors. The most noticeably useful member of Sunday's staff in this regard was Rodeheaver. His genial character gave the tabernacle an atmosphere of enthusiastic friendliness that made the revival a powerful competitor of secular amusements even in the largest cities.

Rodeheaver was the epitome of twentieth-century evangelism. Born in Cinco Hollow, Ohio, in 1880, he grew up in Jellico, Tennessee. There his father ran a sawmill, and his brother Yumbert opened a music store. He learned to play the cornet as a boy. When he went to college at Ohio Wesleyan in 1896, he took music courses, played in the college band, acted as cheerleader, and switched from the cornet to the trombone. Interruptions to earn money and to serve in the Spanish-American War with the Fourth Regiment Band of Tennessee lengthened his stay at Ohio Wesleyan until 1904. In that year he left college without his degree in order to work for an up-and-coming evangelist named William E. Biederwolf.

Five years as Biederwolf's chorister provided the training which made Sunday bid for Rodeheaver's talent. When he met Sunday in 1909, he possessed a soothing baritone voice, an ingratiating personality, a vaguely handsome face, dark wavy hair, and the stage presence of a veteran trouper. He also had considerable skill as a trombonist, was able to give evangelistic talks, had a knowledge of magic which helped him conduct children's meetings, knew how to direct a large choir, and, above all, had developed the smiling, affable sociability of the professional chorister as Charles Alexander had established the role.

Unlike Fischer, Rodeheaver was eager to use new hymns and to experiment with new group-singing practices. As Biederwolf's chorister, he had replaced Sankey's conservative hymnal with the "songbook" of E. O. Excell, an expositor of modern, twentieth-century gospel songs. Rodeheaver was also more adept than Fischer at warming up a crowd by telling a funny story, doing a magic trick, making odd noises on his trombone, or playing a joke on another member of the party. Fischer would not have understood Rodeheaver's advice to his choirs that in singing they must "go at it like selling goods."

Rodeheaver's role was aptly characterized as that of "a jollier." When he instructed the women to remove their hats, he made the incident a cause for good humor by saying that this would prevent envy among them. He encouraged audience participation, and, when a group of local singers pitched their song too high and broke down in the middle of it, he turned their embarrassment into triumph: "This is certainly a fine, high-toned organization," he said. "We like high-toned organizations, and I thank you for this mistake because it reminds me of the old lady down in my section of the country . . . ," and he told a long-winded joke. After the crowd laughed and the group regained its self-possession, he asked them to sing the song again. When they successfully completed it, he led the applause as they proudly took their seats.

Newspaper writers called Rodeheaver "a wonder" and stated that without him Sunday could never have succeeded: "Rody is one of the greatest adjuncts a revivalist ever had. His musical ability, his sense of humor, his southern accent, his ability to catch the feeling of the crowd, and his sympathetic smile . . . make him as appealing a figure on the platform as Bryan was in the freshness of his career." Privately many reporters felt that he was a little too suave, too unctuous, to be sincere. But to the crowds he was affectionately known as "Rody" just as Alexander had been "Charlie." Like Alexander, he provided a contrast to his evangelistic counterpart. It was Rodeheaver's grace and politeness which gave tone and polish to the meetings, while Sunday's acrobatics and hoarse shouting provided the emotional fervor. If Sunday had the reputation of being a red-blooded man's man, Rodeheaver, a bachelor, was undoubtedly a lady's man. According to one of Rodeheaver's former secretaries, his mail during each campaign consisted largely of letters from lovesick women whom he had never met.

Rodeheaver's ability to find new, spirited gospel songs particularly pleased Sunday, who, said Rodeheaver, "loved a song with a lively lilt and rhythm. . . . He was a good judge of the kind of song that would be liked eventually and we always respected his judgment. . . . He wanted a simple, direct, practical message."[13] There was little basic difference between the doctrinal content of the hymns of Sankey's day and the gospel songs of Rodeheaver, but the spirit of the latter was livelier and more lighthearted. Rodeheaver used some of the Sankey hymns, but he depended more on songs which emphasized the optimistic aspects of the gospel. The difference may be implied from the fact that the favorite Moody and Sankey hymn was the heart-rending "The Ninety and Nine," while the most popular song of Sunday's revivals was the joyous "Brighten the Corner." "Ring the Bells of Heaven" was popular in both eras, and so were "Bringing in the Sheaves" and "Pull for the Shore," but many old favorites like "Safe from the Law," "Christ Is My Redeemer," and "There Is a Fountain Filled with Blood" were sung less often in the twentieth century. Like the professional evangelists, the writers of gospel songs were more interested in reaching a broad audience than in promoting sectarian doctrines. Hymns which glorified particular aspects of theological dogma were not likely to be understood by Sundays audiences or, if they had been, might have promoted disharmony among the denominations co-operating in the revival.

Something of the difference between Moody's and Sunday's revivals was revealed in the musical preferences of the two evangelists. Moody disliked the self-confident tone of "Onward, Christian Soldiers" and forbade Sankey to sing it; he preferred, instead, the humility of "Oh, To Be Nothing."[14] But Sunday disdained "Oh, To Be Nothing" and favored the triumphant "I Walk with the King, Hallelujah!" "Onward, Christian Soldiers," "The Battle Hymn of the Republic," and "The Fight Is On." Those who sang in Sunday's crusades were more self-righteously confident than Moody's followers that they could persuade the rest of the nation to accept their brand of Christianity. The singing in Moody's revivals resembled the lonely wailing of the saving remnant; that in Sunday's sounded like the militant trumpeting of the tyrannical majority. "I love the sweet old gospel songs," said Sunday, "but we need to have some like 'Hold the Fort for I Am Coming!' The church must be martial and we need martial music."[15] Rodeheaver revived interest in "Hold the Fort," an old Sankey hymn, as well as in other martial hymns of earlier days; the hymnbook which he compiled and published to replace Excell's contained a special section in its topical index devoted to "Warfare."

When not militant, the singing as Rodeheaver directed it was almost "jazzy." As one reporter noted at the first meeting, the hymns were "hustled along with a swing that makes them refreshing." "Imagine," he wrote, "hearing 'He Leadeth Me' sung like a popular song." The two pianists who provided the background for the choirs were under Rodeheaver's direction, too, and most observers agreed that "in the accompaniment their is just a hint of syncopation." But the more tender songs were by no means omitted. The sentimental aspects of evangelism, though not so prominent in Sunday's sermons as in Moody's, were still effective in moving an audience, and Rodeheaver frequently made use of old favorites like "Where Is My Wandering Boy Tonight?" "Tell Mother I'll Be There," and "We Shall Meet, By and By."

When Rodeheaver went into the hymn-publishing business in 1910, he not only began to write hymns himself but employed the services of much better gospel song-writers like B. D. Ackley and Charles H. Gabriel. To create a market for the songs which his company published, he stated that in the half-hour song periods which preceded each revival service, "We usually started off with

some of the old familiar hymns which everybody could sing, then
mixed in some of the newer gospel songs, which we would teach
the people, interspersing these with a solo, duet, or special numbers
by the great chorus." By dint of constant plugging, many of
Gabriel's and Ackley's songs became popular. Gabriel's "Glory
Song," "Sail On," "Since Jesus Came into My Heart," and "Brighten
the Corner" soon rivaled old favorites, and the same was true of
Ackley's "I Walk with the King," "If Your Heart Keeps Right,"
"Mother's Prayers Have Followed Me," and "I Am Coming Home."
The words of these hymns illustrated the optimistic, nondoctrinal
content of Rodeheaver's hymnbook:

BRIGHTEN THE CORNER

Do not wait until some deed of greatness you may do,
Do not wait to shed your light afar,
To the many duties ever near you now be true,
Brighten the corner where you are.

> Brighten the corner where you are.
> Brighten the corner where you are.
> Someone far from harbor you may guide across the bar,
> Brighten the corner where you are.

Just above are clouded skies that you may help to clear,
Let not narrow self your way debar,
Tho' into one heart alone may fall your song of cheer,
Brighten the corner where you are.

[Copyright 1913, renewal 1941, The Rodeheaver Co., owner]

"We were criticized for introducing a song of this kind into a religious service," said Rodeheaver. "It was never intended for a Sunday morning service, nor for a devotional meeting—its purpose was
to bridge that gap between the popular song of the day and the
great hymns and gospel songs, and to give to men a simple, easy,
lilting melody which they could learn the first time they heard it,
and which they could whistle and sing wherever they might be."
Compare the equally popular "If Your Heart Keeps Right":

If the dark shadows gather as you go along,
Do not grieve for their coming, sing a cheery song,
There is joy for the taking, it will soon be light—
Ev'ry cloud wears a rainbow, if your heart keeps right.

> If your heart keeps right,
> If your heart keeps right,
> There's a song of gladness in the darkest night;
> If your heart keeps right,

If your heart keeps right,
Ev'ry cloud will wear a rainbow, if your heart keeps right.

Is your life just a tangle full of toil and care:
Smile a bit as you journey, others' burdens share;
You'll forget all your troubles making their lives bright,
Skies will be blue and sunny if your heart keeps right.

[Copyright 1912, renewal 1940, The Rodeheaver Co., owner]

The similarity of content and often of tune between the gospel hymns which poured by the thousands from the pens of semitrained or untrained choristers and church workers in these years often led to heated controversies concerning plagiary and breach of copyright. Torrey once remarked of the songbook which Alexander issued in 1907, "I wish that Charlie had a little more conscience";[16] and there were some who declared that a few of Charlie's hymns were practically pirated. But such accusations, while they produced heated quarrels within evangelistic circles, were seldom aired in public. They were symptomatic, however, of an increasingly commercial and secular approach to revivalism.

The growing popularity of phonograph records was one cause of this trend. The song-writing and copyright business became much more lucrative. Recording brought increasing competition from secular music, and Rodeheaver rightly emphasized the necessity of "bridging the gap" between the secular and the religious in his songbook. He took another step to meet this problem by going into the phonograph recording business himself in 1916, and soon his gospel hymns were making more money from record sales than from sheet music.

The increasing number of patriotic and outright secular songs in evangelistic hymnbooks was apparent in the topical index in Rodeheaver's tabernacle edition of *Songs for Service*. Three of the categories in the topical index were "Patriotic," which included "America" and Ackley's "Song to the Flag"; "Intermediate," which included "Brighten the Corner," "If Your Heart Keeps Right," and "Help the One Next to You"; and "Children," which included such songs as the following:

SWING LITTLE BLOSSOMS

Swing little blossoms the sunshine is falling
Into your golden hearts dewy and sweet,
Lift up your golden heads, lo, the warm winds are calling,
As they sweep o'er you with joyful wings fleet.

Swing, swing, little blossoms, swing,
As neath the sunshine your golden hearts glow,
Swing, swing, little blossoms, swing,
Breathing love's fragrance, swing high, swing low.

[Copyright 1915, renewal 1943, The Rodeheaver Co., owner]

A fourth category in the book was "Temperance," which included "Pure White Ribbons," "Yield Not to Temptation," and "De Brewer's Big Hosses." The latter was by far the most popular. Written in 1887, it was first introduced into revivalism by Rodeheaver in 1911. It had a stirring tune, fighting words, and for some unknown reason was written in Negro dialect.

DE BREWER'S BIG HOSSES

Oh, de brewer's big hosses comin' down de road,
Totin' all around ole Lucifer's load;
Dey step so high, an' dey step so free,
But dem big hosses can't run over me.

Oh, no, boys, oh, no!
De turnpike's free wherebber I go,
I'm a temperance ingine, don't you see,
And de brewer's big hosses can't run over me.

Oh, de licker men's actin' like dey own dis place,
Livin' on de sweat ob de po' man's face,
Dey's fat and sassy as dey can be,
But dem big hosses can't run over me.

Oh, I'll harness dem hosses to de temp'rance cart,
Hit 'em wid a gad to gib 'em a start,
I'll teach 'em how for to haw and gee,
For dem big hosses can't run over me.

Rodeheaver noted in the score of this work: "A good effect can be obtained if the male voices will imitate escaping steam and whistle, while the female voices sing."

Such songs not only were calculated to provide a more spirited, freer atmosphere than had formerly been associated with religious revivals, but they were frankly intended to entertain the audiences. Rodeheaver prepared special "artistic" and "unusual" effects for such songs. Like Alexander, he gave the audiences an active part in the singing by having them compete with the choir or among themselves, by assigning various lines of a song to males and females or to alternate areas of the tabernacle. He also enjoyed secretly placing members of the choir in the back of the tabernacle in order to provide answering echoes for certain songs.

The tremendous size of the choirs in the years 1912–18 provided new opportunities for a man with Rodeheaver's artistic pretensions. "We popularized many new songs and revived interest in many old-time favorites by the unusual rendition made possible by these great mass choirs." Typical was Rodeheaver's arrangement of "Hallelujah, What a Saviour!":

> Let a choir of two thousand voices sing this along at a moderate tempo, good rhythm, and when they come to the "Hallelujah" bring it out with the full power of all the voices, cut it off suddenly and sharply drop from this tremendous crescendo to the faintest pianissimo as they start on the next phrase, "What a Saviour," then let the whole chorus make a tremendous crescendo on the vowel "a" in the word "Saviour" bringing it up to the top of the wave and then letting it die again to the faintest featheredge, and you can get some slight conception of the unusual possibilities with a singing organization of this size.

Rodeheaver also liked to add "tone" to his song periods by having soloists sing semiclassical songs, but Sunday's attitude toward this type of artistry kept it in check. "He said," wrote Rodeheaver of Sunday, "it always gave him a nervous chill when he saw someone start to the platform unrolling a piece of sheet music."

As part of the entertainment aspect of the tabernacle music, Rodeheaver often sang Negro spirituals or played solos on his trombone. Unlike Sankey, he seldom prefaced his songs with a prayer, though he frequently told a funny story about them. Local singers and instrumentalists were encouraged to perform from the platform. In Boston a group called "The Lotus Quartet" sang "Take the Stars and Stripes Away from the Saloon" and a parody entitled "It's a Long Way to Prohibition, but We're Almost There." Rodeheaver, like Alexander, arranged to have young children of six or seven sing solos to the vast tabernacle audiences. Army, Navy, Marine, and Salvation Army bands were asked to come, as well as church fife-and-drum corps and high-school bands. During the Washington, D.C., campaign Secretary of the Navy Josephus Daniels gave the Sunday party free use of the Navy and Marine bands. Singing organizations, especially of immigrants, such as Welsh, Swedish, or German singing societies, were brought to the tabernacle to compete with each other. In Boston in 1916 the chorus girls from Al Jolson's Winter Garden troupe were persuaded to sing at the tabernacle. In return for this publicity, Jolson deleted his burlesque of Billy Sunday, which had been a featured part of his current musical revue, "Robinson Crusoe, Jr."

The most important use for the choir came not in the preliminary song period, however, but after the sermon was over, when it was up to Rodeheaver to supplement Sunday's call for converts with appropriate background music. "I believe more mistakes are made here than in any other part of the music," said Rodeheaver. Some choristers had the choir sing the same "invitation hymn" after every sermon, but, said Rodeheaver, "if the preacher closes his sermon with a challenge to men, literally daring them to come and take their stand for Christ, then we certainly do not want to pick out something like 'Softly and Tenderly Jesus Is Calling' or 'Just as I Am,' but a song like 'Stand Up for Jesus,' 'Onward, Christian Soldiers,' 'I Am Resolved No Longer To Linger.'" And, conversely, sermons which ended on a tenderly appealing note "need a quiet song like 'Jesus, I Am Coming Home,' 'Just as I Am' or 'Where He Leads Me, I Will Follow.'" He also discovered that "it was never wise to change the invitation song as long as people were coming forward, even though we had to use it over and over." If the song was abruptly changed, it seemed to break the chain of feeling, to spoil the mood, or to imply a change in the meeting. But "if you start a certain song at the beginning of the invitation and people do not seem to respond, then it is wise, while the preacher is making an additional appeal, to change to another."

Rodeheaver was more than a choir leader and soloist. He was also a master of ceremonies and a host. As the host he welcomed each evening the delegations which had special seats reserved for them. The delegation system, originally a spontaneous idea on the part of certain groups, was encouraged by Sunday and his party and soon became as vital a factor in the attendance at the tabernacle as Rodeheaver's inspirational song periods.

As Sunday's fame increased and as the cities he visited grew larger, he had the double problem of finding sufficient seats during the early meetings to seat all those who were curious and then to see to it that the attendance kept up continuously throughout the revival. He also wanted to reach as wide a cross-section of the city's population as possible. The Sunday party was basically created to answer these problems. "While he was preaching twice daily in the tabernacle and occasionally in outside meetings," wrote Rodeheaver, "his associates were speaking several times each day in different places to different groups and at the close of their message inviting the groups to come in a body to the tabernacle." Sunday's authorized biographer frankly admitted that "at the outset, Mr. Sunday's assistants had to 'work up' these delegations."[17]

The primary purpose of the delegation system was to appeal to group solidarity. By setting aside special seats for a group which had established traditions and loyalties among themselves, Sunday induced many to come who might not otherwise have done so; they came to be with their friends or to show their loyalty to their association or club rather than to support Sunday or his aims. The tabernacle meetings became, to a certain extent, melting pots which united many social groupings upon certain broad emotional terms common to each.

The delegations from the co-operating evangelical churches were, naturally enough, the backbone of the meetings, the hard core of individuals whose constant and well-nigh unanimous support could always be counted on to set the tone of the meetings and carry the burden of the emotional excitement. With regular attendance of delegations of Bible classes, Sunday-school classes, Christian Endeavor Societies, Epworth Leagues, men's and women's church social groups, and even whole congregations, Sunday could, by directing his sermons toward the known quantity of their loyalties, create an emotional atmosphere which the rest of the crowd would unconsciously reflect and imitate or, at least, one which it would be difficult for them to openly reject. These church delegations were the key to Sunday's proficient manipulation of crowd psychology.

Critics of the campaigns complained that the church delegations were purposely planted in the tabernacle to lead the other sheep forward, but, while this was true enough, it would have been difficult for Sunday to refuse to give special seats to the church members who had worked so hard to prepare for the revival and who had invited him in the first place. However, there were times when he found the vast number of church delegations embarrassing. Just as Moody tried to issue tickets for his meetings to unconverted persons only, in order to avoid preaching to the same people night after night, so Sunday instructed his reservation secretary in Pittsburgh to give no more special attention to church groups in order that other groups in the community might be reached. In Boston Sunday scolded from the platform: "Some of you churchers had better stay home for awhile so as to give other folks a chance to come here and get front seats." Generally, however, church groups were more than welcome.

It was one of the boasts of the Sunday party that its revivals reached more elements of the city than any other revivals had ever done. The delegation system extended far beyond the church groups. The most obvious and willing sources of group support outside the churches were the fraternal lodges, such as the Masons, the Odd Fellows, the Knights of Pythias, the Redmen, the Woodmen, the Ben Hurs, and the Knights Templar. These groups readily accepted invitations to the meetings and often came in full regalia, accompanied by their bands or drum corps. Business groups like the Rotary Clubs, the Lions, Elks, and Kiwanis, and the local chambers of commerce were equally willing and eager to come to the tabernacle. Since most of these associations had counterparts for wives, daughters, and sisters, women's groups were also frequent attenders.

Groups of a civic nature, "do-gooders" and reformers, were always welcome. The WCTU and other temperance groups seized the opportunity to advertise their cause. Even a bipartisan political organization like the Suffragettes was told that, in return for its support of Sunday, he would say a good word for it. Members of the town council and state legislatures were often present in a body, and sometimes local political clubs, usually Republicans in the North and temperance-Democrats in the South, were given special seats. Veterans' groups, with their uniforms, bands, and flags, were diligently courted. Civil and Spanish War veterans were told about Sunday's patriotic father and Rodeheaver's service in Cuba. During World War I members of the armed forces were particularly favored by good seat reservations, and the American Legion groups in later years were always stout Sunday supporters. No organization with even the slightest tinge of radicalism was welcome, however.

Moody and other predecessors of Sunday had recognized the importance of making an appeal to special groups outside the church in order to extend the scope of the revival. But Moody seldom got beyond holding special meetings for men only or women only or for children, young men, businessmen, the unemployed, and, once or twice, "fallen women." Sunday included all these types of meetings (except the one for "fallen women"), plus special nights for businesswomen; out-of-towners; veterans; students of colleges, business colleges, and high schools; and "old folks." Moody had done little more to prepare for such meetings than to trust to a general announcement at the tabernacle or in the newspapers. Sunday's staff made a definite effort to go out and bring in the persons to be favored. When Rodeheaver announced the coming "Old Folks' Day" at the tabernacle in Boston, he told the audience, "Now here's the scheme. You find the old folks, and when you find them, you make sure that they will come. Then you get their addresses and send them to Chester I. Campbell, 5 Park Square, Boston. He will arrange for the autos to get them and take them to the service."[18]

The desire to reach businesswomen was even more carefully organized. During the preparatory work for each revival, "preliminary surveys were made of stores, office buildings, telephone exchanges, business colleges, factories, laundries, hospitals, hotels, restaurants, and among household workers." In each of these groups the female workers were organized into prayer meetings and Bible classes: "two young women volunteers were secured to act as councillors in buildings where others were employed; through them interest was created and tickets were issued for the business-women's section at the tabernacle."[19]

When the party's businesswomen's experts, Miss Miller, Mrs. Asher, and Miss Saxe and their assistants arrived, they organized daily meetings in these establishments and held rallies at the YWCA's in the evening which brought each working girl face to face with the revival. Miss Miller pointed out to co-operating ministers and businessmen that her work helped to keep young working girls from falling into sin: "This organization of the business women into groups," she said, "will do more to improve social conditions than all the vice commissions ever conceived." During the revival the local committee for businesswomen gave ten-cent lunches at certain downtown churches, where businesswomen heard gospel talks, hymn-singing, and special pleas for attending the meetings. It was not accidental that the tabernacle was jammed with working girls on "Businesswomen's Night" or that delegations from one store or office building after another came night after night to the tabernacle.

The directors of men's work undertook the same organization in the factories and among clerks and salesmen in stores and offices. Occasionally, large delegations of one or two thousand attended, representing various steel mills in Pittsburgh, silkmills in Paterson, Baldwin's locomotive works in Philadelphia, and textile-mills in Boston. More than once local AF of L unions came in a body. The Junior Order of United American Mechanics frequently attended.

The director of Bible study organized Bible classes on a neighborhood as well as on a church basis and brought to the meetings groups of housewives and their husbands whose principal relation to one another was the proximity of their habitations. The directors of boys' and girls' work organized the children of the neighborhoods regardless of denomination and even if their parents were not church members. Boy and Girl Scout groups were persuaded to come in uniform. The director of students' work visited the colleges in the area to get the help of Student Christian Associations, student choirs, and other student organizations.

Another cross-section of working people was obtained by appealing to occupation. Subway conductors came in a group in New York. "City Employees' Night" was observed in most cities. Firemen and policemen came and were rewarded by having the collection from some meeting turned over to them. An appeal which intermeshed many loyalties was that to groups of a particular national origin. Norwegians, Swedes, Germans, Scotch, Welsh, and Italians were given special nights at the tabernacle and were asked to wear native costumes and sing songs in their native languages.

Some idea of the work undertaken by the members of the party to "work up" these delegations may be seen by the list of one day's revival activities published in the *Boston Herald* on November 23, 1916:

SUNDAY REVIVAL ACTIVITIES FOR TODAY

TABERNACLE SERMONS

2 P.M. Personal Work—"A Wise Man"

7 P.M. For Men Only—$1 Night—Subject to be announced

10 A.M.—Cottage Prayer Meetings.

11 A.M. to 2 P.M.—Miss Miller will meet with "Council Women" of the invitation committee at Park St. Church.

1 P.M. to 2:30 P.M.—Mrs. Asher will meet businesswomen at Park St. Church.

3 P.M.—Miss Saxe will give instruction Bible Class at the Tabernacle.

3:30 P.M.—Mrs. Asher will speak to young women employed with private families at YWCA, 40 Berkeley St.

3:45 P.M.—Miss Gamlin will meet the boys and girls of the district at the Allston Methodist-Episcopal Church.

4:30 P.M.—Miss Fetterolf will meet high-school girls of the Dorchester District at the Second Congregational Church.

6:45 P.M.—Miss Miller will meet "Council Girls" at Park St. Church. Lunch will be served at 10 cents.

7 P.M.—More than 11,000 seats have been reserved at the Tabernacle for a group of men's Bible classes. Mr. Sunday will speak to men only.

7:45 P.M.—Miss Saxe begins a series of talks on "Methods of Bible Study" at Prospect St. Congregational Church, Cambridge.

7:45 P.M.—Miss Lamont will hold a Bible Rally at the Second Congregational Church, Dorchester.

7:45 P.M.—Miss Saxe will meet the Community Bible Class at the Washington Baptist Church, Lynn.

This list of activities was a regular daily feature in local newspapers in every campaign. The above list failed to mention the meeting for women only which Mrs. Sunday conducted at 7:00 P.M. and the meetings that went on at the lunch hour in various factories led by Sunday's men's work specialists.

As a result of such activities, Rodeheaver welcomed ten to twenty different delegations at the tabernacle each night. They ranged in size from a dozen persons to three or four thousand, and "Rody" always had a word of praise for each and encouraged the applause of the crowd as he asked each group to rise in a body. Usually these groups met at some prearranged spot and marched to the tabernacle, singing, carrying signs and banners, often with a band, and wearing some sort of uniform or identifying badge. The general public, which took the seats left over after the delegations had made their reservations, was at least treated to a spectacle, even if it did not receive any special attention.

To unite the varied delegations which made up the audience, Rodeheaver let each one perform an act or sing a song. Schools and colleges gave their football cheers. Rodeheaver always asked each delegation to name its favorite hymn and promised to sing it during the song service. It became the custom for groups to name a hymn which had some joking reference to their profession or company. Insurance salesmen called for "Blessed Assurance"; real estate agents asked for "Higher Ground"; a flourmill delegation asked for "Why Not Now"; automobile mechanics announced as their favorite song "Get Out and Get Under"; laundry workers wanted "Wash Me and I Shall Be Whiter than Snow"; sailors asked for "Sail On"; and once a delegation of milkmen inadvertently requested "Shall We Gather at the River?"

Rodeheaver pointed up these jokes to the crowd and made additional jokes himself. Often the groups sang a parody of a hymn or popular song. A group of visiting ministers from New Hampshire sang these words at the Boston tabernacle to the tune of "Brighten the Corner":

> We're from New Hampshire, don't you know
> We stand by Sunday hearts aglow.

94

Up along the river where the churches want to grow,
We're from New Hampshire, don't you know.

A Christian Endeavor society from Middlesex, Massachusetts, sang
this song at the Boston tabernacle:

Came a man to Bean Town—Billy Sunday his name,
He sure is a corker—he merits his fame;
He lambastes the Devil with uppercut blows,
Slams boozers and sinners, too—high brows and lows;
Middlesex does not care—we are here for our share—
Good luck, Billy—God is with you.

Middlesex, Middlesex, now is here for your best;
We want you to slam us hard, just like the rest.
We are Christian Endeavorers but bum ones we know;
We admit it, we regret it—so fill us with go.
We'll take our full due, for we sure like you—
Good luck, Billy. We're strong for you.[20]

The laughter and crowd participation from such demonstrations
quickly united the diverse elements into an enthusiastic mass-
responsive unit.

At the height of Sunday's fame the requests for special reservations often deluged the reservation secretary. Usually some local
person was asked to assist in arranging the priority of these reservations in order to give the best seats to the most influential groups.
Groups were permitted to make reservations by telephone, and
their seats were held by the ushers until just before the sermon. In
Philadelphia such interest was worked up by the party and the
publicity that, when the meetings closed after eleven weeks, there
were enough requests for reservations on hand to have filled the
tabernacle for another three months.

Sunday did not leave all the extra-tabernacle mechanics to the
party, for he was able to reach audiences which they could not. In
every city but two which he visited in the years 1906–18, he obtained permission from the local board of education to address the
high-school students in their school auditoriums. He had no objection to obeying the stipulation that his talk must not deal specifically with any religious creed. He gave his special talk for boys
and girls entitled "The Forces That Win," a triumphant restatement
of the dogma of O. S. Marden and Horatio Alger. Frequently he
spoke at various colleges and theological schools in the vicinity.
Here he was not forbidden to preach his creed and call for converts.
Sometimes the invitations to colleges originated with the students,

but for the most part they were instigated by trustees or faculty members. The University of Pennsylvania asked Sunday to come because a number of student suicides began to undermine parental faith in the institution.[21] Dartmouth, Cornell, Rutgers, Wesleyan, Brown, Northwestern, Drew, the Episcopal Theological Seminary in Cambridge, all invited Sunday in the years 1912–18.

Sunday was invited to speak to three hundred different organizations during his New York campaign. He could accept only a small proportion of these invitations. There were two groups, however, which he was always willing to address: the convicts of state and federal penitentiaries, and temperance meetings. On his day of rest he often went a hundred miles or more to give his "Booze Sermon" if he thought it would help in some local or state election for Prohibition.

Two social groups which Sunday alone in the party could reach and which were of prime importance in promoting the revival were the wealthy and the *nouveaux riches* of "Society." Albert J. Saunders reached some of these in the preparatory work, but Sunday was of far greater interest, and his support by the Rockefellers, Biddles, and McCormicks gave him a certain prestige value among those who had recently gained entry into the social register. A few of the wealthy men in this set could be persuaded, like Rockefeller and Wanamaker, to sit on the platform, but their wives and daughters seldom if ever came to the tabernacles.

To satisfy the curiosity of the society women, Sunday began after 1908 to conduct "parlor meetings" or "society meetings" on Thursday mornings. These meetings were conducted in the homes of the socially self-conscious, and attendance was by engraved invitation only. Sunday gave special sermons free of slang and acrobatics and based on the theme that the primary obligation of the wealthy was to become converted and to support Christianity. While in Paterson, New Jersey, Sunday was persuaded by Mrs. Thomas A. Edison to talk to her friends at the East Orange Woman's Club; in New York he spoke at the homes of Mrs. Rockefeller and Mrs. Thorne; in Philadelphia he spoke at the homes of Mrs. Wanamaker and Mrs. Biddle; in Montclair and Paterson his hostesses were Mrs. E. H. Wells, Mrs. Hobart, and Mrs. Quackenbush; in Washington, D.C., he was the guest of Mrs. Marshall Field; in Boston, of Dr. and Mrs. Houghton; in Pittsburgh, of Mrs. Donner and Mrs. Heinz; and, in Chicago, of the McCormicks, Armours, Farwells, Swifts, and Mrs.

Dawes. At one meeting in New York he addressed Mrs. J. P. Morgan, Mrs. Andrew Carnegie, Mrs. Hamilton Fish, and Mrs. Cass Gilbert. Sunday's sincerity in preaching to these people was exemplified in a remark he made at one of his parlor meetings in the home of a wealthy society matron in Denver: "Let me ask you ladies something. Have you accepted Jesus Christ as your Saviour? Are you attending these meetings to be benefited spiritually? I'll quit if you come to see me or to visit beautiful homes or to get a nice ride in your autos."[22]

Other activities outside the tabernacle by Sunday seem to have been undertaken more for publicity than for increasing the tabernacle attendance. In Boston he addressed a group of Unitarian ministers. In New York he rode on a special train with Governor Whitman and Marshal Joffre to visit West Point. He often umpired college and charity baseball games. In Philadelphia, at the age of fifty-three, he hit a home run in an "old-timers" game in Shibe Park on St. Patrick's Day and rounded the bases in sixteen seconds. In Washington he gave an opening prayer at the House of Representatives, and he did the same for the state legislatures in Massachusetts, New Jersey, and Illinois.

All these meetings outside the tabernacle, all the organizing by the party, all the music, publicity, sermons, and delegations, were undertaken to build up the tabernacle attendance, but a large attendance was useless unless it produced "trail-hitters." "Hitting the sawdust trail" was the expression for walking down the aisle to profess conversion by shaking Sunday's hand. It originated in the campaign in 1910 in Bellingham, Washington, where the sawdust floors and the wooden tabernacle touched a responsive chord in that lumber community. According to Mrs. Sunday, the term had long been used by lumbermen: "The men who had the job of going out into dense, dark woods to scale the timber," she said, "often carried large gunny sacks of sawdust and as they went from one location to another would scatter a handful in their path—when work was done they would say 'Now if I can only find that sawdust trail I'll be safe and get home.' "[23] The religious implications were so apt that the term immediately was adopted by revivalists and newspapermen in referring to those who walked down the sawdust aisle to "come home to Christ."

Moody and Chapman, like Finney, had made every sermon a plea for conversions, but Sunday discovered early in his career that, if he delayed his calls for converts until after the first week of the revival, the anticipation built up to a climactic pitch which created a greater number of trail-hitters and a new flood of publicity in the newspapers. The delay helped to weed out those who came the first week merely out of curiosity, and also gave the party time to consolidate the activities of the local committees and to "work up" delegations. In his early revivals, as in Fairfield, Sunday needed the first week to stir up sufficient interest in the revival to fill the tabernacle. It would have been foolish to call for converts in a half-empty hall where there was little enthusiasm and a good chance that none would come forward. Consequently, Sunday's sermons the first week were among his most spectacular and "were calculated," as Rodeheaver said, "to attract attention, arouse discussion, and draw people to the tabernacle," not to win converts.

Sunday himself did not know exactly when he would give the first call, nor did any of the members of the party. "As the time drew near," wrote Rodeheaver, "his concern and anxiety would become apparent." The call might be expected any time after the first eight days and usually followed his sermon "The Hour Is Come." But Sunday was a shrewd judge of crowd psychology and refused to give the invitation until he intuitively felt that the emotional pitch was just right. Often the party was kept on edge night after night while Sunday waited for the proper moment.

In Boston in 1916 the first call came on the tenth night at a meeting for men only in which 11,000 seats had been reserved for members of men's Bible classes in the churches of Boston and vicinity (just as in New York, where the audience on the first night of trail-hitting consisted mostly of Bible-class delegations). Twice during the course of the sermon Sunday stirred the crowd to action by demanding that they stand if they were opposed to the liquor traffic and if they were ready to die for Christ. The speed and enthusiasm of their response convinced him that the crowd was with him. He concluded the sermon with a story of the Scotch hero Douglas, who threw the heart of Bruce into the ranks of an opposing army of Saracens and ordered his men to follow it to victory.

Then Sunday "leaped to the chair, standing high above the sea of faces toward which he extended his hands," and shouted, "I seize the Cross of the Son of God and I wave it over this audience and hurl the heart of the Saviour out into the ranks of the manhood of Boston and as I do I cry aloud, 'On, on Christ, and we will follow.' How many of you will walk out and give me your hand and say, 'I

Billy Sunday shaking hands with trail-hitters in Philadelphia, March, 1915. This lithograph by George Bellows, drawn to illustrate an article by John Reed in the *Metropolitan Magazine,* presents an exaggerated view of this aspect of the revival. (*Reproduced courtesy of Mrs. George Bellows.*)

☞ SUBSCRIPTION 50 CENTS A YEAR—SINGLE COPY 5 CENTS

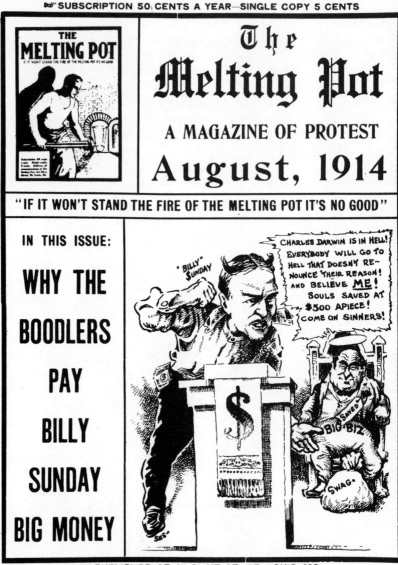

☞ PUBLISHED AT 411 OLIVE ST., ST. LOUIS, MO.

Sunday sued the editor of the *Melting Pot* for this libelous cartoon, but the case was settled out of court. The *Melting Pot* was devoted to promoting "free thought" and claimed in its article that Sunday was hired by Big Business to teach the working class to be content with its lot.

will live for Christ from now on the best I know how?' Come on. Come on. Come on."

Rodeheaver was ready; signaling the choir of fifteen hundred, he yelled a hymn number, and they burst into "Stand Up, Stand Up for Jesus." For a fraction of a second the crowd hesitated, and then it surged forward together. Men poured down the aisles by the hundreds. Immediately the trained ushers, personal workers, and secretaries sprang into action. Their every move had been rehearsed. The ushers, who were stationed on each side of the two central aisles at five-row intervals, stood up and faced toward the center of the aisles urging the converts forward, assisting persons in their rows to reach the aisles, and keeping the trail-hitters moving. Another group of ushers at the front of the hall rapidly cleared the first five rows of all persons, asking them to move quietly to the rear via the aisles along the walls.

As soon as he saw the stream of converts start down the aisles, Sunday pulled up the trap door beside the pulpit and jumped into the well to greet the first comers. "Two ushers stood back to back as two streams approached from opposite directions. One usher seized the right arm of each approaching person from the one direction and placed the hand in Billy's right; the other usher placed the hand of the person approaching from the opposite direction in Billy's left; so Billy was continually swaying now to the right, now to the left rapidly." He gripped the upstretched hands at the rate of fifty-seven per minute and said a quick "God bless you" to each.

"As the streams turned back after the hand-shaking two other ushers at the head of each stream urged the people into seats" in the recently vacated front rows. When the first five rows were filled, the next five were vacated and their occupants sent to the rear. Once the converts were seated the secretaries descended upon them giving each one a decision card and a special leaflet with the message from Sunday entitled "What It Means To Be a Christian."

Meanwhile, the choir continued to sing the same hymn over and over until the trail-hitting began to slow down. Then Sunday jumped out of the well and back onto the platform. He urged the rest of the crowd to come forward to take their stand for Christ and for Boston. The choir switched to "We're Matching to Zion." Sunday called to the personal workers to get busy. "Galvanized into action the be-badged and be-ribboned officers speedily found, as Billy had assured them, that there were plenty of persons needing only a word of invitation to hit the trail and in a twinkling, proud ushers were gently leading willing captives up to Billy's outstretched hand."

After twenty-two minutes the trail-hitting dwindled and stopped. The choir sang "Ring the Bells of Heaven, There Is Joy Today." Tired, perspiring, but smiling, Sunday announced, "I've never seen anything like this. I know God is proud of you and I know the devil isn't. Millions of people the country over are watching Boston." He concluded with a brief prayer for the converts in the front rows. "O, Christ, put your arms around the manhood of Boston. Sweep through the cities about us and through New England. Hear us and bless us until New York City is staggered . . . and, O, Jesus, let thy spirit leap across the seas to Australia to which we have had a call."

He smiled again, nodded, waved his hand, and disappeared off the platform into his rubdown room. The crowd poured out of the tabernacle as the last converts filled out their decision cards. The reporters stayed long enough to learn that 1,441 persons had come forward and then rushed to telephone the headline that a new record for first-night trail-hitting had been set.

The first night of trail-hitting in Pittsburgh was just as dramatic but netted only 476 converts in 1914. In Philadelphia in 1915, 1,300 hit the trail, for the record which stood until the Boston campaign the next year. Then in 1917 the New York first call broke all records by producing over two thousand trail-hitters.

To get a large number of converts on the first invitation in these years was not difficult if the preparation had gone well. The problem, as with the attendance, was to keep up the trail-hitting pace day after day at both the afternoon and evening meetings. The importance of the delegation system in this regard was clearly demonstrated when Sunday experimented for three days in Detroit by omitting any special reservations. The average number of trail-hitters on those three nights was 260. The average on the next three nights, when special reservations were made by various groups, was 800.[24]

It was clear that group loyalty was a valuable asset in bringing people down the aisles, and Sunday made the most of it in his invitations. Instead of making his appeal a general one, as he had the first night in Boston, he frequently picked out some delegation and called upon it to demonstrate the high quality which its name implied by taking a stand for all that was decent, Christian, and respectable. If one or two members of this group started forward,

Sunday would urge the others to follow them to show that the group stood together. "Come on, you Masons" or "Come on, Sailors" or "Come on there, Wanamaker store, you're a fine looking bunch" were typical of this type of group appeal. He was particularly eager to appeal to railroad men, since he had worked on the railroads himself. When railroad workers were present, he would shout, "Come on, Erie" or "Come on, Boston and Maine" and wave a green lantern. As the son of a veteran, he appealed to GAR groups and made arrangements to have their flag-bearer hit the trail in hopes that the rest of the group would follow the colors.

On out-of-town nights Sunday knew which suburban towns had sent delegations and called to them, "Come on, Boston; Come on, people. Come on, Roxbury. Come on, Somerville. Come on, Newton. . . . Don't, I beg of you in the name of the Lord, refuse." When young people's church groups were present, he invited them with a challenge: "Come on, Epworth Leaguers, Christian Endeavorers, everybody. What'll you do? What'll you do?" Sometimes he stood on top of the pulpit waving two American flags or a large church flag in order to stimulate the trail-hitting. On "Scotch Night" in Boston he called to the large Scotch delegations which had come with bagpipes and kilts, "Come on, Scotchmen. Show some of the grit of Wallace and Bruce." And he waved a Scottish flag from his perch on the pulpit. To a Swedish delegation one night he shouted, "Come on, Swedes. The Swedes have never been cowards yet. So come on."

On occasion Sunday virtually bribed or threatened groups to make them hit the trail. In Boston, when continuous pleas one evening had netted only a dozen trail-hitters, Sunday turned to a large delegation from Providence which had come that day to ask him to hold a campaign in their city. "You, Providence, if you want me to come there in 1918, show it now." The group of ministers, church members, and businessmen dutifully came forward in a steady stream and boosted the trail-hitting figure from 12 to 417 for the meeting.[25]

Since Sunday was interested in reviving the churches, he naturally expected them to show their support by coming forward to shake his hand. "Come on, whether you are church members or not," he said. "We know you are in the church, but we want you to get out fully for God." It was explained to the crowd that there was a place on the decision card for persons already saved to check the word "Reconsecration" and thus indicate their reawakening but not imply that they had not been saved hitherto. "Your pastor will be glad to know of your reconsecration," they were told, and the pastors sitting on the platform nodded their approval. Some critics complained that the ushers, secretaries, and personal workers were secretly told to come forward in groups when the trail-hitting lagged, but there was no secret about this. Sunday often said, "Will you accept Christ? Will you come down you ushers, you choir singers, you door-men, and all of you church people? Come choir. Come get up and walk down."[26]

Sunday expected the fullest co-operation in promoting the trail-hitting from the ushers, personal workers, and ministers who were stationed in the tabernacle for that purpose. Frequently he chastised them from the platform if they failed to do their jobs. "Don't let them stand there in the aisles. Get the preachers down there to take names. There aren't enough secretaries. Ministers get into it. Oh, this is enough to drive a man to drink." In Denver he threatened to quit the campaign if he did not get more co-operation from the local committees. In Wichita he used his closing prayer one night to berate the lazy church workers. "Oh, Lord, I am discouraged over the way these church people are doing. I never saw such laziness and indifference on the part of Christians before. . . . Lord, these people have no right to expect us to come here and do their work for them. . . . Oh, Lord, help these Christians to do their duty by getting out into these vast crowds and inviting men and women to come to Christ." In Detroit he set them an example by dramatically coming down from the platform to convert two old baseball cronies whom he had spotted in the audience.

At least once in each campaign Sunday held a special meeting of the volunteer campaign workers to tell them they were falling down on the job and that, unless they worked harder, the campaign would be a failure. This constant pressure often led to overzealousness among the workers. A reporter from the *New York Times* said that there were three types of trail-hitters: "Those who came by themselves"; those so affected "that the guidance of an usher was necessary"; and "those who came, unaffected, with the arms of workers around them, often two workers to one convert," who were "literally shoved" down the aisle. Sometimes, said this reporter, these captive converts broke away from the ushers by main force and "fled to the exit."[27]

Ushers frequently led the same man forward three or four times.

A woman named Hattie Harris confessed to reporters after Sunday's Boston campaign that she had hit the trail fourteen times. A different type of zealousness in this regard was exhibited by John Wanamaker, who was so eager to help Sunday win converts in Philadelphia that he went from the platform into the audience one night and came back up the aisle leading a staggering drunk.[28]

All this was carefully calculated to increase the trail-hitting statistics upon which Sunday's performance was judged, but it would be unfair to assume that Sunday was cynically hypocritical about the process. On the contrary, he was convinced of the urgency of his mission. "Listen to me," he would say. "You've got to. I have a tribunal to which I must answer." Many times he interspersed his calls for converts with the remark, "Don't come down to shake hands as friends. I'm calling for those who are really ready to live for Christ. Don't come if you don't mean it." When persons tried to leave the tabernacle during the trail-hitting, he cried, "Please don't go out. I'm preaching to get people to come to God, not to amuse you nor entertain you nor instruct you. This service is still going on. Don't drift out. I'll not keep you long. Don't fill up the aisles." One night in Baltimore his call for converts brought only a handful forward. He pleaded again and again in vain. Then, with tears streaming down his face, he turned exhausted to his son George and a local committee member on the platform: "I've done my level best and they're not coming as they should. Are you praying George? Stuart, pray!"[29]

Usually, however, there was no cause for disappointment. Afternoon and evening, day after day, year after year, his carefully organized system ground out its regular quota of trail-hitters. The average numbers of trail-hitters for the campaigns of 1906–18 were as follows:[30]

Cities of under 30,000 (22)	3,381
Cities of 30,000–50,000 (9)	5,724
Cities of 50,000–100,000 (10)	8,304
Cities of 100,000–500,000 (14)	15,238
Cities of over 500,000 (9)	42,968

The cities with the five largest trail-hitting totals were as follows:

New York	98,264
Boston	64,484
Chicago	49,165
Philadelphia	41,724
Buffalo	38,853

103

In the twenty-three cities of over 100,000 population which he visited in this period, he averaged 567 trail-hitters each day—about 300 per sermon; in the forty-one cities of under 100,000 he averaged 161 per day. Neither Moody nor Finney approached these figures, and Sunday's contemporaries were hopelessly outdistanced.

The fact that each of Sunday's campaigns lasted longer than those of any other post–Civil War evangelist except Moody accounts in some measure for his large convert statistics. The revivals of Mills, Torrey, and Chapman seldom lasted over four weeks even in the largest cities. Chapman's Boston campaign lasted exactly three weeks. Even though these evangelists began calling for converts the first night, they could not match Sunday's totals. By careful experiment Sunday learned the length of time which would produce the maximum trail-hitters and still end the campaign with a climactic final day. He found that "generally there is a falling off in attendance during the middle of the campaign." In fact, almost immediately after the first hectic week of trail-hitting the daily totals both for attendance and trail-hitting began to drop, until in about the fifth week the campaigns were at their lowest ebb. Then the interest slowly revived, until by the eighth week it reached and surpassed that of the opening weeks. In some cities the crowds on the last day were so large that four meetings had to be held to accommodate them. Sunday usually stayed eight weeks in cities of over 100,000, and in the largest cities he stayed ten weeks. Had he closed his campaign in Pittsburgh after six weeks, he would have obtained only 11,160 trail-hitters. By continuing for two more weeks, he reached a total of 26,602. The final two or four weeks were not always as spectacular as this, but they often doubled his total converts.

The trail-hitting in New York and Boston followed the typical pattern. As shown in the accompanying tabulation, the first ten days of trail-hitting attained a peak which was not matched until the conclusion of the campaign:

AVERAGE NUMBER OF TRAIL-HITTERS PER DAY

	New York	Boston
First 10 days of trail-hitting	1,826	1,446
Second 10 days	1,559	1,002
Third 10 days	1,641	742
Fourth 10 days	1,812	856
Fifth 10 days	1,818	1,340
Final 10 days	3,319	(Last 3 days) 2,867

The slump in trail-hitting after the first ten days corresponded to the slump in attendance which came in the middle of every campaign. As the attendance picked up in the closing weeks, the trail-hitting figures slowly built up again until in the last week a new peak was reached which surpassed that of the first ten days.

As in most campaigns, New York and Boston had peak trail-hitting on the days when the "Booze Sermon" and other well-known sermons were given, since these days were announced in advance and special efforts were made to pack the tabernacle. The largest total of trail-hitters for one day, as in every campaign, was on the final day (which always came on a Sunday). The New York total of 7,238 for the three meetings that day was the largest of Sunday's career.

The genius of Sunday's organization in producing trail-hitters was equaled only by its genius in extracting money. There were two financial phases in each campaign (in addition to raising the guarantee fund). The first was the raising of money by collections to pay off the expenses; the second was the free-will offering, with which the party was ostensibly not connected.

Until 1912 Sunday used the system for raising money which had worked so effectively in Jefferson, Iowa, in 1903. Collections were taken at every meeting, and Sunday would devote part of one of his meetings to a special fund-raising. In Wichita, Kansas, in 1911 this fund-raising technique was described as follows: At the meeting on the next-to-last Sunday of the campaign the evangelist began by asking all those who would subscribe ten dollars toward meeting the legitimate expenses of the revival to give their names to the ushers. The ushers relayed these donations to "tellers" on the platform who kept a running total. For a hectic half-hour Sunday pleaded, threatened, and cajoled subscriptions out of the audience. "What's the matter with you Masons?" he asked making his usual appeal to group loyalty. "You've got the finest building in the world, why don't you make a subscription?" Some Mason stood up to make a pledge in the name of his group. "Now you Odd Fellows come across. . . . Where's the Country Club? Why can't it come across with ten dollars? . . . Good, there's the Rock Island. Guess I'll have to go home on that road. What's the matter with you Frisco folks and Missouri and Pacific? . . . Good for the Boston Store. Wake up Inness and you other big stores. Get in the game."[31] The *Wichita Beacon* reported that "it is pretty certain that few stayed out of the giving game." Sunday went from ten-dollar subscriptions to five, then two, and then one. "Rev. Sunday did not miss a church or church organization in his calls for money." Often a member of an organization which was called on by Sunday would rise to protect its good name by pledging so much in its behalf and stated that "if other members did not agree with him he would stand for the pledge himself."

Sunday did not spare himself. "His collar was melted, his cuffs protruding from his coat sleeves, his coat was awry, and his trousers had lost their crease." From time to time his assistant, after consulting with the tellers, would come up to Sunday and, in an undertone, say, "Go after them, boss, things are coming our way." Finally, after half an hour every cent needed to pay off the remaining debt of the Wichita campaign was subscribed, a total of $4,123. The *Beacon's* report concluded: "Mr. Sunday's actions were rather spectacular," but "he had raised the coin."

This was a wearing and unpleasant ordeal. Sunday often could not raise the entire sum in one session and had to devote part of his afternoon and evening meetings to more fund-raising. He also had to preach his three sermons that day. While this technique could raise the money for small campaigns like Wichita, where the total expenses were only $8,134.31, it was impractical in large cities where the cost ran into tens of thousands. One solution which he tried was to lengthen his campaigns. Another was larger tabernacles. Both of these increased the collections. But the most important revision in this system was a combination of increased pressure on the part of local committees and an increased psychological buildup for the collections. Ministers were expected to impress upon their church members that it was their duty to meet the expenses and that no one could rest easily until the great burden of debt was lifted from their collective shoulders.

The precampaign publicity was increasingly directed toward making the public aware of the fact that collections would be taken at the very first meetings, that as soon as the expenses were met the collections would cease, and that it was customary for each city to try to better the records of preceding cities in the amount of the first day's contributions. Newspapers were provided with statistics of first-day collections, and it became customary to try to exceed the record of towns of equal size. The preparatory buildup in Buffalo was so effective that $10,181 was produced the first day. Boston contributed $9,337.95, and Philadelphia $7,500. Sunday frequently apologized for the fact that collections had to be taken, for those who remembered Moody's revivals knew that Moody had had such generous financial support from wealthy laymen that he had seldom taken collections at his meetings. But Moody held less than ten revivals at which special tabernacles were built; Sunday had to find a way to make ten score tabernacle campaigns pay their own way.

Sunday always reminded his audiences that he got not one cent from the collections, and he promised that, as soon as the expenses were met, the collections would cease. Every effort was made to have the expenses paid off at least in time to have the final week of the revival free of collections. Sunday continually railed at "cheapskates" who put pennies or nickels in the large tin dishpans which were used as collection plates. "You expect to pay your carfare up to the tabernacle," he would say; "why not expect to pay for your religion, too? This isn't a taber-nickel, you know."[32] Constant references were made to local pride in order to increase the contributions: "Other cities are watching Boston's collections," Sunday said; "I know you have too much local pride and wealth to let Boston fall back along this line." The final touch was to announce that the next three nights would be ten-cent, twenty-five-cent, and dollar nights. It was a hardened man who would place in the tin collection pan on dollar night a coin whose clatter would betray his miserliness.

The *Providence Journal* described a money-raising trick which Sunday tried on his audience in that city when the patriotic fervor of World War I was at its height. After asking for those who would donate $25.00, $10.00, and $5.00 toward the expenses, he asked for those who would give one dollar: "Billy repeated his call of 'How many of you will give a dollar? Stand up,' and the two pianists broke into 'The Star-Spangled Banner.' No need of telling what happened. Everybody [stood up and] broke into a roar of laughter and it was noticeable that when the dishpans came back greenbacks were more in evidence than silver."

Sunday claimed that never, throughout his whole career, did he fail to raise the money to pay off the expenses and release or repay those who raised the guarantee fund. He meant by this that he left no unpaid debts behind him, but he exaggerated when he implied that the collections taken in the tabernacle were always sufficient to do this. It was obvious that the church members who put up the guarantee usually came to the tabernacle and paid themselves back by the money they put in the collection pans, and in many cities the wealthy backers did not require that the money they donated to the guarantee fund be repaid. In Boston the members of the executive committee donated from $500 to $2,000 apiece to increase the collection total.[33] Moreover, it became a matter of record that contributions were actively solicited outside the tabernacle from individuals and corporations in order to supplement the collections. The Washington, D.C., and New York campaigns were notable in this respect.

From the outset of the Washington campaign in 1918, Sunday denounced the lack of interest and the meagerness of the collections. The Liberty Bond and other war fund drives had apparently drained away much that would have gone into the meetings. After four weeks, only $12,000 of the $62,000 expenses had been met. The local committee openly began to solicit private individuals to help raise the money, and in one week $12,000 was given in this manner, while Sunday's pleading brought another $10,000 in collections. But $28,000 was still needed, with only three weeks left.

The drive for funds continued both inside and out of the tabernacle, but at the outset of the final week the expenses were still unpaid. It was decided to abandon the attempt to raise the expense fund by tabernacle collections and to rely solely on the solicitation of wealthy individuals. Nevertheless, it seemed inevitable that the campaign would still end ten thousand dollars in debt. Then W. K. Cooper and John Letts hit upon a solution. The Washington YMCA would buy the tabernacle from the Sunday citizens' committee for ten thousand dollars and use it as a servicemen's center for the duration of the war; the ten thousand dollars would be credited against the expenses. By this scheme the committee closed its books in the black, but the newspapers reported that only about 50 per cent of the expenses had been paid out of tabernacle collections.[34]

A similar situation occurred in New York. With expenses that totaled over $200,000, the collections had reached only $64,000 after eight weeks had gone by. The committee decided four days later to cease the collections anyway and announced to the papers that the expenses had been met. The auditor's statement which appeared later revealed that the total amount received from "collections" had been $67,834.32 and that the remaining $133,392.31 had come from "Contributions."[35] As the committee had stated before the campaign, "persons interested in the evangelization of New York City" had given their money without any hope of a return from the collections.

In short, Sunday's largest campaigns were not, as he boasted, self-supporting. It was beyond the limit of voluntary public collections to meet expenses of over $50,000. Pittsburgh's $39,000 in expenses were met almost entirely by the tabernacle collections, but in every city where the amount was higher, private subscriptions were necessary. To this extent Sunday had improved little upon Moody's system. Revivalism was backed by the wealthy and hence bore the odium of possible ulterior motives on the part of this particular class of society toward the lower classes.

Except in the five or six largest cities, however, Sunday's campaigns from 1906 to 1918 did not often cost over $50,000. In fact, none of his campaigns prior to 1914 cost more than $25,000. On the whole, however, Sunday's efforts to increase the efficiency of revivals did not extend to making them less expensive. His expenses from 1912 to 1918 averaged almost $10,000 per week, as compared to Moody's $5,000 per week. Sunday's five most expensive campaigns were as follows:

New York (10 weeks)	$200,168.87
Chicago (10 weeks)	135,000.00
Philadelphia (11 weeks)	105,889.95
Boston (10 weeks)	93,000.00
Buffalo (10 weeks)	66,795.90

A list of the expenses of the New York campaign, though larger than all others, explains some of the items involved in these vast sums:

Tabernacle (including $11,139 for running expenses, $6,552 for insurance, $12,750 for ground rent)	$ 95,091.56
Cafeteria	13,596.00
Comfort building	3,503.17
Salaries and traveling expenses of party	21,163.65
Household expenses for party	7,093.07
Transportation expenses of party in New York City	2,850.81
Headquarters (suite of 12 rooms in Metropolitan Building and $13,535 in salaries)	29,496.62
Traveling expenses of volunteer helpers	1,294.71
Committee expenses	16,597.78
Publicity	5,732.29
Dinner meetings for promotion of campaign	2,937.16
Discount and interest on notes	822.05
Total expenditures	$200,168.87

The New York tabernacle was exceptionally elaborate, with its cafeteria, comfort rooms, and headquarters expenses. It also was the only city which paid the full amount of salaries for the party, though the accounts carefully noted that Sunday received "not a penny listed under the expenses."

Except in New York City, Sunday chose to pay part of the salaries of his staff himself even when local committees volunteered to pay them all, not only because it kept the staff under his control but also because it assured their working for the success of the revival. A successful revival meant a large free-will offering, and it was out of this that Sunday paid his share of their salaries.

Evangelistic remuneration had always been a touchy problem. Moody was usually rewarded with a check placed in an envelope and quietly handed to him, as he left the city, by one of the members of the local committee. Torrey used this same procedure. B. Fay Mills had his local committee pass out "Offering Envelopes" in which might be placed, he said, "such free will offerings as individuals desire to make to the Lord for our services"; the envelopes were mailed or given in person to the evangelist. Chapman was one of the first to accept the collections at the final day's meetings as his salary; his co-workers received the last day's collections in their districts. Before Sunday's era the amount of remuneration given to an evangelist was always kept in strictest secrecy. Perhaps because the sums were not large, the newspapers never considered this aspect of revivalism worthy of mention. But with Sunday's advent the question of religion and money suddenly became news.

When his staff had been small and his campaigns short, Sunday had left the work of raising the free-will offering for himself to the local ministers. The audiences were informed during the last week of the campaign that a special effort to reward Sunday suitably for his labors would be made on the final day of the campaign. On that day, imitating Sunday's fund-raising technique and undoubtedly coached by him as to the process, several ministers acted as tellers on the platform, the ushers were given pledge cards or blank checks to pass out, and an "auction" began to see which individual or group would make the largest donation. This was done prior to each of the three final services before Sunday reached the tabernacle. It was an undignified and often embarrassing process, especially if the ministers were not adept at coaxing donations. However, the system produced sizable results. Washington Gladden reported in 1913 that Sunday had recently stated, in comparing his high-pressure "auction" technique for raising large free-will offerings to that used by other evangelists, "I've got all those other fellows skinned a mile in the free-will offering."[36]

In Springfield, Illinois, in 1909 the morning auction netted $6,229.84 for Sunday; the afternoon, $2,521.74; and the evening, $1,943.25. An additional $260 was raised at a women's meeting in the afternoon, and $100 in small amounts was given to Sunday personally outside the tabernacle. The total was $10,734.84, a thousand dollars more than the expenses. Still, it was $5,000 short of the goal which the ministers had set for themselves—or which had been set for them. This sum was modest in comparison with later offerings, but it seemed excessive to many. The previous year, during the campaign in Ottumwa, Iowa, the mayor and ten leading citizens signed a petition respectfully asking Sunday to take only $1,000 for his services and to give anything above this to charity. Sunday did not answer their petition, but the local ministers flew into a rage. They wrote, and read at the tabernacle, a blistering reply to the petition, in which they accused four of its ten signers of holding stock in breweries and stated that none of the signers ever gave anything to charity themselves. On the closing day of the campaign these ministers carried out the usual offering system, and Sunday took the entire $7,353.77 collected.[37]

There was a limit to the amount which could be coaxed out of the audiences on the final day. In Columbus, Ohio, in 1912, the local committee decided that Sunday deserved more than could possibly be raised by such collections. During the last week "a large committee headed by one of our prominent businessmen," said the Rev. A. E. Isaac, one of the co-operating ministers, "took charge of the collection the last day for Mr. Sunday. . . . They telephoned to some of the leading businessmen and gave them the opportunity to subscribe in advance." As a result, Sunday received $20,929 in Columbus, the largest offering of his career up to that time. Collections were taken at the tabernacle as well, but the bulk of the money came from private subscriptions made beforehand. "I do not think," said Isaac, "you can find a businessman in Columbus . . . that has any criticism to offer. They will tell you he is entitled to all he gets."[38]

The following year, in Denver, during the last week of the campaign the co-operating ministers asked that contributions to Sunday's offering by check or in cash be deposited in his name at the Interstate Trust Company, in which the committee had opened an account for him. It was suggested that a suitable goal for this drive would be $24,000, and Dean H. Martyn Hart, a co-operating Episcopalian minister, asked the audience one night, "Surely Denver does not want to fall behind other cities?"

In succeeding years the emphasis was less and less upon the last day's collections, except for publicity purposes, and the auction system ceased altogether. In Pittsburgh in 1914 each of the three-hundred-odd churches co-operating were asked to make a special contribution toward Sunday's remuneration. On the day after the campaign closed, the offering was announced as $29,000, of which only $10,400 had been taken in the last day's collections. But two hundred churches had not yet been heard from. During the next week the contributions from these churches brought the total to roughly $46,000. One church alone, the Rev. Maitland Alexander's First Presbyterian Church, donated over $2,300.

The churches were not the only outside contributors in Pittsburgh. $18,498.97 had been given to Sunday by various individuals and corporations. One check came to him for $2,000 and ten others for $1,000 each, but the names of the donors were withheld from the public.[39] Some of these undoubtedly came from individuals at whose homes he had held Thursday morning "parlor meetings," such as Mrs. W. H. Donner and Mr. H. J. Heinz. Others came from corporations which, as the *Lutheran Observer* noted, were pleased to contribute because of the improved work in the steel mills.[40] During the 1913 campaign in Johnstown, Pennsylvania, the Johnstown Traction Company and the Cambria Steel Company were so pleased by the increased sobriety and industry of their workers that they donated $500 and $1,000, respectively, to Sunday's offering.[41]

By 1917 the mechanics of obtaining a large free-will offering had been thoroughly reorganized. In almost every city after 1912 an offering committee was an integral part of the local organization. Thoroughly coached by Sunday and his assistants, this group of ministers and businessmen took the initial steps toward securing a large offering several weeks before the concluding date of the campaign.

The Boston offering committee was made up of members of the executive committee and was extremely diligent. Throughout the entire final week, offering envelopes were passed out at the tabernacle in order to reach "those who desire to give something but do not expect to be present on the last day." The Rev. Cortland Myers admonished the local citizens, "Boston must not blush with shame because of small figures a week from next Monday." Allan Emery described the four methods by which a person could contribute: he could mail a check to the evangelist (when indorsed, cashed, and returned, it was pointed out that the check would provide the donor with Sunday's autograph); he could give a check or cash to the committee's treasurer, William T. Rich; he could make a donation through any of the co-operating churches, which were taking special collections for the offering; or he could give his offering at the tabernacle on the final day.[42] It was not surprising that fifteen to twenty thousand dollars had been received for the offering on the Saturday before the final day of the campaign.

The question of how much solicitation was done by the local committees, how much was voluntary, and how much was undertaken directly by the Sunday party was hotly debated by Sunday's friends and critics. Philip Loeb, of Montclair, New Jersey, complained in a letter quoted in the *New York Times* in May, 1915, that the Sunday party had resorted to "organized begging" in order to get money for the offering in Philadelphia. He claimed that only $2,000 of the $53,000 Sunday received came from the last day's collections and that the other $51,000 was obtained from personal solicitation of the wealthy.[43]

Loeb's statements were corroborated by the Rev. Dr. Longsworth's experience in the Paterson campaign that same year. Longsworth, a co-operating Congregational minister, said that the Sunday party had tried to compel the ministers to use high-pressure methods to solicit the wealthy residents of the city for the offering. A member of the Sunday staff had presented the ministers with a twenty-eight-page list of influential citizens who were to be approached. Some ministers complied with the party's request, but others balked.[44] Longsworth also stated that the delegations which received reserved seats were urged to bring gifts to the Sundays, which were presented prior to each service. Of the $24,000 that Sunday received from Paterson, only $7,800 came from the final day's collections. Among the prominent donors of $1,000 and $500 checks were Mrs. Hobart, Elbert Gary, and George Arnold.[45]

Leonard W. DeGast, the treasurer of the Washington, D.C., campaign, said that the committee was compelled to pass out blank checks at every meeting during the final week of the campaign because the Sunday party felt that the local committee had been slothful in soliciting private individuals. When DeGast told Mrs. Sunday ten days before the campaign was to close that nothing had been done yet about the free-will offering, she demanded angrily: "Do you mean to say you're going to let us work our guts out for nothing?"[46] It was reported that Sunday was expecting a free-will offering of $40,000 in Washington, but the war and the lack of outside solicitation resulted in an offering of only $16,332, the smallest Sunday had received in five years.

Probably the most influential attack on Sunday's offering system came from the Rev. Hamilton Schuyler, of Trinity Church, Trenton, New Jersey. Writing in the *American Church Monthly* in March, 1917, he described Sunday's methods in Trenton as "polite blackmail." He told how the party had divided the city into districts and sent out a host of solicitors to canvass each section. Foremen and superintendents in factories were instructed to tell the workers under them that a certain minimum donation was expected from each. Individual businessmen were put on lists and given a financial rating according to what was expected from each. "Pressure of every sort is employed to induce the giving of the sum fixed upon as representing their proper share." Appeals were made to "civic pride" and "the fine advertisement which the city will get" if the offering surpassed other cities.

Such charges as these caused John D. Rockefeller, Jr., to look into the question of Sunday's finances prior to the New York campaign. He reported:

I studied Mr. Sunday's financial methods—I had an investigator follow his work and make a report to me—and I found that no effort was made anywhere to get contributions. The people whom he had helped gave what they felt like giving. No one was asked to give a cent.[47]

But the weight of the evidence was against Rockefeller, and apparently it weighed upon Sunday's conscience. One month after Schuyler's article Sunday announced on the opening night of his New York campaign that he would give his entire free-will offering in that city to the Red Cross and the YMCA. This, said Mrs. Sunday, "had a great effect. [The] Press were swept off their feet and balance and everybody's mouth was closed that [had said that] he had come to New York for money." Whether his offering would have been as large as $120,500 had he not done this seems doubtful. The sum was turned over officially to Sunday in order to let him make the gift, but the requests by donors that their gifts go also to the YWCA indicated that the donations were regarded more as a charity gift toward the war effort than as offerings to the evangelist. It was in order to permit Sunday to donate this entire sum without any deductions that the New York committee agreed to pay the full salaries of the Sunday party. Though little was said about it, the

114

New York Times reported that certain prominent citizens saw to it that Sunday did not go entirely unrewarded for his labor.[48]

Whether to quiet further criticism or to palliate the Chicago public for his frequent postponements of the campaign, Sunday gave his entire free-will offering in Chicago to the Pacific Garden Mission. A list of some of the donors to this fund of $56,000 is significantly reminiscent of Moody's backers: $5,000: Mrs. Cyrus McCormick, Louis F. Swift, Mrs. G. F. Swift; $2,500: J. Ogden Armour, Victor Lawson, H. P. Crowell; $2,000: Illinois Steel Company, by E. J. Buffington; $1,000: W. A. Peterson, S. B. Chapin, George W. Dixon, Thomas Smith, A. M. Johnson, Mel Trotter, J. V. Farwell family, Bryan McKinnon; $500: G. M. Webb, John Murveen, Robert Stewart, Charles E. Holt, Marvin Hughitt.[49]

The increasing size of his free-will offerings after 1906 was responsible for a large measure of Sunday's publicity. Newspapers all over the nation followed his record and listed his earnings over the years. The year-by-year totals were as shown in the accompanying tabulation.[50]

Year	No. of Campaigns	Total Offerings
1907	6	$ 24,508
1908	6	46,664
1909	6	45,204
1910	6	53,489
1911	6	67,603
1912	6	71,306
1913	5	83,009
1914	6	102,310
1915	4	122,370
1916	5	204,825
1917	4	200,695
1918	5	117,332
Total		$1,139,315

Even if the total of $176,490 which Sunday gave to charity in New York and Chicago is subtracted, the gross income for these dozen years (excluding income from chautauqua lectures, government bonds, real estate investments, gifts, and royalties on his biographies and sermons) was close to a million dollars and averaged over $80,000 a year.[51] Critics were not impressed by the fact that Sunday paid part of the salaries of his staff out of this or by the fact that he gave one-tenth of his earnings to charity. According to Rodeheaver, Sunday was a millionaire by 1920, when Dun and

115

Bradstreet rated him as worth $1,500,000.[52] Sunday's only comment was that it was nobody's business how much money he had or what he did with it. Like another contemporary millionaire, John D. Rockefeller, Sr., Sunday believed that the Lord gave him his money.

Sunday defended the high cost of his revivals by stating that he produced more converts more cheaply than any other revivalist and even than the churches themselves. Speaking in Columbus, Ohio, in 1912, he quoted some figures on total annual expenditures by the Protestant churches in various cities; then he divided these staggering amounts by the small number of new members officially received into the churches in these cities in one year. The result showed that most denominations spent several hundred dollars for each new member gained. "In spite of all these high figures," said Sunday, "you kick about what I get. What I'm paid for my work makes it only about $2 a soul, and I get less proportionately for the number I convert than any other living evangelist."[53] He sarcastically told eastern audiences that one hundred thousand dollars was spent on tickets for a single football game at the Yale Bowl, and he pointed out to western audiences that, if his offerings were graft, so was the one hundred thousand dollars a year that William Jennings Bryan was making from chautauqua lectures.

According to the available statistics, Sunday was correct in claiming that two dollars was the average cost for each trail-hitter in the years 1906–18 if the expenses alone were considered the cost of the revival. Prior to 1906 Sunday obtained trail-hitters for less than a dollar each. In a few large cities, like Chicago and Washington, D.C., the cost was nearer three dollars apiece. If the free-will offering were considered part of the revival expenses, the cost of a trail-hitter would have averaged nearly four dollars for the 1906–18 period. Some critics added not only the expenses and the free-will offering but the money spent for hymnbooks, religious pamphlets, Bibles, biographies, postcards, and other literature sold at the tabernacle, plus the gifts of clothes, jewelry, and bric-a-brac made to the party—all these things were money taken out of the city by the revivalist. Others, noting that all those who shook Sunday's hand did not join churches, felt that Sunday's cost-per-trail-hitter criterion of success was purely academic.

But during the years 1906–18 Sunday suffered little from such criticism. Invitations poured in upon him. The vast majority of evangelical churchmen had nothing but praise for his efficient organization, and even those old-fashioned ministers who were over-

whelmed by the "big statistics" or the "man-made look" of tabernacle evangelism admitted that he got results. To his supporters the
importance of spreading the religious and social message which
Sunday's sermons embodied justified all the mechanical aspects of
his campaigns. And, just as he had perfected his organization by
years of experience, so Sunday developed his message until it fitted
his technique, his personality, his backers, and his audience. For a
decade or more he was the voice of the evangelical churches in the
United States.

4

"GOD'S MOUTHPIECE"[1]

The mechanical efficiency of Billy Sunday's revivals would have amounted to little had he not preached what people wanted to hear. His creed, though it became associated with the Fundamentalist movement in Protestantism after 1916, consisted of a broad, non-denominational form of evangelicalism which represented the average American's conception of Christianity. His social views were formed by a rural, midwestern background and changed little, if at all, in the years after he left Iowa to live in the big city. Self-interest may have modified Sunday's public expressions on certain contemporary issues, and he undoubtedly catered to the prevailing opinion upon occasion, but for the most part his attitudes were so similar to those of his audience that he could speak with complete spontaneity and sincerity and know that his words would be applauded.

Sunday's religious and social views were a logical historical outgrowth of that inherent conflict in Protestantism between the pessimistic determinism of Calvinism and the optimistic faith in free will implicit in the Arminianism of Wesley and Finney. At the moment when Sunday appeared on the scene, these two views were once again in open conflict, and the theological pendulum which had swung so sharply toward Arminianism in Finney's day was slowly returning to the neo-Calvinism of the post–World War I period.

When Charles Finney formulated in the 1830's the systematic theology which underlay most nineteenth-century revival preaching, he gave authoritative evangelical sanction to the rejection of the Calvinistic dogma of the innate depravity of human nature. In rejecting this dogma, Finney climaxed a century of revolt against the pessimistic views which had denied the benevolence of the Deity, the goodness of man, and the ability of human reason to fathom the secrets of the universe. Finney maintained not only that man could effect his own salvation but that, by the use of his divinely given ability to reason, he could grow in wisdom and goodness until he achieved a state of perfection. In fact, said Finney, "the re-

118

generate habitually live without sin, and fall into sin only at intervals so few and far between that, in strong language, it may be said in truth that they do not sin."[2] This doctrine, known as "Oberlin Perfectionism," represented the extreme limit of the swing away from Calvin's pessimistic view of human nature. But the 1830's and 1840's were decades of philosophical extremism and experimental utopianism; in preaching Perfectionism, Finney was merely expressing that ebullient optimism which characterized the American scene throughout the nineteenth century.

The acceptance of Darwinism by Henry Ward Beecher and of Herbert Spencer's "Social Darwinism" (with its corollaries of inevitable and continual progress) by most of the better-educated Protestant clergymen in the last quarter of the nineteenth century was a consequence of this same optimistic outlook. Though Finney died in 1875, sixteen years after the publication of the *Origin of Species,* he never accepted Darwin's theory. But the optimism voiced in his Perfectionism made the way easier for evangelical clergymen of all denominations to accept evolution on the grounds that it was simply God's way of bringing about that state of perfection which would permit his kingdom to come "on earth as it is in heaven."

The significance of this compromise with science dawned very slowly upon most evangelical clergymen, and few revivalists prior to 1900 were sufficiently aware of the warfare yet to come between science and theology even to mention evolution in their sermons. It was not until the 1890's that Moody began to find conflicts arising among his followers regarding the irreconcilability of certain scientific theories of the creation of the world and the explanation of the creation given in the Bible. And when Moody was faced with the historical inaccuracies unearthed by the "higher critics" regarding the authorship of the Bible, he dodged the whole issue by saying, "What's the use of talking about two Isaiahs when most people don't know there's one?"[3]

Billy Sunday, however, was not able to avoid the struggle between the literal view of the Bible upon which Finney and Moody had based their theology and the "liberal" or "Modernist" view of the Bible which evolved from the theistic concept of evolution. By the second decade of the twentieth century the issues were too clear cut for any minister to avoid taking a stand. The younger generation, reading Darwinian and Spencerian theories in the schools, were no longer willing to accept the compromise that the Book of

119

Genesis was a "metaphorical" interpretation of the geological and astronomical laws governing the creation. Either the Bible meant what it said, or it did not. If Genesis was an elaborate scientific riddle, then the whole Bible was a riddle, and if there were two Isaiahs, then there may have been two or more authors of every book in the Bible. The evangelical clergy found their authority slipping away as the authority of the Bible slipped away, and the time came when the compromise with science was utterly repudiated by many ministers who chose to stand upon the older and firmer ground of a literal interpretation of the Bible as "the infallible word of God."

However, the crisis which faced the evangelical churches at the turn of the twentieth century concerned more than theological dogma. It concerned a whole philosophy of life. The social outlook inherent in Finney's Perfectionism was challenged by the fact that all was not going well with the American system of free enterprise and laissez faire capitalism. The rugged individualism and self-reliant optimism of the early nineteenth century suffered more and more frequent shocks and disappointments. The farmer found himself caught in the meshes of monopolistic railroads and unscrupulous price speculators who seemed to be robbing him of the just fruits of his labor. The farmer's sons and daughters who went to the city found themselves either without jobs or without any chance of working their way up from the drudgery of factory or clerical employment into the longed-for financial success and independence. The small businessman was unable to compete with the ruthless large-scale manufacturer. The country as a whole seemed at the mercy of unpredictable and uncontrollable panics and prolonged depressions. In short, America was in the throes of a gigantic transformation from a primarily agrarian to a primarily industrial economy, and no one knew how to manage the transfer without causing great suffering to millions of hard-working and honest men and women. Though the old optimism did not give way to despair, many Americans were sorely troubled.

Moody expressed strong doubts about the inevitability of progress and the perfectibility of human nature. He was converted in 1855 under the preaching of the Rev. Edward N. Kirk, a Boston Congregationalist minister noted even at that late date for his Calvinistic views, and, consequently, although both Moody and Finney tried to interpret the Bible as literally as possible, the element of pessimism was much stronger in Moody's preaching. On the other hand, Finney's optimism, though not his literalism, was quite noticeable in the preaching of ministers like Henry Ward Beecher, whose background was of a much more liberal Congregationalism than Moody's and whose sermons Billy Sunday often read and quoted. Beecher, secure in a wealthy suburban pulpit, could accept the economic difficulties of the era with equanimity and could complacently express the strongest faith in God's evolutionary process of survival of the fittest. Moody, struggling to convert the poorest elements of Chicago's South Side, was convinced that the world had been getting steadily worse since Adam's fall.

With this view Beecher categorically disagreed. After talking to Moody one day, he told a friend: "I thought I saw the secret of his working and plans. He is a believer in the second advent of Christ, and in our times. He thinks it is no use to attempt to work for this world."[4] Moody searched the Bible for God's views on progress and concluded: "I don't find any place where God says the world is to grow better and better. . . . I find that the earth is to grow worse and worse. . . . I look upon this world as a wrecked vessel: God has given me a lifeboat and said to me, 'Moody, save all you can.'"[5]

Although Beecher was convinced that the world would get better and better, he willingly co-operated with Moody's revivals. The struggle between Fundamentalism and Modernism was still many years off, and both men shared a common belief in a laissez faire type of government. Moody favored it because he considered any attempts at social reform a waste of time which might better be spent in soul-winning. Beecher favored it because he believed governmental interference with the natural functioning of economic laws would lead to the survival of the *un*fittest and a consequent disruption of progress.

Billy Sunday's preaching in the days of his greatest success was an amalgamation of the views of Finney, Moody, and Beecher. Like Finney and Moody he was a literalistic conservative in his theology, and like Finney and Beecher he was an optimistic believer in progress. He was at war with science and learning whenever they conflicted with a literal interpretation of the Bible, but he was a staunch admirer of them when they stood for mechanical progress: "If by evolution you mean advance, I go with you," he said; "but if you mean by evolution that I came from a monkey, good night!"[6] Unfortunately for Sunday, the two views were not mutually exclusive, and eventually he rejected science and learning and progress altogether. Like Moody, he came to believe that the world was a wrecked vessel, or, as he expressed it in twentieth-century terms: "This sin-soaked world is going to hell so fast it is breaking the speed limit."[7]

When Sunday was converted in the Pacific Garden Mission in 1886, he accepted the orthodox evangelical theology of Finney and Moody. But this conversion, despite its references to the sinful world and the evil human heart, could not erase the firmly imbedded beliefs in the divine potential of the individual and the manifest destiny of the nation which Sunday had imbibed in childhood. If it ever occurred to him that there was any conflict between the pessimistic doctrine of human depravity and the optimistic doctrine of progress, he undoubtedly resolved it by reference to those equally cogent evangelical doctrines that salvation gave the sinner a new heart and that constant devotion to soul-winning by all believers made it a definite possibility that the world, or at least the United States, could be redeemed and made perfect.

It may have been the unconscious urge to still this latent conflict which led Sunday to devote his life to trying to convert all America. After all, Moody, whose living example was before him in Chicago until 1899, was not so pessimistic as to withdraw completely from the world: not only by his revivals, his schools, and his YMCA's was Moody trying to leaven the American loaf, but he went so far as to proclaim his profound belief in the Republican party as the nation's bulwark and to demand that no Christian should fail to do his duty at the ballot box.

During the first decades of the twentieth century Billy Sunday devoted himself to promulgating his religious and social views from the tabernacle platform without ever resolving, any more than the nation as a whole resolved, the conflicts between American ideals and American practice. Sunday held up the mythical "American way of life" as the goal to be sought after by all Christians; he defined it in nineteenth-century terms, and, in his frequent references to "the good old days," he implied that the myth had been reality then and could be so again.

In spite of, or perhaps because of, his intellectual limitations and inconsistencies, Sunday's sermons successfully expressed the views not only of the majority of the evangelical clergy who supported him but also of a large segment of the American people. His crusading zeal against contemporary ills symbolized to many the buoyant faith of Americans in themselves and in their country despite the temporary malfunctioning of free enterprise; his dynamic revivalism represented a form of that aggressive spirit of business enterprise and efficiency in coping with current problems that appealed directly to the American urge to "do something about it"; and the simple terms to which he reduced all issues and the colorful way in which he presented them aroused the reforming zeal of the average American to new activity reminiscent of the antislavery and other reform crusades of Finney's era.

Sunday, however, did not lead or form public opinion; he merely gave it voice. That the shy, uneducated, and simple baseball player from the cornfields of Iowa should come to express in blatant and dogmatic terms the deeply felt troubles of a confused nation could be explained to those who accepted his leadership only as a direct manifestation of God's use of humble human agents to make known his will. Or, as Sunday phrased it: "If I am not God's mouthpiece, come up and show me."[8]

As God's mouthpiece, Sunday succeeded in reducing the systematic theology which Finney had taken five hundred pages to elaborate into a single sentence of ten words: "With Christ you are saved; without him you are lost." He made no attempt to elaborate or develop a systematic theology of his own. "I don't know any more about theology than a jack-rabbit knows about ping-pong, but I'm on my way to glory," he exclaimed proudly. The extreme simplicity of his theological beliefs was one of Sunday's greatest assets as a revivalist.

By "saved" Sunday meant saved from the eternal punishment in hell-fire, which in strict justice should be the inevitable lot of all men since Adam brought sin into the world. "You can't argue against sin," Sunday declared. "It is in the world and men and women are blighted and mildewed by it." To fulfil his law God should, and could in all righteousness, send all men to hell not only because of Adam's sin but because, since that time, no man could live without committing some sins. But God was merciful and benevolent, and though he realized that man would "do wrong," said Sunday, he realized also that "there had to be some way whereby we could get right with Him, so He established the plan of salvation." This plan was to permit Christ to pay the penalty for the sins of all men. Christ "came into this world" and "gave up His life that you and I might be reconciled to God through our faith in Jesus Christ." To be "saved" one had only to believe in the truth of Christ's birth, death, and resurrection as it was set forth in the Gospels. "Salvation is escape from the punishment of sin . . . everyone who accepts the sacrifice of Christ as his own is released from the penalty of the law. That is

God's method of salvation." And that was the essence of Sunday's theology.

In order further to simplify his message, Sunday frequently employed the terminology of the contemporary businessman. He explained that in Christ's death God had "paid a price" for men's souls and that those who refused to believe in Christ were "withholding from God what he paid for on the cross. . . . When you refuse you are not giving God a square deal." Or, put another way, Christ was a "mediator" between God and man just as "a retail merchant is a mediator between the wholesale dealer and the consumer"; "because of His divinity He understands God's side of it and because of His humanity He understands our side of it."

There was nothing in this reduction of Christianity to its simplest evangelistic terms to offend any denomination. "As an evangelist of a union meeting," Sunday said, "I always steer clear of anything about which there is a controversy. It is my business to get men to take a stand for Christ." Unlike certain sectarian revivalists, he took no stand on doctrinal or liturgical quibblings, such as the proper form of baptism. "I want you to understand I am not here preaching baptism. I am not here preaching sprinkling, immersion, or pouring." These questions Sunday left up to the regular pastors who supported him, while he concentrated entirely on persuading sinners to "accept Christ."

The principal obstacle in the way of man's giving God "a square deal" was the devil. The devil, said Sunday, "is the most formidable enemy the human race has to contend with." Whenever a man hesitated to hit the trail, he was told: "That's the real, genuine, blazing-eyed, cloven-hoofed, forked-tail, old devil hanging on to your coat-tail." Sunday denounced as "time-serving, hypocritical ministers" those Modernists who played down the old-fashioned belief in the devil. Ministers who say that "there isn't any devil—that he is just a figure of speech, a poetic personification of the sin in our natures, are calling the Holy Bible a lie," he maintained. Yet in other sermons he seemed to adopt this very attitude himself: "If there is no devil why do you cuss instead of pray? Why do you lie instead of telling the truth? Why don't you kiss your wife instead of cursing her?" The answer, he said, was simple: "You just have the devil in you, that is all." Finney, in his *Memoirs,* told of personal encounters with the devil, who on several occasions tried to kill him, but Sunday had no such encounters. He was, in fact, quite willing to accept the common view that the world was governed by fixed natural laws with which God no longer interfered: "God doesn't throw the universe out of gear to stop and punish one sinner," he said.

Nevertheless, Sunday was not so modern as to concede away the existence of heaven and hell. "There is a hell and when the Bible says so don't you be so blackhearted, lowdown, and degenerate as to say you don't believe it, you big fool!" The flames might not be literally flames, said Sunday. "What difference does it make whether the fire in hell is literal or not?" It may be, he conceded to the metaphorical interpretation of the Bible, that "God used that term as figurative to convey to you the terror of hell."

And the same was true of heaven: "It doesn't make any difference whether the gold on the streets in heaven is literal or not." The fact of the matter was that "God said 'streets of gold' in order to convey to us the highest ideals our minds could conceive of beauty." To deny the existence of heaven and hell was to deny the whole structure of reward and punishment upon which God's control over the free human will was based—and also the main force behind the evangelist's control over his audience. "You are going to live forever in heaven, or you are going to live forever in hell," Sunday declared. "There's no other place—just the two. It is for you to decide. It's up to you, and you must decide now!"

With considerable relish Sunday populated hell with all the great freethinkers and "sinners" of history. The list included persons as dissimilar as Nero and Darwin, Henry VIII and Robert Ingersoll, Mme de Pompadour and John Stuart Mill, Catherine of Russia and Mary Baker Eddy. Heaven was portrayed in glowing terms as the direct opposite of the torments of hell. In heaven they dig no graves, no one gets sick, nobody cries, "the flowers never fade, the winter winds and blasts never blow." All friends and families are united. The hardhearted rich are not allowed into heaven. The saved meet and talk on equal terms with the saints and the prophets, the disciples and the Holy Family. In heaven there is no hard work, no poverty, no hunger. A home is provided for everyone. "I never like to think about heaven as a great big tenement house, where they put hundreds of people under one roof as we do in Chicago and other big cities. 'In my Father's house are many mansions.' . . . Don't let God be compelled to hang a 'For Rent' sign in the window of the mansion he has prepared for you."

Billy Sunday, like Moody, devoted at least one sermon in each revival to the Imminent Bodily Second Coming of Christ, though the dogma was not popular among the more liberal clergy. Sunday

likened the Second Coming to the imminent but unpredictable
arrival of a "Bank Inspector"—than which, he said, nothing else does
so much to "keep us right." At the moment of Christ's return, so the
doctrine went in Sunday's version, the saved would immediately be
separated from the unsaved; the saved would be snatched up into
heaven, and the unsaved would be left to live for seven (or seven
hundred—Sunday did not know which) years under the terrible rule
of Satan. Then Christ and the saved would return again, Satan
would be locked up in the pit, and the saints would rule the earth
for a thousand years. Think of it, Sunday told his audiences, "Think
of coming here and reigning over the people that used to slander
and vilify you. Think of coming back to this world as a ruler where
you have been reviled!" He presented a picture of Christ dividing
the world and saying to him, " 'Bill, you take Massachusetts.' If He
says 'Reign over Massachusetts' there'll be something doing. . . .
I've got it in for that gang."[9]

At the conclusion of the millennium Satan would be released from
the pit, and the battle of Armageddon would take place. Satan and
his forces would be defeated and sent back to hell forever. Then God
would make his Last Judgment, and all souls, living and dead,
would be divided into those who must spend eternity in hell and
those who would spend it in heaven. Sunday pointed to passages in
the Bible which predicted that Christ would return when the world
was steeped in sin, and who could deny, he asked, that the twentieth
century had brought the world to its lowest depths of immorality
and infidelity? Was it not plain that Christ might come back this
very moment—before the sermon came to an end?

This and the many other appeals to fear and happiness, punishment and reward, were considered by the evangelist to be part of
his divine duty as God's mouthpiece. God "could have sent an angel
here to preach," Sunday said. "That is not God's way. God said,
'Bill, I want you to do it.' " Sunday repeatedly assured his audiences
that if Jesus Christ were to come to the city in which he was speaking, "He would come right down here [to the tabernacle] and say,
'Go to it, Bill.' "

There was little change in the conception of the revivalist's duty
between the views expressed by Finney in 1834 and those expressed
by Sunday in 1916: "It is my duty as a preacher to cry out—Repent—
Repent—to back you up against the wall and hold you there until
you repent." But, though their aims were similar, their methods were

quite different, particularly in regard to the process and significance of conversion.

Finney's revivals in western New York had a reputation for enthusiasm and excitement on the part of the audience which some critics considered excessive and inimical to true religion. Finney spoke of sinners on his "anxious bench" who, "falling under the power of God," were so stricken that they "fell and writhed in agony" on the ground. Finney himself was converted only after long and agonizing nights on his knees, alone in the forest; this was typical of the intense psychological experience expected of conversion in those days. Though his revivals never reached that pitch of orgiastic excitement which Mrs. Trollope described in her report of a frontier camp meeting, Finney's meetings were far from placid.

Sunday's revivals, however, were thoroughly orderly and respectable affairs. In this he profited from Moody's modifications of revivalism. Moody abhorred the hysteria associated with camp-meeting revivals and took great pains to discourage excessive emotionalism in his campaigns. Even "amens" from the audience were unwelcome if they came too frequently or too loudly: "Never mind, my friend, I can do all the hollering," Moody would say to such exuberant auditors.[10] Such excitement as there was took place in the inquiry rooms, where Moody often demanded that all those who wished "to find God" must "get down on their knees until the thing was settled."

Billy Sunday, by omitting inquiry rooms in his revivals, necessitated a higher degree of emotionalism in his sermons. The famous lithographs of Sunday's revivals drawn by George Bellows in 1915 gave the impression that the excitement aroused by Sunday's preaching produced the same sort of hysteria that had taken place at camp meetings. But Bellows' drawings, like the sensational newspaper headlines about Sunday's sermons, were misleading. In reality, Sunday's revivals were models of controlled mass response in which there was no place for idiosyncratic individual reactions. Anyone who did not conform to the limited pattern of unified response, such as laughter or applause or the waving of a handkerchief in "a Chautauqua salute to the Lord," was summarily whipped back into line. This was done sometimes by forcibly ejecting vociferous persons from the tabernacle and at other times by singling the miscreant out for sarcastic ridicule. For example, at one meeting in Philadelphia Sunday stopped short in his sermon and pointed his finger at a woman who had shouted "Amen": "Just a minute, sister," he yelled; "Hold your sparker back and save a little gasoline."

Because of the densely packed crowds, the sawdust-filled air, the excitement, and the overheating of the tabernacles, there were, of course, many cases of individuals who fainted during Sunday's sermons. And some squeamish and guilt-ridden persons undoubtedly fainted from shock at the lurid descriptions of sin and disease which Sunday delighted in. But instances of spasms, shakes, or fainting fits caused by hysteria were few and far between. Dr. Dewitt G. Wilcox, of Brookline, Massachusetts, who directed the tabernacle hospital during Sunday's Boston campaign, declared: "When the campaign started I determined to make a psychological study of the patients at the tabernacle hospital, and I found that of several hundred cases there was but one of hysteria. The only case appeared on the [last] Sunday when a Negress was treated. The other cases were due to over-exertion in reaching the tabernacle and other disorders, none of them serious."[11]

Sunday specifically criticized the violent conversion process of Finney's day:

> Some people think that they can't be converted unless they go down on their knees in the straw at a camp meeting, unless they pray all hours of the night and all nights of the week while some old brother storms heaven in prayer. Some think a man must lose sleep, must come down the aisle with a haggard look, and he must froth at the mouth and dance and shout. . . . What I want and preach is the fact that a man can be converted without any fuss.[12]

To Sunday the plan of salvation was so simple and reasonable that the violent inner conflict with its outward manifestations of hysteria was unnecessary. With ill-concealed annoyance, Sunday once told reporters: "I have no emotionalism [in my revivals]. It's an insult to religion to call it emotional. If nothing in religion appeals to a man's intelligence and judgments he is in a sad way." As Mrs. Sunday explained, regarding her husband's decision to dispense with inquiry rooms: "He made it [the question of salvation] so simple that there was no need for inquiry rooms." Enthusiastic religion had become undignified—a sign of ignorance, lack of manners, and excessive provincialism.

Just as strikingly different from Finney's revivalism as this new attitude toward the process of conversion was the new attitude toward the significance of conversion. To Finney, and somewhat less to Moody, the difference between the saved and the unsaved was as

great as that between good and evil, and it was this great transformation in their lives, this traumatic experience of rebirth, which made
the process of conversion so excessively violent. Sunday was prepared to admit that in some cases this was true: "Salvation to some
men," he said, "is just as big a change as crawling out of a snowbank
and going into a warm room." But in most cases it was different: "To
other men," he continued, "to become a Christian does not mean
much of a change. Multitudes of men live good, honest, upright,
moral lives. They will not have much to change to become a Christian."[13] The tortuous path of Bunyan's Pilgrim was made straight,
short, and soft on Sunday's sawdust trail.

As Sunday stated in the booklet given to each trail-hitter, "You
have by this act of coming forward publicly acknowledge your faith
in Jesus Christ as your personal Savior," and, since this was the sole
requirement of salvation or rebirth, "you may know on the authority
of God's word that you are NOW a child of God (John 1:12) and
that you have NOW eternal life (John 3:36)." The doctrine of "growing in grace," which held that conversion was only the Christian's
first step in working out his salvation, was largely ignored by Sunday
in his effort to concentrate all attention upon hitting the trail. Sunday did say in his booklet to trail-hitters that "it is impossible for
you to become a useful Christian unless you are willing to do the
things which are absolutely essential to your spiritual strength," and
he did suggest that they read the Bible, pray, win souls, shun evil
companions, join a church, and "give to the support of the Lord's
work"; but for all practical purposes the trail-hitter was led to believe
that once he had shaken Sunday's hand he had done all that was
needed to claim his mansion in heaven. The transaction with God
was complete; the contract was fulfilled.

The significance of conversion, reduced to Sunday's simple terms,
had a second aspect beyond this completion of a bargain between
God and man: it signified the trail-hitter's acknowledgment that the
good life was the way of life described in Sunday's sermons and that
the sinfulness which the act of trail-hitting purged was social as well
as spiritual. In fact, it often seemed that Sunday was far more interested in persuading people to conform to the prevailing code of
morality than he was in prescribing any absolute code of Christian
ethics; to him Christian living was synonymous with his own way of
living, and Christian thinking was his way of thinking. "If I positively knew that death was nothing but an eternal sleep, I'd live my life
as I am living it, for the peace and joy and decency that comes to me

now. So it sums up that all God wants is for a man to be decent. Gee whizz!"[14] Or, looked at from the other side of the coin, hitting the trail signified that "all decent people recognize God, and all who won't aren't decent."

Conversion was "simply a question of whether you are interested in decency." Many of Sunday's sermons omitted theological questions altogether in this effort to make conversion simple and reasonable in social terms. "What are you willing to stand for?" he asked the crowd. "Here are the rules. Have a conviction. Take a stand and get into the game." Salvation, like life or a baseball game, was a matter of fair play and good sportsmanship. "All he asked of those who came forward," said H. L. Mencken, describing the trail-hitting in Baltimore, "was that they shake him by the hand and say that they were in favor of the sort of right living described in his sermon: i.e., living purged of murder, embezzlement, delirium tremens, and lues."[15]

From this viewpoint the resolution of the conflict between Sunday's pessimistic theology and his optimistic social outlook depended upon what proportion of the population was "decent." If enough people were, it was simply a matter of time before they all hit the trail (or acknowledged their faith in Christ and decency by some similar public confession) and the world became perfect. If enough people were not decent, it would prove that the world was growing worse and worse.

Up until the end of World War I, Sunday openly leaned toward the more optimistic view and did not even seem to doubt that most Americans accepted the Bible as an authoritative arbiter of human conduct on most issues: "I've never found a dozen men in my life who disbelieved in the Bible but what they were harboring some secret sin." And, far from believing that most men harbored secret sins, he stated: "Most people believe in God. Most of them are honest; most people are truthful; most of them are on the square. The dishonest, the liars, the crooked guys are in the minority. Most people are good." It was no contradiction of his theological doctrine of the inherent sinfulness of man that led Sunday to say: "I am not a pessimist; no, I am an optimist of optimists. . . . I believe a brighter day never dawned upon the church of Jesus. . . . There are more people ready and willing to hear the gospel than ever before."[16]

In spite of man's inherent sinfulness, all men had "that divine spark" said Sunday, that tells them "there is a beyond" and that "gives them an uneasy conscience" when they do not live so as to win God's (and society's) approbation. This being so, it only re-mained for the evangelist to awaken that conscience so that the sin-ner would publicly accept God's way of life: "My aim is to make it easier for you to do right and more difficult for you to do wrong," he often said. "I will try to disgust you with your sin until you turn away from it. That's my business."

It never occurred to Sunday that the criterion by which he judged sin, the social criterion, was a relative one and hence open to ques-tion. Unconsciously he assumed that the American way of life in which he had grown up and which was exalted in all the sermons and patriotic orations he had heard was the way of life approved by God for all men. Though he had the Bible to support him in regard to such basic aspects of right and wrong as lying, stealing, adultery, and murder, on most contemporary issues, such as trade-unionism, municipal ownership, national Prohibition, immigration restriction, and federal regulation of industry, the Bible was silent. But he blithely assumed that his own views, or those of his wealthy and better-informed supporters, were the only correct and divinely ap-proved ones.

Sunday saw the United States as a nation divinely guided by God, who "kept this country hid from the greedy eyes of monarchs 3,000 miles away" until (presumably after the Reformation) it could be settled by "God-fearing" people who would bring it to a state of perfection and power from which it could save the world. He listed the discovery of America and the establishment of free government as two of the four greatest events in history, ranking with the birth of Christ and the Reformation. Americans were "a peculiar people"; they were God's chosen people: "We are citizens of the greatest government on earth and we will admit it," he said.

In his effort to make it perfectly plain that any deviation from the moral code of the nineteenth-century middle-class rural American evangelical churchgoer was sinful, Sunday quoted this passage from Hawthorne's short story "Wakefield" (which in this context was far from what the unorthodox Hawthorne had in mind): "In the seem-ing confusion of the universe, individuals are so nicely adjusted to a system, and that system to another system, that if they step aside for only a moment they are in danger of losing their place forever and becoming an outcast in the universe." Sunday applied this to his belief in the saving influence of society upon all men: "That is what is the matter with the thief, the infidel, the drunkard, the pros-titute—they stepped aside and they have become outcasts, they don't fill their place. They just think they are living alone. They are not."[17] Such persons were to be ostracized from decent society and would, of course, never "get right with God." If they tried to blame heredity or environment, Sunday said: "All right, but weren't there good things in the world? Why didn't you yield to them? . . . God says, 'Sure there's evil, but didn't I provide salvation? Didn't I provide good company?'"

Sunday dismissed the evolutionary concept of the importance of environment upon human development with a simple, dogmatic denial: "I don't believe in the bastard theory that men came from protoplasm by the fortuitous concurrence of atoms." And he denounced the "higher critics" as "highbrows" who "dreamed out" their theories about the historicity of Jesus and the existence of two Isaiahs "over a pipe of tobacco and a mug of beer at Leipzig or Heidelberg." "When the word of God says one thing and scholarship says another, scholarship can go to hell!" With evolutionists and Modernists thus conveniently ostracized from consideration by decent society, Sunday was free to apply the Mosaic laws to contemporary manners. Where he could not quote chapter and verse, he applied his own small-town morality.

The moral standard which, according to Sunday, Christian living prescribed for women forbade the wearing of low-cut dresses and short skirts, the fashionable display of jewelry, "fooling away your time hugging and kissing a poodle dog," playing progressive euchre or bridge-whist, delivering papers at literary clubs, reading novels, and the cardinal sins of smoking, drinking, and dancing. "Let me tell you sister, when I see you smoking a cigarette I don't want to know anything more about you; I've got your number." And "the girl who drinks will abandon her virtue." To the evil effects of dancing Sunday devoted much of his sermon on "Amusements." "Dancing seems to be a hugging match set to music . . . three-fourths of all the fallen women fell as a result of the dance. . . . The swinging of corners in the square dance brings the position of the bodies in such attitude that it isn't tolerated in decent society."

In his sermon to women only Sunday instructed mothers to "talk plain" to their daughters and quoted Theodore Roosevelt's statement that the woman "so selfish as to dislike having children is in effect a criminal." Without hesitation he declared, "The birth control faddists are the devil's mouthpiece." He gave statistics showing that one-third of all pregnancies end in abortions, and he usually claimed that the doctors in the city where he was speaking had come to him to request that he speak out against it. He was particularly hard upon the rich society women in the big cities who asked doctors "to relieve them from the cares and the burdens of child-bearing" and then "just spend their time touring in their automobiles and out at the golf links and drinking wine and playing cards and cruising in yachts with their miserable hands red with blood."

The moral standard for men prohibited smoking, swearing, drinking, gambling, theatergoing, fornication, and telling smutty stories. Sunday had to yield somewhat on the matter of smoking: "A man can use tobacco and be a Christian," he said, "but he will be a mighty dirty one. If you want to smoke, fill up an old briar but cut out the nasty, filthy cigarettes." Billiard-playing also caused him some difficulty when the YMCA's began to instal tables: "I love the YMCA, but I've never yet become reconciled to its adoption of billiard rooms." In his sermon "Chickens Come Home To Roost," given to men only, he warned that "no man can be a good husband, no man can be a good father, no man can be a respectable citizen, no man can be a gentleman and swear." But he devoted the main emphasis in his men-only sermons to attacks upon fornication. Eighty per cent of the men in the nation have, or have had, a venereal disease, he claimed: "It is not alone a moral question, but a question of preservation of the nation." His descriptions of the consequences of sin were so vivid that men frequently fainted and had to be carried out of the tabernacle.

Children were indoctrinated with the social code at the Saturday-afternoon children's meetings, which began with a story illustrating the Ten Commandments. The commandments were symbolized by a row of ten vases, and, as Sunday described the bad little boy who played hooky from Sunday school, he asked the children to call out the number of the commandment which the boy broke in each of a series of incidents. Then, taking a hammer, Sunday would smash one of the vases for each broken commandment. Boys were warned not to flip pennies or read dime novels, and they should not play marbles "for keeps." Little girls were told to play dolls instead of jackstones. "We don't like to see girls playing leap frog," Sunday said; "it don't look right."

Adolescent boys in preparatory and high schools were warned about gambling, drinking, swearing, and smutty stories and were told of the terrible consequences of masturbation. Young men of the courting age were warned against "spooning": "A man would not come to see a girl of mine in the parlor unless I had a hole cut in the ceiling with a gatling gun trained through it." The young ladies of 1917 were warned that "the movies are too suggestive," that they must not "kiss or hold hands," and that only at "the cheapskate dance halls" would you "find young girls with their dresses [up] to their shoetops!" They should never use lipstick or rouge, but "of course, a woman must have her chamois skin with a little powder to keep her nose from getting red."

In addition to the most flagrant and tangible evils, Sunday made frequent references to certain characteristics of temperament and personality which were considered desirable or undesirable in decent society. Pride, gossip, envy, stinginess, a bad temper, grumbling, faultfinding, and general selfishness were frowned upon by society and God alike. They were sinful. Envy or covetousness, in particular, was against God's commandment. "You can measure your desire for salvation by means of the amount of self-denial you are willing to practice for Jesus Christ." You must not, for example, envy your neighbor who wears a "sealskin coat" or drives "a Packard limousine." "As you go by the beautiful homes in the cities and towns, if you only knew the skeletons that hang in the closets; if you only knew the misery that looks out through the French plate glass and hides behind the tapestries; if you only knew all this you would be more content." After all, he said, "The most wealthy man is poor if he hasn't Christ. What do automobiles, servants, silks and candelabra amount to? Nothing!" On the other hand, "there is dignity and nobility in poverty." The rich are more often to be pitied than envied: "To find starvation of the most awful kind today, don't go into the slum, but go to the people who are enormously wealthy. Andrew Carnegie says there are no happy millionaires, and Andy ought to know, for he's got the dough."

This consolation for poverty was not hypocritically motivated to keep the poor in their places, for Sunday was firmly convinced that America was the land of opportunity for all. It was the poor boy, not the rich boy, who was to be envied. The poor boy who was not weighted down with the burden of luxury and slothful ease, the poor boy who had push, tact, and principle, forged to the front, while the rich boy dissipated his wealth, his talent, and his health. "Anyone who says this is a rich man's country lies. It's a hellish lie. Everybody has a show."[18] Sunday's optimism on this score seemed to get the better of him when he claimed, "Everybody can win out if you make up your mind to do it."

Sunday's sermons on "The Forces That Win," "Hot Cakes off the

Griddle," and "How To Be a Man" were eloquent recitals of the American success myth and virtually equated failure with sinfulness. According to his wife, Sunday's favorite reading included the didactic books of Orison Swett Marden, whose anecdotes of the lives of great men of the past reinforced by historical fact the fictitious success stories of his contemporary, the Rev. Horatio Alger. A great deal of the material in Marden's books found its way into Sunday's sermons, usually unconsciously but often by literal borrowing. The carefully underlined moral in Marden's tales of poor boys who made good was "Character is your capital." Sunday, in transposing Marden's stories, modified this to "Christianity is your character and character is your capital." Conversion was, for Sunday, a prerequisite of success.

Conversion was also a guarantee of inevitable success. In the same years in which Sunday was launching his career, the Rev. Russell H. Conwell was telling millions of Americans that there were "Acres of Diamonds" in their back yards; Sunday told them: "Following Christ you may discover a gold mine of ability that you never dreamed of possessing." He himself had done so as a preacher, he said. "Do your best, and you'll never have to wear out shoe leather looking for a job." "God is going to give you a chance." If a man complained that he did his best but still did not succeed, Sunday merely answered, "You have a flaw in your character. They can't trust you. That is the reason you did not succeed." Probably men who failed to become a success were not truly converted: "I never saw a Christian that was a hobo. . . . They that trust in the Lord do not want for anything."[19] Of course, Sunday sometimes admitted, with a touch of unconscious irony, "You may not be able to be a search light or a whistle, but you can be a cog in the machine."

For the unemployed Sunday had no more sympathy than had Moody, who, during the terrible depression of the mid-1870's, told an audience made up of the unemployed of Boston: "Get something to do. If it is for fifteen hours a day all the better, for while you are at work Satan does not have so much chance to tempt you. . . . Work faithfully for three dollars a week, it won't be long before you have six dollars, and then you will get ten dollars, and then twelve dollars. You want to get these employers under an obligation to you. . . . If a man works in the interest of his employer, he will be sure to keep him and treat him well."[20] Sunday, during the depression of 1914–15, told his audiences in words taken from Marden's *Architects of Fate:* "The man that stands around with his hands in his pockets will soon be trying to get them into somebody else's. No trade. Keep them busy. 'No Trade' is the passport by which ninety per cent of the criminals enter the penitentiaries of this country. An idle brain is the devil's workshop."[21]

If it was pointed out that the unemployed were willing to work but could get no jobs, Sunday resorted to the same ludicrous proposition that Moody offered in 1877 when he told Boston's unemployed that they should return to the farm. But Sunday gave it a modern twist: "Go back to the farm and study expert dairying and help save the lives of 200,000 babies that die every year from impure milk that is sold. . . . Go out west and study and be a horticulturist." The belief in the myth of golden opportunity on the western frontier remained strong in Sunday and in his hearers; it perpetuated the belief of middle-class Americans that there was no necessity for reforming the economic system.

Although Sunday's doctrine seemed hard on the unemployed, it was applied with equal rigor to the dishonest employer, provided that his dishonesty was of a kind clearly measurable in terms of Sunday's simple standards of decency. "God will damn in the hottest hell any merchant that will make his clerks lie to sell a few dirty goods." Liquor dealers and bartenders would have to give up their positions. "Crooked business" would have to be "sacrificed" if a man was to take his stand for Christ and decency. "There is many a man grows rich by over-reaching his neighbor. He robs the widow and the orphan. He does it by legal means. . . . Tell me that there is no hell for a scoundrel like that?" This seemed to indicate a weakness in the legal machinery of society, but it was buttressed by punishment after death.

To a man who believed that "the true test of Christianity in a businessman is in his weights and measures" the solutions to monopoly, depressions, panics, and other complex evils of the industrial system were all reducible to questions of personal honesty. "You cannot reform people *en masse*," Sunday stated; "you cannot legislate people out of the slough of despond. . . . The thing to do is to purify the man himself." Sunday's views of religion and society naturally led him to side with those who believed that reform should begin with the individual, and led them, in turn, to support him.

Whenever Sunday wished biblical support for his arguments for rugged individualism, he brought out the doctrine of the Second Coming and, like Moody, declared that "the only thing that pleases Jesus is winning souls." With characteristic inconsistency, he tem-

136

porarily abandoned his faith in American destiny and declared: "There can be no millennium til Jesus comes. Many think the millennium will come gradually by everybody getting better, but the Bible doesn't teach any such thing. It says the world will grow worse." Therefore, "All human schemes of reconstruction must be subsidiary to the Second Coming."

This argument marked Sunday as a conservative not only in his attitude toward social reforms but also in his theology. It placed him squarely in opposition to those Modernists who combined a liberal view of the Bible with a more liberal attitude toward social reform. On the question of the Second Coming the Modernists maintained that the world would get better and better by means of man's efforts to change and improve his environment and that the millennium spoken of in the Bible referred not to a literal return and rule of Christ on earth for a thousand years but to a state of peace and plenty and good will toward all which would indicate a spiritual reign of Christ in the hearts of men; after this, Christ might, or might not, return in person. This view became known as "postmillennialism," and its advocates were clearly opposed to the conservative literalism of the premillennialists.

Even more infuriating to Sunday than the metaphorical interpretation of the Second Coming held by the postmillennialists was their doctrine of "the fatherhood of God and the brotherhood of man." It was this doctrine which lay at the root of the Social Gospel movement at the turn of the century, and it was this movement, with its interest in a certain amount of economic and political reform, which Sunday so virulently opposed in all his preaching: "I do not believe in this twentieth century theory of the universal fatherhood of God and the brotherhood of man. . . . You are not a child of God unless you are a Christian; then you are a child of God—if you are a Christian."[22] To assume that all men were brothers and hence all equally entitled to the help and love of decent society was abominable to Sunday. He held that "a man will be a Christian if he is decent, and if he is not a Christian, he forfeits any claim to decency." And by "a Christian," of course, he meant a converted, saved, or born-again Christian, not merely a church member or a nominal believer in the divinity of Jesus.

In Sunday's mind the whole universal brotherhood and Social Gospel notion, with its doctrine of "social service," was nothing more or less than socialism. The fact that certain of the more liberal ministers like George Herron and Walter Rauschenbusch actually praised socialism and spoke of their work as "Christian Socialism" seemed to Sunday to prove his point, though he was just as vehement against men like Lyman Abbott and Washington Gladden who spoke merely of "Christianizing the social order" and whose social reform ideas were comparatively mild. Sunday called Gladden "that bald-headed old mutt" and damned the whole Social Gospel movement as sacrilegious, un-American quackery.

The view of postmillennialists like Gladden and Abbott that the church must play a role in relieving the distress of the poor by undertaking "social service" and creating "institutional churches" with gymnasiums, dormitories, and educational classes was, declared Sunday, putting the cart before the horse: "It is an entirely good and Christian thing to give a down-and-outer a bath, a bed, and a job," he said, but "the road into the kingdom of God is not by the bathtub, nor the gymnasium, nor the university, but by the blood red hand of the cross of Christ." With an anti-intellectualism which was inherent in all his preaching, Sunday said: "Thousands of college graduates are going as fast as they can straight to hell. If I had a million dollars I'd give $999,999 to the church and $1 to education."[23] The way to help the poor in the downtown slums was to convert them, not to educate them. "The trouble with the church, the YMCA, and the Young People's Societies is that they have taken up sociology and settlement work but are not winning souls to Christ."

Sunday's outlook toward social reform appealed to those middle-class churchgoers whose consciences could not shrug off the poverty and suffering of the workingman simply by attributing it to an abstract scientific principle which declared that the unsuccessful were unfit to survive; it appealed because the average churchgoer feared that economic progress might be hindered if there was too much interference with free enterprise either by trade-unions or by government regulation. The belief that conversion would transform a poor man from one of the unsuccessful and unfit into one of the successfully fit provided a convenient solution to the whole problem. The tender-hearted could exercise Christian charity by helping to win souls while at the same time leaving the economy free from undue interference. Most convenient of all, this approach seemed to make it evident that those poor people who refused to be converted were hardened sinners and therefore deserved whatever punishment or suffering came to them.

Sunday considered that his tabernacle revivals were the best method of "evangelizing the masses" and thus helping the "poor and the wicked" to become successful and respectable. He vigorously denounced ministers and laymen who sold their churches in the downtown areas as soon as the neighborhood "ran down" and moved out into the suburbs, where they erected magnificent new churches. He called these churches "amusement bureaus" and "gorgeous religious club houses for the privileged few." On this particular subject he seemed to be aligning himself with the liberals, for Gladden and Abbott as well as Herron and Rauschenbusch were equally distressed at the churches' desertion of the downtown areas, though for different reasons.

"The downtown church," said Sunday, had become "a passing proposition," and "there is a breach between the masses" and the church. "In board of trustee meetings" in churches throughout the nation ministers and laymen agreed to sell their downtown churches "for enormous prices for commercial purposes" or else "cut down expenses to tally with receipts." "Great God," exclaimed Sunday, "is this a cause and a time for retrenchment or advance? Does a wise general reduce his force in the presence of the enemy?"

With a scorn which some co-operating pastors in his revivals found difficult to bear, Sunday poked fun at suburban pastors, calling them "a hireling ministry" whose sermons were "showers of spiritual cocaine" and whose dignified formality, robed choirs, paid soloists, costly church organs, and upholstered pews were making a hollow sham out of religion. "There never was a time when religion was reduced to such forms and rituals," he said in 1917, as he ridiculed the "black night gowns" and "turned around collars" which many evangelicals were assuming in their respectable suburban edifices. "Lolling in her well fed contentment," said Sunday, "the church is a failure because she is compromising with the men that sit in the seats and own saloons whom she never rebukes; she is compromising with the men who rent their property for disorderly houses and whom she never rebukes." Like many a social reformer and Social Gospeler, Sunday accused the churches of "growing cross-eyed trying to serve God and Mammon."

Unlike the Social Gospelers, however, Sunday was not in favor of the institutional church or social service or any type of legislative reform (Prohibition excepted) that might alleviate the suffering in the slums. The *Watchman-Examiner* printed one of Sunday's sermons in 1915 under the title "Christless Social Service" and commented, "Billy Sunday believes in social service but sees the danger of magnifying it and ignoring Christ and His salvation. He says,

'We've had enough of this godless social service nonsense.'" His only concern seemed to be with soul-winning. "Go from house to house," he urged the suburban church members; "go to the people in your block, in your place of business. . . . Have you said anything to the telephone girl when you called her up? . . . Have you said anything to the delivery boy?"

But, despite this stand against changing the status quo, Sunday was too much a part of his times to be untouched by the wave of social reform in the first decades of the twentieth century which came to be called "the Progressive movement." Agreeing with Theodore Roosevelt, Sunday said that "some people are so busy muckraking that they will lose a crown of glory hereafter";[24] but, like Roosevelt, he could not ignore the fact that Americans were concerned about the malefactors of great wealth, nor did he believe himself that the unsavory facts uncovered by the muckrakers should be condoned. "We are the happiest people in God's world," he said. "I do not believe that there are any people beneath the sun who are better fed, better paid, better clothed, better housed, or any happier than we are beneath the stars and stripes—no nation on earth"; but, he added, "there are lots of things that could be eliminated to make us better." It was characteristic that he should phrase his complaint in negative rather than in positive terms. This was the essence of his "progressive orthodoxy." He was convinced that there was nothing wrong with the American system of free enterprise—that all that was needed was to rid it of certain evil practices by a few unscrupulous individuals and all would be right again. And, on the whole, the American people agreed with him.

The Bible foretold certain "signs of the times" by which the Second Coming might be prophesied, and, when he delivered his sermon on this subject, Sunday pointed to contemporary events which seemed to him to be "signs"—a device which greatly increased the urgency of that particular sermon. One of these signs which reflected the reform spirit of the era Sunday described as "political unrest of the people and concentration of wealth." As he explained this, he revealed a new aspect of middle-class uneasiness: he indicated the growing distrust of the extremely rich and at the same time a distrust of granting excessive power to the government to pass laws curbing the means of becoming rich. The following paragraph was part of the sensationalism by which he attracted headlines, but it was also indicative of the conservatism which kept him from antagonizing his wealthy backers: "Twelve men practically control the wealth of the United States today," he began. "Twelve men can put the United States out of business." And then, without a pause, "I marvel that some of our institutions get along with all the cranky laws we have. With laws of states and the government and the prices of commodities, I don't see how any railroad can turn a wheel. Never was there a time when we had more cranky, asinine laws on our statute books."[25]

This trick of making a sensational statement which, in its full context, amounted to nothing more than cleverly phrased conservatism was highly developed by Sunday. Its most perfect expression came in those sermons in which he outlined the civic duties of the truly converted Christian. Moody had been so intent upon soul-winning that he stated, "The Christian is dead to this world." Sunday, in his reforming mood, maintained that "in order to be not only good, but good for something, a man must get into the world. I want to strike the death blow at the idea that being a Christian takes a man out of the busy whirl of the world's life and activity and makes him a spineless, effeminate proposition."[26] This was reminiscent of Finney's statement about the saved that "their spirit is necessarily that of the reformer. To the universal reformation of the world they stand committed."[27]

In contrast to Moody's withdrawn, otherworldly saints, Sunday proposed "a new type of Christian" who should be "a fighting saint." The "social and political and economic conditions" of the times "demanded" this new type of saint, he said, a saint who would "go on the warpath for purity, sobriety, and righteousness" and who would "draw the sword and carry the war into Africa." In his sermon entitled "The Fighting Saint" Sunday caught the mood of the times and demanded a "progressive Christianity" in which the saved would be as ready as the muckraker to "take up the cudgels for reforms in civic and social life." Sunday pictured the fighting saint as "a fiery spirit," a "fire-eater," for a "man without temper is a man without force." He should be a red-blooded he-man who would resist all compromise with evil: "Moral warfare makes a man hard. Superficial peace makes a man mushy. . . . The prophets all carried the Big Stick." Sunday obviously projected his idealization of Theodore Roosevelt into this symbol and threw in a few aspects of William Jennings Bryan for good measure. It was a combination ideally suited to please his audience, and a role which Sunday portrayed from the platform with great gusto.

To make the social and civic sins against which the saint was to crusade of sufficiently horrible proportions, Sunday approached them in a sensational fashion. The saint was to undertake a kind of police activity which, unlike the reforms Finney advocated for his saints, was violently repressive, not constructive. For this Sunday found precedent in the Bible: "I believe the law of Moses was the best law that was ever given: 'An eye for an eye, a tooth for a tooth; whoso sheddeth a man's blood by man shall his blood be shed.'" He favored capital punishment because, he said, the Bible was in favor of it. "I have no interest in a God who does not smite," he said. No measure could be too strong to wipe out sin.

With unconscious hyperbole, Sunday shocked his audiences out of their complacency by advocating capital punishment for writing novels or swearing: "I wish I could sentence to death fifty popular writers who have been turning the people away from Jesus Christ," he declared, making evident the enormity of "the pernicious influence of fiction." "If I was mayor of this city and had authority to put men on the corners with double-barrelled shotguns to shoot everyone who cussed, you'd see how much cussing there would be." He admitted that he had not yet come to the point of turning the other cheek, for that would show weakness of temper unbefitting a fighting saint: "I haven't got down to the one cheek basis yet. When a fellow swats me on one cheek I don't turn the other. Instead I sail into him like a first class battleship."[28] Spineless effeminacy must give way to red-blooded aggressiveness: "I'd like to put my fist on the nose of the man who hasn't got grit enough to be a Christian."

When this mood of reforming zeal was upon him, Sunday became impatient with his doctrine of reforming the individual. He wanted "a law preventing any boy or girl over twelve years of age from attending dancing schools" and another law "providing that nobody should be allowed to dance until after they were married" and then only with their spouses. There should be a curfew that "drives boys and girls off the street" in every city and hamlet, and a statute on the books of every state in the union compelling candidates for marriage "to submit to an examination" not only of their minds and bodies but of their "morals." Although he swore that he and other fighting saints "will swim our horses in blood up to their bridles before there shall be a union of church and state," he gave vigorous support to those who wanted laws which would "put the Bible on every school teacher's desk and the flag in every classroom."

In urging the saints to undertake these reforms, Sunday disclosed not only the rural origin of his moral code but also the country farmer's distrust of the big city. "The civilization of the future will center more and more in the cities," he believed, and the cities were to him the root cause of all evil. "We have in our jails 98,000 criminals, and they come from the cities, 98 per cent of them." By "civic reform" he meant literally reforming the cities so that they should be like a country town. With the romantic eye of the agrarian, he visualized the rolling sweep of the peaceful countryside, the gentle wooded slopes, and the fruitful plains and valleys and then described with horror the fetid outgrowths upon the beautiful face of nature: "Our cities are carbuncles on the neck of the body politic."[29] "They are like huge magnets drawing all elements and conditions into their great crucibles to melt them up into new and terrible forms." The unspoiled children of nature, the simple, God-fearing farmers' sons and daughters, were caught in the ruthless machine and transformed into drunkards, prostitutes, and criminals.

The cities not only destroyed those whom they attracted, but they reached out to pollute the country around them. "What is enthroned in the cities will give tone to the country that surrounds them. Therefore" (and here the true meaning of civic and social reform was revealed), "a city with the lid off, a city wide open, is a curse, and officials who permit such things are a disgrace to humanity and to the parties that have placed them in office." When Sunday said that "politics—the science of good government—has a proper place in the pulpit," he reflected the views of the Mugwumps and liberal Republicans of the 1880's and 1890's that good men made good government. "The old principles of Christian integrity and honesty," Sunday maintained, were sufficient to prevail against "graft in high places."

The sins of city life were presented in a manner that was sometimes highly sentimental and sometimes salacious. The horrors of gambling dens, fan-tan joints, billiard halls, saloons, and brothels were so vividly portrayed that mothers wept and fathers rose up in anger. Like most professional evangelists, Sunday devoted a great deal of time to portraying the wrecked lives of men and women innocently lured into these haunts of vice in "the wide open" city.

The "white-slave" trade was a source of much sensational preaching. "The king of white slavers, recently arrested in New York," said Sunday in 1917, "confessed that he had trapped 3000 innocent girls and sold them to bawdy house keepers at from $100 to $500 each and received 10% of their earnings afterward"; "Every year 60,000 girls are robbed of their virtue, 5,000 a month, 168 every day"; "No man who deliberately drugs a girl and sends her into a life of shame ought to be permitted in good society. He ought to be shot at sunrise." With eyes blazing, Sunday shouted: "The virtue of womanhood is the rampart of our civilization and we must not let it be betrayed." It was a call to arms which made fighting saints out of normally phlegmatic citizens.

"The social evil," an object of nation-wide and even international interest in the opening years of the twentieth century, was a favorite stand-by of evangelists. Sam Jones and "Gypsy" Smith and even such an unsensational revivalist as Chapman went on slumming trips into the red-light districts during their campaigns. Torchlight parades from tabernacles to the slums and back were spectacular features of most revivals in these years.

For some reason Sunday never led such parades. Brand Whitlock testified that in 1911, while he was mayor of Toledo, Sunday came to that city and showed a much more tolerant attitude toward prostitution than the zealous local committee which had invited him to attack the evil. "Have sympathy with the girl who sins, but not with the sin that ruined her," Sunday remarked. At one time Sunday stated that a segregated vice district was preferable to outlawing the profession; but this attitude did not suit most church members, and he soon dropped it for the less tolerant one: "Look at the girl in the red-light district. Don't she give up her virtue, her purity, her home and parents and everything that is dear to her for a few dollars?"

Sunday attacked not only the lowly but the pillars of society in his demand for conformity. The amoral captains of industry, "whose private lives are good, but whose public lives are very bad," were excoriated with the insight of a muckraker, though here, too, the desire for sensationalism was tempered by a conservative respect for wealth. In his sermon on "Positive and Negative Religion" he chastised the churchgoing, but unsaved, wealthy men "who while they would not shoot a man with a pistol, will sit in New York City and by a vote on the board of directors meeting set in motion forces which ultimately may take a man's life out on the Pacific slope."[30] To persons who were not aware that John D. Rockefeller, Jr., was a supporter of Sunday, this might have seemed a direct attack upon the former's part in the Colorado mine strike of 1914, but Sunday seldom mentioned names, and when he did so, he referred to men like Charles T. Yerkes or the long-dead Cornelius Vanderbilt and

A. T. Stewart, who had been either forgotten or thoroughly condemned by public opinion already.

Sunday played up the public distaste for monopoly in generalized terms by condemning "men who would not pick the pockets of one man with the fingers of their hand" but who "will without hesitation pick the pockets of eighty million people with fingers of their monopoly or commercial advantage." He seemed to be attacking John Wanamaker for the low wages he paid his salesgirls when he denounced "men in whose hands the virtue of your wife or daughter would be as safe as in your own, but who will drive hundreds of cases of virtue over the line into vice by the pressure of starvation wages which they pay." But in the next paragraph he reversed himself completely by arguing that "you can't raise the standards of women's morals by raising their pay envelopes."

Sunday even took up some wordy cudgels against child labor: "Men who will gladly draw their check for $10,000 and give it to a child's hospital see nothing ridiculous in the fact that the $10,000 for the child's hospital came out of $200,000 made from a system of child labor which crushes more children in one year than the hospital will heal in ten." But, instead of demanding laws against child labor and instead of demanding that shotguns be used against these malefactors of wealth, he prayed for their conversion to his form of "progressive Christianity." He begged them to abandon their negative religion for a more positive religion. This, he maintained, would make them more charitable toward their employees and the public.

In his sermon "Jekyll and Hyde" Sunday made his only clear-cut indictment of society at large:

I believe if society permits any considerable proportion of people to live in foul, unlighted rooms where from eight to ten people live, cook, eat, and sleep, working year in and year out from fourteen to fifteen hours every day; I believe if society allows deserving men to stagger along with less than a living wage; if society permits the shoulders of widowed motherhood to be forced down under industrial burdens and throws the unripe strength of children into the hopper of corporate greed to be ground up into dividends, that *society must share the responsibility* if these people become criminals, thieves, thugs, cut-throats, drunkards, and prostitutes.[31]

But no sooner were these words out of his mouth than he returned to the evangelical doctrine of free will or individual responsibility and rejected in one breath both the predestination of Calvinism and the determinism of Social Darwinism in order to deny that the inequalities of industrial society were an immutable part of God's will. "A man is not a mechanical plaything in the hands of an arbitrary God. You have it in your power to say 'yes' to right and 'no' to wrong. Environment is only part of the story of life. . . . If you are right in your heart you will be right whether you live in the North End, Beacon Street, Commonwealth Avenue, or the Fenway."

Sunday was face to face here with the underlying dilemma of his age. He was trying to square the belief in free will and in a national destiny based explicitly on divine favor with the amoral determinism implicit in the scientific laws of evolution and psychology. Many Americans felt that evolutionary progress could be guided and directed by man's growing knowledge of science; Sunday, doubting the efficacy of science to reform either man or society, nevertheless continued to assert the Arminian optimism of man's ability to change his own heart, in the belief that converted men would receive God's help in reforming the world.

Sunday told those reformers who thought that, if slums could be cleared up, perhaps crime, disease, and drunkenness would decrease: "A man is not supposed to be the victim of his environment. . . . I don't like to see you trying to put it all on environment and take away responsibility from the individual who's got a rotten heart." At times it seemed as though a fighting saint would spend most of his energy combating those reformers more radical than he.

In order to explain the evil alterations taking place in the American system, Sunday searched for some particular sin or sinner who could be blamed and against whom he could lead his crusade for decency. With little difficulty he found what he wanted in the saloonkeeper and the immigrant, two scapegoats who could be attacked with virtual impunity and, in fact, with general approval. Both of these culprits were associated with the vicious cities; both were closely associated with poverty and crime; both were hostile to, or at least passive to, orthodox evangelical Christianity. Here were two elements of society which did not conform to the narrowing criteria of the American way. They were clearly the unrespectable and indecent causes of the malfunctioning of the God-given American system; they were the devil's spawn and hence fit objects for the assaults of civic-minded fighting saints.

Since it seemed impossible to convert them, the only solution Sunday had to offer was to exterminate them: to outlaw the manufacture and sale of alcoholic beverages and to lock up or ship back home the "unassimilable" foreigners. The liquor traffic was a more traditional enemy than the immigrant, and the organizational force of the Anti-Saloon League which came into full flower in the first two decades of the twentieth century helped Sunday to focus attention on this crusade. Much of his fame and success was due to the fact that he so thoroughly identified himself in the public eye as the national champion of the Prohibition movement.

It was not until Prohibition became an established fact in 1919 that Sunday turned his full attention to the immigrant, but there were indications of the line he was to take in the postwar period during these halcyon days. Sunday's dislike for the immigrant began during his years as a YMCA secretary in downtown Chicago. The immigrants he met there seemed totally unlike the sober, thrifty, pious, hard-working Scandinavian, German, and Canadian farmers whom he had known in his childhood in Iowa. Chicago's immigrants always seemed to be dirty, poor, ignorant, and frequently unemployed and often had liquor on their breaths. In addition, their inability to speak good English, their adherence to Catholic or Jewish faiths, their "European views of the Sabbath," their suspicion of and antagonism toward evangelization into the Protestant faith, made Sunday quickly adopt the growing prejudice among middle-class Americans for "foreigners," particularly non–Anglo-Saxon (or non-"Nordic" or non-"Aryan") foreigners.

As an evangelist in the Midwest, Sunday early aroused the opposition of German Catholics in his Prohibition campaigns. While these were undoubtedly Nordics, Sunday soon decided that they were not Americans: "Look at the brewers," he exclaimed. "What are the names? No Americans, thank God!" Such people "turn our idea of the Sabbath into the continental idea with their beer gardens and beer drinking." A little research in eastern religious journals and a few conversations with eastern ministers and wealthy laymen like John Wanamaker convinced Sunday that immigration not only was "another influence against Christ" but was a principal cause of poverty and crime. "All over America there are patches of Europe until America has become the backyard in which Europe is dumping its paupers and criminals." Statistics proved, said Sunday, that "sixty-nine per cent of our criminals are either foreign born or of foreign parents."

Sunday was fearful because it looked as if the Americanized Anglo-Saxons were being outnumbered by the new non-Nordic immigrants. "There are multitudes of them," he cried in alarm, "a half million to a million every year—just multitudes of them—coming with just enough money and materials to escape being paupers and criminals." Like the cities in which they live, "they settle here and become a carbuncle on the neck of the body politic."[32] "You walk the streets of New York or Philadelphia or Chicago and not one out of every three faces will have in them the strains of pure Americanism."

Sunday recognized that "we all originally came from across the sea"; his mother, he pointed out, came "from Scotch and Welsh stock," and his father was not from Germany but "of Saxe-Coburg." Such thrifty, hard-working, sober people as these he would be the first to welcome. He was happy to see "any man or woman who wants to come here and assimilate our ways and conditions and live beneath the stars and stripes," but they were not to complain or criticize or try to change the American system. "If they don't like it here, let 'em go back to the land where they were kenneled." Just as the names of the brewers were not American, neither were the names of Socialists, anarchists, and Communists who brought over foreign ideas of government and stirred up the American working-man. "I am glad that the authorities are pinching these old, howling anarchists," Sunday said during World War I. "If they don't like the way we do things let them get out of here and leave. We don't propose to adjust this country to suit a lot of anarchists."

Sunday was convinced that it was because the immigrant refused to conform, to be converted, that he was unemployed. "Take the rube, the boy from the farm, and he's the fellow that makes good." The new European immigrant lacked the unique virtues of push, tact, and sand which brought the hard-working boys from the countryside to the top.

It was not until the Presidential campaign of 1928 that Sunday's sermons revealed any anti-Catholic bias, but there were latent strains of it in such statements as one which he made in Boston in 1916: "I serve notice on this gang of polyglot foreigners if they imagine they can come and spit on our statute books and cherished traditions . . . we will fight for the open Bible, for the free church, and for the free press." There were practical reasons for his failure to play upon the anti-Catholicism of most evangelical church members. In many cities a large measure of political power was held in Catholic hands, and he needed the full co-operation of the city councils and police forces in order to run his city-wide campaigns. Furthermore, openly avowed prejudice was not conducive to the unity of support which he demanded; many of his wealthy backers might well have hesitated to antagonize Catholic business associates and friends.

Often Sunday seemed to court Catholic favor, and Boston was the only city in which a Roman Catholic metropolitan (in this case, Cardinal O'Connell) declared it a sin for Catholics to visit the tabernacle. Sunday claimed that in Baltimore Cardinal Gibbons expressed privately his belief that the revival helped Catholics as well as Protestants.[33] It always drew applause when Sunday said, "I am a Roman Catholic on divorce," and he won a good number of trail-hitters when he told audiences, "If you want to join the Catholic church, join it. I'll help you if I can." In Boston he urged Catholics to come forward and sign decision cards: "We'll see that the priests get them."

The Catholic churches never co-operated in the Sunday campaigns or publicly offered any support, but in Detroit, where Sunday went so far as to say that "if Nell [Mrs. Sunday] had been a Catholic, I would have joined the Catholic Church," the Knights of Columbus permitted him to use their clubhouse for a meeting. In commenting to the press on the fact that Sunday was the first non-Catholic ever permitted to use the building, President Doyle said on behalf of the Knights: "We think he is the greatest evangelist of his kind of all time." Cardinal Gibbons expressed the general attitude of Catholics in a public statement during the Baltimore campaign in 1916: "Mr. Sunday is always kind to the Catholic Church in his references, and we mean no discourtesy to him by keeping away from him and his meetings and his influence." Once, in Boston, during his "Booze Sermon," Sunday stated in regard to Prohibition, "If the priest is against it, I am against the priest"; but more characteristic of his attitude was the statement, "If you're a Catholic, be a good one and you'll never hear a peep from me."[34]

The same may be said of Sunday's attitude toward the Jewish immigrant. Like most evangelicals, he had an ambivalent attitude toward the Jews. The Jews held a high place in the Bible, but, said Sunday, "They are going down. They are turning into a liberal wing; they are going into idolatry, materialism, and infidelity at a rate that staggers you." He held the usual stereotype of the commercial and financial acumen of the Jew: "Jew blood means the capacity for making money," he explained. "They are the greatest financiers on earth." But he was as unwilling to capitalize upon anti-Semitism as he was upon anti-Catholicism. The Jewish faith was infidelity because it did not recognize the divinity of Christ. Sunday took the word of the Bible for the fact that prior to the Second Coming "the Jewish nation" would be "converted in a day" to evangelical Christianity and that they would then become among the most zealous soul-winners in history.

Moody was not above calling the Jews "Christ-killers" and noting that "the blood of Jesus is upon the Jews today"; he even went out of his way to debate publicly with a Jew upon the divinity of Christ;[35] but Sunday steered clear of these controversial issues: "The Jews are a wonderful people," he said. "You'll never find a Jew father and mother in a poorhouse living off the country. . . . It makes my blood boil to hear a man speaking of the Jew as a 'Sheeny' or a 'Christ-killer.' " In his sermon "Jacob's Confession" he pointed out that "it was Jew bankers who stopped the Russo-Japanese war by refusing longer to finance that war. . . . There were three Jews on George Washington's staff, and today when twenty-two million boys rise to salute the stars and stripes 500,000 of them are Jews. . . . You never see a Jew among the hoboes. . . . You seldom hear of a Jew committing a crime. Some of them [he mentioned Nathan Straus] are the best citizens we have and they are the most abused. I say, all hail to the Jew!"[36]

The fact that Jewish immigrants were "shrewd, capable business people" and that they were neither paupers nor criminals nor hoboes gave them a measure of social conformity, of decency and respectability, that raised them in Sunday's eyes above the level of the average immigrant. Throughout his career Sunday managed to keep active anti-Semitism out of his sermons, but the readiness with which he transmitted the stereotype of the Jew made it easier for others less tolerant than himself on this subject to play upon the image.

Toward all other religious groups Sunday was violently hostile. Oriental religions, in particular, were anathema to him, not because of the supposed economic consequences of Chinese or Japanese immigration such as underlay the prejudice of persons on the West Coast but from religious antipathy and from the failure of the Orientals to integrate rapidly into American society. "I think one of the biggest curses that ever came to America was the Congress of Religions held in Chicago during the World's Fair. There were Christian men sitting in with mutts like Hindus, followers of Zoroaster, Shintoists, Parsees, Confucius—they had their pagodas and joss houses and temples and their sun-worshippers in Chicago."

Sunday reserved his most bitter scorn for atheism, Unitarianism, Universalism, Christian Science, Russellism, Dowieism, Mormonism, spiritualism, and Blavatskyism. Though he spoke to a group of Unitarian ministers when he was in Boston, he refused to compromise in his attitude toward them, and in several cities the Unitarians brought Charles Eliot, president of Harvard, and former President William Howard Taft to speak in order to counter the attacks launched against them in the tabernacle. It was reported that Sunday's intolerance toward Unitarians in one revival in Colorado so inflamed the inhabitants against these "infidels" that they drove the Unitarians out of town.[37] Against the Mormons, Christian Scientists, Russellites, and Dowieites Sunday could not bring the charge of infidelity, since they all acknowledged the divinity of Christ, but he attacked them for idolatry in that they raised human beings to sainthood. "The biggest humbug on earth is Christian Science," he said in a typical diatribe; "the biggest humbug on the face of the earth. I am going to rip the thing from hell to breakfast some day. I just hate it!"

Like the attack on the immigrants, these attacks on minority religious groups were based principally upon the failure of such groups to conform to Sunday's fixed image of American behavior. The very vagueness of Sunday's criteria and his assumption that everyone knew what was "decent" contributed to the wide support he received. A fighting saint, aroused by Sunday's lurid sermons, was free to rush forth and express his hate or fear or rage upon almost any person or group which struck him personally as obnoxious. He could raise his big stick against the saloonkeeper, the brewer, the distiller, or the drunkard; he could cudgel the atheists, the anarchists, the Socialists, or the Communists; he could bully the prostitute, the white slaver, the dirty immigrant, the idolatrous Oriental, any number of minor religious groups, or the whole class of "shiftless" and unemployed poor. The hobo was fair game, and so was the striking worker. On a different level, the saint could assault the highbrow, the radical reformer, the "society" woman, the woman who "shirks motherhood," the political boss, and even the big businessman. In short, anyone socially below or above the group assembled in the tabernacle, anyone not a member of an evangelical church and not a saved, born-again Christian, anyone not clearly bearing the traces of "pure Americanism," was to be converted or outlawed.

The fact that in 1917 less than a third of all Americans were church members and that not one in ten of these, according to Sunday, had really been "saved" occasionally gave pause to Sunday's optimism. Despite his faith in America and the general goodness of the people in it, he could not ignore the fact that his revivals drew opposition even from some church members. The doubts which occasionally assailed him were voiced in a sermon entitled "The Inner Wall," which he first delivered in 1916:[38] In this sermon he said, paraphrasing Bunyan's image, that the city of man's soul had two walls around it to protect it from "the assaults of the enemies of the soul": the outer wall consisted of "legislation, education, the home, and patriotism," and the inner wall was salvation. Sunday explained that "if every man in America was a genuine Christian we could dispense with the outer wall of legislation, for it is because the principles of Christianity are not accepted that we need police, jails, penitentiaries, electric chair, and scaffolds."

As proof that very few Americans were truly converted, Sunday declared that "if every man and woman in America was a genuine Christian our periods of unemployment would not be productive of crime as they are now." This sermon hinted that the world might never be perfected, even by American institutions, and that, in order to protect their property and preserve the social order, the truly saved Christians might do well to constitute themselves a ruling minority who would repress by law and by force the evil intentions of the unregenerate majority and preach the gospel to them, while waiting for the ultimate and inevitable state of world revolution and turmoil which would herald the return of Christ. The symbol of the inner wall was, in this sense, the direct opposite to the symbol of the fighting saint who would reform the world and make it perfect; it foreshadowed the terrible disillusionment that was to darken Sunday's final years as an evangelist.

At the outset of the twentieth century Sunday's religious and social views were undoubtedly shared by the large mass of the American people, whether they were church members or not. But, as the century wore on, the climate of opinion changed. Sunday tried to keep abreast of the times, at least superficially, but the road that America was traveling was not his road, and he and his audience came to a parting of the way.

The diverging paths were not discernibly different, however, prior to 1917, when Sunday was at the height of his popularity. From 1908 to 1918 his opinions were warmly approved by the thousands who thronged to his tabernacles. It is obvious that in his dogmatic and colorful sermons Sunday played upon the confusion of an era of transition, and yet his views were rooted deep in the traditions of America, and many of them linger yet. Much of the popularity and success which he achieved was due to the manner in which he stated, or restated, these traditional views. By his rhetoric, his demagogy, and his mimicry—by the sheer force of his personality —Sunday persuaded many persons to come forward and shake his hand who were not really in sympathy with the ultimate implications of his views. Important as the theological and social content of his sermons was, equally important in his rise to fame was the development of his explosive and unforgettable power of expression.

5

"THE CALLIOPE OF ZION"

Sunday once said, "I'd stand on my head in a mud puddle if I thought it would help me win souls to Christ,"[1] and on this ground he excused his unorthodox pulpit technique, which outraged the conservative and endeared him to the multitude. What he lacked in originality of ideas he made up for with a fertility of expressive imagination and a talent for buffoonery which transcended the banality of his message. Conservative clergymen accused him of making a travesty of all that was sacred, but the younger and more aggressive ministers did their best to imitate the style and mannerisms which brought Sunday the widest audience of any preacher of his day.

It was, however, impossible to imitate Sunday. All imitations were bound to be superficial. His style was inseparable from his personality—or, as newspaper reporters often called it, "his charm." Some found this charm in his smile, some in his honest blue eyes, some in the open, friendly warmth of his handshake and the straightforward sincerity of his speech. Newspaper accounts almost always referred to him by the familiar nickname "Billy" rather than by the formal "the Rev. Dr. Sunday," to which he was entitled by virtue of an honorary D.D. conferred upon him in 1912 by Westminster College, a small United Presbyterian institution in New Wilmington, Pennsylvania. Even in a tabernacle crowded with twenty thousand people, Sunday managed to establish an intimacy with each individual which observers could only describe as "magnetic." He drew them out of themselves, out of the crowd, and made each one feel that he, personally, was the one spoken to and chided and exhorted. Even such a self-possessed and hostile critic as H. L. Mencken admitted after hearing Sunday that "many persons in that crowd, I dare say, came away with a certain respect for the whirling doctor's earnestness, and a keen sense of his personal charm—as I did myself."[2]

Speaking to a large and varying congregation at each performance, and lacking any of the technical advantages of electrical amplification, Sunday had necessarily to resort to tactics which were outside the realm of ordinary pulpit presentation. Rodeheaver's preliminary song period helped to achieve the first steps in "warming up" the crowd into a responsive unit, but Sunday had the more difficult task of making that unit follow him through the theological path of a sermon and respond to his conversion call as one mass. At the same time, he had to make each individual in that mass feel that the call was directed specifically to him. It was an innate talent for establishing rapport with his audience that made Sunday a great preacher. The essence of his "magnetic charm" was born in him, not acquired.

Nevertheless, the attention-catching manipulations of Sunday's voice and the gestures and gyrations of his body, which led his authorized biographer to refer to him as "a gymnast for Jesus" and H. L. Mencken to call him "the calliope of Zion,"[3] were necessary adjuncts to his talent. He had to learn to construct his sermons along the lines of a popular melodrama which would build slowly from climax to climax and move his auditors in rapid succession from guilt to fear to laughter to anger to tears to hate to grim determination. He had to learn to use the tricks of the actor and the demagogue.

The printed reports of Sunday's meetings portrayed his talents only imperfectly, but the phonograph, the motion pictures, and ultimately, in his last years, the talking pictures caught the excitement of the evangelist in action and preserved for posterity a record of the genius and skill and personality which combined to make Billy Sunday what he was. He was considerably more than the sum of his parts, yet it is possible only to describe these parts. The whole must be left to speak for itself. He was, said a contemporary observer, "a virile, agile man, sometimes a clown, sometimes a stump speaker, sometimes a minstrel monologuist, sometimes an actor, sometimes a preacher."[4]

Sunday developed his pulpit technique in the early years of the century, when he first began to use wooden tabernacles and to invade the big cities. During this period he spent the summer months speaking on chautauqua platforms, for evangelism was a seasonal trade and, by custom, flourished only from September to June. In order to keep up his income during the "off season," Sunday followed the example of other ministers of his day and hired himself out as a lecturer to those agencies which conducted the lyceum and chautauqua circuits.

Chautauqua meetings evolved out of religious camp meetings and Sunday-school conferences in the 1870's to become a conglomeration of educational, entertaining, cultural, and moralizing programs organized along much the same lines as traveling vaudeville. They were usually held in large tents for two or three weeks in the summer on the outskirts of most of the towns and small cities of the Midwest, and they constituted a combination of social gatherings and culture quests to which the countrypeople flocked from miles around. Preachers like Sunday were sandwiched in between performances by ventriloquists, scientific lecturers, hypnotists, opera singers, acrobats, concert violinists, returned missionaries, traveloguists, minstrels, actors, and magicians. These performers were signed up for a season by a managing agency which provided steady work throughout the summer in one town after another. The fees ranged from the thousands of dollars given to William Jennings Bryan for one lecture to an average of twenty or thirty dollars per performance.

When Sunday first began lecturing, he received the latter fees. He delivered such sermons as those on "Amusements," "The Home," "The Sins of Society," and "The Inspiration of the Bible, or Nuts for Skeptics To Crack." The last was directed against the skepticism of Robert G. Ingersoll, who was himself famous for his chautauqua lectures. Later, as the Prohibition crusade gathered force in the rural areas, Sunday's most popular lecture became "Booze, or Get on the Water Wagon." There was no difference between the versions of these sermons which Sunday gave to his chautauqua audiences and the versions he gave to revival audiences.

Whether the chautauqua technique influenced his revival preaching or whether his experience as a revivalist improved his chautauqua technique, it was clear that Sunday's popularity in both fields increased simultaneously. Soon he was getting one hundred dollars and then five hundred a lecture; in 1908 he received eight hundred dollars plus a percentage of the gate receipts. By 1909 he was so popular that he could virtually name his own terms, but by that time he was no longer in need of either the money or the reputation that came from chautauquas.

During March, 1909, while Sunday was conducting a revival in Springfield, Illinois, Mr. Robert F. Glosup came to see him on behalf of the Chautauqua Managers Association to ask him to lecture under their auspices during the coming summer. After talking to

Sunday, he was interviewed by a reporter for the *Illinois State Register*. Glosup stated: "Sunday is the biggest drawing card on the American chautauqua platform today. . . . He refused a contract for $20,000 for chautauqua dates in July and August and declared to me that he would give us only as many dates as he thought he could spare when the time comes. . . . He does all his booking through us, and I tell you he could get ten times as many dates as he takes if he only would say the word. . . . He is the highest salaried chautauqua speaker in America. I make no exception. . . . He is wanted in the South, North, East, and West, and our bureau has enough calls for him to keep going for months. . . . Notwithstanding the money he receives for his work in the evangelistic field, his chautauqua work would yield him fully twice as much. . . . He has more return calls than any other talent I know. . . . He seems to have a hold on the American people second to no one in the limelight of today." Glosup said he was reluctant to be interviewed regarding Sunday's chautauqua earnings and explained: "I wouldn't do it except that they lie about him, malign him, call him a grafter when I don't think there's a better, more conscientious man in the world."[5]

After 1900 Sunday spent part of each summer vacation at the Winona Lake Bible Conference in Indiana, which described itself as "a kind of religious chautauqua." He bought a home there in 1910 and moved his family from Chicago. Dr. Chapman had helped to start the Winona Lake movement in the late 1890's, and it was to be near Chapman that Sunday first began to spend his summers there. Then, in 1904, the Interdenominational Association of Evangelists was founded at Winona Lake, and Sunday became prominent in promoting the work of this association of professional evangelists which held annual conventions to exchange trade secrets and discuss new techniques in mass evangelism.

After 1910, when he bought an apple ranch in Hood River, Oregon, Sunday gave up chautauqua lecturing altogether. He split his summer vacation between the Bible Conference at Winona Lake, the International Association of Evangelists convention (usually at the same place), and Hood River, where he relaxed and recuperated for the coming season. It is doubtful if in the ensuing years Glosup's view that Sunday could make twice as much from lecturing as from evangelism would have held true, but, even if it had, Sunday preferred his preaching. "I love it as I love nothing else," he declared; "I wouldn't leave it for money."[6] Revivalism was for him a perfect combination of duty and desire, of livelihood and talent. It provided unassailable motivation for the most unabashed self-dramatization, and the results were, to him, so patently approved by the Deity that he, like Finney and Moody, could boldly assert that his ends justified his means. Moody had said, "It makes no difference how you get a man to God, provided you get him there,"[7] and Sunday completely agreed.

To the casual, critical observer who dropped in to hear one of Sunday's sermons at the tabernacle, the means which he used to get souls for Christ were startling: "It was more like an entertainment, or a political meeting than a religious gathering," was the first impression.[8] The observer was struck by the hoarse and rasping quality of Sunday's voice, which, though it never gave out, had, during the years of overstraining, lost all its expressive timbre. Yet, as he shouted, his clipped and rapid phrases were perfectly distinct throughout the whole immense building. "Seldom does he lower his voice for effect," wrote one reporter, "but often he lingers on a word or a syllable, his tone rising in pitch almost to a falsetto and resulting in a wail that penetrates to the air outside the building. It is weird, but effective."

Experienced stenographers who tried to take down Sunday's words verbatim stated that he often spoke at the rate of three hundred words per minute. If his words were ever lost, it was not from the speed at which he uttered them, however, but from the interruptions for applause and laughter. When interrupted prematurely, wrote one newspaperman, "he waits for the handclapping to cease and sometimes repeats a sentence that the people may be certain that they got it all."

Sunday wanted every word to have its full effect, yet often it was not the words themselves but the rapid, rhythmic beat of his curt, alliterative phrases which carried the audience along with him. The acceleration and deceleration of his speaking, like the rising and falling inflection of his voice, helped to create a tenseness in the audience of which they were scarcely aware. With consummate skill Sunday built up this tenseness until, at the psychological moment, he pronounced the word or phrase which broke the spell—the tension snapped, and simultaneously twenty thousand people let out a gasp of pain or broke into thunderous applause or near-hysterical laughter. Yet he never let his audience get out of control. The periods between outbursts might grow shorter as the sermon progressed, but they always came when he wanted them.

The evangelist put every ounce of his tremendous energy into his oratory, and the listeners in unconscious empathy often ground their teeth and clenched their fists and squirmed in their seats, imitating his actions. "Frequently in following the torrent of his own words," a reporter noted, "he closes his eyes as if the better to think in time with the furious pace of his tongue. And as every muscle of his body is involved in movements, so every muscle of his perspiring face takes part in rapid contortions of his features."

The fierce intensity of Sunday's expression gripped even the reporters who watched him day after day. Sometimes it seemed as if something cracked inside Sunday, and he would become a screaming maniac on the platform. One night he was delivering his sermon on "Solomon" and had just asked the men in the audience, "Won't you take home a new daddy tonight?" when, according to one account, "some frenzied impulse seemed to flash into the preacher's overwrought brain . . . suddenly, unaccountably, without an instant's warning came the outburst. With eyes shut tight, knees flexed, his body rising and falling to the rhythm of his words, with perspiration raining from his touselled, tossing head, with clenched fists beating the air, he hurled forth an astonishing torrent of adjectives: 'Bull-necked, infamous, black-hearted, white-livered, hog-jowled, god-forsaken, hell-bound gang!' Dropping like lightning to the carpet he dealt the trapdoor a punishment of clattering blows . . . whirling about on hands and knees with the quickness of a cat and the rage of a tiger, he glanced at the first person who confronted him—one of the newspapermen. His expression was appalling. His contorted face was deep red, his eyes were bulging circles of white with blazing centers of fire, and his lips were drawn back from twin rows of white, tight-shut teeth. His breath came in gasps, and he squealed the impotent anger that no words could voice. Then, leaping to his feet, he dashed across the platform and spit over its edge a mouth-ful of white. As suddenly as it swept over him, his indignation spent itself. . . . Billy was himself again, laughing at his display of emotion and resuming his exposition of the case of King Solomon."[9]

Pounding on the floor of the platform or on his lectern was only a small part of the vigorous action with which Sunday emphasized his points. It was estimated that he walked a mile back and forth across the thirty-foot platform in every sermon—one hundred and fifty miles in every campaign. But it was not merely walking; it was running, sliding, jumping, falling, staggering, whirling, and throw-ing himself around the platform. He did not remain in one spot or one position for thirty seconds. When he was not pounding the lectern or the reinforced kitchen chair on which he sat before he began to speak, he was as often as not standing on one or the other, sometimes with one foot on the chair and one on the pulpit. Then, at the right moment for emphasis, he would leap and come thudding down on the platform. Frequently he picked up the chair and swung it around his head. Once it accidentally slipped from his grasp and hurtled through the air over the heads of the newspapermen and landed in the sawdust-covered aisle below. In earlier days he was known to have purposely brought the chair crashing down upon the pulpit, smashing it to bits in order to express his wrath.

Sunday's movements were not always noisy or startling but usually were nimbly and gracefully executed. "A characteristic movement of extreme emphasis," said one observer, "involves the entire body and suggests a pitcher in the act of throwing the ball." At the conclusion of his sermon to men only he always parodied the famous comic poem "Slide, Kelly, Slide" and made a running dive across the full length of the platform on his stomach. Then he would jump to his feet to imitate "the Great Umpire of the Universe" and yell, "You're out, Kelly!" This scene climaxed his account of a former teammate named Kelly who had taken to booze and thus failed to get home to heaven.

Sometimes, during a vigorous castigation of the backslidden churches and "hireling ministry," Sunday would brandish his fist under the noses of the co-operating clergymen seated at the rear of the platform; to the audience he seemed angry enough to punch them in the nose, but for those close enough to see it "there was a grin on his face that robbed the gesture of any personal meaning."

Another characteristic gesture was to stand at the very edge of the platform on one leg, his body bent forward, his other leg extended behind him, and his right arm thrust out pointing directly at someone in the audience: "You know it, you pup," he would shout with an impish smile. Occasionally his gyrations nearly proved his undoing. During a sermon in Boston "he tore across the platform toward the right, perspiring and screaming invective, his right arm slicing the air in a sweep ten feet long. 'God picked up the Welsh revival,' he bellowed, 'and shook it in the teeth of the merchants and said, "Take that, ye ginks! Take that, ye ginks!"' Billy brought his right foot down with the toe of his shoe touching the very edge of the platform; in his excitement he lost his balance and stood poised for an instant over the fifteen-foot drop to the sawdust and solid earth. Hearts ceased to beat throughout the house. Then whirling

about to face the desk and bending forward with an effort, he recovered his fleeing center of gravity and walked back to the pulpit.
For a moment he lost his self-possession, too, and his face assumed a
surprised expression. A gasp of relief came from the benches.”

During the course of his most exciting sermons Sunday peeled off
first his coat, then his tie and collar, and then his vest, and finally he
rolled up his sleeves. This was both a symbol of pugnacity and an
attempt to keep cool. More than one reporter mentioned the drops
of perspiration which sprayed over him from Sunday's flailing arms
and tossing head. “Just watching these movements is apt to be exciting for the spectator,” said the accounts of his meetings. Despite the
many possible distractions from attention in a crowd of fifteen or
twenty thousand people, “not for a single instant did he fail to hold
their eyes fixed upon him.”

Since Sunday repeated the same set of sermons in every revival
(with occasional new additions) and since he held an average of six
revivals a year from 1906 to 1918, it was obvious that his actions
were not entirely spontaneous. Each sermon had been given at least
thirty times, and some of them a hundred times, by 1912. Persons
who watched him give the same sermon more than once noted with
astonishment that, despite his undoubted sincerity and passionate
fervor, every phrase, every gesture, every pirouette was the same.
Even his most violent outbursts were apparently planned: “He has
himself under control, and after an apparently violent outburst . . .
he steps behind the pulpit and chuckles at the effect his gyrations
have had.” The audiences did not hear the chuckle or the snorting
“Huh!” which Sunday emitted when he was particularly pleased
with the effect he had made, but the reporters did, and conveyed
their astonishment at his self-controlled emotionalism. When questioned, Mrs. Sunday said that, no matter how many times her husband had delivered a sermon, he always went over it again in his
bedroom before each new performance.

The movement in Sunday's sermons was not all rhetorical flourish
or dramatic thumping for its own sake. Most of it consisted of carefully worked-out enactments of the material in his sermons. Sunday
had a superlative gift of mimicry; he claimed that the actor Tom
Keene once asked him to be his understudy.[10] The acting in his sermons made them thoroughly enjoyable to watch simply as entertainment, regardless of their theological implications: “He would be as
entertaining to an audience in a vaudeville theatre as to one that
comes to his revival meetings,” said one reporter, and another wrote,

"Billy's imitation of the prophet Elisha was the greatest fun-producer that he has shown Boston. Perhaps if the collection had been taken after his impersonation instead of before, it might have been larger. This one act alone was worth the average contribution to the offering, and more."

Sunday's sermons often consisted of a whole series of hilarious or sobering imitations of human behavior which made the audience visualize and feel the incidents portrayed. The amount and quality of the mimicry in one sermon was reported in this summary:

Mr. Sunday's interpretations included these characters: a woman singer given to affectation; the Duke of Wellington; a rummy in a saloon smoking a cigarette; a college professor; an intoxicated youth staggering as he walked; the patriarch Issac; Esau going forth to hunt; Jacob afraid to face his brother; King Richard III limping; Abraham Lincoln on his knees in prayer; a photographer posing and making a picture of a child; a pompous physician; his whining patient; a husband; and a man's wife mushily kissing him.

He often acted out several parts in skits which lasted five or ten minutes. Some of these scenes were taken from the Bible, such as Namaan's dipping seven times in the Jordan or the return of the Prodigal Son, and some were scenes from his own life as a baseball player. Others were satirical parodies upon the foibles of modern society, such as this skit:

Drop into a young people's meeting. The leader will say in a weak, effeminate, apologetic sort of way that there was a splendid topic this evening, but he had not had much time for preparation. It is superfluous for him to say that; you could have told that.

He goes along and tells how happy he is to have you there to take part this evening, making this meeting interesting. Someone gets up and reads a poem from the *Christian Endeavor World,* and then they sing No. 38. They get up and sing:

> Oh, to be nothing,
> Only to lie at his feet.

We used to sing that song, but I found out that people took it so literally that I cut it out.

Then a long pause and someone says, "Let us sing No. 52." So they get up and then someone starts

> Throw out the life line,
> Throw out the life line. . . .

They haven't got enough strength to put up a clothes line.

Another long pause and then you hear, "Have all taken part that feel free to do so? We have a few minutes left so let us sing No. 23." Then another long pause.

Billy Sunday and his wife. Taken about 1915. (*Underwood and Underwood.*)

William Jennings Bryan and Billy Sunday. Taken in 1915, when Bryan was Secretary of State. (*Underwood and Underwood.*)

"I hear the organ prelude; it is time for us to close. Now let us all repeat together, 'Lord keep watch between me and thee while we are absent one from another.' "

I tell you God has got a hard job on his hands. Ever hear anything like that?

Applause and laughter greeted every mocking tone, each mincing gesture, "and the encouragement given led him to repeat the impersonations several times."

This dramatic humor was supplemented by Sunday's comments on contemporary social fads, by funny stories about his childhood, and by standard jokes about old maids, Negroes, "Chinamen," and Irishmen told in dialect. Sunday's experience on the chautauqua platform undoubtedly had something to do with this insertion of theatrical humor into religious services. The competition which he met as a lecturer compelled him to enliven his sermons if he wished to build up his gate receipts. He was not the only preacher to popularize his style for this reason.

The most impressive tribute to Sunday's dramatic talent was that paid indirectly by Heywood Broun, drama critic of the *New York Tribune*. In September, 1915, Broun reviewed George M. Cohan's new comedy "Hit the Trail Holliday," in which Cohan played "Billy Holliday," a part he wrote for himself in an obvious attempt to parody Billy Sunday. Broun wrote: "George Cohan has forced a comparison between himself and his greatest rival in the use of dramatic slang, and strange as it may seem, it is George and not Billy who cracks under the strain." The play "was a triumph for Billy Sunday," Broun continued; "George Cohan has neither the punch nor the pace of Billy Sunday. . . . It is true that Cohan waved the flag first, but Billy Sunday has waved it harder. . . . It is in language that the superiority of Sunday is most evident. . . . All in all we believe that Sunday has more of the dramatic instinct than Cohan."[11]

Sunday's use of "dramatic slang," which seemed to Broun to be one of his prime attributes, was to many of the clergymen who co-operated in his revivals the least prepossessing aspect of his preaching. It was certainly one of the predominant aspects and one which no listener could fail to note at once. Criticism of his language dogged him throughout his career and caused him more difficulty than any other attack on his pulpit technique. He tried to meet it in various ways. In 1914 a reporter stated, after interviewing the evangelist, "It grieves Sunday to be pictured as a slangy person"; Sunday told this reporter, "As you see, I use slang scarcely at all in ordinary conversation. I deem it necessary in my work. I try to reach the man on the street and the conversation of the man on the street is made up one-third of cuss words, one-third of obscenity, and one-third of slang. I wouldn't use cuss words or profanity, so I talk slang to him. I want to reach the people so I use the people's language. Some slang is more expressive than pure English and to catch those listening to me I must use expressive language. I am condemned for my slang, but it wins converts."[12]

Sometimes Sunday's answers to criticism by conservative clergymen were more personal: "What do I care if some puff-eyed, little dibbly-dibbly preacher goes tibbly-tibbling around because I use plain Anglo-Saxon words?" he asked. "I want people to know what I mean and that's why I try to get down where they live." Educated, literary preachers who "try to please the highbrows and in pleasing them miss the masses" were not his models. "We've got a bunch of preachers breaking their necks to please a lot of old society dames. Some ministers say, 'If you don't repent you'll die and go to a place the name of which I can't pronounce.' I can! You'll go to hell!"

If, however, the criticism seemed to him to be coming from secular opponents of his revivals, Sunday took an even more vehement tack: "Those who abuse me [for using slang] are trying to divert attention from their own abusive language and iniquity by saying, 'Bill is vulgar, and Bill is crude.' Oh, no, I am not vulgar and crude. You are rotten, that is all there is to it. You doped that wrong my friends."[13] If the attack upon him came from the more respectable members of society, his defense was an oblique attack: "Rotten is a good Anglo-Saxon word, and you don't have to go to the dictionary to know what it means. . . . 'A process in the formation of new chemical compounds' is just the Bostonese way of saying a thing is rotten. It's the society way of trying to keep from holding your nose because it's vulgar, but I like 'rotten' because it gets over the line quicker."

But whatever defense Sunday made, the truth was that he could not, and would not, express himself without using slang. His early attempts at imitating Chapman had proved that he would have to be himself if he was to preach at all, and he proceeded to make a virtue out of necessity. Fortunately, he was able to find good precedents for the use of common language in evangelistic work. Finney and Moody were attacked for their use of the vernacular and wrote notable defenses, pointing out the vituperative language of the Old Testament prophets and the fact that Jesus himself used the language of the common people. Comparison of Sunday's sermons with those of Finney and Moody would have revealed a considerably greater use of slang in Sunday's work, but comparison with certain contemporary evangelists, like the Rev. Samuel P. Jones and Milan B. Williams, indicated that by the turn of the century slang was an established part of revivalism.

In fact, the whole question of Sunday's slangy style was intricately involved with charges that he had plagarized much of his material from these very evangelists. Slang came naturally to Sunday, but not sermon-writing, and to those who took the trouble to unearth the sermons from which he borrowed, it was evident that, while he often altered the form, the substance of his work was the same. The defense against charges of plagiary rested upon the extent to which his dynamic delivery and his vivid phraseology made something new and original out of the material he so obviously borrowed.

Sunday never claimed complete originality for all his sermons. "I am indebted to various friends of mine for some of my thoughts," he would often say, "though I do not always give credit." It became apparent, however, that, had he given credit for all the material he borrowed, there would have been little left of his own. In a talk to the divinity students of the Episcopal Theological Seminary in Cambridge, Massachusetts, in 1916 he described the method he used in writing his sermons: "I attend to them carefully and have a large envelope for each subject, and in this envelope I put clippings or notes of everything pertinent to it from newspapers, magazines, biographies, or histories, once in a while adding a Bible paragraph. In this way I am increasing my sermons at all times."[14]

It is probably a conservative estimate that 75 per cent of the material in Sunday's sermons was borrowed, directly or indirectly, from other sources. In a letter defending himself against such charges, he revealed some of the persons to whom he was indebted:

I was a special student under Professor Lloyd in my early days and have the outline of four sermons he gave me—M. B. Williams helped me in my early days, and I have material I got from him. I have illustrations from Sam Jones. I have no outline of his sermons—I have illustrations from Talmage. I have the outline of one sermon Frank Talmage gave me—I have some outlines that Dr. Chapman gave me and have illustrations and material from Elijah "Ram's Horn" Brown—Morgan—Gypsy Smith—Moody—Pentecost—Munhall—Burrell—Jowett—Hillis—Cadman —and Guthrie—Shakespeare—Bacon—Plato—from editorials by Dana— Greeley—Brisbane—Medill—Keely [sic]—and dozens of others—from states-

165

men—Washington—Lincoln—Garfield—Bryan—Ingersoll. But I am not a thief.[15]

Other sources not mentioned in this letter were Charles Finney, Glenn Frank, Len Broughton, Henry Van Dyke, Henry Ward Beecher, George R. Stuart, B. Fay Mills, and Orison Swett Marden. Sunday claimed that he could not know the source of clippings he used which were sent to him in the mail, and he made this excuse when some freethinkers discovered his plagiary of one of Ingersoll's speeches.[16]

The Ingersoll borrowing was particularly damaging to Sunday for two reasons: first, because he had so consistently condemned Ingersoll to hell for his agnosticism and, second, because the borrowing was absolutely verbatim. There could be no question here that the quotation had come with the permission of a friend or that Sunday had so reworked it that it was something new. Whether he did get this passage from a clipping sent to him in the mail and from which Ingersoll's name was missing or whether it was unidentified material provided for him by Elijah Brown or B. D. Ackley or whether, like "Elmer Gantry," he deliberately lifted the passage from Ingersoll's collected works was never discovered.

The passage borrowed was from a Memorial Day address delivered by Ingersoll in New York in 1882; it was a flowing rhetorical gem glorifying the Civil War's triumphant victory over slavery and sectionalism, complete with flag-waving that much preceded George Cohan's. Sunday used this material as early as 1907 for a Memorial Day address which he delivered in Knoxville, Iowa, and perhaps he had used it even earlier. It was not until 1912 that the plagiary was discovered, when he gave the same address in Beaver Falls, Pennsylvania. The discovery was made and published by a man named Franklin Steiner, who had made a hero out of Ingersoll and a career out of anticlericalism. His report was widely printed in the press in January, 1915, when Sunday denied ever having read Ingersoll's address—though he readily admitted having read all Ingersoll's attacks on the validity of the Bible. No legal action was taken against Sunday by the freethinkers because none was possible, but the revelation seriously hurt him, and he never used the address again.

However, Sunday did not alter his other sermon material, although it contained several lengthy passages of verbatim borrowings from other sources. These passages, however, were from preachers who would probably have made no objection to his using them, though it is doubtful that Sunday actually had their permission. The literal borrowings were all purple passages of flowing eloquence which, presumably, Sunday felt unable to write himself or even to improve upon but which he found useful in his sermons to arouse certain of the more tender or exalted emotions which slang and acrobatics could not elicit. For example, his sermon on heaven incorporated a long passage from T. DeWitt Talmage's sermon on the same subject; his sermon on the home included George R. Stuart's eulogy on "home, sweet home"; his sentiments on mother's love in his sermon to mothers were taken from Sam Jones.[17] He used these without change and without credit, but their incongruity in the midst of his slang made it a simple matter for hostile critics to spot them as borrowings.

But most of Sunday's borrowings were, as he said, merely brief "illustrations"—anecdotes, jokes, supposedly true stories—which he employed to point up some particular moral or doctrine. It was in remaking such illustrations that Sunday's slangy originality justified the claim that he was re-creating the material he borrowed into something new. For example, he took this joke from Jones:[18]

A gentleman asked another some time ago, "How much did Mr. So-and-So leave?" His friend replied, "He left all he had. He didn't take a dollar with him." It is not what we leave but what we carry with us.

He made the story more realistic by giving the dead man a well-known name and phrasing the moral more vividly:

The next day in the street one man said to another: "Have you heard the news? Commodore Vanderbilt is dead." "How much did he leave?" "He left it all." Naked you came into this world and naked you will crawl out of it.

He borrowed these illustrations from Marden:

While a criminal was exchanging his own for a prison suit in the penitentiary of Connecticut he remarked, "I never did a day's work in my life." No wonder that he reached the state prison.

"Out of work" has caused more crime and wretchedness than almost anything else.

These words were found tattooed on the right arm of a convict in a French prison: "The past has deceived me, the present torments me, and the future terrifies me."

But he condensed them into one sentence:

Tattooed on the arm of a French convict were the words, "I never did a day's work in my life."

"The public never knew," said Mrs. Sunday after her husband's death, "how hard Mr. Sunday worked on his sermons. Whenever he came across a big word, he hunted through his book of synonyms for a simpler one which the people would be sure to understand."[19] In most cases Sunday was using material which was twenty or thirty years old, and its style and language were out of date. A typical example of his modernization and vernacularization was his restatement of T. DeWitt Talmage's attack upon science in *Trumpet Peals:*

TALMAGE	SUNDAY
You just take your scientific consolation into that room where a mother has lost her child. Try in that case your doctrine of the "survival of the fittest." Tell her that child died because it was not worth as much as the other children. That is your "survival of the fittest."	Take your scientific consolation into a room where a mother has lost her child. Try your doctrine of the survival of the fittest with that broken-hearted woman. Tell her that the child that died was not as fit to live as the one left alive. Where does that scientific junk lift the burden from her heart?
Just try your transcendentalism and your philosophy and your science on that widowed soul, and tell her it was a geological necessity that her companion should be taken away from her just as in the course of the world's history the megatheriums had to pass out of existence; and then you go on in your scientific consolation until you get to the sublime fact that fifty million years from now we ourselves may be scientific specimens on a geological shelf, petrified specimens of an extinct human race.	Go to some dying man and tell him to pluck up courage for the future. Try your philosophy on him; tell him to be confident in the great to-be and the everlasting what-is-it. Go to that widow and tell her that in fifty million years we will all be scientific mummies on a shelf —petrified specimens of an extinct race. What does all this stuff get her?
And after you have got all through with your consolation, if the poor afflicted soul is not crazed by it, I will send forth from this church the plainest Christian we have, and with one half-hour of prayer and reading of the Scripture promises, the tears will be wiped away and the house from floor to cupola will be flooded with the calmness of an Indian summer sunset.	After you have gotten through with your science, philosophy, psychology, eugenics, social service, sociology, evolution, protoplasms, and fortuitous concurrence of atoms, if she isn't bughouse, I will take the Bible and read God's promises and pray—and her tears will be dried and her soul flooded with calmness like a California sunset.

Sunday's process of simplification and modernization went even further with passages taken from Moody, Chapman, "Gypsy" Smith, and B. Fay Mills. When Moody chastised the worldly condition of the church, he said, "The standard of the church is so low that it does not mean much; it is easy to be a professed Christian." This was not forceful enough for Sunday: "The bars of the Church are so low that any old hog with two or three suits of clothes and a bank roll can crawl through." Moody stated simply, "We don't want intellect and money-power, but the power of God's word." Sunday made the allusions concrete: "The church in America would die of dry rot and sink forty-nine fathoms in hell if all members were multimillionaires and college graduates." It was such slang that shocked evangelists like R. A. Torrey who were trying to maintain the pulpit dignity of the nineteenth century and who consequently failed so dismally to attract audiences in the twentieth.

Sunday's emphasis was not always on the more vulgar aspects of slang. He frequently showed a more ready wit and less sentimentalism in his storytelling than the older evangelists from whom he borrowed. Moody's and Chapman's sermons were filled with stories of dying mothers whose prayers converted wicked sons or of soldiers whose last gasps on the battlefields of the Civil War were confessions of faith. Sunday maintained that "religion lies in the will—not in tears nor in snuffling of the nose." On the whole, he could honestly say to his audiences, "I don't appeal to your handkerchiefs. You don't need to bring your handkerchiefs here very much to wipe your eyes" because "I haven't told you of any death-bed scenes, but I try to show you that religion is the most reasonable thing in the world."

Sunday was keen to see the importance of making his stories coincide with the experience and attitudes of his audience. Moody illustrated the meaning of "Redemption" by a story in Irish dialect about a friend who bought a bird from a boy near Dublin; the friend had tried to persuade the boy to release the bird but was told, "Indade, sur, an' haven't I been chasin' him for half an hour, and d'ye spose I'd be afther lettin' him go?"; so the man "paid the price the little fellow asked" and let the bird go. As the bird fluttered away, it said, "as plain as it could speak, 'Thank you! Thank you!'" And "so my friends," Moody concluded, "we have been in the hands of the devil these 6,000 years," but "Christ has bought us . . . and we ought to fill all the air with songs of thanksgiving." Sunday gave the story an American setting:

I remember when I was in the YMCA in Chicago, I was going down Madison and had just crossed Dearborn Street when I saw a newsboy with a young sparrow in his hand. I said, "Let that little bird go."
He said, "Aw g'wan with you, you big mutt."

I said, "I'll give you a penny for it," and he answered, "Not on your tintype."

"I'll give you a nickel for it," and he answered, "Boss, I'm from Missouri; come across with the dough."

I offered it to him, but he said, "Give it to that guy there," and I gave it to the boy he indicated and took the sparrow. I held it for a moment and then it fluttered and struggled and finally reached the window ledge in a second story window across the street. And other birds fluttered around over my head and seemed to say in bird language, "Thank you, Bill."

The kid looked at me in wonder and said, "Say, boss, why didn't you chuck that nickel in the sewer?"

I told him that he was just like that bird. He was in the grip of the devil. . . . God paid a price for him far greater than I had for the sparrow, for He had paid it with the blood of his Son, and He wanted to set him free.

Borrowings from Chapman were more transfigured, since Chapman was more formal in his speech than Moody. Chapman stated that, after he had lent some of his sermons to Sunday, they were so changed that he could not recognize them. In one of these Chapman told of a boy condemned to die in Pennsylvania and mentioned incidentally that the boy's mother had made a futile plea to "the governor" for a pardon. Chapman's only statement about the mother was, "The boy's mother swooned in his office and they carried her out." Sunday elaborated this scene to astounding proportions:

At last the boy's mother came. Her eyes were red, her cheeks sunken, her lips ashen, her hair disheveled, her clothing unkempt, her body tottering from the loss of food and sleep. Broken hearted she reeled, staggered, and dragged herself into the presence of the governor. She pleaded for her boy. She said, "Oh, governor, let me die. Oh, governor, I beg of you to let my boy go; don't, don't hang him!" And Governor Pollock listened.

She staggered to his side, put her arms around him. He took her arms from his shoulder, held her at arms' length, looked into her face and said to her, "Mother, mother, I can't do it, I can't," and he ran from her presence.

She screamed and fell to the floor and they carried her out.

Sunday made an equally melodramatic revision in the sermon on Mary and Martha which he borrowed from B. Fay Mills. Mills stated that Jesus waited two days after learning of Lazarus' illness before he came to Bethany because "it was necessary for these sisters to have a personal interview with Christ" before he could bless them by helping their brother. "I think," said Mills, "it took more love for Him to stay away than it would have required to go and heal sick

Lazarus." The explanation of Jesus' delay offered by Sunday was self-revealing: "Jesus said to himself, 'I'll let him die. I've been curing people of sickness and giving sight to the blind and still they don't believe in me; but if I raise him from the dead they'll have to believe in me.' I believe it took more love for Jesus to stay away than to go." Mills said, "I am glad to have a good word to speak for Martha. I think poor Martha has been unjustly criticized." Without bothering to question this unorthodox interpretation, Sunday stated: "Mary was one of these Uneeda biscuit, peanut butter, gelatin and pimento sort of women. . . . I am glad to speak for Martha. She was my favorite. Martha was a beefsteak, baked potato, apple sauce with lemon and nutmeg, coffee and whipped cream, apple pie and cheese sort of woman."

Sunday's slangy interpretations of biblical incidents were so popular that he issued a whole volume of them in 1917, entitled *Great Love Stories of the Bible*. It contained, in spite of its title, a version of the story of David and Goliath which he often used in his sermon "The Forces That Win"; it concluded by saying that David "soaked the giant in the coco right between the lamps, and he went down for the count." This, said Sunday in his introduction to the book, is "my effort to make the Twentieth Century more humanly and intimately acquainted with the Bible—from the viewpoint of the Twentieth Century." His famous sermon "The Sins of Society" contained this twentieth-century version of Salome's dancing: "When the entertainment was at its height, Herodias shoved Salome out into the room to do her little stunt. He said to her: 'Go like a twin-six!' She had anklets and bracelets on, but she didn't have clothes enough on her to flag a hand car. And she spun around on her toe and stuck her foot out at a quarter to twelve. The king let out a guffaw of approval . . . and he said, 'Sis, you're sure a peach. You're the limit. You can have anything you want.' "

Such interpretations were certainly original, but Sunday did not deserve credit for first injecting pungent slang into professional revivalism. There were two evangelists whom he very consciously adopted as his models—models who were more in keeping with his own uneducated and flamboyant personality than his early idol, Chapman. The men who most influenced Sunday's style were M. B. Williams and Samuel Porter Jones. Both Williams and Jones began their evangelistic work in Georgia in the 1880's.[20] Williams started as a YMCA worker and Jones as an itinerant Methodist preacher after an unsuccessful career as a lawyer. Williams' career as an

171

evangelist reached its peak when he and Charles Alexander toured Iowa and the surrounding states in tents and wooden tabernacles in the late 1890's. Jones's career lasted from the early 1880's until 1908, and he achieved nation-wide fame, though it was in the South that he was an especial favorite.

As predominantly small-town revivalists, these men considered big-city evangelists like Moody, Torrey, Chapman, and Mills "highbrow." And, conversely, it was reported that Moody considered Jones "uncouth." Moody's son stated that when Jones and his assistant, Sam Small, were speaking in a Chicago church in 1885, they used such language that they "were offensive to Moody's sense of good taste."[21]

But to Sunday, who heard all these evangelists at one time or another and who could never hope to match the rugged dignity of Moody or the sophisticated suavity of Torrey, Chapman, or Mills, Jones and Williams were *beaux ideals*. When he started to build up his sermon repertoire with the type of material used by them, he was himself a small-town preacher touring the prairie villages of Iowa. It was indicative of the provincial-mindedness of the audiences who attended Sunday's revivals in the big cities that the sermons which he wrote for the farmers of Iowa, Illinois, and Indiana were just as effective, with scarcely any alteration, in Chicago, New York, Boston, and Los Angeles.

When he was not busy with Chapman, Sunday worked with Williams in several revivals in the years 1893–96 and learned from him the value of rapid, slangy speech and perpetual pulpit activity. Williams was known to take off his coat and roll up his sleeves, to shout at the top of his voice, to gesticulate vigorously, and to use such language as "if there is anything on earth that I ever hear that uses me up, that converts me into a dishcloth, and makes me feel like a woman who has swallowed a fly" and "some old, fat, red-nosed whiskey seller leans over his bar and blurts it out in my ears with his stinking whiskey breath." Williams was also famous for his talk to men only on "Sex problems . . . as related to health and disease, morality and religion, heredity and environment." A large part of Sunday's well-known sermon on "Amusements" came from Williams' book *Where Satan Sows His Seeds: Plain Talks on the Amusements of Modern Society*. The following parallel passages from their sermons on the text "If Any Man Will" illustrate the similarity between their styles and the lengths to which Sunday had to go to outdo his mentor.

Now carefully look over your chronology. You will find that when Cain went out to court his wife he was a lusty youth of 128 years of age. If you read some of the things in Darwin's writings on population you will find him quoting Malthus, who in turn quotes Euler, the great statistician, regarding population. He says that under favorable circumstances population can double twice in a quarter of a century.

I look back on the circumstances in which man started out life and find they were the most favorable for rapid increase in population. One day I sat down and figured it out for my own satisfaction, and I found in calculating these things, and allowing at the end of twelve years that there were seven pairs on earth and Cain married at 128 years of age, at that time, at that rate of increase, there would be 11,940 people on the face of the earth.

If half of them were females, there would be, as you see, 5,970 buxom damsels out of whom Cain might pick and have his choice for a wife.

There would be enough people on earth to make a chain of cities reaching from the Gulf of Mexico to the Great Lakes, ten miles apart —such cities as they had in those days. And yet men have stumbled over some little thing like that.

It is wonderful so many people take an interest in where Cain got his wife, and the neighbor's wife around the corner bothers you old geezers more than Cain's did. . . . They are hard put to it when they have to go 4,000 years back and try and find a flaw against God. If, however, you will sit down and read the Scripture you will find that Cain was 128 years old when he went courting.

Darwin, that old infidel, quoting from other writers of his like, says that the population will double twice in twenty-five years and allowing seven pairs, when Cain was 128 years old there must have been 11,940 people on earth at that time.

It is reasonable to suppose that half of these were females, which would mean that there were 5,970 buxom damsels for Cain to choose from, and that was enough to satisfy the most fastidious.

There were all kinds, blue eyes, brown eyes, bleached hair—no, not the latter, for in those days they didn't do that. I feel sorry for any girl who dyes her hair. Let it be like God made it. If He had thought you would have looked better with another color, He would have given it to you.

Sam Jones was even more colorful than Williams.[22] While it is usually possible to distinguish Williams' work from Sunday's by its better syntax, its more orderly development, and its less frequent use of slang, Jones's sermons are distinguishable only by their southern idiom. A footnote in one of the authorized editions of Jones's sermons in 1886 stated: "Mr. Jones's disregard of grammatical rules in his pulpit deliverances is always obviously studied; and besides

173

having the merit of popularity, it is one of his most effective means of rightly impressing the multitude." As Jones himself said, "I am trying to get my style and grammar down to your level." He believed, he said, in "scattering the fodder on the ground," where everybody could reach it. Sunday likewise maintained that a good preacher "will put his cookies on the lower shelf," and it was from Jones that he got his defense of using plain Anglo-Saxon words. Jones said, "Now you take the Latin word 'decayed' and it won't faze a fellow. If you take the good old Anglo-Saxon word 'rotten' you can cut his head off."

Sunday's dislike for the cultured minister was another attitude he shared with Jones: "We have been clamoring for forty years for an educated ministry," said Jones, "and we have got it today and the church is deader than it ever had been in history. Half of the literary preachers in this town are A.B.'s, Ph.D.'s, D.D.'s, LL.D.'s and A.S.S.'s."

Both evangelists set themselves up as common men, not so low-down as to have no religion but not so highbrow and snobbish as to think that "the language of the people" was "vul*gah*." They both lumped their opponents into "gangs." "The diamond-wearing bunch, the automobile gang, the silk-gowned—that's the bunch," said Sunday, describing the snobs. "God deliver me from the poolroom gang," said Jones, defining the lowbrows. Being a southern evangelist, Jones had a specific social group in mind when he spoke of "lowbrows": "I hardly ever mention circuses. They are too low down for me. Down South all trashy niggers and low-down white folks go to circuses."

Without exception, each "gang" of opponents to revivalism was the worst. Both evangelists spoke only in superlatives. "The worst thing this side of the gaping gates of damnation is the wide open saloon in a town," claimed Jones; and "The most heartless creature in God's world is a full-fledged society woman." Sunday declared that "the most useless thing on God's dirt is the mere society woman" and "the dirtiest, low-down, damnable business on top of this old earth" is the saloon.

To blacken the enemies of Christianity, both men employed epithets which bordered on obscenity and blasphemy. "Idiots," "damnable mutts," "panderers," and "whoremongers" were among their favorite terms. "They talk about the excitement of a revival meeting being bad for a community," Sunday said. "If you say that, you are a dirty, rotten, stinking liar! Did you get it? They never did any-

174

thing for Christ in their lives. Peanut-headed fools, that's what they are." Neither Jones nor Sunday hesitated to say "you can go to hell," "to hell with you," or "no damned good." Far from shocking the crowds, such denunciations were exceedingly popular. It was only the clergy that was shocked. A reporter in Boston noted with surprise: "Sunday's condemnations of all sorts never fail to evoke applause whether the denunciation be of church members, of representatives of various sects, or just 'Bostonians.'"

A favorite rhetorical device which Sunday adopted from Jones was to embellish his name-calling with long catalogues of adjectives. Rhythmical vigor and variety were obtained by alliteration and by hyphenated words. The extravagance and ridiculous imagery in these catalogues often produced applause and laughter. Sunday spoke of "those ossified, petrified, mildewed, dyed-in-the-wool, stamped-in-the-cork, blown-in-the-bottle, horizontal, perpendicular Presbyterians" and of the "red-nosed, buttermilk-eyed, beetle-browed, peanut-brained, stall-fed old saloon keeper." Pilate's wife was "a miserable, pliable, plastic, two-faced, two-by-four, lick-spittle, toot-my-own-horn sort of woman," and Pilate "was just one of those rat-hole, pin-headed, pliable, stand-pat, free-lunch, pie-counter, politicians." The more ridiculous the catalogue the better: "Lord save us from off-handed, flabby-cheeked, brittle-boned, weak-kneed, thin-skinned, pliable, plastic, spineless, effeminate, ossified three-karat Christianity." Alliteration was sometimes more elaborately developed to provide startling contrasts: "The curse of this age," said Jones, "is we have put gold above God, chattels above character, and mammon above manhood." Sunday denounced city dudes "with shoes more pointed than their intellects, with more collar than character, with more money than morals, and not much of that."

The laughter and applause which such devices produced helped to provide temporary relief from the tension which the evangelist was gradually tightening. "I'm against the world with every tooth, nail, bit of skin, hair follicle, muscular molecule—yes, and even my vermiform appendix," said Sunday. Jones said that his father "fought liquor as long as he had a fist to strike, and kicked it as long as he had a foot, and bit it as long as he had teeth, and then gummed it till he died." Sunday reworked this into a more rhythmical pattern and put suitable motions to it: "I have sworn eternal and everlasting enmity to the liquor traffic: as long as I have a foot, I'll kick it; as long as I have a fist, I'll hit it; as long as I have a tooth, I'll bite it; as long as I have a head I'll butt it; and when I'm old, and gray, and bootless, and toothless, I'll gum it till I go to heaven and it goes to hell."

Whole books of "Sam Jones' Sayings" were published in his day, and long columns of "Sundayisms" were printed in newspapers. These epigrams were very similar to the sayings of Josh Billings, Artemus Ward, Bill Nye, and other professional funny men of the lyceum circuits; both Jones and Sunday occasionally gave credit to one of these for a quotation. How many were borrowed without credit it would be difficult to discover. Typical of Sunday's home-spun philosophy and cracker-barrel wit were the following:

Home is the place we love best and grumble most.

Nearly everybody is stuck up about something; some people are even proud that they aren't proud.

Going to church doesn't make a man a Christian any more than going to a garage makes him an automobile.

Death-bed repentance is burning the candle of life in the service of the devil, and then blowing the smoke into the face of God.

In their efforts to inject humor into revivalism, however, both Jones and Sunday went beyond philosophizing and into pure entertainment for its own sake. They even capitalized upon juxtaposing the sacred and the profane. Jones ridiculed women who went to church to show off their clothes, in this paraphrase of a well-known hymn:

Must Jesus bear the cross alone,
And all the world go free?
No, there's a cross for everyone,
And an Easter bonnet for me.

Sunday chastised churchgoing hypocrites by saying, "You listen to the sermon, pick up the hymn book and sing, 'Jesus paid it all' when you have debts that are outlawed. He doesn't pay them. He doesn't pay for that hat or that set of false teeth you are wearing. You get up and sing, 'I am standing on the solid rock'—you are probably standing in a pair of shoes you haven't paid for yet."

Equally open to charges of sacrilege was the resemblance between Sunday's style and the style of the commercial advertisement. Mrs. Sunday stated that her husband got many of his best ideas for his sermons from reading advertisements.[23] He said that "God is in the greatest business there is," but he also maintained that "it takes more brains to sell goods than to make them." As a salesman Sunday advertised the virtues of his product with the aggressive assurance of the automobile dealer: "Jesus could go some; Jesus Christ could go like a six cylinder engine, and if you think Jesus couldn't, you're dead wrong."[24] Or, in terms of the vendor of patent medicines: "Have you got a boy who is a drunkard, a girl who is frivolous, friends who are going wrong, a husband or wife who is untrue? . . . There is only one who can remedy it, and that is Jesus Christ." His invitations to trail-hitting sometimes seemed to resemble nothing more than the huckstering urgency of a side-show barker: "Hurry, hurry, hurry," he would yell; "enter the kingdom of the Lord before it's too late."

Another source of criticism on the score of sacrilege was the prayers which Sunday delivered at the conclusion of his sermons. Moody, when praying from the platform, always said, "Let us pray" and bowed his head, but Sunday scarcely changed his tone of voice, and, when he began, "Now Jesus, you know . . ." or "Well, Jesus, isn't this a fine bunch here tonight? . . . ," audiences did not even realize that he had begun to pray.

Sunday's critics said that he was overly familiar with the Deity— a charge also leveled against Moody, who answered it by saying that he was not one-tenth as familiar with him as he would like to be. Sunday's defenders claimed, "He just talks with God." The truth was that he often yelled at God, though he apologized for doing so: "O God, you are not deaf. I did not yell because I thought you were, but so that people would hear." Many clergymen not only disliked his tone of voice and his failure to use "thee" and "thou" but also objected to his interrupting the reverential attitude of prayer to call attention to his own activities: "We had a grand meeting last night, Lord, when the crowd came down from Dicksonville (or what was that place, Rody?)" "Dickson City." "Dickson City, Lord, that's right. It was a great crowd."[25]

Even worse, Sunday's prayers were as full of slang as his sermons. "O Lord, there are a lot of people who step up to the collection plate at church and fan. And, Lord, there are always people sitting in the grandstand and calling the batter a mutt. He can't hit a thing, or he can't get it over the base, or he's an ice wagon on the bases, they say. O Lord, give us some coachers out at this Tabernacle so that people can be brought home to you. Some of them are dying on second and third base, Lord, and we don't want that." Most of his prayers were made up ad libitum, but it seemed unnecessarily crude for him to include in them the same type of applause-seeking humor and denunciation he used in his sermons. "Oh, say, Jesus, save that man down at Heron Lake that wrote that dirty black lie about me! You'll have a big job on your hands to do it, Lord, I'll tell you that before you begin—but go ahead. Better take along a pair of rubber gloves and a bottle of disinfectant, but if you can save him, Lord, I'd like to have you do it."[26]

By using sacrilegious humor, common slang, and commercial jargon, Sunday seriously alienated many of the most influential and respectable elements in American Protestantism. It was a severe blow to his self-esteem when, in 1915, President Hibben refused him permission to speak on the Princeton University campus (and not only because his son, William A. Sunday, Jr., was about to enter the Lawrenceville School preparatory to matriculation at Princeton). In 1876 Princeton had been so eager to hear Moody when he came to town that classes were suspended and President McCosh himself sat on Moody's platform and offered prayers for his success.

An official letter by Dean West of the Princeton Graduate School, written on behalf of President Hibben, explained that their distaste for Sunday's preaching was due not to its evangelical doctrine, which they heartily indorsed, but to Sunday's coarse and irreligious language. After quoting some of Sunday's sermons, Dean West said, "No decent person can read these quotations without shame; in the name of decency and of the purity and sanctity of our Christian faith, Princeton University positively refuses to approve of Mr. Sunday's performance as suitable for the edification of our students."[27] One of the "coarse" quotations mentioned by Dean West was this:

> Little girl you look so small,
>   Don't you wear no clothes at all?
> Don't you wear no chemise shirt?
>   Don't you wear no petty skirt?
> Don't you wear no underclothes
>   But your corset and your hose?

But the quotation which irritated the Princeton administration most was this treatment of the Bible in the manner of a cosmetic advertisement:

"And as He prayed the fashion of his countenance altered." Ladies, do you want to look pretty? If some of you women would spend less on dope, pazaza, and cold cream and get down on your knees and pray, God would make you prettier.

"Very funny, no doubt," said Dean West, "and very blasphemous."

Though Sunday's slang and acrobatics made the most immediate

178

impression on observers and roused the greatest criticism of his technique, these elements constituted only the minor aspects of his power as an orator and a demagogue. The purpose of his sermons was not merely to amuse or shock his hearers but to arouse them to the point of leaving their seats and coming down the aisle to make a public display of their agreement with the views he preached. To do this he had to be far more than an entertainer or a clown. He might present himself at the start of each sermon as the personification of the average or the common man, even as a rube, but, before he could expect people to take him seriously, he had to change character. He had to take on the role of an inspiring leader, a man whom men could respect and women love—whose command would be followed without a moment's hesitation.

One of Sunday's methods of building himself up was to play upon the crowd's love for a fight and to assume the part of the leading protagonist. No one, "not even Mr. Roosevelt himself," said one observer, "has insisted so much on his personal, militant masculinity." His well-cut clothes accentuated his slim, athletic figure, and he posed as the example, par excellence, of good health through clean living. "When I was young, I was physically weak," he said, paraphrasing another advertisement, "but through the YMCA and under the best physical directors, I now have as fine a physique as you ever saw." He was "the man who has real, rich, red blood in his veins instead of pink tea and ice water," and he informed young men, "I'm still pretty handy with my dukes." One undergraduate who heard him speak at the University of Pennsylvania wrote, "He appeared to me to be a man in every way, and by his sheer personality he made me strive to be all that is best in manhood."[28] To women he appealed as a preacher, a father, a husband, and a knight-errant who would defend American womanhood against all enemies.

This was, of course, Sunday's personification of the fighting saint. And, to establish the association of this warlike personality with the founder of Christianity, he declared that Jesus "was no dough-faced, lick-spittle proposition. Jesus was the greatest scrapper that ever lived." Born-again Christians were to mold themselves not in the image of Moody's humble saints who desired to be as nothing; Sunday repudiated the view that a Christian must be a "sort of dishrag proposition, a wishy-washy sissified sort of galoot that lets everybody make a doormat out of him. Let me tell you, the manliest man is the man who will acknowledge Jesus Christ."

In order to arouse his audiences to a fighting mood, Sunday

preached hate, not love. And the full weight of his hatred was directed against "the Devil's gang" who ran that "sum of all villainies," the saloon. "I hate it with a perfect hatred," he said, and he instilled his hate into the audience in his famous sermon on "Booze." This sermon epitomized his rhetorical technique; it contained all the invective, pathos, humor, and crusading zeal at his command, and invariably the audience crowded down the aisles at its conclusion.

The text of the "Booze Sermon" was the story of the Gadarene Swine.[29] Sunday began by likening the liquor interests to the "weasel-eyed, hog-jowled lobsters" who owned the swine and who were angry that " a long-haired fanatic from Nazareth" was attempting to ruin their hog business by casting devils out of some madman and into their herds, causing the hogs to run into the sea. "Jesus Christ was God's revenue officer," but "the hog interest" cried out, "You are hurting our business" and told him to leave the country. "That," said Sunday, "is the attitude of the liquor business toward the Church and State and Government and the preacher that has the backbone to fight the most damnable, corrupt institution that ever wriggled out of hell and fastened itself upon the public."

Then, to smooth possible political antagonism, Sunday asserted that, though he was "a temperance Republican," it was the Democrats who had, by 1914, driven booze out of Kansas, Georgia, Maine, Mississippi, North Carolina, North Dakota, Oklahoma, Tennessee, and West Virginia. It was not a matter of party politics: "it is simply a matter of decency and manhood. . . . It is prosperity against poverty, sobriety against drunkenness, honesty against thieving, heaven against hell."

As the sermon continued, Sunday's invective demolished one argument after another against Prohibition and at the same time built up the emotional tension from one climax to another. He asserted that Prohibition did not infringe upon "personal liberty"—particularly the personal liberty of the "patient, long-suffering wife" and children who had to bear the blows and curses of the man who drank. He used statistics to give an appearance of factuality and reasonableness; the taxpayers were not aided by the income from the liquor revenues because the cost of alcohol to the public in terms of wasted money and crime, after deducting this income, was over three billion fifty million dollars a year: "The average factory hand earns $450 a year, and it costs us $1,200 a year to support each of our whiskey criminals." He told true stories from "court records" to convince the farmer that his profit from the sale of corn to the brewer could not be measured against the suffering in human lives resulting from the whiskey brewed out of one bushel of corn. Intoxicated boys and men shot their friends, their mothers, babes in arms, and slew their wives with axes, as Sunday reviewed the records. Statistically, he even proved that business improved in states which prohibited the sale of alcohol.

Shifting from fact to fancy, Sunday launched forth in a panegyric of life in a dry state, where "a man can go from home in the morning with the kisses of wife and children on his lips" and come back sober at night. Then came the grim contrast with life in a "wet" state, where family life was wrecked because the saloon became "a rat hole for a wage-earner to dump his wages into." Then back to more facts to disprove the argument that the saloon could be better regulated by making saloonkeepers pay a high price for liquor licenses than by Prohibition: "You might as well try and regulate a powder mill in hell. . . . See how absurd their arguments are," and more statistics were heaped up.

The absurdity of the arguments gave rise to six paragraphs of virulent denunciation which indicted the saloon as a "coward," an "assassin," a "thief," an "infidel," a "liar," and an "anarchist." "It will steal milk from the breast of the mother . . . it will take virtue from your daughter . . . it would close every church in the land. It would hang its beer signs on the abandoned altars . . . it is waiting with a dirty blanket for the baby to crawl into the world . . . it sent the bullet through the body of Lincoln . . . Garfield . . . McKinley . . . it is the anarchist of the world, and its dirty red flag is dyed with the blood of women and children."

Sunday skilfully relaxed the tension after this preliminary climax by injecting a semihumorous dialogue between himself and "Colonel Politics," a pompous old windbag who blamed the country's depressions and corruptions on "the silver bugbear," "standpatism," "a revision of the tariff," "free trade." Sunday proved to the imaginary colonel's discomfort that all these political vagaries were as nothing compared to the evils of alcohol. "We dumped nearly four times the value of the national bank stock in the United States into the whisky hole last year."

After painting a dismal picture of a funeral procession three thousand miles long with 110,000 hearses containing the drunkards who die each year, Sunday said, "I stand in front of the jails and count the whisky criminals. They say, 'Yes, Bill, I fired the bullet'; 'Yes, I backed my wife into a corner and beat her life out; I am waiting for the scaffold'; 'I am waiting,' says another, 'to slip into hell.' On, on it goes. Say, let me summon the wifehood and the motherhood and the childhood [of America] and see the tears rain down their upturned faces. People, tears are too weak for that hellish business!" It was a fact, he went on, that "in an hour twelve men die drunkards, three hundred a day," in "the land of the free and the home of the brave," and they left behind "865,000 whisky orphan children."

"I hold a silver dollar in my hand," Sunday called. "Come on, we are going to a saloon." Then, for fifteen minutes, Sunday acted out the picturesque story of "John the drunkard," describing how a home filled "with squalor and want" was transformed into a home of sunshine and prosperity when John decided to get on the water wagon and spend his money for beefsteak, calico, and flour instead of for booze.

Building up to a new climax, Sunday described what would happen if all the drunkards got on the water wagon and began to spend their silver dollars on the staples of life. Soon Swift, Armour, Nelson Morris, and Cudahy would be out of meat, he said; Marshall Field, Carson Pirie Scott, and J. V. Farwell Company, would be out of calico; Pillsbury, Minneapolis, and "Sleepy Eye" would be out of flour. The national economy would enter on a perpetual boom, as farmers, packers, ranchers, plantation owners, factory workers, salesmen, all set to work to produce enough to supply the new demands.

Bitter humor was contrasted with this pleasant scene as Sunday personified a sawmill, a gristmill, a paper-mill, and a ginmill. In a dialogue between himself and these personifications he showed that each of the first three mills produced valuable products from raw materials. But the ginmill, when asked what its raw material was, said, "American boys." (Here ten little boys, neatly washed and dressed, appeared on the platform.) "Say, saloon ginmill," Sunday went on, "what is your finished product?" "Bleary-eyed, low-down, staggering men," came the answer. Sunday put his right hand on the head of the smallest of the boys lined up in front of him, and he shook his left fist in the air and shouted in a passionate, throbbing voice: "I would not give up one of these boys for every dirty dollar you get from the hell-soaked liquor business!"

As the boys left the stage, Sunday wrenched his audience from anger to tears with the pathetic story of a little crippled boy whose father was condemned to die and who asked a preacher to come to the jail and "pray for papa." The preacher asked why the father was in jail. "He murdered mama," said the little boy, sadly. "Papa was good and kind, but whisky did it, and now I have to support my three little sisters." The audience shook with sobs and rage.

Sunday felt the twenty thousand persons throbbing as a single mass before him. He stood up on the kitchen chair, leaned forward, and yelled, "I want every man to say 'God, you can count on me to protect my wife, my home, my mother, and my children and the manhood of America!'" And the crowd jumped to its feet screaming and waving its arms. It was five minutes before he could go on.

He started up again slowly, with more statistics to prove the folly of "high license" and the absurdity of the "personal liberty" argument. The repetition did not seem to matter. "I occasionally hear a man say, 'It's nobody's business how I live.' Then I say he is the most dirty, low-down, whisky-soaked, beer-guzzling, bull-necked, foul-mouthed, hypocrite. . . . If I heard a man beating his wife and heard her shrieks and the children's cries . . . I'd knock seven kinds of pork out of that old hog." He ridiculed the man who claimed to be "a moderate drinker" and showed, by a true story of a friend of his, the inevitable result of such foolish toying with danger.

As he neared the end of the sermon, Sunday aroused a sickening revulsion for booze by detailed descriptions of its effects upon the human body. It "knocks the blood corpuscles out of business." "Here's a fellow who drives a beer wagon. Look how pussy he is. He's full of rotten tissue. . . . You punch your finger into that healthy flesh he talks about and the dent will be there a half an hour afterward." With lurid adjectives he portrayed the corruption and decay of each organ of the body from the muscles and nerves to the stomach, liver, and kidney. "That's what booze is doing for you."

The peroration did not try to stampede men into the street to tear down the saloons but subtly turned their attention back to Sunday himself as he stood in his shirt sleeves, tired and perspiring, but still a fighting saint, bloody but unbowed. "I've stood for more sneers and scoffs and insults and had my life threatened from one end of the land to the other by this God-forsaken gang of thugs and cut-throats . . . there is no one that will reach down lower, or reach higher or wider to help you out of the pit of drunkenness than I."

Following the word "I" came the invitation to hit the trail. Usually Sunday was standing on top of the pulpit by this time, waving the flag as he called for volunteers to follow him into battle: "I want the inspiration of taking the hand of every fellow who says, 'I'm with you for Jesus Christ and for truth.' Come on, you've been mighty fine tonight!" As the trail-hitters streamed forward to shake the hand of their hero, the reporters heard them say, "Hurrah for you, Bill"; "I'm with you, Bill"; "Wish you luck, Bill"; "You're a gentleman, Bill."[30]

The "Booze Sermon" displayed Sunday's rhetorical technique at its most emotional pitch; it was the most extreme of all his sermons. But it contained none of the evangelical doctrine expounding the need and meaning of conversion, which was his principal purpose as an evangelist. One of his best doctrinal sermons was "The Three Groups," which drove home the urgency of reviving the church and the individual.[31] The text was from Matthew 26:22, and the sub-title of the sermon was "Lord, Is It I?" He began with a dramatic account of Jesus' entry into Jerusalem, the Last Supper, and the night in the Garden of Gethsemane:

> And the disciples went their way and found the colt tied in front of a house where two ways met, and there was a crowd of men loafing about the place, and if they were anything like the bunch in our day, they were whittling, cursing, chewing tobacco, discussing financial, political and all other public questions.
>
> The disciples began untying the colt, when one fellow who spit tobacco juice enough to drown a rabbit calls out, "Hey, there, what are you doing? What are you going to do with that colt?"
>
> The disciples call back, "The Lord hath need of him." So away they go with the colt.

The modernized and dramatized version of Matthew continued in the present tense until Sunday came to the scene in the garden, where he began an exegetical analysis of the difference between the positions of the three groups: the eight disciples near the edge of the garden; Peter, James, and John farther on; and, finally, Jesus, praying by himself. "The first group is analogous to the position of a large percentage of members in the average church today . . . so near the edge of the garden that they would have only a short distance to go to have been outside where Judas was with the scribes, Pharisees, and the mob." Then followed some examples of loyalty and a denunciation of the churches for being interested only in "dress, strife after wealth, and social life." An anecdote described how a hypocritical church member confessed her own sins and thus was able to convert her husband. "To be able to convict others of sin we must ourselves first get right with God."

Sunday next analyzed the difference in size of the three groups. Just as the largest group was the one farthest from Jesus, so in the twentieth-century church "you will find the largest number nearer

the card party and wine supper." Just as Daniel Webster found
plenty of room at the top of the legal profession, so "the nearer you
get to Jesus the more elbow room you will have." Then, with the
phrase, "please pardon a personal reference," Sunday began a long,
sentimental, and wholly irrelevant description of his departure from
home to an orphanage. Sunday's mother and brother prayed in this
time of trial, but the church members of today, he said, have forgotten how to pray. "Let's get cleaned up for God, and see if the
Lord won't do great things." Then, to change the mood, he gave his
parody of the hymn "Jesus Paid It All" and told a joke about a hypocritical funeral oration.

As the laughter from these jokes died away, Sunday paused and
then shouted, "Crucify Him!" and the audience was once again
plunged into a dramatic recital of the Gospel story. He described
"the relentless rabble" calling for Christ's death and told in horrified
tones of Judas' betrayal. With great detail, he lingered over the
agonies of the Crucifixion. "See, see . . . ," he cried, evoking the picture before their very eyes. Once again he was at a climax, and the
excited audience strained forward on the benches: "How many will
go with Jesus to the last ditch?" he asked, and they jumped to their
feet with a shout. But he was not yet done.

When the audience was seated again, Sunday began another denunciation of those whose "spiritual batting average is not up to
God's league standard." The concluding episode of the sermon was
a melodramatic story of a little boy who asked his father if he could
play on the river's edge while his father chopped trees in the near-
by woods. Suddenly an alligator appeared and swam toward the
boy. He was too terrified to move. "Hurry, papa, hurry," he cried in
his childish voice. "The hideous, amphibious, monster . . . lean, lank,
hungry, voracious" came closer. The boy floundered in the water.
The horror-stricken father, clutching his ax, rushed toward the
river. "Hurry, papa, hurry, the alligator has got me!" screamed the
little fellow. His father rushed into the water, his ax raised to sink
it into the head of the monster. The alligator swished its tail and disappeared; "the blood-flecked foam told the story." "O God," exclaimed Sunday, "what if that had been my boy!" He concluded,
"There are influences in this world worse than an alligator . . . intemperance, vice. Drunkards are crying to the church, 'Hurry faster,'
and the church members sit on the bank and play cards. . . . 'Hurry.'
. . . They are splitting hairs over fool things instead of trying to
keep sinners out of hell. Faster. Faster. Faster. 'Lord, is it I?' "

This was one of Sunday's better-constructed sermons. Fewer than fifteen in his repertoire attempted to develop a theme or exegesize a biblical passage so thoroughly. For the most part, he took some doctrinal subject, such as repentance, faith, heaven, or the atonement or some biblical character or incident as a point of departure for a series of illustrations, denunciations, jokes, quasi-autobiographical stories, statistics, and purple passages which were related only by the constant repetition of the text, if by that. As one Pittsburgh reporter summarized it: "His sermons are disconnected, irrelevant fragments of thought, strung together by invectives, recriminations, quaint stories, and punctuated always by a jumble of acrobatics."

Such differences as there were between Sunday's various sermons were more of emphasis than of subject matter, the emphasis shifting with the audience to which he spoke. Every sermon, he claimed, was written with a particular audience in mind during each stage of the revival. The sermons of the opening ten or twelve days were devoted to arousing the general interest of the community and particularly the regular churchgoers. These were his most sensational sermons, to draw the crowds.

After the first invitation for trail-hitting, Sunday began to hammer at church members, professing Christians, and those who went to church occasionally but did not belong to one. He urged them to "get in the game" and show their support of religion by coming forward at the outset of the campaign. Then, when the most impressionable churchgoers had been won, he divided his sermons between those who were still hesitant but who needed only a little more explanation of doctrinal points before coming forward and those non-churchgoers who did not realize that it was their duty to their family, their community, their country, and their God to join a church. It was here that he used his sermons against skeptics and agnostics.

Sunday did not give all his sensational sermons in the first two weeks of the campaign but kept some to scatter throughout whenever attendance flagged or the newspapers put him on the back pages. Sometimes he repeated the more popular sermons, such as those on "Booze," "The Sins of Society," and "The Home," giving them once to men only and the second time to women only.

As the campaign drew to a close, a note of fear and anxiety was introduced. The sermons bore such titles as "The Unpardonable Sin," "What Shall Be the End?" "How Shall We Escape?" "After Death, Judgment," and "No Second Chance." These awesome subjects were interspersed with more hopeful ones, such as "Not Far from the Kingdom," "God's Promises," and "Hope." The last sermon of each revival was, "And He Said, 'Tomorrow,'" which proved that tomorrow would be too late.

In co-ordinating his sermons to fit particular stages of the campaign, Sunday carefully played upon the fears and anxieties of each particular group. To the unconsecrated churchgoers his tone was one of injured sorrow at their lack of faith: "How little you are doing. Don't you feel ashamed? Aren't you looking for a knot hole to crawl through?" Churchgoers, of all people, he said, should remember what Jesus had suffered for them: "Then tell me why you are indifferent?" "You are robbing God when you spend time doing something that don't amount to anything when you might do something for Christ."

With audiences made up entirely of men or college boys Sunday was more firm. "Do not be so damnable and low-down" as to refuse to come forward, he said. "Are you fellows willing to slap Jesus Christ in the face in order to have someone come up and slap you on the back?" He challenged their courage: "Do you know why you haven't been down here [to shake hands]? You're not man enough. I throw it in your teeth. You're not man enough!" To audiences made up of women he mingled threats and cajolements. He told them that they owed it to their families to come forward, and he brought tears to their eyes with pictures of reunions with departed children and husbands in heaven. He frightened them with the thought that God might "back up a white hearse at your door and take away that baby you are not fit to bring up." Those who did not hit the trail were accused of harboring some hidden, guilty sin: "Has something come into your life, some secret sin, some unholy passion?" All his auditors were warned that "God sees everything. God is writing a book of every life." And they were offered rewards: "Live the Christian life. Men will admire you; women will respect you; little children will love you, and God will crown your life with success."

Whether his calls were directed to one particular part of his audience or whether they were generalized so as to include all "right-thinking," "decent" people, the immediate results of Sunday's pulpit technique were amazingly successful. The sermons carried people by the hundreds out of their seats and down the aisles, though exactly why they went few could say. They liked Sunday; they agreed with what he said; they were in favor of "decency"; they were aroused and wanted "to do something about" wickedness.

The trail-hitter did not know why the shouting of certain words like "mother," "home," "children," "America," "God," "Christ," "blood," "cutthroats," and "fight" made him grow tense and fearful. He only knew that, when the sermon ended, he felt an uncontrollable urge to follow Sunday's commands, to get up and go forward to find "peace," "hope," "assurance," "love," and a warm handshake of comradeship in the battle of life; he felt that by going forward he would come close to a man who wanted to help him, a strong, confident, successful man, who would lead him to comfort, security, respect, and friendship. This strong voice said, "Who will join me? Who will join me and say, 'Here is my hand, and I'm with you in this proposition to live for Jesus Christ.' Come on, if you will. Every man and woman in the building! Everybody rise! Come on! Come on! How many of you will?"[32]

Many ministers and laymen asked themselves this same question before supporting a Billy Sunday revival: "How many will come?" As far as the numerical total of trail-hitters was concerned, Sunday's backers were never disappointed. They might throughly disagree with Sunday's methods of getting them to come, but they were more interested in getting them than in how they were gotten. For the Protestant churches in the big cities faced a serious crisis both in finances and in membership at the turn of the century. If Sunday could pull them out of it, they would hold their peace about his vulgarity, his acrobatics, and even about his blasphemy. But, when the trail-hitting statistics were examined, how many who came stayed, and who were they? It took the churches over twenty years to assess correctly the significance of Billy Sunday's revivalism.

6

"THE HALFWAY HOUSE"

In the year 1910 Ray Stannard Baker, one of the most forthright muckrakers of his day, was doing research for his book *The Spiritual Unrest,* and, after talking with clergymen all over the nation about the critical situation facing the Protestant churches, he came to the ironic conclusion that, "if it were possible to sum up in a few words the one thing that has most impressed me in visiting churches and talking with church leaders in various parts of the country, I think I should say: 'The utter confusion of counsel among the church leaders themselves.'"[1] Everyone was aware of the seriousness of the churches' plight, but no two churchmen could agree on the proper method of dealing with it.

"The problem," as it was usually stated, was how "to evangelize the masses," though the definition of the "masses" was uncertain. When Moody launched the Student Volunteer movement in 1886 to recruit missionaries from the college campuses, the organization adopted as its inspirational motto "the evangelization of the world in our generation"; but twenty-five years later almost every major denomination was reducing the proportion of its funds for foreign missions in order to increase the funds for missionary work at home. "The battle today," warned a Baptist minister in 1907, "is in the larger cities," and he went so far as to propose that his denomination eliminate "superfluous" rural churches in the United States so that more money could be spent on urban evangelization.[2]

Eight years later, in 1915, the Methodists were still making the same complaint: "The two chief problems facing the churches in New England are the rural communities and the alien populations."[3] In reality, these were merely two aspects of the same problem, and it was not limited either to the Methodists or to New England. The nation as a whole, according to the best available statistics, was undergoing a serious religious slump. Not that the church membership did not continue to grow; but it was growing at a very much slower pace than it had in the post–Civil War decades.

The *Report of the Statistics of the Churches in the United States* (issued by the federal government and commonly referred to as the "United States Religious Census") stated in 1890 that Protestant church membership had increased in the years 1880–90 by 42.05 per cent, while the population in that same decade had increased by only 24.86 per cent. In 1912, however, Charles Stelzle, superintendent of the Bureau of Social Service of the Board of Home Missions of the northern wing of the Presbyterian church, analyzed the church statistics for the years 1900–1910 and discovered that the Protestant church membership had increased only 21 per cent—exactly the same as the rate of increase of the national population in that decade. Stelzle published this "alarming" information with the challenging comment: "Holding its own, or 'Evangelizing the World' —WHICH?"[4]

The figures were even more alarming when analyzed according to the density of population. Here the real battle in the cities became apparent. For, while the population was increasing in the cities much more rapidly than in the rural areas, the proportion of church members was not increasing nearly so fast. For example, the federal statistics compiled in 1890 and in 1916 show that over this twenty-six-year period the proportion of Protestant church members in the country as a whole increased from 20.6 per cent of the population to 25.9 per cent, but in twenty of the nation's largest cities the proportion of Protestants in the population increased only from 17.2 per cent in 1890 to 19.7 per cent in 1916.[5] It was not surprising that these twenty cities eventually called for Billy Sunday's services in the years 1913–18, especially since in over one-third of them (marked with asterisks in the tabulation on the next page) the proportion of Protestants actually decreased between 1890 and 1916.

Equally shocking to many clergymen was the decrease in the number of churches. In view of the great exodus from rural to urban areas, it was understandable that some country churches should become "superfluous" and have to close; but what possible justification could there be for a decrease of churches in New York City? Ray Stannard Baker listed seventy-two churches and missions in downtown New York which "moved uptown or perished" between 1867 and 1907. The United States Religious Census for 1916 revealed that the total number of Protestant edifices in Manhattan decreased from 385 in 1890 to 323 in 1916. Yet during this same time the population of Manhattan increased by 50 per cent, or roughly 800,000 people.

Sunday was correct in stating that "the downtown church is a passing proposition." Charles Stelzle bitterly wrote in his autobiography in 1926: "The churches thus practically confessed that they could only live when they followed the well-to-do to the uptown districts or the suburbs." The downtown minister had to confess that, despite the increasing city population, he was preaching to empty pews. He complained that his board of trustees forced him "to cut his expenses to fit his cloth" or to sell the church property altogether and build anew uptown. Federal statistics on the finan-

City	Year of Sunday Revival	Percentage of Protestant Communicants	
		1890	1916
Columbus	1913	18.1	29.0
Scranton	1914	13.3	26.9
*Denver	1914	14.9	13.2
Pittsburgh	1914–15	20.1	24.7
Paterson	1915	15.2	18.0
Syracuse	1915	17.0	20.2
Omaha	1915	7.8	14.5
Philadelphia	1915	15.9	19.2
Trenton	1916	17.5	24.1
Kansas City, Mo.	1916	15.0	23.0
*Detroit	1916	16.9	15.3
Baltimore	1916	22.1	22.4
*Boston	1916–17	12.7	11.9
Buffalo	1917	16.0	17.5
*Atlanta	1917	36.3	34.8
*New York (Manhattan)	1917	8.9	8.6
*Los Angeles	1917	22.0	13.4
Chicago	1918	11.5	12.1
Washington, D.C.	1918	25.2	28.6
*Providence	1918	17.4	16.5
Average		17.2	19.7

* See text.

cial plight of the average downtown church make it clear that the financial problem was intimately related to the membership problem.

Although the value of church property in the United States increased 34 per cent in the years 1906–16, the total debt on church property increased 53 per cent. In cities with populations of 50,000–100,000 the debt increased 84 per cent, while the values increased only 43 per cent. The increased value of the property was merely an incentive to sell before the debts got even more out of proportion. Taking out a mortgage on the strength of the increased valuation merely postponed the day of reckoning and increased the debt. The wealthy trustees who had to make up out of their own pockets what the churches failed to gather in contributions from the few members who still came were too business-like to throw good money after bad in a shrinking market.

The bitter truth was that the churches had taken sides in the nation's social and economic transformation. They had sided with the well-to-do, the successful, the victors in the battle for the survival of the fittest. Now they had no choice but to go where these people went and do as these people suggested, if they wished to survive in an opulent, debt-free fashion. The churches had let their code of hard work, sobriety, thrift, honesty, and piety harden into an economic dogma—a justification, almost a sanctification, of laissez faire capitalism. They had preached what their wealthy members wanted to hear and had shut their eyes to the consequences. They opened their eyes in 1910 to find to their surprise that there was "a gulf between the church and the masses."

At the same historical moment, the god of science was rapidly taking the place of the God of the Bible. Almost without a fight the clergy abdicated their positions as the expositors of a universe governed by the personal words of a personal God and helped to enthrone the scientists as interpreters and administrators of a universe governed by "natural" laws inexplicably attributable to an abstract, remote, and virtually unknowable (although presumably benevolent) "Being." What need could there be for churches in a nation obviously chosen of God to progress by the scientific laws of evolution to ultimate perfection? A few ministers, in defiance, declared war on science and all its findings, but these were no more successful in stemming the tide of secularism than the ministers who limited themselves to the narrow field of expounding middle-class morality from the pulpit for one hour every Sunday morning.

The vast majority of the American people either joined a church perfunctorily or visited the nearest one on Christmas and Easter without bothering to join at all. The membership figures continued to climb numerically as the century progressed, but at a slower and slower rate. It seemed to many church leaders that the statistical summaries of the second decade might well show the figures taking a downward trend. It was an appalling thought after a century of steady, in fact, of precipitous, advance. Smarting from the stinging rebukes of liberals and muckrakers, most ministers wanted a re-examination of the churches' role in twentieth-century society; might there not be, they asked, some way whereby the churches could broaden their appeal without essentially altering their doctrine?

Evangelism was a natural recourse of the churches in this situation. In its simplest terms it meant winning new members, and that was considered the root of the problem. The question was, how? By what possible means could huge cities like Boston, Chicago, and New York be "evangelized"? Moody, Mills, Torrey, and Chapman had made a profession of answering this question, but their answers were not satisfactory. A minister writing in a New England religious journal in 1910, the year after Chapman held his most elaborate simultaneous revival in Boston, stated under the heading "Our Problem Today" that "the prevailing forms of evangelism are not as effective as they used to be." Few evangelists, he said, could "more than scratch the surface of the cities." The problem was to find a new method and a new prophet, he said wistfully: "For such a leader the church is waiting."[6]

There were some ministers in the central part of the United States who thought they had found such a leader: "Several groups of churches, chiefly in the Middle West," reported Ray Stannard Baker on his tour of the country, "under the spirited leadership of men of the type of Billy Sunday, have dashed into Revivalism and by means of the old-fashioned emotionalism have stemmed for the moment the tide of the attack." But many churchmen in other parts of the country seriously doubted in 1910 whether Billy Sunday was the leader they needed to re-establish the churches' waning prestige. "Old-fashioned emotionalism" to most urban clergymen, particularly in the East, was decidedly the wrong kind of evangelism. They wanted something new, not something old; they wanted a solution of their problem in urban terms, not in the provincial terms of the frontier. None of them took seriously Sunday's claim that he had already converted 300,000 people, and when Lindsay Denison reported in the *American Magazine* in 1907 that Sunday employed Barnum and Bailey circus freaks to attract attention to his revivals, that was all the ministers of Boston, New York, and Baltimore wanted to hear about that particular evangelistic method.

It was six years from the date of Denison's article, three years after Baker's *Spiritual Unrest*, before the large cities which were suffering from the strains of the membership and financial crises in the churches were ready to accept Billy Sunday as the answer to their problem. The process by which Sunday was transformed from a self-seeking clown into a God-appointed leader can be traced in dozens of religious journals which managed to do a complete about-face in their attitude toward him. The confusion of counsel gradually changed into a single triumphant "Eureka" as the church leaders sought the easiest way out of their dilemma.

The path of eastern opinion can be readily charted in the *Watchman-Examiner* of Boston, which was typical. In 1907 this Baptist weekly, though it considered Sunday's work "significant," spoke of him as an evangelist who "outrages every accepted canon of religious worship." In 1911 it referred to him as "the baseball evangelist who plays havoc with all the staid religious proprieties," but it admitted that he "appears to have the warm-hearted approval of our strong and level-headed pastors wherever he has been." In 1913 the magazine printed a long article on Sunday's Columbus campaign by one of these strong, "level-headed" pastors who had co-operated in it: A. E. Isaac wrote that "three years ago when asked what I thought of Billy Sunday I said I had little use for him and believed he was only a cheap sensationalist." Then he heard Sunday deliver his "Booze Sermon" and was so impressed that he joined his colleagues in inviting Sunday to Columbus. Now that the campaign was over and 18,000 persons had hit the trail (over two hundred of whom joined Isaac's church), Isaac was "thoroughly convinced that God was working through him."

But still the editor remained skeptical. In 1914 he said that he seriously doubted whether "the Lord really puts the stamp of His approval upon a presentation of the Gospel that is mingled with coarseness and vulgarity." Finally, in the spring of 1914, the editor heard Sunday speak in Carnegie Hall; he was overcome with admiration and reported that "no man who heard him doubted his profound sincerity or questioned his tremendous power." Soon the *Watchman-Examiner* was publishing Sunday's sermons, quoting his "Sundayisms," and doing its utmost to stir up enthusiasm for an invitation to bring Sunday to Boston. Now Sunday was clearly "sent of God," and "whose business is it but God's if He chooses to use Billy Sunday and to pass some of us by?" To criticize Sunday was to criticize God.

It did not take all easterners so long to change their minds about Sunday and to rush to him as the answer to their problems, but roughly the same reassessment was made by dozens of others in the years 1907–14. By 1915 only the most recalcitrant still held out against the general acclaim. In a poll of the religious press taken by the *Literary Digest* that year, 99 out of 127 journals gave either

"Rodey" Plays the Trombone, Too, and Billy Keeps Very Still.

Homer A. Rodeheaver, Sunday's choir leader, with Sunday, as they appeared to the staff artist of the *Boston Herald* in November, 1916.

Billy Sunday and Douglas Fairbanks, Sr. Taken in 1918, when the two celebrities took part in an exhibition baseball game to raise funds to buy sports equipment for the American soldiers in France. (*Underwood and Underwood.*)

wholehearted or qualified support to Sunday's revivalism. The twenty-eight dissenting voices were almost entirely those of Catholic, Jewish, Unitarian, Universalist, Lutheran, and Episcopalian editors.

This revolution in clerical attitude was not due to any alteration by Sunday in his message or his methods; it took some time for the knowledge of his "progressive orthodoxy" to spread eastward, but the real causes of his final acceptance by eastern church leaders were, rather, the increasing state of anxiety in the churches and a growing tolerance of pulpit sensationalism.

Dating from the era of Henry Ward Beecher's slave auctions in Plymouth Church, Brooklyn, in the 1850's, an increasing amount of sensationalism had crept into evangelical church services in the cities. It was usually justified, as in Beecher's case, by the fact that it aroused interest in a worthy cause. The same excuse was made by T. DeWitt Talmage for his diatribes against the theater and other sins of modern society in the 1870's and by the Rev. Charles Parkhurst for his crusades against prostitution and political corruption in New York in the 1890's. With varying degrees of fanatical zeal, self-aggrandizement, and sheer exhibitionism, other city ministers followed this pattern. Men like Russell H. Conwell, Theodore Cuyler, Newell Dwight Hillis, S. Parkes Cadman, A. Z. Conrad, A. K. DeBlois, Christian Reisner, and Cortland Myers found that sensational preaching and vigorous self-advertisement filled their pews and attracted attention. What these orthodox preachers lacked in twentieth-century social and theological enlightenment they made up for by a thorough knowledge of twentieth-century publicity techniques.

Such preachers were praised by the religious press for making their sermons dynamic, for filling their churches, for their virility and their efficiency. While the *Watchman-Examiner* was still hesitant about indorsing Sunday's "coarseness and vulgarity," it praised the ingenuity and talent of a Cambridge minister who filled his church every Sunday night by giving "Drama Sermons," in which he enacted such scenes as the effect of regeneration on a drunkard's home or the conversion of a hardhearted rich man. The old type of sermon on "Purity" or on "Hypocrisy" no longer attracted attention in 1914, wrote one minister in an article entitled "Sensational Preaching": "The ordinary man of the street, as our Sunday evening congregations—or lack of congregations—abundantly prove, cannot be reached by the truth, as a rule, unless his attention is hit by something out of the ordinary." Consequently, said this preacher, "I commend the wise use of sensationalism."[7] By 1916, with Sunday's Boston campaign in the offing, the *Watchman-Examiner*, speaking for all the Baptists, declared: "As a denomination we believe in enthusiastic, red-hot evangelism."

Not only had the clergy changed their views toward sensationalism, but the church members themselves, especially the more successful businessmen among them, had come to feel that the churches could profit by taking a few hints from the world of commerce. They were impressed by Sunday's view of himself as an efficiency expert for the churches.

Since the time of his shift from tent to tabernacle evangelism, Sunday had sedulously paid more court to the laity than to the clergy. His campaigns in the big cities were business enterprises with practical ends and tangible dividends, and he presented them as such to those whose support he needed. John D. Rockefeller, Jr., when interviewed after the Sunday campaign in New York, began by praising the interdenominational co-operation in terms which might well have been used by his father: "In competing sects—as in competing businesses—there is naturally a great wastage of effort. In this campaign all sectional lines were forgotten." He then went on to point out the many religious activities which took place during the revival, but he added: "If the work stopped right there—which it will not—I would consider that a piece of bad business. The expense of the campaign was about $200,000, all of which was raised by public and private contributions. Let us call that our investment. It would not do for us to stop and fail to collect our dividend. That is what we will do in the future. We will be collecting this dividend, I believe, for years in the future."[8]

More than any other aspect of Sunday's revivals, the fact that they were efficiently handled in the financial sense and that they produced "dividends" in the form of new converts served to overcome the scruples of the respectable businessman in regard to Sunday's sensationalism. According to one pastor, Sunday's revivals, in their management and their message, taught the important lesson that the "churches must be run so as to show a profit if they want the respect of the businessman."[9]

For those seeking a simple, ready-made solution to the church crisis the proof that Sunday could "produce results" was copious and seemingly indisputable. For those not convinced by statistics there were numerous leading churchmen and businessmen ready and willing to recommend Sunday. Respected laymen like William

Jennings Bryan, William Allen White, Bruce Barton, Henry J. Allen, Frank Munsey, and Arthur Brisbane wrote in praise of him. Among churchmen, Bishop Luther B. Wilson, Bishop Joseph Berry, Charles L. Goodell, and Russell Conwell were particularly enthusiastic. The testimony of ministers like the Rev. A. E. Isaac, the Rev. Maitland Alexander, and the Rev. Thomas A. Fenton, all of whom told of the tangible results which Sunday's campaigns brought to their churches, was especially convincing. "The Billy Sunday campaign in Syracuse did this for Dr. Thomas A. Fenton, a Presbyterian leader in the campaign," reported the *Watchman-Examiner* to its readers: "It brought his church an addition of 305 members . . . a beautiful $20,000 home . . . increase of $600 in salary . . . two weeks added to his vacation."

As a result of Sunday's campaign in New Castle, Pennsylvania, said the Rev. A. B. McCormick, "our churches are in a prosperous condition. Two large buildings are in process of erection. Four churches have been enlarged. Several others have been repaired and redecorated. Four have purchased new organs. Others have paid debts of long standing. A new hundred thousand dollar YMCA has been erected. . . . A Rescue Mission has been established."

Such reports made many ministers ridiculously eager to obtain Sunday's help. "Why, my dear Sir," exclaimed the Rev. Pearse Pinch, of Fairfield, Iowa, to Lindsay Denison, "the man has trampled all over me and my theology. He has kicked my teachings up and down that platform like a football. He has outraged every ideal I have had regarding my sacred profession. But what does that count against the results he has accomplished? My congregation will be increased by hundreds."[10]

The Rev. Mr. Pinch was almost a caricature of all those gullible, inadequate, and unsuccessful pastors who in their perplexity turned to Sunday. With pathetic hopefulness they clung to the coattails of the wealthy businessmen and the aggressive, publicity-conscious, successful pastors and climbed on the Billy Sunday band wagon. The Rev. Frederick W. Betts, of Syracuse, painted a sorry picture of these ineffective and discouraged ministers.

As a Universalist, Betts had no sympathy for Sunday's evangelism, but he had a great deal of sympathy for his fellow-ministers who joined together in 1915 to invite Sunday to the city. Writing in the *Universalist Leader*, Betts declared that they had turned to Sunday "because they had grown into a definite conviction of the impotence and failure of themselves and their churches."[11] "Not once, or twice, or ten times," said Betts, "but fifty or a hundred times during the past few years in our discussions at the meetings of the Ministers' Association, or in personal confidence at the lunch table afterward, have I listened to statements and discovered minor keys of thought which revealed the fact that the ministers were conscious that they were making only a very small impression upon the community outside the very limited congregations of most of their churches. Some of the confessions of personal inability to reach 'the people' or 'the crowd' have been really pathetic. They were anxious, over-anxious, for anyone who could reach and win the great outside multitude and bring them into the church."

Betts noted also the heavy pressure of financial insecurity. "They wanted and needed, and they still need, a great increase in financial resources." There was a "severe financial pinch" and a "very uncertain" future for many churches in Syracuse unless something was done quickly. Sunday and some of his advance men played upon this fear in their negotiations with ministers. Betts had occasion to hear the inducement offered by one advance man to promote an invitation. "One of the reiterated arguments of the managers of Mr. Sunday's campaign has been this promise of increased pew holders and financial prosperity." In the face of this anxiety, this grasping at straws amidst the "dismal sense of failure," Betts remarked, "a member of one church said to me, 'We expect ——— members from the Sunday meetings.'" (He mentioned a large number.) "And in a moment came the comment, 'We have a big financial load to carry in our church.'"

No objective interpretation of the true effect of a Sunday campaign could take place in an atmosphere of emotional fanaticism. The extravagant publicity, sensational headlines, the evanescent quality of a revival, often obliterated the facts before they could be recorded. Still, an observer not blinded by the bitterness of partisanship could have discovered enough information about the results of a Sunday campaign to cast serious doubts upon its effectiveness in solving the problems of church membership and debt.

Sunday's early reputation was built upon his success in rural towns and comparatively small cities, and here there was no doubt that his success was genuine. In some places, like Audubon and Jefferson, Iowa, between 60 and 75 per cent of the trail-hitters actually joined a church. The average number of trail-hitters was small, only about 700 or 800 per revival in the first ten years of his career; but then the towns themselves were small, and this figure frequently constituted 25 or 30 per cent of a town's inhabitants.

The available statistics for Sunday's early campaigns show that his proportionate effect upon a community varied inversely with the size of its population. In the towns of under 5,000 which he visited from 1896 to 1906 Sunday's converts averaged 20 per cent of the population in each. In cities of 5,000–10,000 he converted 19 per cent of the population; in the few larger cities of 10,000–40,000 which he attempted in these years his preaching netted only 10 per cent. In the period from 1907 to 1918 his technique improved, but it reached the point of diminishing returns when he tried to revive cities of over 30,000. The statistics were readily attainable during these years of nation-wide publicity, and, if they had been investigated, they would have told their own story:

Population	Trail-Hitters
Under 30,000	22%
30,000–50,000	15
50,000–100,000	13
100,000–500,000	9
Over 500,000	4

These percentages for the 1907–18 period are based on trail-hitting totals and are not, as in the 1896–1906 period, necessarily an indication of how many joined a church. It would probably be a fair estimate that, over the whole of the earlier period, approximately 40 per cent of those who walked down the aisle eventually found their way into some church. But it could have been logically assumed, had the clergy wished to be logical, that the anonymity of a revival in a large city would considerably reduce the results in terms of new church members. In a small town, where everyone knew his neighbor, it was a major and almost irreversible step for an individual to come down the aisle under the eyes of family, friends, employer, and prospective pastor. But this was certainly not the case in a big city, where the trail-hitting was much more apt to be a spur-of-the-moment affair which the individual and the crowd soon forgot even if some did happen to know the name of the presumed convert. In small-town newspapers the name of each trail-hitter was often published for all to see; in the larger cities only an anonymous figure appeared in the press.

Ministers who gullibly accepted the statistics published in the newspapers after each Sunday campaign were shocked and confused when the revival in their own city did not measure up to optimistic

199

expectations. The newspapers reported the usual high figures of trail-hitters or converts each night, but when the hopeful co-operating minister hurried to the tabernacle the next morning to pick up the decision cards for his church, he was woefully disappointed to find that, out of the hundreds of converts reported in the paper from the previous day's meetings, he was fortunate if there were half-a-dozen cards waiting for him.

To his sorrow the minister began to realize that the newspapers were more interested in making sensational headlines with their conversion total than in giving an accurate account of the meetings. No two newspapers in the same city carried the same trail-hitting totals, for the simple reason that no official count was made; each newspaper man made his own guess as to how many came forward, and for the sake of his story he guessed generously.

The press was equally careless in differentiating between trail-hitters, converts, and card-signers. An accurate count of card-signers could have been obtained each day, but, since it was so much lower than the number of trail-hitters, few newspapers bothered to publish it. In small cities and towns in the Midwest the correlation between card-signers and trail-hitters was closer than in larger cities, but in the latter the difference was occasionally as large as 50 per cent. A reliable comparison of these statistics is available for only nine of the sixty-five cities visited by Sunday in the years 1907–18, but they confirm the inference:

City	Year of Revival	Trail-Hitters	Card-Signers
Wilkes-Barre	1913	16,584	11,315
Philadelphia	1915	41,724	34,479
Syracuse	1915	21,155	18,419
Kansas City	1916	25,646	20,646
Detroit	1916	27,109	26,450
Boston	1917	64,484	48,903
Buffalo	1917	38,853	32,258
New York	1917	98,269	65,942
Providence	1918	10,119	5,828

The discrepancy was due in part to the inefficiency of the tabernacle "secretaries," or personal workers, in failing to get each trail-hitter to sign a card or in not seeing to it that the addresses on the cards were legibly written; many of the trail-hitters refused to sign a card or did not return the card after they had signed it. In addition, many of the cards which were signed were useless because they were filled out by visitors from "outside the area of the cooperating churches." Saturday, in most campaigns, was called "Out-of-Town-Day" at the tabernacle, and, though the trail-hitting figures were considerably larger than on any other day (except Sunday), the co-operating ministers reaped little benefit from them. The official report of the New York campaign listed almost 40 per cent of the total cards signed as "Out of Town." In Boston 10,281 out of 48,903 cards were in this category. The proportion was significantly high in other cities for which there are statistics: Buffalo, 23 per cent; Kansas City, 22 per cent; Syracuse, 18 per cent; Detroit, 15 per cent; Providence, 13 per cent.[12]

Still, the co-operating minister who received six or seven cards each day for the fifty or sixty days of trail-hitting in a campaign could have sizably increased his congregation had it not been for the fact that the cards bore the names of so many of his own church members who had merely come forward to check the word "Reconsecration" on the decision card. The Rev. C. D. Case commented upon his cards in the Buffalo campaign: "Speaking for my own church as an illustration, about half the cards signed are those of church members, and not, as I had anticipated, of the indifferent, but of the most conscientious workers of the church."[13] Reports from other ministers were the same. In Kansas City "one-third to one-half" of the 20,646 cards were marked "Reconsecration."

The New York editor of the *Watchman-Examiner* said that seven-ninths of the trail-hitters in that city were "active Christian workers" and blamed it on Sunday's trail-hitting invitations for not being "clearer and more definite." "It is a pity," he said, "that he does not say some such word as this, 'Let those who are not church members and who want this hour to confess Christ as their Saviour and King come forward and give me their hand.'" The editor admitted however, that if Sunday did this, it "would greatly decrease the number of trail-hitters."

Sunday made no secret of the fact that he wanted church members to hit the trail, and there were some ministers who claimed that the reconsecrated members were just as valuable as the new converts. Reconsecration provided "an opportunity for the intensification of religious life and activity," said one pastor. But to the average co-operating minister this was not the result anticipated. That he did not foresee it, however, when he agreed to close his church on Sundays so that his members could attend the tabernacle services was attributable only to blind faith and wishful thinking.

It took only a slight examination of the remainder of his cards for

201

the minister to discern that many of them would prove equally un-rewarding. A large proportion of them contained the names of the children in his Sunday school who had come to the special "Chil-dren's Meetings" or of teen-agers who came to the tabernacle on "Young People's Night." These youngsters were enthusiastic trail-hitters, but either they were too young to be accepted as regular church members or, if acceptable, they were hardly financial assets. Moreover, most of them would have become church members any-way in the course of a few years; as it was, Billy Sunday, not the minister or Sunday-school teacher, got the credit for their conver-sion. The Rev. C. D. Case of Buffalo found that "half the remainder" of his cards, after deducting the 50 per cent which were his own church members, were signed by children. Over one-third of the trail-hitters in Omaha were children, according to the *Omaha Bee*. In Columbus 3,000 out of 18,000 were children; in Scranton, 2,500 out of 17,000; and in Atlanta, 1,100 out of 15,000.

Having weeded out 60–75 per cent of his cards, the minister was still far from obtaining the new members he needed. Searching out card-signers was not the triumphant task which he had imagined it to be. Many cards did not list any specific church or pastoral prefer-ence. They merely gave a denominational preference for Methodism, Congregationalism, Presbyterianism, or some other sect. These cards were given to the co-operating minister of that denomination whose church was nearest to the address of the card-signer. Out of 17,540 cards signed for evangelical denominations in Detroit, 4,380 were in this category. The proportion was typical of most cities.

But this was not so unpromising as cards which did not even indi-cate a denominational preference. This group of trail-hitters, who might legitimately be classed as converts to Sundayism rather than to any particular evangelical denomination, often outnumbered the converts to some of the major denominations. In New York the 3,971 "undesignated" cards, those on which the church preference was left blank, outnumbered both the Baptists and the Congregationalists, who obtained only 3,023 and 1,022, respectively. In Boston the "un-designated" outranked the Presbyterians 2,887 to 2,284. They to-taled 3,535 in Buffalo, where the number of cards giving preference for specific evangelical denominations came to only 16,457. They outnumbered the Congregationalists in Detroit and Kansas City and the Disciples in Atlanta and Providence. Such persons were poor prospects. A minister, to win their allegiance, would have had to out-Sunday Sunday fifty-two weeks in the year. And not many churches could compete with the tabernacle services in terms of music, entertainment, and enthusiastic spirit.

The ultimate frustration for the co-operating minister, after running all over the city to find his card-signers, was the discovery that many of the cards contained erroneous or false addresses, false names, or else, as frequently happened, the signer had moved away before he could be reached, leaving no new address.

The Sunday executive committee often hired an associate expert recommended by the Sunday party, who was paid to organize the "follow-up" work. Frequently members of the party stayed on during the week between their campaigns to help. Sunday's advance agents made a great fuss over the efficiency of this work and offered detailed suggestions on how each individual trail-hitter should be personally visited and encouraged to become an active member. But all this proved to be vain and empty promises in view of the material which the cards provided. The follow-up work, in the end, depended entirely upon the minister to whom the cards were given or upon the church members whom he assigned to visit the card-signers.

Few ministers cared to put down in writing a detailed account of their bitter experience in following up their cards, but one pastor did so. The Rev. Daniel H. Martin, of the Fort Washington Presbyterian Church in uptown New York, received 273 cards from the Sunday campaign. Dr. John S. Allen assisted him in following up these cards and made the following reports four months after the campaign ended:

Already active church members	174
Were out whenever called upon or had moved	20
Not known at the address given	19
Fictitious addresses	12
Church members in other towns	11
In the Sunday schools	8
Nonchurch members but frequent attenders (three of these promised to join the church)	12
Had never been to church (four promised to join; six promised to attend some service)	17
Total	273

Out of 273 cards, Martin obtained seven promises of membership, which, after four months, were still unfulfilled.[14]

The Rev. Theodore F. Savage, also of New York, had similarly small success: "As I recall, I received between 100 and 150 cards of those who were undoubtedly statistically reported as converted.

Many of these were wrong names and addresses. The majority, however, were perfectly good members of my church or of some other church in the neighborhood. . . . I followed up all the names of people whom I did not know. As far as I can recall, not a single acquisition came to my church as a result of all this campaign."[15]

In Philadelphia the Rev. Urban C. Gutelius, of the "moderate-sized" Grace Reformed Church, found the net return for his cooperation in the campaign was only three or four members. The Rev. D. H. Edwards, of the Church of the Redeemer in Paterson, stated some years after the revival that not one of Sunday's converts "made good as a member" in his church. Of the 5 per cent of his card-signers who joined the Rev. John Briggs's Baptist church in Washington, D.C., only "a fair number" made good as members; in talking with other pastors, Briggs learned that their experience was the same. Only nine of the seventy-two cards which the Rev. Charles R. Zahniser received in Pittsburgh were new converts.

But for every minister whose discouraging report was published in the years 1907–18 there was another eager to boast of the astounding success which he had achieved. The Rev. Frank Smith, of the First Congregational Church of Kansas City, reported that he received 197 cards, out of which 53 joined his church. In addition, 107 other persons joined his church during or shortly after the revival; Smith credited Sunday with increasing his church membership from 900 to 1,060. The Rev. Cortland Myers, of Tremont Temple, Boston, received 1,000 cards, of which he claimed that half were "a good bunch" and that within two weeks after the campaign eighty had joined his church. The Rev. A. E. Isaac spoke of three pastors in Columbus who, within a year after Sunday's campaign, had taken in, respectively, 311, 400, and 500 new members. John Wanamaker's two churches, Bethany and Bethany Temple in Philadelphia, reported 343 new members between them during the year following Sunday's campaign. The Rev. Harry C. Rogers' Linwood Boulevard Presbyterian Church in Kansas City received 259 new members shortly after Sunday's revival there, and in Spokane the First Methodist Church reported 360 new members the week after Sunday left. The Syracuse South Presbyterian Church of the Rev. John M. MacInnis took in 349 members, 342 of whom were still active four years later. The Rev. Maitland Alexander told ministers far and wide of the 419 members added to his First Presbyterian Church in Pittsburgh.

Such outstanding gains received wide publicity, but they did so not because they were typical but precisely because they were such exceptional cases. The explanation for the tremendous success of three or four churches out of the hundreds which co-operated in every big city campaign lay in the important, but not usually mentioned, facts that they were invariably among the largest churches in the city even before the campaign and that their ministers, almost without exception, possessed the aggressive, salesman-like personality which made the most out of the opportunities offered by the revival crowds and publicity. In short, they were already successful churches, and Sunday's campaign merely pushed them along a bit faster. For example, the average city church in 1916, according to the federal census of religious bodies, had 653 members, but Tremont Temple had over 2,500 members in 1916 just prior to the Sunday campaign. The Columbus pastor who received 500 new members had 1,000 members prior to the campaign, and so did the Linwood Boulevard Presbyterian Church in Kansas City. Wanamaker's Bethany Church had over 3,500 members; Alexander's church, over 1,600; and MacInnis', 978, before the revivals in their cities.[16]

As for the personalities of the pastors, their church membership and national fame spoke for themselves. These pastors were among the most highly paid in the nation and the most influential in their denominations; they attracted persons like themselves, influential business leaders and professional men, who, in turn, attracted lesser citizens seeking the social distinction of religious propinquity. On a purely numerical basis, these churches always had more of their members engaged in the campaigns as personal workers, "secretaries," ushers, and choir members, and it was only natural that the church with the most workers in the vineyard should gather the biggest harvest. Sunday's supporters could have inferred from this the obvious corollary that when three or four churches garnered the majority of the trail-hitters who joined a church, the leavings for the other hundred or more churches in the revival would inevitably be slight.

Within a year after each campaign, general disillusionment had replaced the optimistic hopes which preceded it, and by that time the religious life of the city involved was no longer headline news. The adverse publicity seldom caught up with Sunday in these years, if indeed it appeared in the daily newspapers at all. During the Philadelphia revival, for instance, one of the ministers stated that, if only 50 per cent of the trail-hitters "get into the church," it would be "a catastrophe," but less than a year later the same man reckoned that, of the 42,000 trail-hitters, only 12,000 joined any church, and, of these, only about 5,000 "were confessions for the first time." "I gather from many pastors," he went on to say, "that most of the 7,000 who were revived have slipped back into the world. Many of the 5,000 did not 'stick,' and those who are still in the churches are of a wandering disposition and not very loyal to their pastors."[17]

A year after the Boston campaign, during which its supporters declared that, if only 50 per cent of the 64,000 trail-hitters joined the churches, the revival would be a success, the editor of *Zion's Herald* wrote that the revival fell far short of expectations. The editor of the *Watchman-Examiner*, who claimed before the New York campaign that Sunday would win "thousands" of new church members, wrote six months afterward that "the Billy Sunday meetings were a failure when counted in terms of additions to the churches." Out of 98,264 trail-hitters in New York, in the revival which Sunday considered his greatest success and from which young Rockefeller expected such dividends, it was reported six months later that the three churches which received the largest accessions got a grand total of ninety-two new members between them, and less than two hundred joined any church.[18]

Despite the glowing praise of the Pittsburgh campaign by Maitland Alexander and Joseph Odell, other members of the local committee testified a year later that investigations showed only 3,000 new church members from the 26,000 cards signed. The *Des Moines Register* stated that only 4,000 of the 10,200 trail-hitters had been "non-Christians" and that only "about 25 per cent of the total numbers of non-Christian converts have joined the churches." The Chicago campaign was pronounced a dismal failure by the co-operating ministers within a few weeks after its close: "We have not heard of any pastor reporting conversions," read the Chicago report; "that there is general disappointment over this campaign is an open secret . . . for such vast expenditure and such large publicity and blowing of trumpets the results are entirely unsatisfactory."[19]

Whenever such negative reports were mentioned to Sunday, he immediately placed the blame upon the poor follow-up work of the local ministers, but it was difficult to see what more they could have done. Besides, it could hardly be doubted, as Sunday pointed out, that the revivals did have some effect upon church membership. Even if only 3 or 4 per cent of the total trail-hitters joined a church, this was a considerable boost to the churches' morale. However, instead of heralding an upward trend for church membership, it almost always presaged a serious slump a year or two after the revival.

It is impossible to make more than a general estimate of the effect of Sunday's revivals, because too many other factors are involved— e.g., shifts in population due to industrial or agricultural readjustments, the economic depression of 1914–15, the upheaval in all aspects of national life brought about by World War I, and the postwar reaction; all these had some influence upon church membership which Sunday may have either abetted or counteracted.

As an example of the inadequacy of statistics, there is the following analysis of the fifty revivals which Sunday conducted in Iowa within the ten years from 1896 to 1906. These revivals took place in forty-two of Iowa's ninety-nine counties. Yet the statistics of church membership in those counties where he held revivals show a total increase of only 38.9 per cent in that decade as against an increase of 43.8 per cent in church membership in the fifty-seven counties in which he did not hold any revivals. It would be logical, but hardly correct, to conclude from this that Sunday's effect upon the churches of Iowa was entirely negative.

Complicating the estimation of Billy Sunday's particular influence upon a city is the incompleteness and inaccuracy of the available church statistics. The federal religious census was compiled only at ten-year intervals, and the annual statistics of those denominations which kept them were not even credited by their own members. When the statistics for the New England Conference of the Methodist Episcopal Church for 1917 stated that "at the close of the year of the great [Billy] Sunday campaign the churches of the Boston District report a net membership of 105 less than the previous year," the editor of a Methodist journal wrote, "Who believes it?"[20] Since the report did not agree with what the editor and other Methodists firmly believed was the real result of the revival, they attacked their own statistics as "chaotic" and thoroughly discredited them by pointing out a host of errors and omissions.

The only practical means of estimating Sunday's effect is to choose a number of individual churches which were representative and to let their year-by-year figures stand for their denomination as a whole. By choosing ten or twenty churches in each of the major evangelical denominations in a city and by charting their membership figures for a period of five years preceding the revival and five years after it (including the revival year itself), a rough estimate may be made as to whether Sunday materially changed the rate of growth or decline.

Such charts reveal a significant similarity of pattern. In the majority of cases, whether the measurement is that of a denomination or that of an individual church, the charts show an even rate of growth in membership for the years preceding the revival, then a rapid increase in the rate of growth for the year of the revival and sometimes for the succeeding year, then a serious slump in the rate of growth (often an actual numerical decrease); and then, slowly, the growth picks up again, until, at the end of the fifth year following the revival, the rate is once more about the same as it was in the years preceding the revival. The net result in some cases is that over the ten-year period the total growth has been about the same as it would have been had there been no revival at all.

The deviations from this pattern are numerous, and the pattern itself varies in its steepness of growth from one part of the country to another, with the western states generally showing the most rapid rise. Often the pattern holds for some denominations in a city and not for others. In Kansas City, for instance, the Baptists, Presbyterians, and Congregationalists all followed the general pattern, but the Methodists (North) showed no noticeable effect whatever from the revival, and their membership remained almost stationary throughout the ten-year period. In Springfield, Illinois, the Presbyterians (North) showed a startling recovery from a decline in membership and, following the revival, began a steady increase. In Philadelphia the same denomination sank into a rapid decline after the revival.

The pattern varies widely for individual churches. Maitland Alexander's church in Pittsburgh shows the standard growth, spurt, slump, and recovery in this fashion: in the revival year, 1914, the church added 401 members; in 1915 it gained 334 more; then its membership remained almost stationary, gaining 11 in 1916 and 4 in 1917; for the next three years it increased at the rate of 3 per cent per year, exactly the same rate of growth as in the five years preceding the revival. The spurt in growth in 1914 and 1915, however, gave the church an average rate of growth of 8 per cent for the ten-year period. In Detroit the Presbyterian church of the Rev. Joseph Vance, which co-operated with Sunday's campaign in 1916, increased more rapidly than previously in 1917–18 and then suffered a loss of 54 members in 1919 before returning to its normal rate of growth. In Boston the Old South Congregational Church followed the regular revival pattern, even though it did not take part in the campaign, while A. Z. Conrad's Park Street Church, which worked wholeheartedly in it, showed the same rate of growth before, during, and after the revival.

Other churches, even those with outstanding, aggressive pastors, received a temporary boost, only to slip precipitously downward shortly thereafter, indicating that the crisis which they faced was beyond the power of any revival to solve. The Rev. T. M. Maguire's Ruggles Street Baptist Church in Boston, one of the most actively co-operative during the campaign, gained 201 members during the revival year, continued to grow for two years after Sunday's departure, and then quickly declined, until, three years later, it had 400 fewer members than in the year prior to the campaign. Wanamaker's Bethany Church went into decline almost immediately following the announcement of its great increase in 1915, and five years later it had lost 50 per cent of its peak of 3,800 members. Cortland Myers' Tremont Temple dropped from 3,046 members the year after Sunday's visit to 2,783 in 1922. In Spokane the Rev. H. I. Rasmus' First Methodist Church reached a peak of 1,800 members in 1909, the year of Sunday's revival there, lost 450 members the year following, and by 1914 had only 701 members. The membership of MacInnis' church in Syracuse remained stationary for two years following the rapid increase of the revival year and dropped 200 members in 1919; and, even after Sunday returned to Syracuse for a two-week revival in 1920, the membership in 1921 was 100 less than the year after Sunday's first revival.

It would be as questionable to hold Sunday's campaigns responsible for increases and decreases in individual churches as it would be to do so for state or national fluctuations in church membership. The death of Bethany's pastor, George F. Pentecost, two years after the campaign probably had more effect on the membership decline than any postrevival slump. The great increase in the membership of A. K. DeBlois's First Baptist Church in Boston three years after the campaign was the result of its amalgamation with another church and not of the continuing effect of the campaign.

One statistical feature, however, is worth emphasizing: while downtown churches remained as unstable in postrevival years as previously, uptown and suburban churches maintained a steadily increasing rate of church membership growth after Sunday's revivals. The figures for the four major evangelical denominations in Boston, when separated into downtown and uptown churches, show that the downtown church membership in all four remained virtually static from 1912 to 1922, but the membership in suburban Boston, despite a slight postrevival setback, increased steadily for the five years before the revival, followed by an even greater rate of increase in the five years following it. This same situation holds true for other large metropolitan areas, and it indicates the answer to the much-debated question concerning what class of people were most affected by Sunday's revivalism. Many pastors were far more concerned with the kind of persons Sunday converted than with their number.

One clue to the social status of the trail-hitters can be found in Sunday's own estimate of his work: "I am a halfway house," he said, "between the brownstone church and the Salvation Army. They are both needed and so is the halfway house."[21] The brownstone church symbolized the church of the wealthy; the Salvation Army, the church of the poor. Sunday's tabernacles were filled with neither the very rich nor the very poor. Despite the general conception of revivalism as a lower-class phenomenon, the evidence all points to the inescapable conclusion that Billy Sunday appealed primarily and most strongly to those respectable, middle-class citizens who were already nominal church members or who had often thought about joining a church but who had never had sufficient pressure put upon them to do so.

Contemporary opinion on this subject, however, was not so clear. Sunday's supporters were not even agreed upon whom they wanted him to appeal to. Those who saw the church crisis in terms of the growing gap between the church and the downtown or industrial masses looked to Sunday to bring the masses into the church. Those who saw the crisis as one of increasing secularization, decreasing attendance by church members, or simply as a matter of financial insolvency thought that Sunday would appeal to the solid, substantial citizens who were forgetting their obligation to support the church.

Men like Wanamaker and John D. Rockefeller, Jr., took the former view, while the "go-getter" type of minister generally took the latter. "Our churches do not lay hold of the masses of the people," young Rockefeller told his men's Bible class prior to Sunday's New York campaign. "If he can touch them, there is just one place for me, and that is at his back."[22] "A leading banker" of Columbus expressed the same view when he remarked that, though Sunday's language "seemed coarse and vulgar to me," it undoubtedly "gave him a hold upon the imaginations and consciences of the masses which a more refined and scholarly preacher could not obtain."

Many leading ministers also were convinced that Sunday could reach the lower classes. Bishop John W. Hamilton (Methodist), of New England, claimed that "Billy Sunday is doing his work among some people that no organized church can reach." Bishop Joseph Berry (Methodist) of Philadelphia felt that Sunday was "after the man in the street—the man whom the average preacher cannot persuade to enter his sanctuary." The Rev. George Adams, of Philadelphia, held that "Billy Sunday can get a crowd of the 'riff raff' and 'common mob' anywhere." And the *Watchman-Examiner* believed that Sunday could be counted upon to line up "the cheaper sections" of Boston for Prohibition.

The opposing view of Sunday's influence was expressed by the Rev. W. C. Poole in his description of the results he and some of his colleagues expected from the Philadelphia revival: "Certainly many thousands will turn their attention to Philadelphia as a good place for a home or an investment because of the meetings and publicity. Those people will naturally be the best class of people—generally church folks. There was nothing in the meetings to attract undesirable citizens."[23]

In New York City comparatively few ministers regretted, as did H. D. Brookins, that Sunday's tabernacle at 168th Street was so far uptown, away from "the very class of people that Mr. Sunday likes to reach and to whom he makes his profoundest appeal" (i.e., the downtown masses). The majority agreed with the Baptist editor who attributed the failure of the New York revival to the very fact that the tabernacle was not farther uptown or in a residential area like Brooklyn: "In a more homogeneous community such as Brooklyn the results would have been larger counted in terms of church membership."[24] Sunday was also berated for having extended his New York campaign so far into the month of June that most of the respectable citizens who might have been influenced by it had departed for their summer vacations before it ended.

In the final analysis, the theory that Sunday's revivalism had a great effect upon the mass of working-class people in the cities was not substantiated. Observers of his campaigns, like those who watched Moody's, agreed that his audiences and his trail-hitters were not poor, dirty outcasts but thoroughly respectable citizens. "Only a small percentage" of the trail-hitters, said the Rev. W. M. Walker, of Scranton, "belong to the jetsam and flotsam of society. The great majority live in comfortable homes. They have always been valuable members of society. But through indifference or neglect they have not concerned themselves hitherto with religious matters and through ordinary services the churches have been unable to reach them. The 'trail-hitters,' as they proudly call themselves, are a splendid company of people. Among them are men and women of wealth, of culture, of business and professional standing, and their enlistment is a tremendous gain for organized Christianity."[25]

The same report came from other cities. Even after the "Booze Sermon" given for men only in Philadelphia, the Rev. H. W. Barras noted that those who came forward "were not 'down-and-outers'; they were not booze-soaked men; they were not feeble-minded old men or sobbing little boys. They were fine, bright men, most of them between 25 and 40."[26] The campaign in Columbus scarcely touched the aristocratic or the poor, said one report, but "the churches among the great middle class are almost swamped with new members."[27] The social status of those who joined Maitland Alexander's church was indicated by his statement that, in the weeks following the revival, "it was necessary in my own church, which when packed holds 3,200 persons, to hold special meetings for different groups, such as lawyers, doctors, bankers, etc., and they were always crowded."

That the trail-hitters, and indeed the whole audience, should be "valuable members of society" rather than "jetsam and flotsam" was not only the result of Sunday's style, message, and publicity but also, and most directly, the consequence of his delegation system. Of this system, Mrs. Sunday said, "We had to reach all kinds of people; that was our business." But examination of the delegations which came to the tabernacle shows an overwhelming preponderance of middle- and lower-middle-class groups, corresponding to the general term "white-collar workers" or "the salaried class" as opposed to the "overall" or "blue-collar class" who were paid by the hour or the day.

Those who worked in the Sunday campaigns estimated that 50 per cent of every audience was made up of church members, and the estimate was, if anything, low. It was a favorite custom of Sunday's, as of Moody and Chapman, to try to impress his audiences by asking everyone who was a professing Christian to rise. It apparently did not strike him as anomalous that, whenever he asked this question, according to the reporters, "virtually the entire throng rose to its feet."

The social makeup of the tabernacle audiences can be fairly deduced from the types of delegations which were given reservations. On Sunday mornings the congregations were made up of church members of the co-operating churches, the large majority of them suburban or uptown residents. The seats on "Out-of-Town Day" were reserved for those able and willing to pay train fare and perhaps hotel bills; almost all these groups were church members, usually led by their pastors. The Sunday-school classes which came to the children's meetings and the college groups which came on young people's nights could not be classed as "flotsam and jetsam." Nor could the "bankers, manufacturers, merchants, and professional men" who had seats reserved for them on "Businessmen's Night." Businesswomen were recruited by members of the Sunday party among the stenographers, bookkeepers, department-store clerks, telephone operators, and shopgirls. These came to the tabernacle in delegations, singing,

> Brighten the office where you work,
> Brighten the office every clerk. . . .

If not substantial citizens, these businesswomen had hopes of marrying into a better position; they may have been lower middle class, but they were not lower class.

By far the most numerous delegations were those representing a particular store, business firm, insurance company, or office building. There were office workers and managers from publishing houses, newspapers, manufacturing concerns, and all types of stores; they included petty officials, small shop-owners, floorwalkers, salesmen, filing clerks, office boys, junior managers, and administrative assistants. Most of these persons received regular salaries or at least worked on commission. They all wore white shirts to work, and almost all of them commuted from uptown or the suburbs.

Such delegations looked upon their trips to the tabernacle as office parties rather than as religious pilgrimages. They were noisy and hilarious; the stenographers chewed gum, practiced their shorthand as Sunday spoke, and laughed and giggled as they came forward in groups to shake his hand. To promote group spirit and advertise their company, they wore badges provided by the firm and bearing its name; they carried banners or placards also bearing the company label, and they usually brought Sunday or his wife some gift which, when feasible, represented their company's product. These persons, when converted, were not great financial assets to a church, but they often made hard-working, devout members. They were the core of the true converts, and most of them came from rural, native-American families in which nominal adherence, at least, had always been made to an evangelical denomination.

Among the more frequent and numerous delegations were the

many fraternal orders, businessmen's clubs, church fellowship groups, and their corresponding female societies. These represented "the best class of people," but, unfortunately for the co-operating ministers, most of them already belonged to the churches. There were also such miscellaneous, but obviously middle-class, delegations as women's clubs, suffragettes, temperance organizations, college alumni groups, civic welfare societies, and charity organizations.

In spite of this preponderance of middle-class visitors to the tabernacle, Sunday made some effort to reach the other elements in the city. He used his director of men's work to reach the lower-class workingman, and his parlor meetings to meet the wealthy. With the co-operation of leading local manufacturers, usually those on the Sunday executive committee, the director of men's work held noonday meetings in shops and factories and did his best to persuade those who listened to him to come to the tabernacle. Sunday's director in Boston, the Rev. Isaac Ward, held 163 such meetings during the ten-week revival there, and he reported an attendance of 33,673. But, since these meetings took place in the same shops for four or five consecutive weeks, it seems likely that this total includes many who attended several meetings; the number of different men reached was probably not over five or six thousand. Though some delegations came to the tabernacle from these factories, it was not clear whether they were actually shopworkers or men from the front office. Even had they all been shopworkers, six thousand was a small part of the total million and a half attendance at the Boston tabernacle.

W. J. Hobbs, vice-president of the Boston and Maine Railroad and a prominent Sunday supporter, saw to it that Ward held noon meetings not only in his shops but in those of the Boston and Albany Railroad and the New York, New Haven, and Hartford Railroad. Warren S. Stone, president of the AF of L Brotherhood of Locomotive Engineers, spoke from the tabernacle platform in several cities. It is probable that the comparatively elite workmen of the railroad unions, the engineers, firemen, and conductors, were more frequently seen than the shopmen; the day laborers, who worked on the road gangs, were not seen at all.

Occasionally, local unions of the AF of L came in a body to the tabernacle. In addition to the railroad unions, the Boston revival had delegations from the leatherworkers' union, printers and typesetters' union, and the carpenters and builders' union. Boston also provided reservations for a landladies' association and the Fanueil Market Men. Large delegations of silkworkers appeared at the tabernacle in

Paterson and of steelworkers in Pittsburgh, but, since the press reported that these groups were "led by their officers," it is not certain
whether they came under duress or whether they represented the
office staffs and foremen. The Rev. C. H. Zahniser, who had charge
of the Pittsburgh decision cards, said that he never saw any of the
unskilled steelworkers at the meetings.[28]

There were two concrete reasons why Sunday seldom reached the
unskilled workers, the lowest of the lower classes: first, these people
at the bottom of the social and economic scale were the most recent
immigrants, or the children of recent immigrants, who could scarcely
speak or understand English; and, second, the vast majority of them
were Catholics and Jews, who were unfamiliar with, and unlikely to
be influenced by, Protestant revivalism. That Sunday turned down
an invitation to come to the city of Cleveland because, he said, its
citizens were "foreign—60 per cent or more" constitutes acknowledgment that he could not reach this group.[29] In Johnstown, Pennsylvania, he claimed that "even the great foreign element that can't understand me, has been back of the revival," but how he knew this
or what particular help it was to the co-operating ministers he did
not say.

Though over 1,000 persons signed cards in Boston, Baltimore, Detroit, and Syracuse giving their church preference as Catholic and
3,690 did so in New York, there is no evidence that these were lower-
class Catholics or even that they were thoroughly converted. The
Roman Catholic publication *The Pilot* published the following
report of the 1,381 card-signers who gave their preference as Catholic during the Boston campaign:[30]

     80 Children
    372 Signers for curiosity and fun
    298 Unable to verify because of change of address
    205 Insufficient address on cards
    195 No such person at address given
     66 Not practical Catholics
     46 Non-Catholics
     36 Deny being present and signing cards
     35 No such address
     23 Request of employer
      6 Converts
      6 Not responsible for actions
      4 Perverts
      4 Unable to give any explanation of their actions
      3 Went with Protestant friends
      2 Went to hear sermon on temperance

  1,381

The special nights at the tabernacle devoted to various nationalities were invariably for those of so-called "Nordic stock," which meant Swedes, Norwegians, Welsh, or Scottish of at least second generation in America. They were usually members of evangelical churches, since the Lutheran churches seldom co-operated with Sunday. While these groups covered a wide social and economic range, few of them were from the lower classes, for, with the influx of immigrants from southern European and from Slavic countries after 1890, these groups had risen from lower positions to supervisory or skilled positions, if, indeed, they had not been middle-class citizens doing white-collar work since their arrival. In the coal-mining districts, for instance, Sunday could count upon the avid support of the Welsh, whose skill and organizing ability had made them foremen or union leaders and whose evangelical fervor was well known; like the other union men who attended Sunday's meetings, they believed in his message of opportunity and success because it had worked for them and because they shared his antipathy toward continued immigration.

There is little evidence that Sunday converted many social derelicts or "booze-hoisting" bums, who were the stereotype revival converts pictured in cartoons. Harry G. Saulnier, the present superintendent of the Pacific Garden Mission in Chicago, is of the opinion that mass evangelism of Sunday's type seldom reached the people in the downtown slums. Down-and-outers of American birth who had lost their social status would be unwilling to go to a tabernacle where they might see old friends. Foreign-born and the children of foreign-born, who constituted a large percentage of those dealt with in missions, usually lacked knowledge of English. Perhaps a few "mission stiffs" looking for "handouts" might hit the trail, but neither these nor any other converted down-and-outers would be willingly accepted by uptown or suburban churches, said Saulnier.[31]

There were those who reported that Sunday had a great effect upon the wealthy, the aristocratic, and those in high office. As H. L. Mencken pointed out, however, Dr. Kelly, Joshua Levering, and Daniel Baker may have been wealthy and influential men who took an active part in the campaign in Baltimore, but they had been saved long before. The only influential person to hit the trail in Baltimore for the first time was the Hon. Carl Gray, a friend of John D. Rockefeller, Sr., and the president of the Western Maryland Railroad, and he was already a distinguished church member. In Boston W. J. Hobbs, E. C. Benton, former Governor E. N. Foss, James G.

Ferguson (president of the Fidelity Trust Company), and Charles Thurston (former mayor of Cambridge) were among the trail-hitters prominently mentioned by the press. All these were church members; two of them, Hobbs and Ferguson, came forward with delegations of their employees. Foss came forward to stimulate interest in the Prohibition campaign.

Sunday usually asked such influential persons to hit the trail as an example for others, and undoubtedly many of them did so for this reason. Other public figures, particularly local politicians, like "Boss" Baird of Camden, may be suspected of having had ulterior motives for trail-hitting. Many influential persons were associated with the meetings and were reported as having been "affected" by Sunday when they came to hear him. But, in general, Sunday was, as he said, a halfway house, and the necessity for society parlor meetings indicated that the tabernacle services were not frequented by the upper, or even upper-middle, classes. The actions of J. P. Marquand's character, the late George Apley, who twice attended Sunday's meetings and who gave Sunday a check for $5,000, were not typical of upper-class Bostonians. The reaction of George Babbitt to Sinclair Lewis' Mike Monday is much closer to the mark.

The predominantly middle-class appeal of Sunday's revivals was evident not only in the makeup of the audiences but also in the types of permanent organizations which grew out of the campaigns. Permanent Bible classes were organized from the groups recruited by Sunday's experts. The choirs, made up entirely of church members, were persuaded by Rodeheaver to form permanent singing groups and to give concerts. But most significant were the Billy Sunday businessmen's clubs and the Virginia Asher businesswomen's councils.

After almost every campaign some of the men who had worked on the various committees, usually the ushers, doormen, personal workers, and a few of the leading figures on the executive or finance committee, were inspired by Sunday's preaching and by the good fellowship growing out of the four months of work together to unite for the purpose of promoting evangelistic work. A. B. Nichols, secretary of the Boston YMCA, who helped to organize the Billy Sunday Businessmen's Club of Boston, explained its purpose: "Businessmen can reach businessmen in a different way from what is possible to ministers. The Club has had a profound influence in impressing the power of Mr. Sunday's preaching on the prominent businessmen of Greater Boston." Made up principally of small businessmen, salesmen, insurance agents, and minor managerial assistants, these groups also included some of the more important figures in the city who had worked in the campaign. Franklin P. Shumway was the first president of the Boston club, and he was succeeded by Colonel E. C. Benton. The first president of the Billy Sunday Businessmen's Club of Roanoke, Virginia, was E. R. Johnson, an ex-president of the International Rotary. Sunday boasted that there were forty men in the Billy Sunday Club of Syracuse who "represented forty million dollars."

The principal function of these clubs when first formed was to multiply conversions, much as Moody's "flying squadrons" of soul-winners had done; for this purpose they usually divided themselves into "gospel teams." These teams visited homes in their neighborhoods; spoke at clubs, YMCA's, missions, and churches; or talked to business associates. Two months after the Boston campaign it was announced that 123 such teams, doing follow-up work for the churches, had won 452 "first decisions" for Christ and 3,700 "reconsecrations." In the thirteen months following the New York revival thirty-five gospel teams claimed "5,727 professed conversions while 11,853 persons have renewed their vows of consecration."

After the Wichita, Kansas, campaign in 1911, gospel teams were organized that went all over the state and into adjoining states to win converts. Three hundred gospel teams were organized in the region, and several years later they united to form the National Federation of Gospel Teams. They claimed to have won 11,000 converts by 1915 through the work of "unsalaried, self-supporting" laymen. There is still in existence a group called "Fishers of Men, Inc.," which is made up primarily of Billy Sunday businessmen's clubs which were organized in the southern states in the 1920's following Sunday campaigns. There are 129 separate groups in the affiliation, which has a monthly newspaper and holds annual conventions. The Billy Sunday Businessmen's Evangelistic Club of Chattanooga, Tennessee, which limited itself to fifty members, was formed in 1919 and listed its activities for the first ten years of its existence as follows:[32]

Has had ten members go into the ministry.
Has had one member adopt Christian Life Service.
Has had seven members become Evangelistic singers and assistant evangelists.
Has three members who inaugurated the teaching of the Bible in the Public Schools of Chattanooga; kept it active with expansion each year for eight and one-half years until it includes all the thirty schools of the city.

Has been called upon to engage in every religious campaign undertaken by the church and has performed an important part therein.

Has maintained a religious service every week for two years at the Tubercular [sic] Sanatorium.

Has men who visit the County Jail every Saturday.

Has engaged in a great many Cottage Prayer Meetings.

Has continued, since its organization, to hold personal interviews both by appointment and as opportunity offered with men about their relations to Jesus Christ and done much personal work with people in church services to the end that He should be accepted as their Personal Saviour.

Has conducted religious services when specially invited by ministers.

Has four Pastors elected as associate members who attend our weekly meetings and give us many opportunities for service in religious matters they conduct.

Has held its Club meetings every Wednesday at 12:15 for ten years and three months.

Has taken a leading part in the organization of eight Men's Evangelistic Clubs in the State of Tennessee.

In the first six years had 28,000 personal interviews and 3,000 persons led to definitely declare their faith in the Great Redeemer.

The constitution of this particular Billy Sunday club states that members must belong to an evangelical church and must be "engaged in business or professional life." Membership dues were five dollars per year.

The businesswomen's clubs were generally named after Mrs. Virginia Asher, the Sunday party's director of women's work. Like the Fishers of Men, the Virginia Asher businesswomen's clubs are nationally affiliated and still hold annual conventions. Formed by the volunteer churchwomen who during the campaigns acted as "Council Women" and co-ordinated the work among stenographers, salesgirls, and female clerks, these businesswomen's clubs, or councils, are counterparts of the businessmen's clubs, except that, from the beginning, they worked less among members of their own social group and more among "the less fortunate." The Friendly League for Christian Service, Inc., of New York, which is affiliated with the Virginia Asher Council, continues the work begun in 1917 after the Sunday campaign. Its founders were Mrs. Finley J. Shepard (Helen Gould) and Mrs. Simeon B. Chapin, both active workers in Sunday's revival. It caters to "the great company of businesswomen in New York" who are "in the lower income group"; it employs a salaried, full-time "personal worker" to "visit the sick, to comfort the bereaved, and to help troubled and perplexed business girls solve their many problems."

In contrast to the continued activity of these middle-class groups, attempts to organize permanent shopmen's leagues among the factory workers who had gone in delegations to the tabernacles never had any lasting results.

External evidence regarding the middle-class nature of Sunday's audiences is fully corroborated by the internal evidence of Sunday's sermons. In his sermon on "Home" he revealed his conception of the women to whom he addressed his message: "One of the danger signs of our times," he said, "is the curse of the idle mother," and he then contrasted the idle mothers with the good mothers: "They never go out to help the poor; they never try to do anything in the homes of squalor and want; they never try to bridge the chasm and meet the fellow with the dinner bucket; . . . I tell you what is the matter with you mothers: You are neglecting your home for the lodge, for your clubs, for your literaries, and your society."

Sunday assumed that the men in his audience owned their own homes and held minor executive positions. In his sermon on "Conversion" these assumptions were blandly asserted: "That fine house you live in—have you had to lie and cheat . . . to build that house?" "The devil is always a passenger with you in your auto if he furnished it. . . . There is blood on your hands if you rent your property for a saloon . . . if you are making your clerks work long hours, if you pay them poor wages . . . if you sold that mining stock and knew that it was a swindle." Even when he knew that his audience was made up principally of delegations of shopgirls, telephone girls, and stenographers, as it was on Businesswomen's Night, he delivered his sermon on "Personal Work," which castigated church members for spending "too much time dreaming over 'The Lady of the Lake,' Milton, Bacon, Shakespeare, Chaucer, and a lot of such things." And he demanded that they do personal work by speaking to "the telephone girl," "the delivery boy," "the man who brings your laundry," "the man who hauls away your ashes," "your washerwoman," "your dress-maker."

A composite picture of the man and woman whom Sunday used as the criterion against which he judged the sins of society was a stereotype of the middle-class suburban family: The man was married, had two or three children, and commuted, usually in his car, from his home to his "place of business" in the city, where he had a stenographer and some clerks working for him; he spent his leisure time at his lodge meetings or "Booster Club"; he was a companion to his children, took his wife out for automobile rides, and visited his neighbors; while he might play cards or go to the movies or theater and even drink an occasional "mint julep" or glass of beer, he also went to church regularly and probably belonged to a men's Bible class.

The man's wife was the accepted counterpart of this image, providing the elements of refinement and culture, pampering the children, belonging to a woman's club or literary guild, reading the latest novels, persuading her husband to keep up with the neighbors but also acting as a restraining influence on his manly habits of drinking, swearing, and poker-playing and naturally assuming that he would accompany her to church each Sunday.

These were Sunday's "decent people," who needed only to modify their habits slightly in order to become saints. For him they constituted the overwhelming majority of Americans and the principal objects of his concern. The other caricatures which he portrayed— the hobo, the booze-hoister, on the one hand, and the society woman, the intellectual, and the amoral big businessman on the other—these were always presented as unpleasant contrasts to the decent citizens; sometimes they were beneath contempt, and sometimes hope was held out that even these might, through conversion, reach respectability.

It was to convert this middle stratum of American society that Sunday concocted his multifaceted message, a message which, taken at face value, could and did mean all things to all men. Those who shook his hand at the conclusion of the "Booze Sermon" were not necessarily expressing sympathy with his theological doctrines, and those who reconsecrated themselves after his sermon on "Heaven" were not primarily taking a stand for the moral principles that motivated the trail-hitters after the sermon on "The Sins of Society." All the trail-hitters belonged to roughly the same social position in life, but they did not all see Sunday in the same light.

In fact, it was hard to find any two persons who evaluated Sunday's revivalism the same way. Many of his backers claimed that the effect of his preaching should be measured not at all in terms of conversions, trail-hitters, or church members but in terms of the spirit of righteousness awakened in the community. If all the evidence of Sunday's failure to solve the urgent problems of the churches had been brought forward and proved beyond dispute, he still would have found a host of Americans to back him on the grounds that the churches should think not in the narrow terms of their immediate financial plight but in the broad terms of their responsibility to the general welfare.

It was, said these people, because the churches had forgotten the social aspect of their message that there was a gulf between them and the masses; Billy Sunday was important not because he might win a few new members but because he brought a new emphasis upon civic duty and social morality, because he was shaking the church members out of their complacency and leading them on a great crusade against political corruption and civic apathy. Sunday's revivalism, to these persons, was not a question of helping the churches; it was a question of preserving the fundamental integrity of "the American way of life."

7

"THIS GREAT PLUMED KNIGHT CLOTHED IN THE ARMOR OF GOD"

The confusion over the religious consequences of Sunday's revivals was clarity itself compared to the division of opinion regarding their social and political consequences. Sunday's sermons were so adroitly phrased on contemporary issues that he was for years claimed as a leader by conservatives and liberals alike.

At the same time that ministers all over the nation were heralding Sunday as the one man who could bring the masses into the church, political liberals like John Reed and George Creel were calling him a hireling of the vested interests whose sermons appealed only to the well-to-do. While Socialists accused him of being a tool of the bosses, a group of wealthy society women in Philadelphia wrote to the editor of a local paper stating that Sunday's attacks on fashionable society were attempts to stir up the lower classes against the upper.[1] Reformers like Brand Whitlock described Sunday's revivals as the diversionary activities of corrupt politicians, while the editor of the *New York Times* hopefully looked forward to Sunday's campaign in Philadelphia as the beginning of a reform movement that would oust "Boss" Boies Penrose.[2] A writer for the *Watchman-Examiner* even thought it necessary to point out that Sunday's occasional condemnation of child labor and starvation wages did not mean that he was a Socialist.

Among those most ready to accept Sunday as a great social reformer were some of the nation's most influential business leaders. These men were particularly impressed by such high-sounding statements as this by Sunday: "The great difficulty which confronts America today is the lack of moral principles in business, in politics, and in society. Thoughtful businessmen all over America are awakening to the perils that threaten our country and civilization through disregard of the old principles of Christian integrity and honesty. They are awakening to the fact that if civic righteousness prevails, graft in high places is to be overthrown. If the great avalanche of vice and intemperance is to be beaten back, it must be done by a tidal wave of the old time religion."

John D. Rockefeller, Jr., was so moved by Sunday's moral fervor that he called him "a rallying center around whom all people interested in good things may gather."[3] Henry Leland, president of the Cadillac automobile company, who was instrumental in bringing Sunday to the industrially turbulent city of Detroit and who gave him a new $8,000 Cadillac sedan as a personal thank-offering for the good he felt Sunday accomplished, was inspired to describe him as "this great plumed knight clothed in the armor of God."[4]

When such important and respected men praised him so highly, it was not surprising that the majority of the public was inclined to believe that Sunday was a social as well as a moral reformer. It did not occur to many Americans that there might be a conflict between social reform and moral reform, a conflict which was as sharp as that between progress and reaction. It did not strike them as odd that most of Sunday's support came from the same big businessmen who were constantly under attack by the muckrakers and progressives. Most middle-class citizens found it easier and more comforting to identify themselves with the wealthy than with the radicals or the workingman. Besides, it seemed obvious that Sunday stood for exactly the same things that all decent Americans stood for.

By 1912 the shy country boy from Ames, Iowa, had become a symbol of the American way of life. In the public mind Billy Sunday was an accepted leader in the battle to maintain that way of life against the forces of evil unleashed by the twentieth century. To many people he was as important a crusader for reform as Theodore Roosevelt or William Jennings Bryan, both of whom publicly acknowledged him as their friend. Roosevelt, speaking from Sunday's tabernacle platform, once referred to him as "the most wide-awake, militant preacher of Christianity I know."[5] As a Republican counterpart of Bryan, Sunday must have seemed to some of his supporters as logical a choice for Roosevelt's cabinet, if the latter had been reelected in 1912, as Bryan was for Wilson's.

This exalted position could not help affecting Sunday's personality. At times he seemed to be a blatant, self-righteous zealot who took only too seriously his vision of himself as a fighting saint and a mouthpiece of God. The assault on Babylon had rubbed off much of the freshness and warmth of Sunday's character. "I ask no quarter, and I give none," he challenged his enemies, and there were those who wondered how long it would be before this arrogant knight-errant from out of the West would stumble and impale himself on his own sword.

Yet underneath Sunday was still insecure and ingenuous. Though he seemed a colossal egotist on the platform, face to face he was still a friendly, boyish figure. His magnetic charm had not diminished, nor had his warm generosity and his genuine honesty. As long as the crowds came to hear and applaud him he was easygoing and happy. But the constant adulation of millions of people which kept him in the national spotlight year after year made it inevitable that he would someday face a terrible shock when his popularity dwindled away.

Sunday lived to see the end of progressivism and of the Social Gospel movement, however, before he saw the end of his own fame. What he did not claim, but might rightly have, for his revivalism, was a large part in halting, at least temporarily, the trend which began at the turn of the century toward a re-examination of the traditional beliefs and institutions of America. By playing upon the middle classes' innate fear of change, Sunday's preaching blunted and almost destroyed the keen edge of the reform movement which had seemed to promise so much.

In helping to divert this trend and to make Americans cling even more avidly to the outmoded religious, political, and economic concepts of the nineteenth century, Sunday was thoroughly in tune with the majority of church members in the United States. The activities of the Protestant churches closely reflected the hesitant and halting steps of the public at large in examining the complex problems of industrialism. The founding of the Federal Council of Churches in 1908, for example, seemed a great step forward in bringing the churches into a unified and liberal position from which they could exert a reinvigorated moral force in behalf of reform. The Social Creed adopted by the council that year virtually indorsed the platform of the most ardent progressives in calling for the protection of the workingman against the hardship "resulting from the swift crises of industrial change," for the necessity of "conciliation and arbitration" in labor disputes, for the "abolition of child labor," for the "suppression of the 'sweating system,'" for the "reduction of the hours of labor," for "provision for the old age of workers," for "the protection of the worker from dangerous machinery," and for "the most equitable division of the products of industry."

But this creed was twenty-five years ahead of its time. The churches soon discovered that to enforce it would result in their own destruction before leading to any reform in the industrial system. The businessmen against whom their actions were directed were the very pillars of society upon which the continued financial security of the churches rested, and the businessman did not want to see these reforms put into effect. When Charles Stelzle, the founder of the department of the church and labor in the Presbyterian Church (North), "protested in the name of the church against the unnecessary slaughter of the workingman in the Pittsburgh rolling mills" because of long hours and inadequate safety devices, he was told by a former moderator of the Presbyterian General Assembly that he was "killing the goose that lays the golden eggs." And, when he persisted, his department's budget was drastically cut. In 1913 he was compelled to resign so that the department could be reorganized on the basis of "social welfare work" of the Thanksgiving-basket variety, which posed no threat to the industrial system.[6]

The editor of the *Texas Christian Advocate,* in an article which typified the churches' recoil from the Social Gospel, maintained in 1915 that "social service," rightly understood, "has nothing whatever to do with politics directly or with economics as such." The true role of the church was not to "throw itself indiscriminately into the work of all conceptions of social reforms and make these fads take the place of preaching the old-fashioned Gospel" but "to put into men and women a desire for righteousness and an ambition to develop into the best manhood and womanhood possible. When this is accomplished, then the proper re-adjustment of their conditions will take on shape normally and beneficially."

The fond ambitions of the liberal founders of the Federal Council of Churches were not to be realized so swiftly as they had imagined. When the sociologically oriented evangelism of the Men and Religion Forward Movement in 1912 failed to bring the masses into the church, the conservatives, who had worked with the liberals in the plan, were ready to abandon any type of church action in regard to social work which went beyond the bounds of charity contributions and the preaching of "the old-fashioned Gospel." A split was evident in Protestantism, and during the years 1912–25 this split was to widen into the Fundamentalist-liberal schism.

Billy Sunday voiced the reaction of the conservatives when he said, "Some people are trying to make a religion out of social service with Jesus Christ left out. That is why your Men and Religion Forward Movement was a lamentable failure. They made the Christian religion a side issue." Sunday's theory that the principal purpose of the Christian religion was to save souls and not society was still the basic creed of the majority of American church members, despite their dalliance with the Social Gospel. To conservatives the separation of religion and social reform had become as important a democratic dogma as the separation of church and state.

In spite of Sunday's obvious antagonism toward altering the prevailing political and economic order, his revivals were still looked upon by many as reform movements. This view was based upon a profound faith in three well-publicized aspects of his preaching: his appeal to civic righteousness, his championship of Prohibition, and his supposed ability to convert into respectable citizens the masses of so-called "shiftless, ignorant," foreign-born workers who were looked upon as the pawns of crooked politicians and Socialist agitators. If Sunday could do these things, said his supporters, certainly his revivals would go a long way toward reducing the political corruption which was such a national blight. Revivalism seemed to many to sublimate the inherent conflict between those who wanted to reform society and those who wanted only to reform individuals.

In large part this confused approach to reform was the fault of the progressives themselves. The progressive movement was labeled by some "the ethical revival," and the large element of evangelical religion in the views of most of the leading figures of progressivism from Roosevelt and La Follette to Lincoln Steffens and "Golden Rule" Jones often made it impossible to distinguish secular reform from religious reform. Conservative businessmen could hardly be blamed for confusing "social service" and socialism when men like Steffens could praise socialism while at the same time claiming that the only solution for the problem of capital and labor was the living out of the Golden Rule. In his autobiography, Frederic C. Howe, himself one of the leading progressive reformers, called the "evangelistic psychology," "the early assumptions as to vice and virtue, goodness and evil" which came from a rural childhood and regular attendance at an evangelical church, "the most characteristic influence of my generation. It explains the nature of our reforms, the regulatory legislation in morals and economics, our belief in men rather than in institutions, and our messages to other peoples." Consequently, when Billy Sunday came along mouthing the same phrases as the progressives and playing upon the same "evangelistic psychology" of the American public, it was inevitable that many people should assume that his moral reform theories amounted to virtually the same thing as the political and social reforms of La Follette and his followers.

In the years following his Burlington campaign, Sunday regularly advertised his campaigns as civic reforms. And the newspapers, which, as he did, catered to the market place, took him at his own evaluation. "W. A. SUNDAY USHERS IN 'BIG CLEAN UP,'" read the headlines of the *Ottumwa Daily Courier* of Iowa at the start of his campaign in 1908: "Fiery Evangelist in Opening Sermon Tells of the Good He Will Accomplish in Ridding Ottumwa of Crime," said the subheading. In one of his most popular sermons Sunday indignantly proclaimed that "graft, spoil, and special interests have got a strangle-hold upon our cities." With naïve éclat he announced that "some contractors secure contracts by graft and charge it to the state or national government. . . . The present system of political policy cannot long endure or the government will go down."

By 1915 the *Philadelphia North American,* under the editorial zeal of E. A. Van Valkenberg, did not have to wait to hear Sunday's opening sermon in that city before writing that his "destructive blows against civic corruption, against vice, against greed, against liquor" would make "men pay outlawed debts, abandon habits of hurtful self-indulgence, and give greater consideration not only to their Maker, but to their families, their neighbors, and their cities." Sunday released a statement addressed to the people of Philadelphia on the eve of his revival which read: "Does Philadelphia want to see a 'For Rent' sign hanging in the window of every brewery, saloon, and house of ill-fame? Does Philadelphia want to see thieves made to steal no more? . . . homes of squalor and want turned into abodes of peace and plenty?" The answer and the remedy were obvious.

The claims regarding Sunday's prowess in overthrowing political corruption were astounding. One newspaper said of the results of his revival in Pittsburgh in 1914: "What years of reform work could not do he has wrought in a few short weeks. Old line 'practical politicians,' the men who did the dirty work for the political gang, are now zealous for temperance, righteousness, and religion." Joseph H. Odell, pastor of the Second Presbyterian Church of Scranton, wrote in the *Outlook* that after Sunday's revivals in Pennsylvania "the men who had worked the wards of Allegheny County on behalf of Penrose and the liquor interests for years . . . repudiated Penrose," and, when Odell asked them why, "they frankly ascribed it to Billy Sunday; they had been born again—no idle phrase with them—in the vast whale-back tabernacle under the preaching of the baseball evangelist."

Editorials in cities across the nation proclaimed after each revival that "a new moral tone," "a higher level of civic spirit," and a "newly awakened" or "a deeper sense of spiritual values" were evident in their city. "Drunkards became sober, thieves became honest, multitudes of people engaged themselves in the study of the Bible, thousands confessed their faith in Jesus Christ as Saviour of the world, and all the quiescent righteousness of the community grew brave and belligerent against vice, intemperance, gambling, and political dishonesty."

The concrete results were not quite so evident, but some cities, following the example of Burlington's citizens, formed civic federations after Sunday's campaigns and attempted to enforce Prohibition, stamp out prostitution, and reform the city government. Fargo, North Dakota; Norfolk, Virginia; and Springfield, Illinois, were among these. The citizens in Norfolk, according to one member of their federation, were able to close a number of brothels by exerting pressure upon the owners of the properties, who, it turned out, were respectable church members who had supported Sunday's campaign.

Sunday himself neither joined these federations nor attacked individual evildoers. He considered that he had done his part toward ushering in a cleanup when he denounced sin and advocated virtue. "I never introduce personalities into my sermons," he said, in answer to a demand that he make his political stand clear in Philadelphia by attacking "Boss" Penrose. "I attack corruption in politics itself, not particular men. I would not for any consideration endanger the work I am doing for God by injecting personalities into it at this stage." That it would have endangered his work was obvious. With six or eight revivals in as many different states each year, he could not take any political stand without alienating a large percentage of his support. Had he become embroiled in partisan politics, the churches would have had to withdraw their backing or face the serious charge of "the church in politics." Attesting the validity of his generalized and aloof approach to reform was the fact that, although Sunday was a staunch, conservative Republican all his life, his greatest fame and fortune came in the years of Woodrow Wilson's Presidency. "I never talk politics," Sunday told a reporter in Pittsburgh. "I will preach the Gospel of Christ and if that Gospel is accepted there will be no political trickery, or graft, or anything of the kind."

It was strange that, in the face of this, many of his backers, like Alba B. Johnson, president of the Baldwin Locomotive Works, and the Rev. George Bickley, of Philadelphia, should openly have asserted their belief that Sunday's revivalism would lead to a Republican victory at the polls in 1916. One critic of Sunday went so far as to state that "Rockefeller guaranteed 'Billy' Sunday $300,000 for his so-called religious revival in New York City in 1917 where John D., Jr., was trying to re-elect John Purroy Mitchel mayor."[7]

If this is what Rockefeller meant by calling Sunday a "rallying center" for those who believed in good things, he was doomed to failure. After the election in New York in the fall of 1917, the *New York World* sarcastically commented: "New York City had a Billy Sunday revival in the spring and then elected a Tammany mayor in the fall, thus demonstrating the cumulative effects of righteousness." Harry F. Ward, professor of sociology at Boston University, when asked to comment on Sunday's effect as an inspirer of reform reported: "I have been in seven communities at intervals of from two to five years after these campaigns. . . . In none of these places have I found the community attitude changed toward the fundamental iniquities. 'Booze' and the social evil still continue, and in those places where the longest time had elapsed since the meetings, they continue unabated."[8]

Some acute observers of Sunday's revivals noted that the moral approach to reform which consisted of denouncing the same old sins and vices that had been denounced since biblical times served more to screen iniquities than to expose them. Sunday and his followers believed that the only evils troubling the country were those personal sins committed by unregenerate individuals—stealing, lying, blasphemy, gambling, fornication, murder, intemperance, and Sabbath-breaking. This moral attitude toward reform, which did not even go so far as to name names or political affiliations, was naturally welcomed by corrupt politicians and the interests they served, for Sunday's moral fist-waving provided no real threat to the basic inequalities and underlying values of the competitive laissez faire system upon which they thrived.

"It was odd," said the Rev. Joseph Fort Newton, describing some of Sunday's backers in Dixon, Illinois, "to see a putrid political gang so anxious for the people to get a dose of 'old-time religion,' but it would divert attention from the game they were playing."[9] Brand Whitlock, the progressive mayor of Toledo, noted this same attitude whenever he attempted to arouse the people to undertake some basic reforms in the economic system: "Privilege did what it always does when it is pursued; it tried to divert attention from itself by pointing out a smaller evil. . . . To this 'moral' issue that had served for so many years the 'good' people responded immediately, as they always do, and with certain clergy to lead them rallied instantly about the machine and for six months reveled in an inspection of all the city's vices."[10] Sunday's invitation to Toledo in 1911, said Whitlock, was just one more example of this.

This did not mean that Sunday and his churchgoing followers were not sincere, but it certainly indicated excessive provincialism that they were willing to accept sporadic cases of individual political regeneration or of renunciation of corrupt practices as evidence of Sunday's power to reform the wicked cities. Or, put another way, it indicated such complete faith in the values and institutions of the United States that it never occurred to these people to question them. Such blind devotion was not even shaken by the repeated failure of Sunday's revivals to produce the effective civic reforms expected of them.

Another, and more important, reason for the continued faith in Sunday was that the Prohibition movement was reaching its exciting and unbelievably successful climax in these years. The most talked-of aspect of Sunday's revivalism was invariably his attack on "Booze." Here, it seemed, there was real evidence of the fruitful effect of his preaching. His attempts to reform politics might fail, his attacks upon white slavery might prove useless, but his denunciations of the liquor interests frequently led to immediate and startling results. It was said that "wherever Sunday went a great temperance awakening followed."

Of all the complaints of the rural folk against the city, that against the evils of alcohol was the most virulent. The Prohibition movement was symbolic of the rural distrust of the cities and of the industrial civilization which they represented. The driving force behind the temperance crusade was the sanguine belief that the liquor traffic was, as Sunday said, "the sum of all villainies" and that once it was prohibited, all social, political, and economic troubles would vanish. It was the simple panacea of simple people transformed into a powerful political instrument by the machinations of devout fanatics like Wayne B. Wheeler and the other leaders of the Anti-Saloon League.

Founded in 1893, the Anti-Saloon League's rise in the ensuing quarter-century coincided with the progressive movement and with the rise of professional evangelism. Sunday's connection with the league was one of close co-operation in a common cause, but, though he often spoke under its auspices, he was never, as were other evangelists, on its payroll. He maintained that Prohibition was secondary to revivalism and that preaching against saloons was only "a part of saving souls." It was never clear, however, whether those who came down the sawdust trail to shake his hand after the "Booze Sermon" were being "born again" or were merely promising to get on the water wagon.

Partly because of this attitude and partly because of the partisan political stands which the Anti-Saloon League took in every local, state, and national election, Sunday never became a member of the league's organization. Even in the heat of denouncing booze, Sunday would not depart from his political neutrality on the platform. In fact, he was so nonpartisan that sometimes, as in Burlington, Iowa, it was suspected that he had been duped by the local politicians into supporting the "wets." In Boston he waged a vigorous campaign prior to a Prohibition election, while at the same time referring to Mayor James M. Curley, who could hardly be called a "dry," as "our good stout-hearted friend."

Sunday followed the Anti-Saloon League in its transition from a program of local option to its demand for state-wide and finally for national Prohibition. In such early campaigns as Keokuk (1904) and Burlington (1905) he attempted only to compel city officials to enforce the already existent laws regulating saloons. Then, in Muscatine (1907), Ottumwa (1908), Decatur (1908), and Jacksonville (1909), Sunday used his campaigns as springboards for local-option movements, starting petitions at the tabernacle which demanded referendums for that purpose. In Spokane in 1909 he began to advocate state-wide Prohibition. A senator who was being thwarted in an attempt to push a Prohibition bill through the state legislature asked Sunday for help. Sunday closed his revival for three days and went with a delegation of ministers to the state capital at Olympia on a special train paid for by Spokane businessmen. There he preached his "Booze Sermon" at two mass meetings in order to put the pressure of public opinion upon the legislature. Finally, in 1917 in New York he was saying from the platform, "This whiskey business is a question for the government, not the states to battle, and you know it." It was evident then that the large industrial cities would never go "dry" unless the Constitution itself was changed. Here, at least, Sunday was willing to alter the system, but he did it in the name of the Bible and of moral reform.

If, as often happened in these years, a town, county, or state voted for Prohibition within a year after a Sunday campaign, Sunday and his supporters took full credit for it. William H. Anderson, the New York State superintendent of the Anti-Saloon League, claimed that most of the cities in which Sunday spoke went "dry" as a result. Even C. A. Windle, editor of the *Iconoclast*, who followed Sunday around the nation to deliver for the "wets" his speech entitled "The Answer to Billy Sunday's Booze Sermon," admitted that in at least one state Sunday "fooled them and the state went dry."

There is substantial evidence that in many midwestern towns and smaller cities Sunday played a large part in arousing public interest in Prohibition and in influencing subsequent elections. Cities like Mason City, Muscatine, and Ottumwa, Iowa; Jacksonville, Bloomington, Decatur, and Charlestown, Illinois; and Steubenville, Ohio, went "dry" shortly after his revivals. In West Virginia in 1912 and in Michigan in 1916 Sunday was provided with special trains and cars at the expense of the Anti-Saloon League in order to deliver his "Booze Sermon" at various points throughout the state during the day and still be able to return to the cities of Wheeling and Detroit to conduct his revivals at night. Both West Virginia and Michigan voted "dry" shortly thereafter.

But Sunday's victories for Prohibition could be easily matched by his defeats. Although the state of Michigan went "dry," the city of Detroit voted heavily against it. Although several of the suburbs of Boston went "dry" while Sunday was there in 1916, Boston itself went "wet" by several thousand more votes than it had two years before. Despite six separate revival campaigns and numerous single addresses throughout the state of Ohio in 1911–12 by Sunday and despite the utmost efforts of Wayne Wheeler and the league, that state went "wet" in the fall of 1912 by a majority of 84,000. Sunday's Baltimore revival in 1916, sponsored by such ardent "drys" as Joshua Levering, Daniel Baker, and Dr. Howard Kelly, primarily to promote Prohibition (though Sunday did not admit it), was a dismal failure, and so was his Providence campaign. It is possible to list dozens of such defeats, but as indications of Sunday's importance they are as inconclusive as his successes. In an era when the cause of Prohibition was successful and popular, its prominent advocates were considered successful, too. From the amount of money and energy spent by the "wets" in opposing Sunday, it was evident that they certainly considered him influential.

Sunday's role as a martyr and crusader for Prohibition made him a hero to those who accepted it as the panacea for the nation's ills; but to those who did not, Sunday and his friend Bryan merely became symbols of blue-nosed puritanism. To some of the more radical reformers, the Prohibition movement, like the moral reform movement, was simply the diversionary tactic of politicians and vested interests. It was in this regard that Sunday began to come under attack as a tool of Big Business. The connection, for Sunday's critics, was not hard to make. They said that the National Safety Council had been formed by the largest manufacturers in the nation to promote Prohibition, that the recent enactment of workmen's compensation and liability laws in many states had been opposed by manufacturers who blamed all accidents on drunken workers, and that many companies enforced Prohibition among their employees by hiring spies to report those with alcohol on their breath. Prohibition was simply an employers' plot to get more work out of labor without raising wages or bettering conditions. Some employers were known to have said of Prohibition, "I'm against it for myself, but it's fine for the working classes."

This hypocritical attitude was not that of the majority of the tee-totaling businessmen who supported Sunday, but it was sufficiently prevalent to lead radicals to cast suspicion upon the whole movement. A list of the most prominent supporters of the Anti-Saloon League, men like the Rockefellers, Wanamaker, the Bakers, S. S. Kresge, Leland, and Levering, was so strikingly similar to the list of names appearing on Sunday's local executive committees that his implication in this "plot" against the workingman seemed irrefutable.

The suspicion was reinforced by the arguments used in behalf of Sunday's revivals by certain backers. In an article called "Industry vs. Alcohol" in the *Outlook* in 1914, Lewis E. Theiss told of the vice-president of "one of the great steel companies" who said that his company "could have afforded to pay its employees a quarter of a million dollars more than their wages during the period that Billy Sunday was working among them" because of "the increased efficiency" and the decline in accidents. Another employer, "a manufacturer of railway cars," stated that "booze has got to go. We are not much interested in the moral side of the matter as such; it is purely a matter of dollars and cents." Speaking for industry as a whole, this manufacturer told Theiss that backing Sunday was a profitable venture.

This theory that Sunday and Prohibition were useful to Big Business assumed that his revivals had a direct effect upon the workingman. Some of Sunday's critics rather inconsistently denied that his preaching actually influenced the workers themselves, but there were few of Sunday's supporters who did so. The pious promoters of the panacea of Prohibition eagerly, in fact, overeagerly, emphasized the claim that Sunday would convert the foreigners, the "politically dangerous" masses, into "decent Americans." By this they meant that Prohibition, or voluntary temperance induced by religious regeneration, would free the lower classes from their addiction to beer, wine, and whiskey and thus release them from the wicked domination of the liquor traffic and of the big-city political machines.

The following analysis of a Prohibition defeat in Texas was typical of the growing bitterness of the evangelical churchgoers toward the immigrant: "In districts where the foreigners predominate," said the editor of a religious journal, "the saloon vote was almost solid. It will take a great Anglo-Saxon majority to overcome this foreign influence. . . . Broadly speaking the lower elements of all the foreign peoples among us will be controlled by the liquor interest." The editor concluded that this was not only proof of the superiority of Anglo-Saxons but also "a tremendous argument for home missions," which might convert these misguided and ignorant people from their sinful ways.[11]

Such statements disclosed a growing apprehensiveness and hostility among respectable, middle-class citizens toward the lower classes (whom they variously identified as "the masses," "the workingman," "the dangerous elements," or, simply, "the immigrants" or "foreigners"). Since the immigrant was connected with the factories and cities, he became the scapegoat held responsible for all the evils of the industrial system. Even before the turn of the century the evangelical churches began to blame their insecure position upon "the immigrant hordes" who drove decent people out of the downtown areas, who lowered the standard of living, and who increased crime, corruption, and infidelity.

It was reported after Sunday's "recent presence in Pennsylvania" that "even up in Pennsylvania's coal regions, with their large foreign population, many communities are going 'dry,'" and those who wished to save civilization from the barbarians were willing to believe it. Like Leland and the younger Rockefeller, John Wanamaker saw in Sunday a plumed knight in this regard. "Billy Sunday is no longer an individual only," Wanamaker wrote in 1915. "He is the center of a great Gospel work, and he cannot do that work without organization and assistance." This assistance was needed to protect America from "the tremendous tenderloin interests and infidelity of the combined nations that inhabit New York," Wanamaker told Sunday.[12] Beneath the fervor of revivalism lay a mixture of fear and duty, hatred and hope. And Sunday became its focal point.

Most of the immigrants who were held in such low esteem were inarticulate in their own defense. But a few of them, plus a handful of radical American reformers, spoke out against Sunday and the leaders of civic righteousness. These critics pointed to certain sinister implications in the crusade for moral reform and social conformity which seemed specifically directed against labor unions.

In his book *The Profits of Religion* Upton Sinclair accused the people who backed Sunday of gross hypocrisy in their attitude toward the lower-class workingman, for whom they affected such Christian concern. He offered the following explanation of the real purpose of Sunday's revival in Paterson in 1915:

> After the big strike in Paterson, New Jersey, the employers, Jews and Catholics included, all subscribed to a fund to bring Billy Sunday to that city; and it was freely proclaimed that the purpose was to undermine the radical union movement. This was never denied by Sunday himself, and his whole campaign was conducted on that basis.

This explanation was repeated by Elizabeth Gurley Flynn, Frank Tannenbaum, Carlos Tresca, Charles Ashleigh, Ted Frazier, and Jim Larkin. Tresca, however, reported that the silkworkers gave Sunday "a cold frost" and that the employers had failed in their attempt to convert them from active unionism to submissive Christianity.

Emma Goldman and Ben Reitman agreed with Sinclair, but, after hearing Sunday, they, too, dismissed him as an ineffective "clown"; yet they were worried enough about his activity to hold protest meetings. During the Paterson campaign Reitman interviewed Sunday's advance agent, the Rev. E. H. Emett, on the philosophy underlying revivalism. The *New York Times* printed their conversation:[13]

REITMAN: Has any man who has been converted ever bettered himself in any way?

EMETT: Yes, lots of them. They have increased their efficiency as employees.

REITMAN: Ah, that is just what I wanted you to say. They have been able to give more to the bosses. Has hitting the trail ever caused a boss to treat his employees better?

EMETT: I'm not sure that it would.

REITMAN: Do you know of any specific case in which a converted employer has raised the wages of his men?

(To this Emett was unable to give any definite reply.)

Further evidence of the antilabor aspects of the Paterson revival was unearthed by John Reed, who was told by Sunday's private secretary, Bentley D. Ackley, "You see, Paterson has always had the name of being a turbulent and unchristian city; and they think that Mr. Sunday will turn the thoughts of the working population to the salvation of their own souls and regenerate Paterson."[14]

The radicals' distrust of Sunday found additional confirmation when Sunday's director of men's work, the Rev. Isaac Ward, explained the purpose of the shop and factory meetings to a group of Boston ministers: "We never touch labor troubles," said Ward. "We teach only that old-time gospel of the cross. It's amazing how men who have never gone inside a church are ready to respond to that old gospel. It's the only solution to the problem of capital and labor. The great gospel of Jesus Christ finding its way into the hearts of men makes man love man, makes capital appreciate labor and labor appreciate capital. Labor agitation disappears in some places because of the meetings in the plants and factories. That is its moral and economic value. In some places strike agitation has been eliminated altogether."[15]

The fact that Sunday's assistant claimed that the revivals eradicated strike agitation did not mean that it was so, but there was a definite conviction on the part of many besides the radicals that it was. Helen Keller reportedly described Sunday as "a monkey wrench in the social revolution." Irvin S. Cobb wrote sardonically that, if Sunday's voice ever gave out, he knew that he could always turn to Elbert H. Gary, John D. Rockefeller, Jr., George W. Perkins, or Theodore Roosevelt for help.[16] Rabbi Stephen S. Wise called Sunday "the greatest theological strike breaker in history." The writer of the "Topics of the Times" column in the *New York Times* stated that Sunday's vulgar sermons were approved by his businessmen backers "as a police measure—as a means of keeping the lower classes quiet."[17]

During the depression of 1914–15, when Elbert Gary was heading an emergency committee to find jobs for the unemployed in New

York City, the *Wall Street Journal* said that a revival of religion was needed, since only religion "brings employer and employed together on the common platform of love and fear of God." And Gary himself stated in an interview that Sunday's revivals had done much good among working men. It was shortly after this that Sunday was given a formal invitation by the leading citizens of New York to hold a revival there.

The Billy Sunday campaign in Philadelphia, said the Rev. W. C. Poole, helped business because "business was taught that religion was profitable." "A better understanding has developed between the church and big business," he went on, because of Sunday; "a better comradeship exists between employer and employees of the same firm. These are the things which cause businessmen to rally around Mr. Sunday and consider him a good investment for individuals, cities, or business."[18] It was not until the red-baiting era of the 1920's that Sunday's antagonism toward labor reached its peak, but there were several incidents in his prewar career which seemed to point to this.

Sunday's revivals in Philadelphia and Denver seemed to the radicals to prove beyond a shadow of a doubt that his preaching represented the views of America's reactionaries and that Sunday himself was their dupe, if not actually their willing tool. Though it would be unfair to judge Sunday's whole career on the basis of these two campaigns, they did epitomize the tangled threads of strikebreaking, Prohibition, civic reform, and religious and political conservatism which characterized the whole profession of evangelism. To what extent the results of these particular revivals were coincidence and to what extent they were the direct product of careful manipulation by those who sought to profit from a wave of religious enthusiasm, it was difficult to determine.

The Philadelphia revival in the early months of 1915 attained nation-wide prominence as the result of a celebrated case of the abridgment of academic freedom which was connected with it. The trustees of the University of Pennsylvania always denied that there was any abridgment of academic freedom in the case of Scott Nearing, but the public thought otherwise.[19]

Scott Nearing had been an able and popular teacher of economics at the Wharton School of Finance at the university for eight years when, without warning and contrary to the desire of the dean of Wharton, he was notified by the trustees on June 15, 1915, that his appointment would not be renewed for the ensuing year. Nearing's friends immediately charged that the trustees had fired him not for incompetence or budgetary reasons but in response to external pressure and in order to punish him for liberal views which he had expressed outside the classroom. In the ensuing debate Sunday's recent campaign in the city assumed a large role.

John Dewey, president of the American Association of University Professors, denounced the trustees for assuming that a university professor could be treated like a "hired hand." But the newspaper headlines were devoted to the charges that "views and utterances on economic subjects considered too radical by members of the board of trustees of the University and faculty and which several times in the past jeopardized his position, are believed to be the cause of his removal." Nearing and several of his friends on the faculty had been active in local politics and reportedly had been of "vast use to the present mayor and his directors in showing up the wrongs done the city by corporations whose most powerful directors sit on the board of trustees of the University." The trustees had told Nearing to curb these extracurricular activities. When he refused, promotions had been withheld from him, and finally he had been dropped.

The trustees, led by Randal Morgan, John C. Bell, E. T. Stotesbury, J. Levering Jones, and George Wharton Pepper, refused to make any public statement regarding their action except that Nearing was "a greater liability than an asset" to the university and that because of Nearing's radical views "the University was beginning to feel the backfire. People began telling us that if the University accepted the views of Nearing it was not the place to send their children."

One of Nearing's extracurricular activities was his fight against child labor exploitation. He had praised the bill against child labor which Governor Brumbaugh was trying to get through the state legislature. Brumbaugh's chief antagonist in this was Joseph R. Grundy, a wealthy manufacturer. According to the *Philadelphia North American*, "Grundy's senator, Clarence J. Buckman," who was chairman of the state senate appropriations committee, had put pressure upon the university officials to drop Nearing. "When the University trustees came before the Grundy committee as applicants for $1,000,000 of the state funds, they are said to have been reminded of the fact that Dr. Nearing had unpleasantly antagonized 'influential men' in the state who had much to do with granting or withholding state appropriations."

239

Billy Sunday's name entered the controversy at several points. Sunday had spoken to the students at the university in 1914 at the special request of Provost Edgar Smith and George Wharton Pepper, both of whom were active in support of Sunday's Philadelphia revival in the spring of 1915. During the campaign Nearing had written an open letter to Sunday, which read in part:

The city is filled with unemployment and poverty; multitudes are literally starving; thousands of little children toil in the city's factories and stores; its workers, a third of a million strong, have no workmen's compensation law for their protection. Meanwhile the railroad interests which control the hard coal fields are reaping exorbitant profits; the traction company exacts the highest fares paid by the people of any American city; the manufacturers intrenched at Harrisburg are fighting tooth and claw to prevent the passage of up-to-date laws, and the vested interests are placing property rights above men's souls. . . .

The well-fed people whose ease and luxury are built upon this poverty, child labor and exploitation, sit in your congregation, contribute to your campaign funds, entertain you socially, and invite you to hold prayer meetings in their homes. . . .

Has it occurred to you that their kindness is a return for your services in helping them to divert attention from real, pressing, worldly injustice to heavenly bliss?

It was generally believed that Nearing, being somewhat socialistic in his politics, was an atheist. One of the trustees, John C. Bell, stated that Nearing had once remarked, "If I had a son I would rather see him in hell than have him go to the Episcopal Academy." This, said Bell, "invites dismissal."

Raymond G. Fuller wrote in the *Boston Transcript* on June 26, 1915: "It is the Billy Sunday crowd that is responsible for the Nearing case." He explained that "the Billy Sunday crowd is the crowd which prevents the overthrow of Penroseism in Pennsylvania, which permits the political debauching of Philadelphia, which keeps the university from being a positive and helpful force in public affairs." Fuller divided the "Billy Sunday crowd" into three groups: "One represented by most of the university trustees . . . another represented by the majority members of the Billy Sunday campaign committee, the men of secondary strata of business success and financial powers, and the third, represented by the political bosses and their henchmen." All these were "men who regard as Socialists all who see injustice and wrong in the present economic order of things." Sunday, Fuller concluded, "could have worked miracles for the purification of political conditions in the city and state, but . . . he was paid for other work. He was paid to put a 'quietus' on 'social unrest.'"

John Reed gave further corroboration of the conservative attitude of the "Billy Sunday crowd" in Philadelphia when he asked the Rev. George Bickley, vice-chairman of Sunday's executive committee, whether the revival would cause a prominent textile manufacturer who backed it to raise the wages of his employees. Bickley answered: "You don't seem to understand. Raising wages is a question of economics, not of religion. It would be utterly ridiculous anyway to raise wages in the textile industry with conditions as they are. What we need is the Republican Party in power before we can hope to do that."

Alba B. Johnson, of the Baldwin Locomotive Works in Philadelphia, told Reed: "You know the widespread Social Unrest is largely due to the workingman's envy of those who make a little more money than he does. Now Billy Sunday makes people look to the salvation of their own souls, and when a man is looking after his own soul's good he forgets his selfish desire to become rich. Instead of agitating for a raise in wages he turns and helps some poorer brother who's down and out." As for unemployment, said Johnson, "if the Republicans were in power, the problem of the unemployed would settle itself."

Nearing was not reinstated, but one final headline came out of the incident. On July 9, 1915, the *Philadelphia Evening Ledger* carried the following front-page headline: "BILLY SUNDAY BROUGHT HERE TO HALT STRIKE!" The article contained a special interview with Roger W. Babson, the statistician, who charged that "Billy Sunday was brought to this city not for the purpose of evangelism, but to avert a strike on the Philadelphia Rapid Transit Co." After giving Babson's reasons for this charge, the article continued:

Confirmation of the reason for bringing Sunday to this city was made by P. J. Kerrane, secretary of Local 477, Amalgamated Association of Street and Electric Railway Employees.

Mr. Babson's remarks were read to Mr. Kerrane. "We have been working for two or three years to get a strike for higher pay," he said. "The reason given by Mr. Babson for bringing 'Billy' Sunday to this city is correct in my opinion."

Babson himself was quoted as saying, "Billy Sunday is the best strike breaker the country has produced."[20]

Prohibition was also an element in the Philadelphia campaign, and petitions demanding a referendum for local option were signed at the tabernacle under Sunday's exhortation. Clarence D. Antrim, Republican leader of the Thirty-second Ward and a member of the Sunday committee, declared that the revival had added 50,000 men to the Bible classes in the city and that these men, realizing that the Republican machine was dominated by the liquor interest, could all be counted on to fight the machine and restore the party to the control of decent citizens.[21]

It appeared that some of Sunday's backers, like Antrim, Wanamaker, and Van Valkenberg, were using the revival to engage in what Penrose's predecessor, Matthew Stanley Quay, had called "Sunday School politics."[22] These would-be reformers had supported the local-option movement in Pennsylvania and had helped elect Mayor Blankenburg and Governor Brumbaugh as reform candidates to try to overthrow the Penrose-dominated Republican machine. But their intraparty revolt was unsuccessful. Few of Governor Brumbaugh's reforms got through the state legislature, and the bill for a referendum on local option was easily defeated in April, 1915. What was worse, a Penrose candidate was elected mayor in the fall of 1915.

All in all, it looked either as though Sunday's attempt at civic reform in Philadelphia had been totally ineffectual or else as though the whole revival had been taken over by the vested interests and their politicians, and the "Sunday School" reformers had been beaten at their own game. John Reed found some evidence for the latter view when he discovered that Penrose's henchmen were surreptitiously lending their full support to Sunday's meetings. "How," asked Reed, can Sunday "accept as converts the 130 members of the Thirtieth Ward Republican Club who hit the Sawdust Trail under the leadership of City Treasurer William McCoach, a prominent member of the Penrose gang?" And "Why is it that members of the Penrose machine who are tied up with the liquor interests of the state of Pennsylvania support Billy Sunday?" The only answers to these questions were found in the results of the revival.

More concrete evidence of collusion between machine politicians and Big Business in putting Sunday's revivals to good use was unearthed after Sunday's revival in Denver, Colorado, which attached Sunday's name to the Colorado mining strike and the infamous Ludlow Massacre.

On November 3, 1914, the citizens of Colorado voted in favor of an amendment to the state constitution to prohibit the manufacture and sale of alcohol. The result reversed a majority of forty thousand who had voted against the same amendment in 1912. This Prohibition victory also swept the Republican party into office in the state on a platform which advocated the vigorous suppression of the mining strike that had raged for over a year throughout the state.

Sunday's role in this election was indicated from the Prohibitionist's side in an appraisal by the Rev. A. H. C. Morse, a Baptist pastor in the state. Morse, in thanking divine Providence for the victory, listed three causes for it: the first was the activity of the Anti-Saloon League; "the second contributory cause—maybe the first—was the work of Billy Sunday in Colorado Springs and Denver. His mighty philippics against 'the whiskey bunch' created a new conscience in those cities and changed the votes of many thousands. . . . The third contributory cause—or surely the first—was the providence that permitted industrial strife in the spring; that led the Democrats to nominate for Governor an advocate of a 'wet' state and that led Mr. Sunday to fix his dates for Colorado before the great election. In these things it will be seen that the stars in their courses fought against 'the whiskey bunch.' "[23]

George Creel, who was a reporter in Denver during the course of the strike and the election, summarized the situation from the viewpoint of the liberal reformer in an article in *Harper's Weekly* in June, 1915. Sunday, said Creel, was the tool of "special privilege" and was invited to Colorado by the mine operators in order to distract public attention from the strike. "As a result of his revivals, the industrial issue fell from sight. Prohibition became the one great over-whelming importance. The operators gave unstintedly to the 'dry' campaign and sent word down the line that every controlled vote must be cast for the 'dry' candidate." Then, when the "dry" candidate was elected, "the fact became apparent that he was a 'coal company man.' " In this way, Creel concluded, the coal and steel operators "had 'put one over,' thanks to the aid of Billy Sunday. They had used the prohibition mania to sneak in their governor and their legislators." The truth of the matter lay somewhere in between the views of Morse and Creel, but there was nothing really contradictory in their stories.

The strike had begun in September of 1913 and was directed chiefly against the Colorado Fuel and Iron Company, whose mines were located at Walsenberg, Ludlow, and Trinidad, about one hundred miles south of Colorado Springs (which, in turn, is seventy miles south of Denver). This company was controlled by the Rockefellers, who had appointed Jesse F. Welborn as its president and

Lamont W. Bowers as chairman of its executive board.[24] Many years of oppressive working and living conditions lay behind the strike, but the growing power of the United Mine Workers Union made recognition of the union the main issue. As the heads of the leading mining company in the state, Welborn and Bowers took the lead in organizing the other operators in resisting the union's demands. The Rockefellers gave their full support to this policy and hired Ivy Lee as their press agent to see that the most sympathetic view of their case and the least sympathetic view of the union's was publicized across the nation.

The striking workers were evicted from the company-owned towns soon after the strike began. They moved into tent colonies set up and maintained by the union in the open country near Walsenberg, Ludlow, and Trinidad. As the strike dragged on through the winter and spring, numerous incidents of armed conflict between the strikers and company guards compelled Governor Ammons, who was a Democrat, to call out the state's National Guard to maintain the peace.

In the spring of 1914, while the strike was still in this indecisive stage, Billy Sunday was invited by the ministers of Colorado Springs to hold a revival in that city in June, 1914. The leading figure in obtaining Sunday's consent to hold a revival on such short notice and during his normal vacation period was the Rev. A. J. Finch, the Colorado superintendent of the Anti-Saloon League. Finch told Sunday that a revival would greatly aid in the movement to work up interest for a Prohibition referendum in Colorado in November of that year. There was no evidence that any particular partisan politics were involved in this invitation to Colorado Springs by Finch or that the mine operators, whose principal offices were in Denver, had any part in it.

Then, on April 20, 1914, shortly after Sunday had agreed to come to Colorado Springs, the Ludlow Massacre occurred. An armed battle between the National Guard and the strikers led to the death of thirteen women and children when the miners' tent colony near Ludlow was set on fire by the Guardsmen, who at this time consisted largely of professional strikebreakers imported from the East by the operators and enlisted in the Guard. As the violence increased, Governor Ammons finally had to request President Wilson to send federal troops of the regular Army to restore peace. The nation was so aroused by the incident that a congressional investigation followed.

Three weeks after the massacre the ministerial association of Denver, following the example of their brethren in Colorado Springs, voted to invite Sunday to hold a revival in their city, too, that same year. Once again, the Rev. A. J. Finch, representing the Anti-Saloon League, was a powerful factor in persuading Sunday further to shorten his vacation to come to Denver that summer.

That political considerations were mentioned in this invitation seems more than likely, for it was well known that the ministers in Denver had, since the start of the strike, taken the side of the operators against the strikers. Lamont Bowers testified at the congressional inquiry that the ministerial alliance of Denver had joined with the operators, the chamber of commerce, the real estate board, and the rest of "the best citizens" of the city in persuading Governor Ammons to call out the National Guard in the early stages of the strike. A number of prominent clergymen, including H. Martyn Hart, dean of St. John's Cathedral in Denver; Charles S. Olmsted, Methodist bishop of Colorado; and Charles G. Williams, pastor of Capitol Heights Presbyterian Church in Denver, had written a letter to the United States Secretary of Labor denouncing the "bad faith" of the strikers and the "76 violent deaths, most of them unprovoked murders," which, according to the one-sided view of these ministers had been entirely the fault of the strikers.[25]

That Finch made some political allusions in regard to the Prohibition campaign he was waging when he talked to Sunday about the Denver invitation seemed evident from Sunday's angry response to his advances: "I don't care about politics," Sunday told him. "I will not permit, not for one instant, the use of my name or of my services by any parties to a political campaign."[26] Nonetheless, Sunday agreed to come to Denver in September and October of 1914 for a revival.

When he arrived on September 5, Sunday reiterated to reporters that he would "keep away from politics." And Mrs. Sunday chimed in, "He sticks to his knitting." Throughout the whole seven weeks of his Denver revival he never once mentioned the strike or the political campaign taking place. Nor had he done so during his six weeks in Colorado Springs earlier that summer. He did not visit the miners' camps, nor were his meetings attended by delegations of the strikers. Delegations from the Denver offices of the Colorado Fuel and Iron Company, led by the company's attorney, were on hand, however.

Sunday's only political activity was to lend his vigorous support to the Prohibition movement. This in itself, however, virtually negated his surface neutrality, since the Prohibition question in Colorado that year was inextricably involved in partisan politics and also in the fate of the striking miners. At the outset of the campaign the state seemed so inevitably "wet" that neither party considered the issue of prime importance. The Democrats by-passed Governor Ammons to nominate Senator Thomas M. Patterson, who favored local option, as their candidate for governor. The Republicans nominated George R. Carlson, whose views on Prohibition were unknown. Little was made of the fact that Carlson had barely beaten out Sam D. Nicholson, an avowed "wet," for the nomination and that Carlson had been indorsed by the Anti-Saloon League (which by 1914 considered local option too "wet"). Patterson did remark, however, that the coal companies, who were backing Carlson, had formerly been notoriously "wet" in their politics.[27] But neither he nor anyone else attached much significance to this.

The central issue of the campaign was the strike; here the lines were clearly drawn. The Republicans stood for what was termed "law and order" or "the restoration of state sovereignty." By this they meant the withdrawal of federal troops, whose presence in the strike zone, though requested by Governor Ammons, was considered by the Republicans, as by the mine operators, to be an invasion of states' rights. Carlson's platform called for the policing of the strike zone by the National Guard, and, since the Guard was controlled by the mine operators' strikebreakers, this meant virtual suppression of the strike on the companies' terms.

The Democrats favored the acceptance of a compromise settlement of the strike on terms which had been voluntarily set forward by President Wilson. These terms had been accepted by the union but had been curtly refused by the coal companies. Paterson stated that, if elected, he would see to it that the companies accepted Wilson's proposals.

Public opinion in Colorado was undecided. There was a definite desire to put an end to the intolerable state of affairs, and there was no doubt that the Ludlow Massacre had alienated many people from the mine operators. But it was also felt that Governor Ammons had aggravated the situation by his hesitant and indecisive actions, and the Democrats, as the party in power, bore the onus for the public's discomfort.

While the two candidates were waging verbal warfare on this issue, the Rev. A. J. Finch quietly and efficiently organized the Prohibition movement. He not only got petitions signed which put the

Prohibition referendum on the ballot but also brought delegations to hear Sunday at the tabernacle, saw to it that local ministers played up the issue in other parts of the state, created the Dry Colorado Campaign Committee, and obtained funds to flood the newspapers with quotations from Sunday's "Booze Sermon." Most important of all, he saw to it that twenty thousand new voters were registered in the rural areas.

So efficient was Finch and so eloquent was Sunday that certain local businessmen in Denver began to fear that Prohibition might win out. Although these men were ardent Republicans, they were also in favor of local option because they felt that the liquor trade was essential to Denver's important tourist and convention trade, and Denver was a tourist center, not an industrial center. It was to gain the support of these men, most of them on the local chamber of commerce or real estate board, that Carlson had kept quiet on the Prohibition issue.

These businessmen and bankers of Denver decided to counter Finch's activity by organizing a Home Rule League. They spent a great deal of money advertising the dire warning that, if Prohibition were enacted, it "would reduce the tourist trade by fully 75 per cent." The situation had its amusing side in the fact that some of the more prominent members of this Home Rule League were also active supporters of Billy Sunday's revival. They put themselves and Sunday in a ludicrous position by their anti-Prohibition activity. "Denver, Colorado, is the only place where I have ever been," said Sunday, "where bankers have contributed to the campaign fund of the damnable saloon business." But there was more at stake than the tourist trade in Denver, and the activity of the city-controlled Home Rule League merely added to the piquancy and interest of the Prohibition movement in the rural districts.

On October 3, one month before the election, Finch and Sunday organized a Prohibition parade. Ten thousand persons marched through the streets of Denver to the tabernacle. Among them were the active members of the Anti-Saloon League; the choir of the Episcopal church, led by Dean H. Martyn Hart; the leading ministers of the city, heading their congregations; one hundred Protestant Italians carrying banners saying "Give Back to the Italians the Holy Bible" and "The Italians Are Returning to the Gospel and Christianity"; a delegation of Welshmen carrying a banner which said "The Welsh Are with Billy Sunday"; and three brass bands playing "The Brewer's Big Horses Can't Run over Me" and gospel hymns.

247

Leading the parade with Sunday and Finch was Major Leo Kennedy, of the National Guard.

The next day Sunday gave his "Booze Sermon," during the course of which he injected this statement: "Say, are you in favor of a Constitutional amendment prohibiting the sale of liquor in the United States? If you ever get a chance to do it, boys, will you do it? If you will, stand up with me. . . . Vote the saloon out of Denver and the tourists won't come, you say. . . . You're a black-hearted liar! . . . It's not a religious or a political question that confronts you November third, but a question of decency in the home."

Though Sunday also said that it was possible to vote "Yes" on the Prohibition referendum and still vote for either the Republicans or the Democrats, prompt action by Carlson, plus his indorsement by the Anti-Saloon League, served to associate Prohibition with the Republicans and to label Patterson and the Democrats as "wets." On October 5 Carlson made a speech in which for the first time he took a definite stand in favor of Prohibition. The astonishment of the Democrats at this turn of events was voiced by Patterson: "It was not until that imposing parade of Mr. Sunday's converts with Denver's church congregations and Sunday-school scholars under the lead of the indomitable Mr. Sunday himself that Mr. Carlson took the plunge into prohibition. The Republican managers, realizing that as the issues stood Mr. Carlson and the rest of the ticket were badly defeated, decided that they might possibly be washed into the statehouse on the top of the prohibition wave which they hope is sweeping the state. . . . I never heard of Mr. Carlson's making a public speech in favor of statewide prohibition until the present campaign."

The Democrats tried to remedy the situation by persuading Secretary of State William Jennings Bryan to come to Denver to speak on behalf of Patterson, but again they were outmaneuvered. Bryan spoke for Patterson, all right, but he also allowed himself to be persuaded to speak at the Denver auditorium in behalf of Prohibition. Moreover, his known friendship for Sunday served more to confuse the issue than to clarify it.

Sunday left Denver on October 25. "My last word to you," he told the citizens of Colorado, "is don't forget November third. Watch out for the whiskey bunch." Finch ably continued to agitate for Prohibition during the final week of the election campaign. The Democrats, with the betting odds five to one that the state would go "wet" and five to three that Patterson would win, continued to underestimate the Prohibition movement.

Lamont Bowers told the congressional investigating committee six months after the election that, on November third, "I turned out 150 men, out of my offices, and saw to it that they got out and worked for the going dry of the State and turned everybody out I could." He referred, of course, to the Denver offices of the Colorado Fuel and Iron Company. Presumably the other mine operators were just as zealous in their electioneering.

In the Republican victory which followed, the vote for Carlson was an overwhelming 128,476 to 90,133. The vote for Prohibition, though carried by only about 9,000, showed a tremendous shift in votes since the "wet" victory in 1912 and revealed that forty-eight out of fifty-six precincts in Colorado voted for Prohibition. Finch's rural votes were the deciding factor. Denver had voted against Prohibition by 10,000 votes, justifying the evangelical distrust of the cities and indicating something less than success for Sunday's activities there. But the city also voted strongly for Carlson, indicating the connection between the Home Rule League and the chamber of commerce. The "best people" of Denver had split their vote, refusing to accept Sunday's pleas for Prohibition but joining in what Creel had declared was the ulterior motive of the revival—the defeat of the strikers.

In those areas of the state where the coal companies controlled the political machine the vote was also solidly for Carlson. Strikers who tried to vote in the Walsenberg area were told by the company-appointed election judges that they "were all foreigners and had no right to register." The voting in the district of the Colorado Fuel and Iron Company was so fraudulent that the supreme court of the state later threw out the Republican sheriff and declared that his Democratic opponent had rightfully won the election.

When Carlson was installed in office, it became apparent, as Creel said, that he was "a coal company man." He immediately put a bill through the Republican-controlled legislature permitting him to appoint a new district judge to sit in the cases for the prosecution of the strikers. The man he appointed, Granby Hillyer, a former coal-company attorney, was so manifestly prejudiced against the strikers whose cases he tried that, shortly after he had sentenced John Lawson, the principal union leader of the strike, the Supreme Court of Colorado issued a writ prohibiting him from trying any further strike cases.

But the strike had been broken long before this. The federal troops had been withdrawn, and the strike officially came to an end on December 10, 1914; but its real conclusion had been election day, November 3. That the mine operators successfully manipulated both the primary election and the election to suit their own ends was indisputably proved not only by the course of events but by the testimony before the congressional investigating committee. Senator Frank P. Walsh put the question directly to Bowers: "Didn't you use the Prohibition sentiment that was strong in the State to get support for what you called the law and order platform, that was for the Colorado Fuel and Iron Company and others to aid in the ruthless prosecution of the strikers and the union officers, and a relentless policy of suppressing these men?" Bowers replied: "It was all interlinking and locked together."

Billy Sunday was one of the links in this chain, though he never admitted it and perhaps never realized it. He told Carl Beck, managing director of the Labor Forum, in New York three years later that if the men responsible for the Ludlow Massacre could be identified he would denounce them in the tabernacle, but he was astounded that Beck placed the blame upon the Rockefellers. Sunday did not even consider denouncing them; the younger Rockefeller was sitting on the tabernacle platform nightly as a member of his executive committee in New York.

Sunday took full credit for having made Colorado "dry"; but, when George Creel asked him during the revival in Denver if he were not acting on behalf of the mine operators in promoting Prohibition, "he could not," said Creel, "be induced to believe that the operators were using him, and I gave him credit for sincerity."

Despite the apparently conclusive evidence in Denver and Philadelphia that Sunday's revivals were used for ulterior purposes by politicians and businessmen, the arguments of Sunday's critics that "Sunday is being manoeuvred from industrial centre to industrial centre as the result of a very shrewd plan" seems highly untenable.[28] Sunday's career extended over forty years; his itinerary covered forty states and over three hundred separate revival campaigns; from 1908 to 1920 his schedule was always fixed for at least two and sometimes three years in advance. It is difficult to see how even the shrewdest group of politicians and businessmen could have manipulated this program to suit themselves. Except in Colorado, Sunday never altered his schedule to fit in extra campaigns.

Even in those cities where, by coincidence, Sunday's revival oc-

250

curred simultaneously or shortly after some labor trouble, the prominent men who backed him did not use him to quiet the workers. Rockefeller did not send him out to speak in the mining towns or at the camps of the striking miners in Colorado; Gary and Frick did not send him to speak in company-owned steel-mill towns like Gary or Homestead; the Swifts and Armours did not request him to hold mass meetings among the slum dwellings which housed the stockyard and packing-house-plan workers of Chicago. Of all the towns in which Sunday campaigned, only a few had labor trouble directly preceding his coming, and many industrial centers which did have serious strikes in these years, like Bayonne, New Jersey, and Fall River and Lawrence, Massachusetts, made no call for his services.

The argument that Sunday's revivals were all planned by industrial tycoons was as far-fetched as the argument that Prohibition was a plot hatched and fostered by Big Business to exploit the workers. Such a theory ignored the deep-seated rural and evangelical roots of the temperance movement in American history. It also ignored the fact that many unions, like the railway unions, and many labor leaders, from Terence Powderly to John Mitchell, were strong advocates of Prohibition, and they were hardly tools of Big Business. Many businessmen obviously did favor Prohibition from purely mercenary motives, and some of them did believe that Sunday not only would promote Prohibition but also would attract their workers to his tabernacle or convert them by means of the shop and factory meetings conducted by his assistants. But this was more a fanciful and nebulous hope than a carefully organized plan.

The only legitimate basis for the view that Sunday was a tool of reactionary business elements is the fact that he did, by influencing the middle classes, indirectly prolong a conservative resistance to political and economic change and thus hinder the development of sympathetic understanding which might have promoted basic and necessary social reforms on behalf of the workingman. As Creel put it in 1915, "With his revivals Billy Sunday has dealt the social sense a body blow. The spirit of service that was beginning to be a significant feature of modern life has been turned into its ancient channels of emotionalism. Altruism is being frittered away on 'experience meetings' and 'hitting the sawdust trail.' "

Sunday's influence and aims were neither so black as they were painted by his radical critics nor so glorious as they were portrayed by his admirers. The worst that might be said of Sunday would be quotations from his own provincial, but sincerely held, beliefs regarding the significance of poverty and unemployment. These views were clearly set forth by Sunday's wife in an interview in Philadelphia: "I haven't got any patience for a man that can't find a job," she said during the height of the depression of 1914–15. "He has usually wasted his strength and his brain through drink or cigarettes or women." If an unemployed man gets converted "and shows by his actions that he is trying to do good and live cleanly, the well-off Christians in that town will help him. . . . I say that a Christian can always buy his own shirt no matter how poor he has been. . . . I've seen thousands and thousands of people get converted and begin to make money right away. A good Christian is always successful."[29]

The question raised by Sunday's critics was really one of motive. Their view of Sunday implied that he was not sincere or, if he was, that he was being used by others who were cynical, hypocritical, and selfish. The former belief was held by relatively few persons. For the most part there was little question of Sunday's sincerity—though how this could be squared with forty years of constant manipulation by others was not clear. Despite Creel's dislike for what he called Sunday's "Salvation Circus," he stated: "To attack Billy Sunday as insincere and hypocritical is as false as it is unfair. The man has made too many sacrifices. . . . Criticism of him on the score of cupidity is likewise without foundation. He has made money, to be sure, but not one-tenth of the money he could make if he were greedy and self-seeking." John Reed agreed completely. "Is Billy Sunday sincere?" he asked. "I think he is. . . . I do not believe he could put the fire and passion and enthusiasm into his words and actions if he were not sincere. He is generous, even reckless with his money—he seems to have no idea of its value. Everyone who talks with him loves him. . . . I think he is just ignorant, that's all."

In general, the same may be said for most of those who supported Sunday: they were sincere but ignorant. For example, with absolute sincerity former Governor Foss of Massachusetts, who helped bring Sunday to Boston and who was an employer of five thousand men in his private business, explained how Prohibition would prevent panics and depressions:

Brewing and distilling are destructive industries. They lower the purchasing power of the masses for legitimate products to a very serious degree. This means that great quantities of clothing, shoes, food, furniture, and manufactured articles remain unbought. The result is stoppage in industrial production until the stocks on hand are lowered. In this way drink plays an important part in producing periods of depression and industrial crisis.[30]

John D. Rockefeller, Jr., in defending his company's actions in Colorado, asserted with the utmost sincerity his belief that for the Colorado Fuel and Iron Company to have recognized the United Mines Workers Union would have been contrary to America's most cherished tradition of freedom of contract. To compel a man to join a union was contrary to the Constitution; it was immoral and un-American, and men who promoted strikes in order to advance unionism deserved to be prosecuted as criminals. He stated that he was willing to lose every cent that he and his father possessed in order to protect the rights of the workingman against the unions.[31]

The wealthy men who backed Sunday's revivals were motivated principally by the general belief that religion was good for all people, but especially for the poor. These businessmen were devout churchgoers; their fathers, if not they themselves, had won their places in society by practicing the principles of honesty, industry, sobriety, and perserverance which Sunday preached. They were less interested in keeping the workers in their places than in wishing them converted so that they might become respectable American citizens. John Wanamaker assumed that the clerks in his stores could work their way up in the world precisely as he had done. He supported Sunday's meetings, just as he had those of Moody, Torrey, and Chapman, because he thought that they would instil into his workers the virtues which would insure their success. This belief was much more likely of fulfilment in the case of the native-American, white-collar clerks in Wanamaker's stores than in the case of the masses of industrial workers, but, despite the vanity of their hopes, the businessmen were no less sincere in their attitude toward the lower classes.

Though an increasing number of businessmen, like Wanamaker, began after 1915 to have fears about the non–Anglo-Saxon foreigners, their main interest in evangelism sprang from a deep sympathy with the poor and a sincere desire to do all they could to help them to help themselves. To these men Sunday's doctrines constituted the vital core of American democracy and the divine assertion of the social mobility of the deserving individual. Billy Sunday was more to his backers than a colorful evangelist. He represented a way of life which was slowly passing and which thus became an object of redoubled poignancy, to be grasped more tightly even as it slipped away. Their faith in Sunday was based on the essentially nostalgic desire to re-create the past in the present—to bring back the carefree youth of American enterprise.

When industrialism finally replaced agriculture as the main source of American livelihood and the urban center replaced the small town as the symbol of America, the wickedness of the city became a dead issue in revivalism, for to condemn the city was to condemn America.

After 1918 Billy Sunday fought a desperate battle to retain his popularity against the changing times. The churches still were badly in need of active and financially generous members, and secularism was still increasing rapidly, but new methods of evangelism were replacing Sunday's sawdust trail. The last years of the plumed knight provided a sad contrast to these years of his triumph. As scandals and lawsuits began to hound him and family tragedy sapped his strength, a shadow of doubt fell over his faith in himself and in the destiny of America. But his role as a prophet in postwar America was still powerful and, if anything, more vociferous.

8

JUST "PLAIN BILLY SUNDAY"

The first World War proved to be a turning point in the career of Billy Sunday as it was a turning point for the United States. When the war ended, the warm climate of reform turned to the chilly winter of reaction, and while, superficially, the latter seemed more congenial to professional evangelism, it proved to be otherwise. The mood of the 1920's not only was cool toward social reform; it was equally cool toward evangelical moral reform. Sunday strove desperately to ride the crest of reaction as twenty years earlier he had mounted the crest of reform, but he was only partially successful.

Like most other Americans, Sunday was slow to realize the tremendous effect which the outbreak of the war in Europe in July, 1914, would have upon the United States. The immediate reaction was one of surprise and horror, followed by a tendency to condemn or ignore the whole affair; if European nations were so foolish as to get themselves into a mess, it only proved how decadent they were, and a progressive, modern, Christian democracy like the United States might well congratulate itself on being outside the conflict.

There were a few who immediately took sides in the struggle and demanded that the United States give its moral, if not its material, support to the more righteous of the two sides, but it took three years for the nation to make up its mind which was the more righteous. Billy Sunday nowhere showed himself more typical of the middle class than in his reactions to the war. Had he felt that it was a clear-cut issue, he would have been quick to sense and express the prevailing view; but from 1914 until the very month of America's entry in April, 1917, he rarely mentioned the war, and, when he did, it was to express the opinion held by the great mass of Americans that Europe should be left to stew in its own juice. It is worth while to trace his statements regarding the war, not only because his views were so in tune with public sentiment, but also because there was a new note of frenzy in his war sermons which foreshadowed the tone he was to adopt in the 1920's.

When the war broke out in the summer of 1914, Sunday was vacationing at Hood River, Oregon; but upon his arrival in Denver for the campaign on September 5, he was immediately pressed by reporters to give his opinion of it. "There'll always be wars," he said. "God is the God of love and the God of war too." When asked if the devil was not involved in starting this conflict, he replied, "Oh, yes, I think the devil has supernatural powers and sometimes I believe that the Lord lets him go on ripping things up just to see how far he'll go."[1] But he made little mention of the war during the Denver campaign. In one sermon he said casually, "A lot of fools over there are murdering each other to satisfy the damnable ambitions of a few mutts who sit on thrones," but the main attention of the campaign was focused upon the coming Prohibition vote in Colorado. Without causing a ripple in the audience, Sunday stated that "the war in Europe is a sideshow compared to the damnable effects of the saloons."

Eight months later, in April, 1915, he refused during his Paterson campaign to pray for the end of the war on the grounds that the Lord had planned it in order to punish all the participants:

Never will I try to rearrange God's plan. How do I know that he isn't using the Allies to punish Germany for the higher criticism and heresies. . . . How do I know that God isn't using the Allied fleets storming away at the moslem fortresses of the Dardanelles to drive the Turks out of the Holy Land that Palestine may be restored to the Jews? How do I know that the Almighty isn't using the Kaiser's troops ravaging against France as a vengeance upon her licentiousness and immorality and her driving out of the believers. Do you mean to tell me that the Civil War was not planned by the Almighty?[2]

Even the sinking of the "Lusitania" could not make him publicly commit himself. Like the public at large, he was shocked, but not yet willing to fight. Even after two years of the war, in September, 1916, when Sunday was in Detroit, he still refused to pray for its conclusion or to take sides but merely repeated his Paterson statement. Mrs. Sunday told Detroit reporters that war was a necessity—that there had always been wars and always would be. She refused to express any opinion on the moral implications.

When Sunday reached Boston in November, 1916, he sensed the growing belligerency of the people along the Atlantic seaboard, but he was still noncommittal except in tone. "We are a mixture of all races, hence we are not a nation in the sense France, England, and Germany are nations though we have got them skinned, take it from me, and we can whip hell out of the bunch. I hope we won't have to, but if it comes to a showdown, look out!" On the night of the first call for trail-hitters in Boston he said, "You talk about a moral equivalent for war; you can develop more backbone by fighting devils in your neighborhood and city than you could if you were on the firing lines in Europe."

By December, 1916, Sunday had evidently come to some decision, but he did not announce which side had his allegiance. In talking of the need for outright surrender to Christ, he said, "There's no more neutrality about it than in the war. There's nobody in the United States that's neutral. A neutral man is a nonentity. He is a cipher. Nobody's neutral. I know I'm not." Finally, in Buffalo in March, 1917, just a few weeks before the United States entered the war, he was reported to have made the following statement in one of his closing prayers:

Jesus, you are surely taking a lot of back talk from the Kaiser. I wish, Lord, you would tell America to help wipe Germany off the map. Count Billy Sunday in up to his neck when war comes—I'll raise enough of an army myself to help beat the dust off the Devil's hordes. Jesus will be our Commander in Chief and he has Hindenburg beaten to a frazzle.[3]

On the day after war was declared, Sunday's statement indicated that he and the people of the nation were relieved that the die was cast:

Well, it has come at last! I am surprised that we have kept out of the war this long, President Wilson has certainly shown lots of patience. We were just forced to fight.

Sunday revised his sermons for the New York campaign which was about to begin and told the newspapers that patriotism would be the keynote of the revival. The headlines on the front page of the *New York Times* the day after the campaign opened read:

16,000 Cheer for War and Religion Mixed by Sunday
Sermons Brought Up to Date To Sink the Kaiser
with the Devil as an Enemy Alien

Quotations from the opening sermon revealed the new note which professional revivalism was to take for the duration. "In these days," said Sunday, "all are patriots or traitors to their country and the cause of Jesus Christ."

In order to mollify those of German ancestry or who were otherwise not enthusiastic about the war, Sunday at first adopted the prevailing attitude of American war propaganda to the effect that it was

257

Prussian militarism or German imperialism and not the German people which was the real enemy:

I never said either in private or in public that the German nation should be blotted off the map. What I did say and now repeat is that German imperialism should be blotted off the map. For the German people I have nothing but love, nothing but sympathy, nothing but pity. In these days of conflict I believe you'll find no more loyal, brave, or patriotic people beneath the Stars and Stripes than those with German blood in their veins.[4]

For several months Sunday followed this policy: "It was the salvation of the German people that led us to enter into this great conflict" he said. "Our flag has never been unfurled for conquest. . . . We're unfurling the flag for the liberty of the world."

But before long, as the war propagandists whipped up the emotion of the public, Sunday, like other patriots, forgot the distinction between the German people and the German militarists: "All this talk about not fighting the German people is a lot of bunk," he declared in February, 1918. "They say we are fighting for an ideal. Well, if we are, we will have to knock down the German people to get it over."[5]

The same hyperbolic exaggeration that marked his denunciations of the liquor traffic was employed against everything that was German: "I tell you it is [Kaiser] Bill against Woodrow, Germany against America, Hell against Heaven. Germany lost out when she turned from Christ to Krupp and from the Cross of Calvary to the Iron Cross. Either you are loyal or you are not, you are either a patriot or a black-hearted traitor." He had no use for "that weazen-eyed, low-lived, bull-neck, low-down gang of cut-throats of the Kaiser."

When Sunday was asked in April, 1917, how he thought the war would affect his revivals, he replied with one of his last touches of optimism, "You know all things work together for good. I have no idea how the war will affect my campaign, but I am not worried in the least." It seemed as though the heightened emotionalism and the clear-cut wartime distinction between good and evil would provide complete psychological reinforcement for his message. The surcharged atmosphere provided a host of new scapegoats for his attacks: pacifists, conscientious objectors, slackers, anarchists, Socialists, and "that God-forsaken crew of I.W.W.'s" who "would have a firing squad at sunrise if I was running things."

Ironically, however, this situation which found Sunday with no real opposition, with everyone clearly on the same side of each issue, was a detriment to his revivalism. He could not pose as the embattled underdog in this crusade; for the first time in his career he began to feel that he was losing that close rapport with the vital spirit of America which he had shared so intimately for two decades. Try as he would, he could not make personal salvation seem like part of the war effort.

In the spring of 1918 Sunday was making plans to go to France to preach to the boys in the trenches when he received a summons from President Wilson to come to the White House. When he arrived, Wilson politely asked if he would not put off his trip. As Sunday described the interview, Wilson said: "We have speakers, and singers, and entertainers enough overseas. Not everyone here at home is doing his part like the soldiers are, and you have the ears of the people and can go from city to city." Sunday replied as he shook Wilson's hand, "Mr. President, your wish is law with me."[6] Sunday stayed at home, and, by his own reckoning, he helped to sell $100,000,000 worth of Liberty Bonds, but he was sadly disappointed to be left out of the war, and he and his wife always carried a deep resentment against Wilson for his action.

As the war continued, Sunday's hatred of the German "Hun" seemed to become less a patriotic attitude than a personal feud; it was as though he thought the devil had produced the war for the sole purpose of diverting people's attention from soul-winning. Sunday was not conscious of this, but his personal frustration was apparent; it reached a peak in the campaign in Providence, Rhode Island, in the fall of 1918, when the Federal Priorities Division of the War Industries Board declared, in a letter published on August 10, "This committee advises that the building of a Billy Sunday Tabernacle does not lead directly toward the winning of the War," and hence "this committee will not consider priority for material entering into such operations unless there may be an abundant supply." The Providence revival committee was able to find sufficient lumber for the tabernacle, but Sunday had hardly been preaching for two weeks when the virulence of the Spanish influenza epidemic compelled the state health authorities to recommend the closing of all theaters, schools, and churches and the Billy Sunday meetings. Sunday yielded to necessity, but, in praying for the speedy end of the epidemic, he accused the Kaiser of inaugurating germ warfare: "We can meet here tonight and pray down an epidemic," he said the day before his tabernacle was closed, "just as well as we can pray down a German victory. The whole thing is part of their propaganda; it started over there in Spain when they scattered germs around. . . . If they can do this to us 3,000 miles away, think of what the bunch would do if they were walking our streets."

The war years produced one incident which perhaps marked the high point of Sunday's career. On January 10, 1918, he was invited by Champ Clark to give the opening prayer at a session of the House of Representatives. The prayer was characteristic of his rhetoric and his philosophy. In it he referred to the Germans as "one of the most infamous, vile, greedy, avaricious, bloodthirsty, sensual, and vicious nations" in history and described them as "that great pack of wolfish Huns whose fangs drip with blood and gore." His opening words were a paean of praise for the United States of America, where "the compact signed in the cabin of the Mayflower by our ancestors was for democracy, freedom, and the right to worship Thee according to the dictates of our consciences," where "there is not a stain on any star or stripe in Old Glory," and where "we have never gone to bed hungry or scraped the bottom of our flour barrel." He closed with the hope that "every man, woman, and child from Maine to California and from Minnesota to Louisiana [would] stand up to the last ditch and be glad and willing to suffer and endure until final victory shall come . . . until Thou shalt dispel the storm clouds that hang lowering over this sin-cursed, blood-soaked, and sorrowing world."

By the time the war ended, Sunday had begun to lose his grasp on the American public. His rhetoric and demagogic technique had not changed, but his audiences had. The great crusades for liberty abroad and Prohibition at home were over. The movies, the radio, the automobile, and organized sports provided better entertainment than the tabernacle. People were tired of the symbols which Sunday flaunted; they were tired of world-saving, civic cleanups, and personal salvation, and they were tired of professional evangelism.

For twenty years evangelists of all types, most of them crude imitators of Sunday, had been touring the country, leading their crusades, promoting clerical disunity, sowing discord in the wake of their frenzied denunciations and their commercialized sensationalism. Charles Stelzle estimated that in 1911 there were 650 active professional evangelists in the country and that over 1,300 more were engaged in part-time evangelism.[7] If a conservative estimate of 1,000 evangelists undertook an average of five campaigns a year between 1912 and 1918, it would mean that a total of at least 35,000 towns and cities held revivals in these years. One historian of religion declared that the evangelical churches spent $20,000,000 a year on professional tabernacle evangelism in the peak years from 1914 to 1917.[8]

As early as 1915 the overcrowding in the field was evident. Sunday's secretary, Bentley Ackley, whose two brothers Alfred and Kilmer were evangelists, reflected the growing uneasiness and unemployment in the profession when he wrote to Sunday that summer: "I would deeply appreciate it if at any time when you may hear of some small places, anything from three or four hundred to a couple of thousand population, if you would let me know so that I can post Alfred and Kilmer. The evangelistic situation for the little fellow this season is going to be mighty hard."[9]

There were not only too many "little fellows," but there were too many medium-sized and would-be big fellows in the trade. By far the greatest number of evangelists were engaged in tent and small tabernacle campaigns in the rural areas. Among these minor figures were men like the Ackley brothers, the Fife brothers, Dan "Cyclone" Shannon, J. M. Linden, Earle D. Simms, Franklin W. Swift, "Joe" Bennett, and Thomas Needham. Among the middling figures, those who occasionally visited cities of 20,000–25,000, were men like Charles Forbes Taylor, J. Scott Dawkins, Albany Smith, J. Q. A. Henry, George W. Taylor, A. W. Spooner, Charles T. Schaeffer, Herbert C. Hart, C. L. Evarts, John M. Dean, and D. L. Schultz.

In this same category were the part-time evangelists, ordained ministers with pastorates who had attained some fame, or wanted to, as pulpit orators and who took occasional leaves of absence from their regular work to capitalize on the exciting and lucrative field of mass evangelism. Among the best known of these were J. C. Masee, G. Campbell Morgan, George W. Truett, A. C. Dixon, W. B. Riley, and J. Whitcomb Brougher. Southern evangelists, who patterned themselves after Sam Jones, or Negro orators who called themselves "The Black Billy Sunday," stayed for the most part in their own section of the country. Such men as Major Burke Culpepper, "Cyclone Mac" McLendon, Lockett Adair, Tillman Hobson, "Bob" Jones, "Sid" Williams, Mordecai Ham, George R. Stuart, and "Sin-Killer" Griffin were seldom heard in the northern and eastern states.

There was a great ambition among all these figures to be "big-timers," to invade the wealthy eastern cities and suburbs, for that was where fame and fortune lay. As the small-town evangelist Clyde Fife wrote to Mrs. Sunday from his campaign in Billings, Montana, in 1915, "I have had a hard time and gone through a great deal out here on this western tour. Tell Mr. Sunday he was right. Billings is a dandy town. But say, it is not like the East for our business. I have done both and know."[10]

Few evangelists reached sufficient stature to be called to cities of over 25,000, and none ever rivaled Sunday's popularity. But there were five of second-rank importance who had sufficient fame and personal connections to be invited to cities which could not afford or were not attractive enough for Sunday. These five were Rodney "Gypsy" Smith, William E. Biederwolf, Charles R. Scoville, Milford H. Lyon, and Henry W. Stough. Of them, only Smith, an Englishman, did not adopt Sunday's style.

The evangelists modeled after Sunday who were turned out by Bible schools like the Moody Bible Institute were so numerous that they had to adopt nicknames so that they could be told apart. They not only called themselves "Bob," "Bud," "Cyclone," "Gypsy," or "Joe," but they added titles like "The Cowboy Evangelist," "The Labor Evangelist," "The Singing Evangelist," "The Businessman's Evangelist," "The Railroad Evangelist," and, if they looked young enough, "The Boy Evangelist." These sobriquets, however, became so common that at one time there were at least three different "Boy Evangelists," five "Singing Evangelists," three "Cowboy Evangelists," and five men, apparently related, each calling himself "The Gypsy Evangelist."

Since most of these were members of the Interdenominational Association of Evangelists, they all shared trade secrets and technical information. Sunday's success led to the imitation of his system in every detail, though on a reduced scale: the advance man, the chorister, the guarantee fund, the businessmen backers, the precampaign publicity and committee organization, the wooden tabernacle with sawdust floor, the spectacular arrival and opening night, the paid specialists, the delegation system, the trail-hitting, the society parlor meetings, the collection for expenses, the buildup for the free-will offering. Every evangelist tried to follow the formula.

Biederwolf, the most successful of those who followed Sunday's pattern, held a revival in Lawrence, Massachusetts, in 1917 which lasted for six weeks; thirty churches co-operated and provided a guarantee fund of $38,000; the expenses came to $15,000 and were paid off out of the tabernacle collections by the end of the fourth week; six thousand people jammed the tabernacle nightly, and the total attendance was reported as 260,000; 6,233 decision cards were signed, of which 3,350 were "reconsecrations," 2,432 were "first decisions," and 451 were signed by children. Besides unsolicited gifts from office and shop delegations, Biederwolf received a free-will offering of $6,175.

Like his colleagues, Biederwolf gave the standard sermons on booze, civic reform, "The Pure Life" (for men only), "Motherhood" (for women only), and the sins of society. Some of Biederwolf's sermons were so similar to Sunday's that plagiarism or permissible borrowing must have taken place. In his "Booze Sermon," for instance, Biederwolf brought a little boy to the platform and, laying one hand on the child's head, declared, "I would not give this boy for all the dirty dollars ever coined out of your damnable rotten liquor traffic." Even Sunday's hyphenated style was followed: "I'd rather be a dog with gratitude enough to wag his tail," said Biederwolf, "a foul-featured orang-ou-tang of the jungle, a leather-hided rhinoceros, my jaws dripping with the blood of slaughtered prey, a dodo, an ichthyosaurus, a hippopotamus, or any sort of cloven-hoofed, web-footed, sharp-clawed creature of God's earth, than to be a man with a soul so contemptibly mean as to sit down at the table three times a day and gulp the food that God has provided and never once lift my heart in thanksgiving to God who gives all."[11]

Few evangelists possessed the vital and inimitable qualities of personality and talent which alone could make tabernacle evangelism of Sunday's variety successful. In trying to imitate or outdo Sunday, many made fools of themselves and of the churches which backed them. What was worse, they brought the whole tradition of evangelism into disrepute. Biederwolf, for example, seemed to lack Sunday's diplomacy in handling the question of the Jews; he openly declared, "My father was foreign born, but I say if a European don't like the laws of this country let him stay at home. . . . If atheists and infidels and Jews and other rebels don't like our public schools where the word of God is read let 'em take their kids and hike out!"[12]

H. W. Stough was described in the *Philadelphia Ledger* as the preacher who "out-Billies Billy Sunday" and who "invariably makes personal attacks on saloonkeepers, politicians, distillers, and brewing magnates." In June, 1915, Stough became involved in a libel suit in Hazelton, Pennsylvania, by denouncing an alderman, a liquor dealer, and two city officials, whom he called "riff raff" and "plug uglies" and accused of being political bosses. Other evangelists shocked the churches by standing on their heads in the pulpit, by leaving town with debts unpaid, or by walking out in the middle of a revival because of an imagined insult or lack of co-operation. The ministerial association in one city wrote to the Federal Council of Churches: "It was a sad day for our churches when Evangelist —— came to ——. He is utterly unfit for such work. He is a disturber of the peace. His lightness and cheap imitation of Billy Sunday were pathetic. He is ignorant, stubborn, and untruthful. He has hurt woefully the influence of our churches in this community. Is there not some way to warn us pastors of struggling churches against men of this type?"[13]

The venality, commercialism, and incompetence of such evangelists in countless similar situations led to a crescendo of protest against the profession, a protest which had begun to make itself heard even before the war. Bishop Joseph F. Berry, though a staunch supporter of Sunday in 1915, voiced this rising antagonism the year after Stough's trial. "Advance agents of evangelists' parties are running to and fro in the land seeking to make engagements for their chiefs, in some cases actually offering liberal commissions to pastors who will assist them to get into their communities," he said. "How far is that removed from attempted bribery?"[14]

Berry condemned not only the evangelists but the religious press which catered to them by accepting their advertisements. In one such advertisement, said Berry, "Bob" Johnson claimed that he got decisions from 34 per cent of the population in every town he visited; another evangelist advertised that, singlehanded, he "converted a whole town in Oklahoma;" a third stated that he was a "thriller" but that his terms were so reasonable that any town could afford him. Others, like "Tom" Jones and "Bud" Eckels, or the "Cowboy Evangelist," boasted of their soloists from New Zealand or of the fact that they had two "harp evangelists" in their parties.

In summarizing his objections to mass evangelism of the Billy Sunday type, Berry listed the complaints which were heard with increasing regularity after 1915: the "two weeks of vitriolic attack upon ministers and church members" at the start of every campaign; the exaltation of the evangelist, with small credit, if any, given to local ministers for their efforts in the campaign; the "superficial and perilous" " 'shake-my-hand' method" of dealing with converts; the "vulgar display" of gifts to the evangelists; and the commercially worked-up remuneration for the evangelist. The weight of Berry's criticism led to the appointment of a Commission of Evangelism by the Federal Council of Churches which attempted to set up certain standards for "vocational evangelism." But the code which the commission drew up was too strict, and the council lacked the means of enforcing it.

Furthermore, as some opponents of this "astounding mania for organization" in evangelism noted, a large part of the blame for the uncontrolled and uncontrollable situation lay at the door of the regular clergy, who, by their overeagerness to hire someone to solve their problems, encouraged the unsatisfactory state of affairs. An example of this occurred in Cincinnati, Ohio, in the winter of 1916–17. The spectacle of the clergy rushing headlong into an expensive and laborious undertaking with little or no thought as to its consequences was ludicrously revealed in a letter written to Sunday's wife by the Rev. F. N. Riale, who had been appointed by the ministers of the city to try to persuade Sunday to rescue them:

> 315 BRYANT AVENUE
> CINCINNATI, OHIO
> February 8, 1917

Mrs. Wm. A. Sunday
Buffalo, N.Y.

MY DEAR MRS. SUNDAY:—

I wish it were possible for us to meet you again and lay before you the most unprecedented [*sic*] and in a way most calamitous situation we are facing here. I cannot help but believe if we could talk this all over face to face both yourself and Mr. Sunday would hear the Macidonian [*sic*] call in thundrous [*sic*] tones, and be willing to book up at the earliest possible date an engagement for Cincinnati.

When it seemed that you did not see your way clear for some reason or other to give us an exact date, some of the ministers on Walnut hills—and these too representing some of our strongest churches, closed up without much serious forethought with Dr. Stough. There are perhaps fourteen churches in the engagement. They built a tabernacle seating 7,000. The campaign was started the last Sunday in December. It will close in another week, the most colossal failure and representing one of the greatest religious trajedies [*sic*] ever seen in Cincinnati. This I am saying not because it clearly appears thus to myself, but it is the general concensus [*sic*] of most, if not all. Almost these exact words were said of it by Mr. Fagely, the Sect. of the Federation of churches as I was with him the other day in his office.

Last night I was over at the meeting and there could not have been more than 1000 there. At no time that I have been there—and it must be ten times at least—I never saw the tabernacle more than a third or at the most half full. Night after night has Dr. Stough appealed with all the physical earnestness a man could for decisions, and very often there was not *one* responce [*sic*]. Reports that two or three hundred responded at times meant nothing, as they only showed the number who went up after all appeal for a changed life ended in a desire for Christians to reconsecrate themselves more thoroughly to God's service, or to the definite tabernacle work.

One can feel the awful deadness in the whole situation; with the look of dispare [sic] on the faces of the clergy that had been prematurely drawn into it. The collections have not met the actual running expences [sic] of the heat, light and board bills of the party. The $14,000 expences [sic] of building the tabernacle and advertising &c. have not been met; and the men who have underwritten the amount are of course broken hearted or "mad as hornets" over the experience. . . .[15]

This abdication of personal responsibility by many pastors was pointedly emphasized in an editorial in the *Watchman-Examiner* which told of a self-seeking evangelist who, having been informed that an awakening was taking place in the town where he was scheduled shortly to appear, sent a telegram to the ministers saying, "Hold back the revival until I come." The ministers of Chicago, said the editor, were adopting this same attitude when, having arranged in 1915 to have a Billy Sunday campaign in 1917, they decided that they would cease all evangelistic activity until he came. Union meetings by special evangelists, said the editor, should "supplement the regular activities of the church," not "substitute" for them. "Shall we hire an evangelist and put upon him the burden," asked the Rev. George Stair, "or shall we rouse the entire church to the responsibility of the matter?"

Other church leaders joined in this call for a return to pastoral responsibility. In the search for a new, a less costly, and a less sensational method of evangelism, experiments were made in various cities with a new system called "visitation evangelism." Cities like Indianapolis, Bridgeport, St. Louis, and Lowell, which either had had unhappy experiences with tabernacle evangelism or had opposed it altogether, began city-wide house-to-house evangelistic campaigns in the years 1913–17. In 1914 the Rev. E. T. Clark described the St. Louis system as a "One-to-win-one" campaign in his book *The New Evangelism*. It was this system, ironically similar in many respects to the work undertaken by the Billy Sunday businessmen's and businesswomen's clubs, which eventually replaced Sunday's type of revivalism.

These "visitation" campaigns began with a budget of several thousand dollars being contributed by as many churches in the city as cared to co-operate. Then a careful "religious census" of the city was undertaken to determine how many persons were not church members and where they lived. Volunteer church members were trained by their pastors in the art of soul-winning, and then, during a fixed two- or three-week period, usually culminating at Easter, they were sent out in teams in their areas to visit a certain number of homes where nonchurch members lived. These visitors attempted to convert the nonchurch members and to get them to pledge that they would join some church. All the co-operating churches held special weekday services in the evening during this period, and the converts were asked to attend the church of their choice and let the pastor prepare them for membership.

The plan, it was claimed, worked wonders. St. Louis won 10,000 new members by using it in 1915. There was no expensive tabernacle to build, no need for headlines or publicity, and the face-to-face work was considered by many a far more effective method of winning church members than mass evangelism, with its vague, anonymous, and unpredictable consequences. Shortly after the war this new system became professionalized.

Experts in visitation evangelism, like the Rev. Guy H. Black and the Rev. A. Earl Kernahan, gave up their pastorates to devote themselves to organizing these campaigns in cities throughout the nation. Kernahan established an office of Directed Survey and Visitation Campaigns in Washington, D.C., and hired a staff of associate experts to help him. For a fixed fee he would come to any city, institute a thorough religious census, make a card catalogue of "prospects," and train the volunteer church workers (or, if there were not enough volunteers, he would provide "paid visitors" who were professional personal workers); he would himself direct the two weeks of visitation and would personally visit the leading social, political, and business figures in the city to convert them.

Kernahan was an expert at publicizing his ventures and published several books on the subject in the 1920's. He claimed that from 1923 to 1929 his campaigns won 185,867 decisions out of 370,750 prospects.[16] He was only one of many visitation experts, who were soon as popular as tabernacle evangelists had been before the war. The praise for this new type of visitation or personal evangelism (sometimes called "lay evangelism") was as lyric and overwhelming in the 1920's as had been the praise of tabernacle evangelism a decade earlier.

Cortland Myers, writing on "The New Evangelism" in 1920, said: "Old methods of evangelism . . . must give place, on the whole, to something better; that is face-to-face work, whether by pastor or Sunday School teacher, or ordinary church members." Charles L. Goodell, speaking for the Federal Council of Churches, said in

1921, "This has been the greatest year in evangelism which America has ever seen . . . and not by any feverish campaign or by a few remarkable personalities, but by a steady and constant emphasis on pastoral and personal evangelism."

In 1922 a conference held by three hundred churches of Pittsburgh met to discuss the relative merits of tabernacle and visitation campaigns. Since Pittsburgh had held four of the former in the twentieth century (Chapman, 1904; "Gypsy" Smith, 1906 and 1921; Billy Sunday, 1914) and one of the latter (Black and Kernahan, 1920), the representatives spoke from experience. With only three dissenting voices, the Pittsburgh Federated Council of Churches went on record to the effect that "imported" professional evangelists of the "Gypsy" Smith and Billy Sunday type were "too high-priced, too much commercialized, obsolete, false in stimulation, and ineffective."[17] Pittsburgh henceforth adopted visitation evangelism. By 1930 two-thirds of the city church federations in the United States were using this new method as their major evangelistic activity each year.

But by that time it was becoming evident that this new system had as many defects as the old. It relied on similarly false or misleading statistics which confused the pledges of converted "prospects" with new members; its expenses were high because there were no tabernacle collections to repay the churches for the money they invested in Kernahan or in other experts; the religious "census" or "directed survey" automatically eliminated as "prospects" all who were registered as members of any sect, no matter how infrequently they attended church; and the home-to-home visiting was done entirely in suburban or uptown middle-class districts—no attempt was made to reach the masses.

The appeals to join a church used by the "visitors" were based on the same ideas of "decency," "getting in the game," and good citizenship that Sunday had used. The personal workers were trained to be as sentimental, as sensational, as domineering as necessary in wringing a pledge from the prospect; the face-to-face confrontation by one's neighbors was often more emotionally uncomfortable than listening to Sunday. And the commercialism implicit in the system of paid directors and visitors was made explicit in Kernahan's statement that "a successful personal evangelist must be a good salesman. The same principles which enable a man to sell his goods are applicable to a personal evangelist." In short, the new methods simply replaced department-store evangelism with door-to-door salesmanship.

The effect on Sunday's career of the church's evangelistic fickleness was telling but not so great as it was on the hundreds of minor professional evangelists who were forced out of business altogether. Sunday did not condemn the new system, for personal work was an acceptable method of working for God; but he did feel that clergymen like Berry, Myers, and Goodell, who not only abandoned his system but also attacked it, were being personally disloyal. These particular men did not mention Sunday by name in their attacks, but the similarity of their charges lent the weight of authority to those of persons who did mention him by name. As the leading exponent of professional evangelism, Sunday received the major share of the abuse turned against it.

Sunday's reputation was not so free from stain that he could place the blame entirely upon the misdeeds of others. His sensationalism, commercialism, and misleading statistics were as subject to criticism as were those of his imitators. Though he avoided the gross blunders of men like Stough, he made others almost as bad, and the scandals attached to members of his party inevitably affected him.

It turned out that a large part of the book which Sunday permitted to be issued under his name in 1917, called *Great Love Stories of the Bible*, had been ghost-written by a man named Hugh A. Weir, and in 1918 Weir sued him for alleged failure to live up to an agreement regarding the royalties. The charges of plagiarism which had hounded Sunday throughout his career also came to a head in 1918, when a suit was brought against him for this offense by Sidney C. Tapp. His private secretary, B. D. Ackley, in a fit of depression resulting from chronic alcoholism, denounced the commercialism of Rodeheaver in June, 1915, and threatened to write a series of articles exposing the whole profession of evangelism. Rodeheaver was sued for "alleged breach of promise" in 1914, and the jury awarded the plaintiff $20,000. Another member of the party, Fred Seibert, was sued for divorce in 1915. In May, 1915, Charles Keegan, who had rented his home to the Sunday party for the Philadelphia campaign, brought suit against them for $1,754 worth of damage to the building and for the destruction of wine and champagne glasses during the party's occupancy.[18]

The accumulated weight of these incidents and of reiterated charges of "polite black-mail" in regard to the free-will offerings could not be shrugged off. Even the conspiratorial silence of most of the religious press regarding derogatory information could not offset the obvious failure of the campaigns to live up to their advance claims. A cartoon in the *Washington Evening Post* during Sunday's campaign in Washington, D.C., in 1918 was indicative of the change in the public's attitude. Instead of the usual picture of Sunday hurling hot shot at a cringing devil, the cartoonist portrayed a small boy clinging to his mother in the crowded tabernacle and saying, as he pointed to the men selling hymnbooks, Bibles, and authorized biographies, "It's jes like a circus, ain't it, Ma?"

Sunday's revivalism suffered additional shocks from the bitter fight between the Fundamentalist and Modernist wings of the Protestant churches which broke out in its full fury in the early 1920's. Almost every denomination was rent from top to bottom over questions of correct interpretation and proper emphasis of certain aspects of the Scriptures. Sunday, like every other evangelist, sided with the Fundamentalists, particularly on the issues of the imminent Second Coming of Christ and the literal inerrancy of the Bible. In some cities his revivals came to be looked upon as propagandistic moves by the conservatives in the battle for control of the denominations.

But, regardless of which side Sunday had been on, the very fact that the churches were split so deeply and so fanatically in this struggle made it virtually impossible to produce the united harmony so necessary to mass revivalism. One of the great advantages of visitation evangelism was that its manipulators took no public stand whatever on the problem; they left the whole question of doctrinal interpretation entirely up to the individual visitors.

The gradual decline of Sunday's popularity after 1918 was evident in the diminishing size of the cities which invited him, in the shift of his activity to the South and the Midwest, in the modifications in his technique, and in the decreasing mention of his name in both the religious and the secular press. The *Watchman-Examiner,* which had mentioned Sunday several times in almost every one of its weekly issues from 1914 to 1918, carried his name only five times in the first six months of 1919 and only once in the last six months; he was mentioned six times in 1920 and five times in 1921. The references were brief, usually one-sentence summaries of his campaign statistics. The *New York Times,* which carried 116 articles on Sunday in 1917, had only 6 in 1918 and none in 1919. The *Truth Seeker* printed a series of articles in 1919 entitled "The Collapse of Bill Sunday" and then ceased to consider him worth combating as an enemy of free thought.

Part of this decline in attention was due to Sunday's infrequent appearances in the East. Local papers in the South and the Midwest gave his campaigns wide publicity, but he was no longer of national interest. Of the sixty-seven campaigns which Sunday held between January, 1919, and May, 1930, thirty were in southern states, eighteen in the Midwest, thirteen in the East (including five in West Virginia), three in the Southwest, and two in the Far West. The size of the cities visited dropped considerably below the average for the prewar decade. Thirty-eight of the sixty-seven cities were under 50,000 population, and thirteen of these were under 10,000. In the spring of 1919 Sunday was in such straits that he accepted an invitation to hold a two-week tent campaign in St. Augustine, Florida, a city of about 6,000.

Sunday grew increasingly less demanding in the requirements to be met before an invitation was acceptable. Unanimity among the evangelical churches of a city ceased to be necessary shortly after the war. By 1927 he was accepting invitations like that from Bangor, Maine, tendered by only eleven churches. Specially constructed tabernacles were still preferred but not required; tents, auditoriums, tobacco or cotton warehouses, armories, and finally churches were considered sufficient. Return visits were no longer taboo; one out of every eleven campaigns in the postwar years was a return to a city already revived. His last full-length campaign lasted four weeks and took place in Mt. Holly (then Northhampton), New Jersey, in 1930, a town of 6,753 persons.

By 1920 the Sunday party was reduced from its peak of seventeen experts and nine assistants in 1917 to five experts who did double duty. Only Rodeheaver, Matthews (secretary-pianist), Mrs. Asher (businesswomen and Bible study), Miss Kinney (students' and children's work), and Albert Peterson (custodian of the meeting hall and advance man) were considered essential. From time to time a business manager was employed, but for most campaigns Mrs. Sunday took this position. Local ministers did the committee work. The party no longer required a private home for its accommodation but was content with hotel rooms.

The smaller size of the cities meant shorter campaigns: four weeks in the small towns and five or six in the cities of fifty or sixty thousand. Return visits lasted only two weeks. The co-operating churches were not required to close their doors every Sunday morning, though they sometimes agreed to do so on alternate Sundays.

Despite the more modest scope of his activity, however, Sunday was far from inactive during the 1920's. The fact that twenty-nine of his campaigns were in cities of over 50,000 (including Cincinnati, Dayton, Memphis, Portland, and Nashville) indicates the remarkable adaptability of the profession to the changing times and the stubborn perseverance of the tradition of mass evangelism. In a poll of 90,000 clergymen in the nation in 1924 the *Christian Century* asked, "Whom do you regard as the most influential minister in the American Church?" and, out of 1,146 ministers named in the 21,843 replies, Billy Sunday ranked among the top twenty-five. (The editors refused to give the exact order of popularity.)

Sunday was most influential in that section of the country which H. L. Mencken derogatively called "The Bible Belt" and "The Sahara of the Bozart." As the stronghold of the Fundamentalists, this part of the nation, principally the southern states, was the natural retreat of professional evangelism after 1920. It was especially so for Sunday, since he had, during his twenty-two years of preaching prior to the war, held only one revival in this area, in Atlanta, in 1917. At the time, this campaign was described by some members of his publicity committee as "Billy Sunday's only appearance in the South," but, with the revivals in Washington, D.C., and Fort Worth in 1918, Sunday began eleven years of almost constant activity there. The rising industrialism of the South; its basically united evangelical orthodoxy, centering in two major denominations, Baptist and Methodist; and its growing urban and suburban middle class made the area fertile ground for Sunday's type of evangelism.

There were two reasons why Sunday had hesitated to go South prior to 1918. One was his deep-rooted Republicanism, with its emotional hangovers from the Civil War; the other was the question of segregation. The first of these difficulties wore off over the years, and Sunday came to consider the South the bastion of Christianity because, compared with other sections, it had a higher percentage of church members, a smaller number of Catholics and foreigners, and a more rural and conservative social system. The South, he observed in one sermon, was the home of "more true-blue Americanism" than any other part of the country: "There's more pure-blooded Americans south of the Mason-Dixon line than anywhere else in this country." But the problem of segregation he never solved; he faced it only when forced to do so by his general ostracization from the North.

"We don't know what to do about the color line," one member of the party said before the Atlanta campaign. "We've all been in conference several days seeking spiritual guidance. We don't know whether to have a Jim Crow tabernacle or to alternate meetings of blacks and whites. It's very difficult."[19] Moody held few revivals in the South for the same reason, and on one occasion, when he was preaching in Chattanooga, the Negroes boycotted a meeting which he had set aside especially for them because they had been prohibited from attending his other services.[20] Sam Jones and other southern evangelists had no qualms about preaching in tabernacles or auditoriums where Negroes were restricted to a special section or were excluded entirely. After a long debate Sunday decided to follow Moody's example and exclude Negroes from the tabernacle except for one or two services which would be solely for them. "We always fell in with the custom," said Mrs. Sunday, regarding segregation.[21]

Sunday claimed that Negroes and whites were both equal before God, but he was unwilling to accept their equality among men. He stated his views on the Negro's inequality most clearly in Springfield, Illinois, in 1909, the year after the race riots there. He denounced the riots in one of his sermons and was cheered when he said that, if he had been in charge of the police during the riot, the streets would have been "crimson with the blood of the members of the gang" that had lynched the Negroes. But then he went on to state: "I am not going to plead for the social equality of the white man and the black man. I don't believe there is an intelligent white man who believes in social equality or an intelligent and reasonable colored man who believes in social equality. But before God and men every man stands equal whether he is white or whether he is black."

Sunday brushed aside this typical inconsistency in his next remark that he would not want his daughter to marry a Negro, and "I do not think any sensible Negro would want to marry my daughter." He finally passed the whole question off with a bit of sophistry: "We haven't equality even among the white folks. Mrs. Potter Palmer gave a magnificent reception in her palatial home on Lake Shore Drive in Chicago. She didn't invite me."[22]

It was not until the labor shortage during the war necessitated the employment of Negroes in many northern factories that Sunday seemed to oppose the assumption of white supremacy. In Providence, in 1918, he noted that some workers were refusing to work next to Negroes in the war plants. He agreed with the factory owners that this was unpatriotic and un-American. "If the Negro is good enough to fight in the trenches and buy Liberty Bonds, his girl is good enough to work alongside any white girl in the munitions factories."

This remark was quoted by the *Richmond Planet,* a Negro paper of Richmond, Virginia, when Sunday campaigned there in January and February of 1919. John Mitchell, Jr., the paper's editor, led a vigorous protest among the city's sixty thousand Negroes against the revival because "somebody blundered" and "colored people are absolutely barred from attending these meetings." Sunday's managers, said Mitchell, "have deemed it advisable to show only white people the way to heaven."

When Sunday attempted to mollify the Negro population by offering to hold a special meeting during the revival at which they would have all the seats in the balcony reserved for them, the Negroes refused. "If the Negroes of Richmond," said Mitchell, "have as much self-respect as the fourth part of a grain of sand or mustard seed, they will respectfully decline the invitation and stay away from the unclean feast." And they did stay away; only twenty-one appeared at the tabernacle on the night reserved for them. The Negroes of Richmond placed the blame for their exclusion not upon Sunday but upon the local committee which had invited him without seeking the advice or aid of the Negro ministers. It was not long after this show of independence that a branch of the Ku Klux Klan was organized in that city.

Sunday's connection with the Ku Klux Klan was probably as indirect in general as it was in this particular instance. However, the Klan was made up of people who shared his social and religious attitudes, and its program of pure Americanism and superpatriotism was very similar to his in its broad outlines. Those who promoted professional evangelism could quite consistently promote the platform of the Klan just as they had the platform of the Anti-Saloon League. Although not so well co-ordinated or so carefully directed as the Anti-Saloon League on a national basis, the Ku Klux Klan had similar motivation and emotional fervor, was made up largely of the same class of people, and used its power politically in a similar nonpartisan, or bipartisan, fashion. At the outset of its renascence in the twenties, the Klan numbered among its leaders many of the most respectable and substantial men in the communities in which it flourished. Many ministers took an active part in it. "It is probable," said one investigator at the time, "that the majority of the Baptist ministers in the small towns and countryside are either secretly or openly sympathetic to the Klan."[23]

The rank and file of the Klan in the South "was made up of the common whites, industrial and rural," and in the North, especially in Indiana, Ohio, Illinois, and Oregon, the same middle-class leadership and following made the Klan as strong as, if not stronger than, in the South. The secrecy of the Klan's membership lists prevents verification, but it seems undeniable that there was a high degree of correlation between Sunday's supporters in the 1920's and the members of the Klan. There is nothing in Sunday's sermons praising the Klan, but neither is there any record of his attacking it. Mrs. Sunday stated that "he never expressed himself much about it—they attended a meeting in a tabernacle in a body once, I remember, but I do not know where."[24] It is probable that this took place in Tulsa, Oklahoma; Portland, Oregon; or Richmond, Indiana, since these cities contained particularly active and prominent Klan branches in the early 1920's, when Sunday was invited. Wherever the Klansmen came to the tabernacle, and it may have happened more than once, it was not to threaten Sunday but to applaud him, for his preaching in most respects advanced their views.

Examination of the Klan's program in its general outline explains why Sunday saw no harm in accepting its open support. This program can be summarized negatively as anti-internationalist, anti-bolshevist, anti-immigration, anti-alien, anti–naturalized citizens, anti-Negro, anti-Semitic, anti-Asian, and anti-Catholic. Or, stated positively, the Klan's motto was "100 per cent Americanism." Sunday was perhaps principally pleased, however, by two other aspects of the Klan's program: its aggressive evangelicalism and its staunch Prohibitionism. Its evangelicalism was proudly in favor of the Fundamentalist movement and it stood for anti-evolution, anti-higher criticism, anti-atheism. Its Prohibitionism, like Sunday's, favored vigorous reprisals against those who broke the Volstead Act.

In broader frames of reference, the Klan, like Sunday, associated atheism with bolshevism and with un-American attitudes toward private property and free enterprise. It also associated bolshevists, or "Reds," with unionism and strikes, both of which were disapproved of by the businessmen in the Klan as they were by Sunday. (When a railroad strike was threatening in 1921, Sunday made it clear that, despite his professed friendliness for the railway unions, he would never permit them to disrupt the nation's business: "If we have a railroad strike, I'll probably get out and run an engine."[25]) In northern industrial centers the Klan looked with suspicion upon the working class not only for its susceptibility to labor agitation but also for its Catholicism and its anti-Sabbatarian desire for Sunday baseball and Sunday movies. To many Klansmen the very inability of the industrial worker to rise to middle-class respectability was looked upon as proof of un-Americanism.

When United States Attorney-General A. Mitchell Palmer began his famous raids against "radicals" in 1919–20, the Klan vigorously supported him, and Sunday told the Attorney-General that deporting the radicals was too good for them: "I would stand every one of the ornery, wild-eyed I.W.W.'s, Anarchists, crazy Socialists, and other types of Reds up before a firing squad and save space on our ships." The unfounded and largely manufactured "red scare" of these years was made to order for this type of demagogy, and Sunday made the most of it.

After 1925, when immigration restriction laws had been enacted, when the Scopes trial held up to general ridicule the narrow theological views of the Fundamentalists, when it became certain that isolationism and disarmament were firmly established as national aims, and when congressional investigation threatened to expose the Klan, "a rapidly growing exodus of all the more decent elements from the rank and file of the Klan" began.[26] The nomination of Alfred E. Smith, a Roman Catholic, for President in 1928 caused a brief resurgence in Klan activity, but after the election this, too, died out. It was not entirely coincidental that Billy Sunday's career came to an end shortly thereafter.

Sunday's sermons in the 1920's were still directed principally toward reviving the complacent church members and arousing non-members to repentance and the need of salvation; but the social overtones, the political asides, and the scapegoats he used to arouse the emotions of his audiences, these elements underwent a subtle metamorphosis in the postwar reaction. The wickedness of the city was transformed into the wickedness of foreign entanglements. Prohibition was still a main theme, but instead of the saloonkeeper and the booze-hoister, Sunday now attacked the bootlegger and the rum-runner. Hoboes, anarchists, and "the man with the dinner bucket," instead of being isolated individuals, were stereotyped into a class and lumped together under the term "foreigners"; atheists, skeptics, agnostics, evolutionists, Unitarians, and other nonevangelicals all became "Modernists" and, if not made synonymous with "Bolsheviki," were at least closely associated with them.

The tone of Sunday's sermons became steadily more frenetic, more uncompromising, more bitterly extremist. Faced at last with the fact that his influence was rapidly waning, Sunday abandoned any attempt to be tolerant or open-minded. His transformation is apparent in the hastily scrawled revisions, the crossings-out, the insertions, and the rearrangement of phrases, paragraphs, and pages in the sermon notes which he used during the last fifteen years of his life. The process by which Sunday gradually lumped together his three principal scapegoats, the "wets," the "Bolsheviki," and the "Modernists," can be readily followed in the abbreviated, elliptical phraseology of these sermon outlines.[27]

After the enactment of Prohibition, Sunday's "Booze Sermon" was replaced by a sermon entitled "Crooks, Corkscrews, Bootleggers, and Whiskey Politicians—They Shall Not Pass." This sermon advocated the complete and strict enforcement of Prohibition and was given many times for the Anti-Saloon League as well as in each revival. It began by describing the blessings that Prohibition had brought to the workingman and the nation. The incomplete fragments of sentences in the sermon outlines read: "Prohibition is making capitalist out of workingman. There are fewer strikes—any other time. A sober nation consumes everything its workers produce." According to Sunday, Prohibition had proved to be just the blessing the "Booze Sermon" predicted. It had aided American industry because of the demand it made for more manufactured goods. It also cut costs. "From everywhere in industrial America come reports from great industrial plants: 'We no longer fear Blue Mondays with their train of accidents!'" Sunday took care to paint this glowing picture of the effects of Prohibition because the main point of his sermon was its attack upon those who sabotaged or opposed it. Since Prohibition aided workers and business and since it made America prosperous and happy, the enemies of Prohibition were clearly enemies of America.

This was easily proved. "I made a list of nearly 500 names of men recently arrested for violating Prohib. It reads like a page of directories from Italy, Greece—sprinkling of Irish. Senator Reed said Prohib. has created a new class of criminals," said Sunday, but "it merely diverted the criminal class. . . . For nearly everyone of the 500 was a confessed crook before he became a bootlegger. Not one was in favor of the 18th Amendment." Of course, a man who violated the Eighteenth Amendment had broken the law, but what Sunday wished to show, and did, to his satisfaction, was that these law-breakers were a separate and distinctly un-American "class."

"It is estimated," he went on in the sermon, "90 per cent of the gangsters, racketeers, and boot-leggers of Chicago are foreign-born —and further that 75% of the 90% have never been naturalized." This not only proved his point, but it provided the simple solution to the problem of enforcement. "The answer to Chicago's problem is largely the answer to our enforcement problem. 1. Deport every unnaturalized law breaker. 2. Take away citizenship papers of every foreign born man—who proves himself a criminal—and 3. on second offense deport him also."

The simplicity of this argument led to less obvious conclusions in other sermons. In his sermon on "The Ten Commandments," for example, Sunday found that the same group of persons who broke the Prohibition law was responsible for labor unrest and radical views on government ownership. They were part of a great foreign plot to undermine America. "It so happens," said Sunday, "that America is placed in a position where the fate of the world depends largely on our conduct. If we lose our heads down goes Civilization. Woe to the world if this nation wabbles [sic] out of the orbit of Liberty. The mission of America is [to] salvage the world from the wreck of war."

This was to be done not by any international commitments, not by the World Court or "the mutts League" of Nations ("I'm not for League of Nations or World Court," he penciled into a sermon outline in 1920), but by setting the world a good example of what true democracy was like. It was to be accomplished by maintaining the old American virtues and morality and by adhering strictly to the rugged individualism which made the nation great.

This did not require any changes in the American system. On the contrary, it required a rigid adherence to "normalcy," to the status quo. "No man who swerves in the slightest degree from absolute loyalty should be called American citizen," and by "loyalty" Sunday meant adherence to the political and economic policies of the Republican party, which he called "the party of Grand moral ideas," as exemplified by Harding, Coolidge, McKinley, Grant, and Theodore Roosevelt. He came to the conclusion in this sermon that "America is not a country for a dissenter to live in."

With the zeal of a Klan member, Sunday lashed these dissenters and, in doing so, laid bare the irrational fear underlying the "Palmer raids" and the hysteria which produced the bigoted immigration laws. "I believe the 10 million aliens in this country who have been content to seek fortune under protecting folds Stars and Stripes but who have refused to be assimilated should be dug up—to the last man and make to kiss American flag or go back to lands from which came." He did not maintain that all these had violated the Prohibition amendment, but he did maintain that they were dissenters, since they did not immediately adopt the religious and political views and customs which he considered the only true indication of Americanism.

There is a "class coming" to this country, Sunday continued, in the curt notations for his "Ten Commandments" sermon, which is "injurious—dangerous—bring heresies—Continental customs. Do not come [to] become Americans—. . . . Every drop blood beats to music Sabbath desecra. Many come tags telling destination—Not build American homes—Not learn language—Undermine honest labor—flaunt red flag. I say Rip off tags—tag back."

The mere fact of nonassimilation implied disloyalty and hence revolution and the overthrow of America. "Our country crowded with anti-American — [anti-]church — [anti-]God — [anti-]marriage. Laying eggs Unrest and Rebellion. They call us the melting pot world. It is up to us to see that the slag and scum which refuses to melt into Americanism—is skimmed off."

The atrocity stories of what was happening to religion and the sacred bonds of marriage in Russia under the Bolsheviki made Sunday see in every immigrant a potential atheist and advocate of free love and in every proponent of birth control a Communist. It was, he claimed, a well-established fact that the country was being overrun by "this radical spawn trying capture U.S. Govt. Turn stars stripes—red rag rebellion." The evidence was clear in the unrest stirred up among honest American labor by the Socialists and the IWW. Sunday aroused the superpatriots: "This country is going to be run by Americans. . . . Not by brood of foreign vultures—smell steerage. Not by howling wolves communism trying build for themselves prosperity. Socialism is the sulphur—I.W.W. [later crossed out and replaced by "Communism"] niter which radicals would mix into the T.N.T. of Rebellion and blow this Govt. into atoms. They are tunnelling under Constitution. Keg powder one hand—Fuse. Trying to write into our Jeffersonian Ideals of Government the God-forsaken mental and moral twists of Carl [sic] Marx the socialist."

This whole "dangerous class" of radicals who were pouring into the country from Europe to "spit their venom on church—flag" was bent upon undermining free enterprise. "They sneer at private ownership. They would tear down boundary fence. They would tear up every deed." Such persons were lacking in the American drive to work their way up in the world. "I never knew anyone to disparage wealth except the man who did not possess it," and, in this land of opportunity for all, "the man who saves nothing is like a man walking through a valley of diamonds without fingers or hands to pick them up." It was no wonder, Sunday concluded, that, with such men stirring up the workers, "thoughtful businessmen are awakening to perils that threaten our civilization in the widespread disregard for law and integrity." This was a sentence left over from a prewar sermon, but it had a new significance now.

In his sermon "What Think Ye of Christ" Sunday explained the alarming situation to the honest American workingman, the members of the Junior Order of United American Mechanics or of the AF of L who were only too ready to agree with him, that this scum of Europe would lower the standard of living: "We can't compete with the promiscuous importations," he told them. It was tantamount to admitting that his revivals had not and could not reach the lower classes when Sunday finally inserted in his sermons a stereotype of the day laborers as "dangerous radicals" or "the criminal class" who should be sent back to Europe immediately. It was as though Sunday at last realized that there was a lower class in America, a proletariat that could not rise to be captains of industry simply by means of push, thrift, and honesty. To recognize it was to reject it as un-American and to seek means to be rid of it.

Sunday compared the native-born American laboring man to this unassimilated foreigner with whom he could not compete: "We must have meat once a day. A bath once a week. We can't compete with man who takes up belly-band [for] breakfast. Eats rye bread, hot dog, spagetti [sic]—lunch. Sucks in [his] limburger [and] garlic breath [for] supper. Calls crummy-buggy blanket a bed." Such men, if not Communists or criminals already, soon would be. And, even if they became naturalized citizens, Sunday did not think that they would change. "We have made American citizenship too cheap. We allow every creature calls self man to sway the sceptre of American soverignty [sic]—To become factor framing public opinion." To allow such dirty, lazy, unsuccessful men to vote might mean the overthrow of private property by democratic means. Immigration must be stopped, and the alien, even the naturalized citizen, must be deported.

The principal bulwarks of Americanism to Sunday were the Protestant religion, as preached by Fundamentalists, and the public school, provided that it had compulsory religious training in conservative theological doctrines and prohibited the teaching of evolution. "The Preachers of America have done more to civilize it than all armies and sheriffs," he maintained in his sermon "In the Beginning, God." "When you destroy the church you destroy civilization." "We can never be grateful enough for the church. From it we get all that is best." But, unfortunately, said Sunday, "two opposite religions are being proclaimed from pulpits. One is the great redemptive religion known as Christianity founded upon supernatural birth Jesus and that he died on the Cross as a sin offering. . . . The other is anti-Christian—Agnostic—Naturalistic—Modernism—Represented by Fosdick—Grant—their breed of cats."

During the war Sunday had been quick to trace the origin of the higher criticism directly to the Kaiser's orders. "Oh, this higher criticism! Listen!" he confided to a Providence audience in October, 1918. "In 1895 at the Potsdam Palace the Kaiser called his statesmen together and outlined his plan for world domination, and he was told that the German people would never stand by and endorse it, as it was not in line with the teaching of Martin Luther. Then the Kaiser cried, 'We will change the religion of Germany, then,' and higher criticism began."

After the war Sunday decided that it was Lenin or Trotsky and not the Kaiser who was really behind the spread of religious Modernism. To his mind there was no difficulty in associating Harry Emerson Fosdick and Percy S. Grant with the garlic-smelling, bomb-throwing, unassimilated immigrant, even though John D. Rockefeller, Jr., had deserted Sunday to take Fosdick's side as a Modernist. "Atheism marches with Communism—Bolshevism—Socialism," and Modernism was atheistic, since it denied, or quibbled over, the tenets of conservative orthodoxy. "I have more respect for the gang of cut-throats [in] Russia in their attitude toward religion than for these Modernists," he declared. "There isn't a convention, a conference, a Presbytery, a YMCA, a YWCA, a General Assembly or a religious gathering of any sort that you do not find poisoned and saturated and shot through with Infidelity—clothed in Modernism and swathed in Liberalism."

Religious liberalism became subtly equated with political liberalism and even radicalism. The words were used almost interchangeably in the sermon notes. The Federal Council of Churches, which was largely in the hands of the Modernists, was associated in Sunday's mind with many radical causes, and, though he did not specifically call it "communistic" or label any of the Modernists "Reds," he did say that many such persons were pitiable dupes who "looking for something humanitarian to do fall for" Communist propaganda "and enlist unconsciously in the ranks of the Reds."

In one sermon Sunday listed some of the organizations with "pseudo-social titles" which liberals were duped into joining: the American Civil Liberties Union, the Christian Social Order Conference, the *International Socialist Review,* the Young Pioneers of America, the Youth for Peace Movement, and the Fellowship of Reconciliation. All these were the same, he said; all were Communist-dominated. Among the supporters of these groups, he listed such "Red Anarchists" as Roger N. Baldwin, William Z. Foster, Elizabeth Gurley Flynn, J. H. Maurer, William Haywood, Scott Nearing, Morris Hillquit, Upton Sinclair, Charles Garland, and Felix Frankfurter. "There is no question," he said, "the intention of this gang is to overthrow this government and establish Soviet Rule."

From this attack upon those whom he considered to be the enemies of American liberty, Sunday occasionally departed in order to advocate a return to the "old time religion of our fathers." "America, I call you back to the Bible—back to God," or "America needs a tidal wave of Old Time Religion." After painting a lurid picture of the "drift into the Boom-Boom—Whoopee—Jazz—Bootlegging—Joy-riding current" of the postwar generation, he asked rhetorically, "Now what's the remedy?" and answered, "Preach the Gospel of Jesus Christ. Evangelistic work. Rebuild the family altar. Greater care of the young."

Sunday's program for greater care of the young was the enactment of laws prohibiting the teaching of evolution and requiring the teaching of conservative evangelicalism.[28] "Education if divorced from religion leads to the spread of depravity and is a greater menace to Christianity than Socialism—Communism—Bolshevism. Education without religion is a false philosophy. We must not surrender our schools to atheism. Evolution is atheism with a new name. The state is in danger if it encourages no-religious [*sic*] teaching in the schools."

Only by indoctrinating the young with the dogma of the Fundamentalists could Americanism be kept pure. "Children enter school not as Prot.—Cath.—Jews. As future American citizens. Without Religion they miss the most important equipment." The inherent anti-intellectualism of the rural evangelist, which had formerly smoldered beneath the surface with only occasional eruptions, now emerged violently and vindictively. "We are confronted with conditions which justify statement that much of modern learning is undermining faith in God—Morality . . . ," he said. "The subversive educational forces are distorting the thinking of young people to make it coincide with the warped views of the Communists, socialists, the lawless pagan, the moral anarchist." The choice was obvious: "Faith in God without an education is better than an education without faith in God." Though he still professed to believe in the separation of church and state, it was evident that, if he had had the power to enact his will into law, the United States soon would have become a Fundamentalist theocracy.

Firm in his belief that "only Christians should be allowed to teach in the schools," Sunday became in the 1930's a trustee of Bob Jones College, an archconservative Bible school which started in Cleveland, Tennessee, and later moved to Greenville, South Carolina. It was one of many such interdenominational colleges and Bible schools founded in the 1920's and 1930's to take the place of schools and universities where unconverted (hence non-Christian) teachers taught evolution. "Schools," said Sunday in 1931, "are worse than useless if they bring students under the influence of those who do not believe in Jesus Christ upon which the church and schools were built."[29] At Bob Jones College, Americanism of Sunday's variety—the variety which said, "There can be no religion that does not express itself in patriotism"—could be promoted, and the youth of America could remain free from any ideas of dissent.

Sunday did not originate the views which he preached in these years. Dwight L. Moody and Sam Jones had attacked the Communists and the anarchists and the unassimilated immigrant in the post-Civil War years, as had a good many of the more learned and genteel Americans. Postwar anxieties in the 1920's merely provided a congenial climate for the first fruition of these seeds of thought. The Moody Bible Institute adopted the title of "The West Point of Christian Service" and advertised itself in the 1920's as "The Answer to Labor Unrest," where "'agitators' for righteousness" were trained to combat the "agitators of class hatred and revolutionary radicalism" who "are busy from coast to coast."

Sunday's sermon notes reflect the political conservatism of the era. He crossed out his attacks, such as they were, on starvation wages and child labor and on those men whose monopolies picked the pockets of eighty million people. He expunged the reference in his sermon on the Second Coming to the fact that "the concentration of wealth in the hands of a few" was a significant sign. The rise of

Franklin Roosevelt to national prominence brought a revision in Sunday's notes on the need for a national leader who would be "as (1) resolute as Washington; (2) patient as Lincoln; (3) modern as Roosevelt; (4) cautious as Coolidge." The third attribute, a reference to Theodore Roosevelt, he changed to "(3) conservative as Cleveland," in order to avoid confusion.

Sunday completely altered the emphasis in this passage: "There is a conspiracy on foot to discredit, defy the Constitution and laws— Let us show the crooks and whiskey politicians [he crossed out the words "whiskey politicians" and wrote in "Radicals"] that this nation is not so weak that it cannot enforce its own laws against a few thousand crooks, bootleggers, pimps [the word "pimps" was crossed out], ex-convicts, rum-runners [the word "Radicals" was added], who are often aided and abetted in their criminal acts by officials— Big Business [this whole final clause, beginning with "who" and ending with "Big Business," was crossed out]." As he rewrote this, Sunday was waking up to the fact that the "Radicals" and not the "whiskey politicians" or "Big Business" were the scapegoats of the moment.

In 1920 Sunday's son George campaigned actively for the nomination of General Leonard Wood as the Republican candidate for President, and Sunday lent himself to the cause. A letter of his was printed in the *New York Times* indorsing Wood because "he believes in America for Americans. He is heart, soul, mind, and body against the spirit of Bolshevism which strikes at the body politic and spits on the flag." When Harding won the nomination, Sunday wrote to him to say that he was his second choice: "I am an American Republican," he began, and the "platform as set forth by the Republicans will be for the best interest of the people of the United States and the nations of the world. . . . I believe in a League of Nations," he said, modifying his opinion to fit the party platform, "but not without reservations. I do not believe in turning this nation over to a foreign committee and throwing the Constitution and the Monroe Doctrine upon the international scrapheap."[30]

Throughout the rest of his career Sunday did not hesitate to take a pronounced stand in party politics, though he sometimes did so on the nonpartisan basis of Prohibition enforcement rather than on the grounds of "American Republicanism." He supported Theodore Roosevelt, Jr., for governor of New York in 1924 and Coolidge for the Presidency. He chastised the Republicans in New York for attempting to straddle the Prohibition question in the nomination of

Charles H. Tuttle for governor. He attacked Governor Ritchie of Maryland, Governor Edwards of New Jersey, and Governor Smith of New York for their "wet" sympathies. He announced in 1928 and in 1932 that if both parties adopted a "wet" platform, he would run for President himself.

As the 1928 election neared, Sunday grew increasingly outspoken against Alfred E. Smith, whom he called "the mouthpiece of the Liquor Interests," and against John J. Raskob, whom he called "a renegade Republican." When he was accused of being anti-Catholic for his abuse of Smith, his reply was quoted in the *New York Times:* "I don't find fault with him just because he's a Catholic, but because he's a Tammanyite, a Catholic, and a wet."[31] His anti-Smith sermons in the South prior to the election caused some Democratic spectators to throw rotten eggs, but they also brought this approving letter from Vice-President–elect Charles Curtis after the election:

UNITED STATES SENATE
WASHINGTON, D.C.
November 10, 1928

MY DEAR REV. SUNDAY:

I greatly appreciate your kind congratulations and good wishes upon my election to the Vice-Presidency.

I know you were of great help in the campaign, and I am thankful for your valued assistance. I heard of your good work in the South. It was a great campaign, a wonderful victory, and Mr. Hoover and I are under great obligation to you for your good work.

Again thanking you, I am,

Very truly yours,
[*signed*] CHARLES CURTIS

Though there is ample evidence in various statements by Sunday to show his distrust of and prejudice against Catholicism, Sunday never adopted the rabid anti-Catholicism of the Ku Klux Klan and its supporters and, except during the Smith campaign, never publicly expressed his prejudice. A pamphlet entitled *Billy Sunday Unmasked,* published by William Lloyd Clark, of the extremely anti-Catholic Rail Splitter Press, in 1929, attacked Sunday for being too pro-Catholic. Clark pointed to Sunday's friendly remarks about Cardinal Gibbons and the Catholic church and noted that many cards signed by trail-hitters who signified their preference for that church were turned over to the local priests: "Mr. Sunday's attitude toward Roman Catholicism is so compromising and so void of red-blooded patriotism," said Clark, that it was probable that he was actually a Jesuit in disguise.

285

Sunday was also under attack in the twenties, as previously, for his alliance with Big Business. In 1921–23 he held five campaigns in West Virginia during the mining strikes that caused violence and bloodshed in that state similar to that in Colorado in 1914. The Ku Klux Klan was active in the same area, terrorizing the strikers. When Sunday accepted two invitations to campaign in the small mining towns of Beckley (population, 4,149) and Logan (population, 2,998) in the heart of the strike area, Rabbi Stephen S. Wise called it a "loathsome instance of the attempted prostitution of the Church. We all know what it means—that he is to use all the power of his eloquence to lead men back to work" who were "rightfully dissatisfied with their conditions."[32]

Sunday ignored the charge, and the evidence was purely circumstantial, but Wise's assumption seemed even more justified than that made after Sunday's Colorado revivals, for here there was no Prohibition campaign, and even in these lean years of evangelism it was strange that Sunday should hold campaigns in such small towns. There is no doubt that professional evangelists of minor stature were used during the 1920's by employers in industrial mill towns to preach contentment with their lot to the workers.[33] There is little doubt, however, that Sunday felt just as sincerely innocent of Wise's charges in 1922 as he did of those made by Creel in 1915.

Sunday remained active in tabernacle revivalism much longer than any other professional evangelist. The majority turned to other professions, took up pastorates, or attempted to form their own churches. The last was the most common choice, and the professional evangelists were joined in this by the graduates of Bible schools and by Fundamentalist ministers who were at odds with their denominations. In city after city, interdenominational "gospel tabernacles" of cinderblock, concrete, wood, and corrugated steel were erected in the twenties and thirties. They were built in the poorer areas of the city—not actually in the slums but somewhere between the slums and the suburban or uptown areas.

Typical of these were the Churchill Evangelistic Tabernacle, built by a convert of Sunday in Buffalo in 1921; the Chicago Gospel Tabernacle, founded by Paul Rader of the Moody Bible Institute in 1922; and E. Howard Cadle's Gospel Tabernacle in Indianapolis, built in 1927. There were literally hundreds of smaller tabernacles similar to these erected in these years; they became known as "storefront churches," since they frequently were located in made-over stores. All their pastors preached the conservative theology associated with Fundamentalism and devoted a great deal of time and money to their "radio ministry," the newest form of revivalism. But their principal activity was to serve as permanent centers for evangelistic meetings. E. Howard Cadle, in founding his tabernacle, publicly announced that it would be only one of a nation-wide chain in which professional evangelists would make periodic tours like traveling vaudeville teams; he planned, he said, to have Billy Sunday and Aimee McPherson as the "headliners" for his circuit.

Aimee Semple McPherson was a part of this settling-down of revivalism into permanent establishments. She started her career in 1917 as a traveling professional evangelist but realized after five years of touring small towns and cities with a tent that the itinerant phase of the profession was over. In 1922 she founded a permanent tabernacle in Los Angeles, which she called "Angelus Temple," and shortly thereafter built her own radio station. Unlike most of the professional evangelists, she decided to propagate her own variety of Fundamentalist theology and formed a completely new sect, which she called "The International Church of the Foursquare Gospel." According to the United States Religious Census, her denomination had 205 branch churches and 16,147 members by 1936.

Sister Aimee did not, during her brief career as a professional evangelist, obtain the support of the major evangelical denominations for her tent meetings. Her flamboyant personality, her "faith healing," and the fact that regular churches were no longer hospitable to mass evangelism at the late date of her arrival on the scene all contributed to make her course difficult. Sunday himself was hostile to her sensationalism, her flowing robes, and her tendency to melodramatize her sex. According to his wife, Sunday refused to allow Mrs. McPherson to sit on the platform during his campaign in Tampa, Florida, in 1919, when she, too, was holding a revival in that city and was being escorted to the bathing beaches by Rodeheaver. But Sunday did not object to her doctrines or her "faith healing"; in fact, said his wife, "Mr. Sunday sometimes said he wished he had the gift of healing."[34]

Aimee McPherson represented the last giddy spasm of the profession's attempt to perpetuate itself. The necessity she felt to establish her own private denomination was indicative of her separation even from the Fundamentalists. Following Sunday's Mt. Holly campaign in May, 1930, professional tabernacle evangelism disappeared from public interest for almost twenty years. Sunday and his wife, with Harry Clarke as their song leader and general helper, were all that remained of the party. They continued to hold revivals, but these were only one- or two-week affairs held in a single church or gospel tabernacle at the invitation of a pastor or former evangelist. Tremont Temple in Boston; Calvary Baptist Church in New York; Moody Church in Chicago; the Baptist Temple in Philadelphia; the tabernacles of Cadle, Churchill, E. J. Rollings, and the Rader brothers, were typical of the places visited by Sunday in the last five years of his life. To most of them he returned more than once.

The stock-market crash of 1929 and the subsequent depression seemed to Sunday to justify his dire predictions of the nation's decline: "Sometimes I'm glad God knocked over the heavens to put America on her knees before she became too chesty," he said in 1931. "Our great depression is not economic, it is spiritual and there won't be a particle of change in the economic depression until there is a wholesale revival of the old time religion."[35] But the election of Franklin Roosevelt, the repeal of Prohibition, the diplomatic recognition of Russia, and the rise of Hitler came as a series of shattering blows which made him begin to doubt whether America could ever be saved. "America must turn to God to avoid a revolution," he wrote in his "Autobiography" for the *Ladies' Home Journal* in April, 1933. "Man cannot put the world right; our hope is in God."

Sunday's loss of confidence and his bitterness were in large part due to the personal problems which overwhelmed him in these years. His mother, remarried and widowed a third time, died as Mrs. Mary Jane Stowell in Sunday's home at Winona Lake in 1916. His best friend, Dr. Wilbur J. Chapman, of whom Sunday said, "Next to the members of my family, I loved him more than anyone else," died in 1918. Two of Sunday's sons took the proverbially wicked path of a minister's children. His eldest son, George, attempted suicide in 1923, was arrested for auto theft and bail-jumping in 1929, was divorced by his first wife in 1930, married a Los Angeles model in 1931, and jumped from a window to his death in September, 1933. The youngest son, William A. Sunday, Jr., was divorced in 1927, remarried in 1928, and was divorced a second time on grounds of extreme cruelty in 1929.

The death of Sunday's only daughter, Helen, in 1933, further saddened his life. He was sixty-eight in 1930, and his health failed fast in the five remaining years of his life. A heart attack in 1933 and another in May, 1935, left him seriously weakened, but he would not give up preaching. He continued to answer invitations to speak at various churches until the very end.

In one of his last sermon revisions, some time in 1934, Sunday re-wrote his interpretation of the Second Coming and entitled it "The Coming Dictator." In this sermon he reached the ultimate stage of pessimism, and, rejecting all his faith in the American heritage and destiny, he expressed his agreement with Moody that the world was doomed. He went even beyond Moody by setting the date for the end of the world in the year 1935.

The signs of the "approaching end" were evident in the rise of dictatorships, he wrote, for the Bible predicted that immediately preceding the Second Coming the world would be ruled by a super-man, the antichrist. "Russia has her Stalin, Italy has her Mussolini, Germany has her Hitler . . . and Colonel House thinks 'even America seems ripe for one—if we haven't already got him.'" He pointed to the tottering governments and crumbling economic systems of the day as further evidence of the approaching end, and he described the antichrist as "a Mussolini—a Stalin and a Hitler all rolled into one. He will give the world a 'New Deal.' A wizard in finance, he will stabilize the currency of the world and all industry will be brought under his control. He will issue a compulsory code for every commerical enterprise." The similarity to Franklin Roosevelt became almost too pointed, but Sunday avoided it: "And his 'mark'—not the swastika of Hitler, nor the bundled axe of Mussolini, nor the hammer and sickle of Stalin, nor the Blue Eagle of Roosevelt," but "a mysterious number," 666, as described in the Book of Revelation. By an involved statistical interpretation of the statement that the world would end when "the Times of the Gentiles" ran out, Sunday presented evidence to show that the era of the gentiles would end in 1935 and that the last dispensation of God "is about to close."

There was a significant internationalistic note in the sermon, re-flecting the uneasy feeling of many Americans that, despite their utmost efforts at isolationism, America might yet be dragged into the horror of another war across the seas. In the depths of his de-spair Sunday's prophetic vision seemed more clear than it had ever been before:

A few years ago the relation between the Orient and the Occident was well fixed—the East was not ambitious and worshipped the past. The West was aggressive—worshipped Future. Progressive they said, and con-sidered themselves superior.—That was ten years ago—and so confident were we of our superiority that we passed exclusion laws—we deliberately slapped the face of the Orient. Ten years later the echo returns—and it is our face that is being slapped. Japan now runs the Orient—and is telling the Occident what it may and may not do in that section of the world.

He blamed the Versailles Treaty for the rise of Hitler and the muni-
tions-makers for the world armament race in progress. "Nations are
glaring at each other across disputed borders. War in Europe and
the Orient seems certain. Will America and Japan come to grips?"

Unlike the problems of the 1920's, such as bootlegging, Modernism, evolutionary teaching, and bolshevism, these new international
problems could not be terminated by punitive or restrictive action
by the Congress of the United States or even by a determined army
of fighting saints. It was impossible to deport the Communists or the
Japanese or the Nazis off the face of the earth, and Sunday resolute-
ly opposed rearmament. "One thing is certain, if world war comes
again the last one will seem like child's play compared with it," he
said. "Another world war would mean [the] cemetery of civilization."

For once Sunday could not find a tangible scapegoat against
whom he could direct his attack. Though he held Franklin Roosevelt
responsible for most domestic ills, he could not blame him for the
war in Manchuria or the rise of Hitler, Mussolini, or Stalin. "Who is
to blame?" he asked, and then he answered, sadly, "The human race
is to blame." The sinful human race could find its way out of the
world dilemma by only one road, "a mighty sweeping revival." But
in 1934 the American people were too busy with the problems of the
depression and too hopeful in their isolationism to be excited by the
warnings of a dishonored prophet.

It is possible that, had Sunday lived a few years longer, he would
have become involved in the various neo-Fascist groups in the
United States which had such close ties with some of the more extreme Fundamentalists. Many of those with whom Sunday associated in the 1930's—Clinton H. Churchill, Paul and Luke Rader,
E. J. Rollings, and J. Frank Norris, for example—were on friendly
terms with Gerald B. Winrod and directly or indirectly lent their
support to his Bible Defenders of America group, which after 1935
became violently pro-Fascist.[36] But the majority of the evidence
points the other way.

In 1934 Sunday wrote a sermon entitled "Hitlerism," in which he
denounced Hitler for "his determination to cut Christianity loose
from its Jewish rootage and substitute Teutonic mythology for the
word of God." He accused "the German Dictator whose ruthless
warfare against the Jews has aroused the indignation of [the] civi-
lized world" of "Hitlerizing" "the pulpit of Protestantism." He denounced "Rudolph Hess, chief head hunter for Hitler" and "the gov-

ernment controlled press, radio, and other agencies of propaganda" which had "proscribed the Old Testament and forbidden its use in Protestant churches." The election of Ludwig Mueller, "Primate of Protestantism in Germany," was "one of the most astounding events in the history of Christianity," said Sunday. It presaged "the fall of Protestantism and the rise of Godless monarchy or Communism in Germany."

It is true that, prior to his trip to Germany in 1935, Winrod, too, was hostile to Hitler and "Reich Bishop" Mueller, but it seems unlikely that Sunday would have countenanced the anti-Negro and anti-Semitic attitude which Winrod and his followers adopted in later years. Never in his search for scapegoats did Sunday pick on the Jews. In the last version of his sermon on "The Coming Dictator," which he delivered in 1935, the notes contain the phrase "Hitlerism doomed for anti-Jew."

Mrs. Sunday, who shared Sunday's views in many respects and who continued after his death to work actively as a speaker at evangelistic meetings, did not become associated with Winrod or with any other neo-Fascists. William E. Biederwolf, who, together with Mrs. Sunday, ran the Winona Lake Bible Conference until 1939, did not fall into these associations. Paul Rader spoke several times at Winona Lake conferences, but neither Winrod nor any other neo-Fascist was ever invited to do so. Winrod still continues his anti-Semitic activities, but today the Winona Lake Bible Conference actively supports a movement to evangelize the Jews.

When Sunday had his first heart attack in 1933, he was in the middle of a sermon at the First Federated Church in Des Moines, Iowa. As the attack seized him, he staggered on the platform, and Harry Clarke rushed to catch him. It was typical of Sunday's devotion to his calling that at this moment, which he believed to be his last, he pointed to the crowd and gasped to Clarke, "Don't let them go. They're lost. Give them the invitation. I'd rather die on my feet seeing them come than quit." Clarke hesitated. "Harry, don't let the people go without me having at least one from this meeting to go into the presence of God with." The choir struck up an invitation song, and Sunday held out his hand. "I put my hand in his hand," said Clarke, "and he must have thought somebody had taken his hand to make a decision for Christ, for he said, 'Thank God!' "[37]

But Sunday recovered from this attack and continued to preach for two more years. His last sermon was delivered at a small church in Mishawaka, Indiana, on October 27, 1935. He died after a third heart attack on November 6, 1935, at his brother-in-law's home in Chicago, across the street from a saloon. His will was registered in probate at $50,000; there were trust funds for his wife and his two remaining children; $150,000 in government bonds made up the bulk of his state. Telegrams of condolence poured in to his widow from all over the nation—from President Franklin D. Roosevelt, Fiorello La Guardia, Kenesaw Mountain Landis, John D. Rocke-feller, Jr., and countless individuals who remembered his generosity and his earnestness. Memorial services were held in Chicago, Buf-falo, and Sioux City. He was buried in Forest Lawn Cemetery in Chicago in a plot he had bought in 1918.

Little remains of Sunday's life's work: some businessmen's and businesswomen's clubs, some Bible classes, a few YMCA buildings and rescue missions in various cities built from funds he helped to raise; there is a Billy Sunday tabernacle at Winona Lake and an-other in Sioux City, founded by his last chorister, Harry Clarke; a few of the last tabernacles he used in the South are still standing and are used for occasional revival services. But mostly there remain just the fading memories of aging men and women who were stirred by his preaching. Neither his children nor his grandchildren have followed in his steps. His wife alone has kept alive the memory of his evangelism. "Mr. Sunday," she wrote at his death, "was a typical, great-hearted, sentimental American husband." But, she went on, "He really had no social life. He was a lonely man. Take his preach-ing away from his record and 90 per cent of his life would be gone."[38]

Sunday wrote out his own estimate of himself in a brief, charac-teristically self-defensive apology shortly before his death. It is a self-revealing appraisal of his life and personality:

"Most people resemble their reputations and if a life famously spent is in the mind of one who visits a person of wide repute you naturally look for the peculiarities of conduct—of facial expressions —or physique which appear to account for their reputation. Whether that person be soldier—Philosopher—actor—athelete [sic]—Reformer —Preacher or Bootlegger.

"The reputation which has been built up for me regarding slang and uncouth humor has been done by the old whiskey crowd in re-taliation for the fact that they blame me as being largely responsible for the 18th amendment. I do use the common vernacular of the campas [sic]—the club—the street to impress the truth on those who think and talk in that vernacular. But its [sic] only an occasional in-cident, not a regular diet. I am charged with saying things I never said and with doing things I never did—It is all done by the enemies of the Gospel which I believe and preach.

"I do not conceal the fact that I am in this world for the purpose of making it easier for people to do right and harder for them to do wrong. I care not what is said about me unless its [sic] a lie so great as to call for my rebuke.

"I am not a mountebank, I am not an aper [sic] or a reprint of some one else. I am and always have been plain Billy Sunday trying to do God's will in preaching Jesus and Him crucified and arisen from the dead for our sins."

In the obituaries Billy Sunday was referred to as "a colorful character," a "picturesque evangelist" with "a flare for the spectacular." The real meaning of his career was buried under the reminiscences of his sensational preaching and the statistical summaries of his campaigns. He conducted over 300 separate revivals; he spoke to over 100,000,000 people in the days before radios and loud-speakers; he brought 1,000,000 down the sawdust trail, and he received, so it was said, millions of dollars in free-will offerings.

But the significance of Sunday's career and of professional evangelism did not lie in statistics. In the years between 1862 and 1935, while revivals and declensions in church membership roughly canceled each other out, the steady over-all growth in membership (although at a diminishing rate) continued. In 1936 the United States Religious Census revealed that, for the first time in history, more Americans were church members than were not. But the principal reasons for the growth of the Protestant churches in America were social rather than religious.

Joining a church had become the socially respectable "thing to do"; a crisis conversion was neither necessary nor expected. A watered-down version of Horace Bushnell's doctrine of Christian nurture had successfully replaced the ecstatic regeneration of the frontier camp meeting, and Billy Sunday's revivalism had played an unwitting part in the transformation. Despite his emphasis on conversion through the agency of the Holy Spirit, Sunday's trail-hitters were primarily expressing the acceptance of the prevailing morality, not undergoing any fundamental spiritual change. This new interpretation of conversion was indicative of an increasing social conservatism in America, a conservatism which, while it claimed to believe in political and economic individualism, denied the intellectual and social individualism which Emerson called "self-reliance" and which Jacksonian democrats called "equality." In this sense, the optimistic, self-reliant individualism which characterized America in the first half of the nineteenth century had undergone a radical change. By 1900 it was replaced by growing feelings of uncertainty and insecurity which produced in the 1920's a compulsive desire for conformity in taste, thought, and action which has not yet run its course.

But to place Sunday's career in its true perspective, it is necessary to go back even further. The evangelical awakening that began as "pietism" in Europe early in the eighteenth century was part of a universal cry for individual self-expression and self-development in the Western world; it was part and parcel of the industrial revolution and the concomitant laissez faire doctrine of free enterprise. By breaking with Calvinism's emphasis on the predestination of the elect, Wesley and his admirers in America made religion more democratic, but they also separated it from its important concern in the secular affairs of business and the state. Americans were quick to unite the doctrine of free will in salvation with the egocentric opportunism which characterized the philosophy of Franklin's Poor Richard and later of Herbert Spencer's melioristic Social Darwinism. In theory a man's business activity, his calling, was an aspect of his religion, but in practice business went its own amoral way while religion was left to the relatively secondary tasks of sanctifying free enterprise and saving souls. After reaching high tide in the last quarter of the nineteenth century, both evangelicalism and laissez faire capitalism, with which it had so successfully merged, began to ebb in the early years of the twentieth. The theology of the former and the economic theory of the latter had hardened into rigid dogmas which were fast becoming unrealistic, impractical, and outdated. And, as they did so, their advocates in America sought desperately to identify them with the ideals of American democracy in order to maintain the status quo. To alter any part of these dogmas, ran the argument, was to undermine everything the country stood for—everything that had made it great.

Perhaps the most important and yet the most easily forgotten fact about Billy Sunday is that he entered manhood in the year 1883, at the moment when these dogmas were near the peak of their influence, pervading the whole of American life from top to bottom with a unanimity of acceptance which they never held before or since. By the time Sunday tried to reform New York, in 1917, he was fifty-five. Whatever his physical agility, his mental processes were stiff and inflexible. He was unwilling and unable to modify the religious and economic beliefs which he had adopted as the ultimate truth at the time of his conversion in 1886.

In the days of his prime, in the years 1896–1912, Sunday's revivals gave expression to the dilemmas of the American middle class. He made some effort then, however haphazard, to reconcile the nineteenth century to the twentieth. Although the absolute equalitarianism of the frontier had been replaced by the limited "equality of opportunity" of the city, Sunday could still confidently give voice to the American success myth. Coming as a "plumed knight" out of the West, in the years 1912–18 he was hailed by evangelical leaders as the savior of the national heritage. They looked to him to fill the empty churches and thereby to defray the increasing costs of an overexpanded institution. They looked to his revivals as the solution for the social, economic, and political ills which plagued the nation: He was to reform the country without changing its institutions; he was to refute science without denying progress; he was to bring back the good old days merely by reasserting the old-time religion. In short, he was to perform miracles—or to induce divine providence to do so. That Sunday's revivals did not accomplish these ends was less a stigma on his ability or faith than it was a testimony to the intellectual and spiritual bankruptcy of the churches and their leaders. High-pressure mass evangelism was not the way to solve either the churches' or the nation's problems.

After 1919 the churches of the East and West rapidly abandoned Sunday's technique and his Fundamentalist theology. Sunday moved southward and revised his message to fit the new mood of "normalcy." The activistic reform element in his preaching, which had never been strong, disappeared entirely with the accomplishment of his one great crusade, national Prohibition. Now the whole weight of his message was restrictive and intolerant; he preached with an almost hysterical insistence on conformity, based on an ever narrowing definition of 100 per cent Americanism. And many Americans, in their desire for a return to "the good old days," continued for a time to agree with him.

Sunday's indorsement by the urban clergy, the small businessman, and the suburban white-collar worker had a large element of nostalgia and make-believe in it. It represented a hope that the American success myth had not become just a myth. But attempts to reconcile the myth with the fact necessitated an increasingly frantic effort to find scapegoats and to resist change. It was in this effort that Sunday became a rallying center and a fighting saint. His revivalism made church membership a test of Americanism and salvation a ritual of acceptance of the myth. It limited membership to those whose native birth, education, occupation, and social status conformed to a strictly defined stereotype. In his fanatical self-righteousness he asserted that those who did not conform were not only damned to hell but were ineligible for citizenship or acceptance in respectable society, and his audiences applauded.

The increasing discrepancy between the traditional American ideals and Sunday's ideals became abundantly clear in his sermons. Freedom of speech applied to all—except to pacifists, Socialists, anarchists, Bolsheviki, IWW's, labor agitators, and "pinko" liberals. Freedom of religion applied to all—except to Unitarians, Universalists, atheists, Mohammedans, Hindus, Confucianists, Mormons, Christian Scientists, theosophists, Russellites, and Modernists. All men were born equal—except Negroes and foreigners. Church and state must be separated—except that Christianity should be written into the Constitution, no Roman Catholic should be eligible for the Presidency, there should be a Bible in every schoolroom, all teachers should be converted Christians, and anything contrary to the most literal interpretation of the Bible should be prohibited by law from the curriculum of the public schools. The fact that Sunday continued to find widespread support throughout the 1920's despite the reactionary extremism of his message indicates the extent to which the nation had turned aside from its principles.

Then, in 1929, a new phase began in American history. The great depression shattered the make-believe world of perpetual prosperity in the 100 per cent American way. As the nation faced up to the necessity of making its business enterprise more adequately serve the general welfare, Sunday lost touch completely with the public temper. He had excluded so many from his definition of "true-blue Americans" that he found himself in a dwindling minority. He decided not only that the twentieth century had broken the speed limit but that it could never put on the brakes short of hell. At the time of his death he was ready to abandon America for heaven unless the quick advent of Christ, by inaugurating the millennium, should put an end to the nation which had changed beyond recall.

His message aside, it is easy to see why those who knew Sunday liked him. As an individual he had many laudable traits. He was generous to a fault; he was courageous and honest. He was trusting to the point of naïveté yet extremely sensitive to any ridicule or rebuke. Quick to anger but equally quick to apologize, he had a keen sense of humor, a vivid imagination, a gift for words, and a positive genius for catching the eye and ear of his generation. If it were possible to sum up all his individual acts of kindness and all the personal reformations in character that his preaching effected, an imposing portrait of him as an agent of Christian charity and love might be presented.

But, as John Wanamaker had said, Billy Sunday was more than an individual; he was a force in American life. The religious movement which he led from 1908 to 1918 was not a revival in the usual sense of the word, for, on the whole, it failed to win the large numbers of new converts to Christianity which the term generally implies. But in the broader sense of the word—in the sense of an emotional upheaval caused by a major dislocation or transition in social action and intellectual currents which finds expression in traditional religious forms—Billy Sunday's career deserves an important place in the religious history of America. His revivals were a product of the profound struggle of Americans to cope with the challenge and the responsibility of a new and inconceivably more complex industrial civilization than they had ever dreamed of. That they gave up their old beliefs with difficulty and looked for a time to the simple answers which Sunday offered was only natural.

For Billy Sunday was a symbol of the American dream, a living embodiment of the mythical farm boy who went to the city and made good, an orphaned bricklayer's son who rose to fame and wealth, whose name became a byword throughout the land, and who lived on familiar terms with the leading figures of his day. Although Sunday was an almost forgotten man at his death, he had been a representative spokesman for the time in which he lived. He won recognition and fame precisely because he embodied so accurately the cultural pattern of his era. If Billy Sunday's career was, in the long run, a failure, it was a failure shared by a generation of Americans.

NOTES

PROLOGUE

"BILLY'S RUBICON"

1. This quotation is the title of an article in the *Literary Digest*, LIV (April 21, 1917), 1168. The majority of the quotations in this chapter are taken from the *New York Times*, supplemented by a few quotations from the *New York World*, the *New York Globe*, and an article by Joseph Collins, "Revivals, Past and Present," in *Harper's Monthly*, CXXXV (November, 1917), 856 ff.

My insights here, as elsewhere, have been greatly enriched by conversations with Mrs. William A. Sunday, and by friends of the evangelist who are mentioned in the "Note on the Sources."

CHAPTER 1

"A RUBE OF THE RUBES"

1. The principal sources used for biographical data on Sunday are Elijah Brown, *The Real Billy Sunday* (New York, 1914); W. T. Ellis, *Billy Sunday: The Man and His Message* (Philadelphia, 1936); T. T. Frankenberg, *The Spectacular Career of Rev. Billy Sunday, the Famous Baseball Evangelist* (Columbus, Ohio, 1913); and Sunday's "Autobiography," which is included in the Ellis volume. Supplemental information and various corrections were supplied by personal interviews and correspondence with Mrs. Helen Sunday, the evangelist's widow.

2. *Jefferson Bee* (Jefferson, Iowa), December 17, 1903, p. 1.

3. *Boston Herald*, December 4, 1916, p. 4.

4. Quoted in Brown, *op. cit.*, p. 51.

5. See the *Northwestern University Alumni News*, November, 1924, pp. 11, 25.

6. *Family Call* (Philadelphia), November 23, 1896, p. 6.

7. Frankenberg, *op. cit.*, p. 8.

8. *Hancock Signal* (Garner, Iowa), January 15, 1896, p. 3.

9. *Sigourney News* (Sigourney, Iowa), January 23, 1896, p. 3.

10. From Sunday's *Autobiography*, as printed in Ellis, *op. cit.*, pp. 503–4.

11. *Sigourney News*, January 30, 1896, p. 3.

12. This quotation and that from the Elliott, Iowa, paper are quoted in Brown, *op. cit.*, pp. 88 and 91.

13. *Semi-weekly Telegraph* (Atlantic, Iowa), April 1, 1902, p. 3.

14. W. R. Moody, *D. L. Moody* (New York, 1930), p. 420.

15. *Audubon Republican* (Audubon, Iowa), January 23, 1902, p. 5.

16. Quoted in Brown, *op. cit.*, p. 103.

17. *Jefferson Bee,* December 24, 1903, p. 5.
18. *Ibid.,* January 7, 1904, pp. 1–2.
19. *Daily Gate City* (Keokuk, Iowa), October 1, 1904, p. 1.
20. This account is contained in a letter to the author from Mr. N. C. Nelson, curator emeritus of the American Museum of Natural History in New York, September 22, 1951.
21. *Daily Gate City,* October 11, 1904, p. 1.
22. *Ibid.,* October 1, 1904, p. 1.
23. *Jefferson Bee,* December 24, 1903, p. 5.
24. Quoted in Brown, *op. cit.,* p. 86.
25. *Centerville Daily Citizen* (Centerville, Iowa), February 2, 1905, p. 1, and *Daily Gate City,* October 2, 1904, p. 1.
26. *Audubon County Journal* (Exira, Iowa), September 12, 1901, p. 3.
27. *Centerville Daily Citizen,* February 3, 1905, p. 2.
28. This and the following quotations on the Burlington, Iowa, campaign are taken from the *Burlington Hawkeye,* October 26, 1905–December 31, 1905.

CHAPTER 2

" 'BIG BUSINESS' FOR THE LORD"

1. A detailed and documented examination of Finney's contribution to professional evangelism and of the subsequent developments outlined below in regard to Moody, Torrey, Mills, and Chapman can be found in the author's doctoral dissertation, "Professional Evangelism: The Social Significance of Religious Revivals since 1865" (Harvard University, 1953), chaps. i–iii, which is on file in the Harvard University archives.
2. This quotation from Torrey's letter is taken from the Torrey–A. P. Fitt correspondence on file in the Moodyana Room of the Moody Bible Institute in Chicago and is used with permission of the Moody Bible Institute. This letter is dated Liverpool, November 29, 1904.
3. See "The New Attitude toward Evangelism," *Current Literature,* XL (February, 1906), 163 ff., and the *Watchman-Examiner* (Baptist, Boston), February 6, 1908, p. 32.
4. See Sunday's "Autobiography," in W. T. Ellis, *Billy Sunday: The Man and His Message* (Philadelphia, 1936), pp. 487–88; and Elijah Brown, *The Real Billy Sunday* (New York, 1914), p. 200.
5. See *The Life and Labors of Rev. William A. (Billy) Sunday, "the Great Modern Evangelist," with Selected Sermons* (Decatur, Ill.: Herman, Poole Co., 1908), p. 344.
6. Lists of Sunday's revivals are contained in Brown, *op. cit.,* pp. 206–7, and in Ellis, *op. cit.,* Appendix. Details of conversions, expenses, and free-will offerings were obtained from the newspapers of the cities involved and from tabulations published from time to time in publicity releases. No claim for complete accuracy in regard to these details is possible.
7. Brown, *op. cit.,* p. 130.
8. This is the Herman, Poole edition mentioned in n. 5 above. The

only available copy is in the Library of Congress, Washington, D.C. For the statement about Sunday's destruction of the plates see T. T. Frankenberg, *Billy Sunday: His Tabernacles and Sawdust Trails* (Columbus, Ohio, 1917), p. 168.

9. T. T. Frankenberg, *The Spectacular Career of Rev. Billy Sunday, the Famous Baseball Evangelist* (Columbus, Ohio, 1913). Sunday's repudiation of this book is quoted in the *Pittsburgh Press*, December 15, 1913, p. 19.

10. See the *New York Times*, January 19, 1915, p. 5.

11. See *ibid.*, April 16, 1915, p. 8; October 19, 1916, p. 7; April 8, 1915, p. 5; April 9, 1915, p. 20; and Frankenberg, *The Spectacular Career of Rev. Billy Sunday, the Famous Baseball Evangelist*, p. 162.

12. See *Zion's Herald* (Methodist, Boston), April 19, 1916, p. 491.

13. The data on Sunday's invitation to Boston were taken from the files of the *Watchman-Examiner, Zion's Herald,* and the *Congregationalist* for 1915–17. See, especially, *Zion's Herald,* February 10, 1915, p. 162; February 17, 1915, pp. 198 and 206; March 3, 1915, p. 261; March 17, 1915, p. 344; *Watchman-Examiner,* February 18, 1915, p. 202; September 21, 1916, p. 1226.

14. The data on Sunday's invitation to New York were taken from the files of the *New York Times,* 1914–17, and from material in the Sunday papers at Winona Lake, Indiana, used by permission of Mrs. William A. Sunday. See, especially, *New York Times,* March 10, 1914, p. 9; March 17, 1914, p. 9; April 14, 1914, p. 4; January 19, 1915, p. 5; January 26, 1915, p. 5; January 29, 1915, p. 5; May 22, 1915, p. 11. The letter from Wanamaker quoted on p. 56 is dated June 23, 1915, and is among the Sunday papers at Winona Lake, Indiana; there is also a copy of this letter in the Wanamaker files, Wanamaker Store, Philadelphia, Pennsylvania.

15. Data on the Washington invitation were provided by Leonard W. DeGast, of Washington, D.C., in a personal interview with the author, August 19, 1951, and from the files of the *New York Times* and the *Washington Evening Post,* 1915–18. See also *New York Times,* January 19, 1915, p. 5, and *Zion's Herald,* February 17, 1915, p. 206.

16. *Pittsburgh Sun,* March 2, 1914, p. 2.

17. *Zion's Herald,* February 17, 1915, p. 206.

18. *Watchman-Examiner,* April 9, 1914, p. 450.

19. *Ibid.,* May 4, 1916, p. 565.

20. *Pittsburgh Press,* November 23, 1913, Editorial section, p. 10.

21. This information was given to the author by Mrs. Sunday in a personal interview, October, 1950.

22. *Wichita Beacon,* December 2, 1911, p. 1.

23. Compare the accounts in Sunday's "Autobiography," in Ellis, *op. cit.,* p. 506, and in the *Illinois State Register* (Springfield), February 27, 1909, p. 1.

24. *Pittsburgh Press,* November 23, 1913, Editorial section, p. 10.

25. *Rocky Mountain News* (Denver, Colo.), May 12, 1914, p. 3.

26. *Watchman-Examiner,* February 24, 1916, p. 232.

27. *Zion's Herald,* November 8, 1916, p. 1413.

28. *New York Times,* May 19, 1916, p. 1, and December 12, 1916, p. 12.

29. *Ibid.,* April 24, 1915, p. 8.

30. This and other details of the preparations and expenses in New York are contained in an official report of the New York William A. Sunday evangelistic campaign issued by the William A. Sunday Evangelistic Association (New York, 1917); a copy of this report is among the Sunday papers at Winona Lake, Indiana.

31. See the *Pittsburgh Press,* December 29, 1913, p. 1.

CHAPTER 3

"TWO DOLLARS A SOUL"

1. H. A. Rodeheaver, *Twenty Years with Billy Sunday* (Winona Lake, Ind., 1936), p. 119. (The Rodeheaver Co., owner. Used by permission.)

2. *New York Times,* April 10, 1917, p. 22.

3. W. T. Ellis, *Billy Sunday: The Man and His Message* (Philadelphia, 1936), p. 339.

4. Taken from Sunday's sermon notes, which are among the Sunday papers at Winona Lake, Indiana.

5. Quoted in Ellis, *op. cit.,* p. 436.

6. *Boston Herald,* November 26, 1916, Editorial section, p. 1.

7. See T. T. Frankenberg, *Billy Sunday: His Tabernacles and His Sawdust Trails* (Columbus, Ohio, 1917), p. 97, and *Spokane-Spokesman Review,* February 6, 1909, p. 9.

8. *Pittsburgh Sun,* March 2, 1914, p. 2.

9. *Ibid.,* February 20, 1914, p. 16.

10. *Pittsburgh Press,* December 29, 1913, p. 1.

11. Ellis, *op. cit.,* p. 294.

12. Lindsay Denison, "The Rev. Billy Sunday and His War on the Devil," *American Magazine,* LXIV (September, 1907), 451 ff.

13. For this and much of the information that follows regarding Rodeheaver's work with Sunday see Rodeheaver, *op. cit.,* passim.

14. See Ira D. Sankey, *My Life and the Story of the Gospel Hymns* (Philadelphia, 1906), pp. 244–47.

15. *Boston Herald,* November 20, 1916, p. 5.

16. Letter from Torrey to A. P. Fitt, September 23, 1908, in files of Moody Bible Institute, Chicago. Used by permission of the Moody Bible Institute.

17. Ellis, *op. cit.,* p. 299.

18. *Boston Herald,* November 24, 1916, p. 4.

19. Quoted from the official report of the New York William A. Sunday evangelistic campaign, issued by the William A. Sunday Evangelistic Association (New York, 1917).

20. See *Boston Herald,* December 3, 1916, p. 4, and December 7, 1916, p. 3.

302

21. Ellis, *op. cit.*, p. 346.
22. *Rocky Mountain News*, October 9, 1914, p. 3.
23. Letter from Mrs. Sunday to the author, December 30, 1951. Used by permission.
24. *Watchman-Examiner* (Baptist, Boston), November 23, 1916, p. 1507.
25. *Boston Herald*, December 24, 1916, p. 4.
26. *Ibid.*, November 27, 1916, p. 4.
27. *New York Times*, January 17, 1915, Sec. V, p. 3.
28. *Ibid.*, March 6, 1915, p. 1.
29. *Watchman-Examiner*, May 4, 1916, p. 569.
30. Only sixty-four of the sixty-five campaigns Sunday held in this period are included here, since no statistics are available for the Duluth, Minnesota, campaign. The statistics of trail-hitting which follow are taken from the local newspapers of the cities concerned. No claim for complete accuracy is possible because no two newspaper accounts agree, and in most cities no official statistics of trail-hitters were released by the Sunday committees.
31. *Wichita Beacon*, November 27, 1911, p. 1.
32. *Boston Herald*, November 16, 1916, p. 5.
33. *Ibid.*, January 7, 1917, p. 2.
34. *Washington Evening Post*, March 4, 1918, pp. 2 and 10.
35. Official report of the New York William A. Sunday evangelistic campaign. Since the total from collections and contributions exceeded the expenses, the surplus was used in "follow-up" work (see above, chap. 2, n. 30).
36. T. T. Frankenberg, *The Spectacular Career of Rev. Billy Sunday, the Famous Baseball Evangelist* (Columbus, Ohio, 1913), p. 162.
37. See *Ottumwa Daily Courier*, December 11, 12, 13, 14, 1908.
38. *Watchman-Examiner*, April 10, 1913, p. 12.
39. *Pittsburgh Press*, February 23, 1914, p. 1.
40. Quoted in "Billy Sunday in the Big Cities," *Literary Digest*, XLVIII (April 4, 1914), 761–62.
41. "Billy Sunday's Results," *Literary Digest*, XLVIII (April 25, 1914), 990; *Pittsburgh Press*, December 15, 1913, p. 1.
42. *Boston Herald*, January 15, 1917, p. 1.
43. *New York Times*, April 28, 1915, p. 12.
44. *Ibid.*, May 10, 1916, p. 24.
45. *Ibid.*, May 18, 1915, p. 22, and May 25, 1915, p. 7.
46. Leonard W. DeGast to the author, in a personal interview, August 19, 1951.
47. *New York World*, June 18, 1917, p. 16.
48. *New York Times*, June 17, 1917, Sec. I, p. 8.
49. *Chicago Tribune*, May 20, 1918, p. 1.
50. I have interpolated figures for six of the sixty-five campaigns for which I have not been able to obtain figures; hence this chart must be considered only a rough estimate.
51. Sunday's income from other sources might be conservatively estimated at $5,000 a year.

52. Rodeheaver, *op. cit.*, pp. 117–18.

53. Quoted in Frankenberg, *The Spectacular Career of Rev. Billy Sunday, the Famous Baseball Evangelist*, p. 213.

CHAPTER 4

"GOD'S MOUTHPIECE"

1. Since Sunday never edited for publication an authorized collection of the one hundred and fifty or so sermons which he repeated with only minor variations throughout his career, the quotations of his views used in this chapter were in the main taken from among the following sources: *Life and Labors of Rev. William A. (Billy) Sunday, with Selected Sermons* (Decatur, Ill.: Herman, Poole Co., 1908 [hereinafter referred to as "Sunday, *Sermons* (Poole ed.)"]); W. T. Ellis, *Billy Sunday: The Man and His Message* (Philadelphia, 1936); Elijah Brown, *The Real Billy Sunday* (New York, 1914); *New York Times*, January 1, 1915– June 20, 1917; *Boston Herald*, November 11, 1916–January 25, 1916. Occasionally quotations were taken from other newspapers as noted and from manuscripts and copyrighted, but unpublished, sermons among the Sunday papers at Winona Lake, Indiana. The reader interested in more detailed annotation is referred to the author's doctoral thesis, "Professional Evangelism: The Social Significance of Religious Revivals since 1865" (Harvard University, 1953), chap. vii.

2. Charles G. Finney, *Lectures on Systematic Theology*, ed. J. H. Fairchild (Oberlin, Ohio, 1878), pp. 317–18.

3. Quoted in A. L. Drummond, *The Story of American Protestantism* (Edinburgh, 1949), p. 345.

4. Quoted in E. J. Goodspeed, *A Full History of the Wonderful Career of Moody and Sankey in Great Britain and America* (New York, 1908), p. 234.

5. D. L. Moody, *Moody: His Words, Work, and Workers*, ed. W. H. Daniel (New York, 1877), pp. 474, 476.

6. *Boston Herald*, November 14, 1916, p. 1.

7. *New York Times*, April 5, 1915, p. 4.

8. Taken from Sunday's copyrighted sermon "Mighty Man Who Cannot Save" (1917), which is among the Sunday papers at Winona Lake, Indiana.

9. *Boston Herald*, December 14, 1916, p. 5.

10. *Boston Advertiser*, February 9, 1877, p. 4.

11. *Boston Herald*, January 23, 1917, p. 4.

12. Ellis, *op. cit.*, p. 151.

13. Sunday, *Sermons* (Poole ed.), p. 324.

14. *Boston Herald*, December 15, 1916, p. 14.

15. Quoted in the *Truth Seeker* (New York), April 15, 1916, p. 246.

16. *Boston Herald*, November 13, 1916, p. 5.

17. From Sunday's copyrighted sermon "Thou Shalt Be Missed" (1917), which is among the Sunday papers at Winona Lake, Indiana.

18. *Washington Evening Post*, January 12, 1918, p. 2.

19. *Boston Herald,* January 17, 1917, p. 9.
20. D. L. Moody, *"To All People"* (New York, 1877), pp. 490–94.
21. Cf. *Boston Herald,* December 3, 1916, p. 4, and O. S. Marden, *Architects of Fate* (Boston, 1895), p. 411.
22. Ellis, *op. cit.,* p. 362.
23. *Boston Herald,* November 23, 1916, p. 6.
24. *Ibid.,* December 1, 1916, p. 12.
25. *Ibid.,* December 14, 1916, p. 5.
26. *Ibid.,* December 9, 1916, p. 3.
27. Finney, *op. cit.,* p. 312.
28. *Rocky Mountain News,* September 7, 1914, p. 1.
29. *Boston Herald,* December 3, 1916, p. 4.
30. *Ibid.,* December 9, 1916, p. 3.
31. *Ibid.,* Janaury 12, 1917, p. 5. (Italics mine.)
32. *Ibid.,* November 20, 1916, p. 5.
33. *Ibid.,* November 25, 1916, p. 2; *New York Times,* January 18, 1917, p. 6; *The Pilot* (Boston), November 11, 1916, p. 5, and January 23, 1917, p. 4.
34. *New York Times,* April 11, 1915, Sec. II, p. 6.
35. See *Liberal Christian* (New York), January 22, 1876, p. 3, and April 1, 1876, p. 4.
36. *Boston Herald,* November 16, 1916, p. 4.
37. See F. M. Davenport, "The National Value of Billy Sunday," *Outlook,* CX (June 9, 1915), 311–15.
38. See *Boston Herald,* January 5, 1917, p. 4, and January 12, 1917, p. 5.

CHAPTER 5

"THE CALLIOPE OF ZION"

1. *Ottumwa Daily Courier* (Ottumwa, Iowa), November 11, 1908, p. 1.
2. Quoted in the *Truth Seeker* (New York), May 20, 1916, p. 326.
3. *Ibid.,* April 15, 1916, p. 246.
4. *Boston Herald,* November 19, 1916, Editorial section, p. 1.
5. *Illinois State Register,* March 4, 1909, p. 2.
6. Elijah Brown, *The Real Billy Sunday* (New York, 1914), p. 218.
7. *Boston Daily Advertiser,* February 3, 1877, p. 4.
8. It does not seem necessary to annotate this and other quotations from newspaper reports of Sunday's meetings unless they are of a particularly controversial sort; almost every account of his meetings contains remarks similar to those quoted here. (For a generalized statement of sources used in this chapter see n. 1, chap. 4.)
9. *Boston Herald,* January 4, 1917, p. 9.
10. Brown, *op. cit.,* p. 215.
11. Quoted in "Dramatizing Billy Sunday," *Literary Digest,* LI (October 2, 1915), 713.
12. *Rocky Mountain News,* September 6, 1914, p. 4.

13. From the copyrighted sermon "Repentance" (1917) among the Sunday papers at Winona Lake, Indiana.

14. *Boston Herald,* January 7, 1917, p. 4.

15. Two rough drafts of this letter addressed to a Mr. Fenley and written in June, 1915, are among the Sunday papers at Winona Lake, Indiana.

16. See *New York Times,* January 31, 1915, Sec. II, p. 11. The notes for this address are among the Sunday papers at Winona Lake, Indiana. There is no indication in them that the address was taken from Ingersoll.

17. Cf. W. T. Ellis, *Billy Sunday: The Man and His Message* (Philadelphia, 1936), pp. 128, 245, 246, with T. DeWitt Talmage, *Trumpet Peals* (New York, 1890), p. 462; S. P. Jones, *The Popular Lectures of Sam Jones* (New York, 1909), p. 35; and G. R. Stuart, "The Christian Home," quoted in W. L. Clark, *Billy Sunday Unmasked* (Milan, Ill., 1929), pp. 20 ff. Clark's work is a 47-page exposé of Sunday's literary borrowings.

18. Annotation for all the following comparisons of Sunday's work with that of other writers may be found in the author's typewritten doctoral dissertation, "Professional Evangelism: The Social Significance of Religious Revivals since 1865" (Harvard University, 1953), chap. viii.

19. See Ellis, *op. cit.,* p. 446.

20. A more detailed discussion of the careers of Williams and Jones is contained in the author's doctoral thesis, *op. cit.,* p. 469 ff.

21. See W. R. Moody, *D. L. Moody* (New York, 1930), p. 469. The allusion is indefinite, but circumstantial evidence supports the assertion here.

22. Most of the quotations from Jones which follow are taken from Jones, *op. cit.; Sam Jones' Sermons, with Biography by Theodore Smith* (Philadelphia, 1886); and *Sam Jones' Own Book, with Autobiography* (Cincinnati, 1887).

23. Personal interview with the author, October, 1950.

24. Quoted in the *Truth Seeker,* April 17, 1915, p. 248.

25. For this and other examples of Sunday's prayers see Ellis, *op. cit.,* pp. 274 ff.

26. Quoted in the *Truth Seeker,* March 16, 1907, p. 169.

27. *Ibid.,* April 24, 1915, p. 261. For the background of the squabble over Sunday's invitation to Princeton by the faculty of the Princeton seminary see Ned B. Stonehouse, *J. Gresham Machen: A Biographical Memoir* (Grand Rapids, Mich., 1954), pp. 222–28.

28. *Old Penn* (magazine published by the University of Pennsylvania), April 11, 1914, p. 839.

29. This sermon is printed in Ellis, *op. cit.,* pp. 86 ff.

30. *Boston Herald,* December 11, 1916, p. 12.

31. This sermon is printed in Brown, *op. cit.,* pp. 237 ff.

32. *Boston Herald,* November 29, 1916, p. 1.

CHAPTER 6

"THE HALFWAY HOUSE"

1. R. S. Baker, *The Spiritual Unrest* (New York, 1910), pp. 261–62.
2. See *Watchman-Examiner* (Baptist, Boston), May 16, 1907, p. 10.
3. See *Zion's Herald* (Methodist Episcopal, Boston), August 4, 1915, p. 969.
4. Charles Stelzle, *American Social and Religious Conditions* (New York, 1912) p. 192.
5. For more detailed annotation on the research methods underlying the statistical analysis in this chapter see the author's doctoral dissertation, "Professional Evangelism: The Social Significance of Religious Revivals since 1865" (Harvard University, 1953), chap. ix and Appendix III.
6. *Watchman-Examiner*, December 29, 1910, p. 9.
7. See *ibid.*, April 16, 1914, p. 492.
8. *New York World*, June 18, 1917, p. 16.
9. *Zion's Herald*, July 26, 1916, p. 942.
10. Lindsay Denison, "The Rev. Billy Sunday and His War on the Devil," *American Magazine*, LXIV (September, 1907), 454–55.
11. See F. W. Betts, *Billy Sunday: The Man and Method* (Boston, 1916), pp. 9–11.
12. For annotation of these statistics, which were obtained from local newspapers and periodicals, see the author's doctoral dissertation, *op. cit.*, pp. 550 ff.
13. I have not thought it necessary to annotate this and similar quotations by clergymen regarding the effects of Sunday's campaigns unless they are of a highly controversial nature. Such quotations are fully annotated in the author's doctoral dissertation, *op. cit.*, chap. ix.
14. *New York Times*, August 12, 1917, Sec. VI, p. 6.
15. Letter to the author, April 19, 1951. Used by permission.
16. The official statistics of the denominations involved are used throughout this chapter in references to membership in individual churches.
17. *Watchman-Examiner*, June 15, 1916, p. 777.
18. *Ibid.*, December 20, 1917, p. 1648, and "Abjuring the Sawdust Trail," *Literary Digest*, XCV (October 8, 1927), 32.
19. *Zion's Herald*, July 3, 1918, p. 846.
20. *Ibid.*, July 4, 1917, p. 853.
21. W. T. Ellis, *Billy Sunday: The Man and His Message* (Philadelphia, 1936), p. 201.
22. *New York Times*, April 2, 1917, p. 13.
23. *Zion's Herald*, July 26, 1916, p. 942.
24. *Watchman-Examiner*, January 3, 1918, p. 3.
25. *Ibid.*, May 14, 1914, p. 651.
26. *Ibid.*, January 21, 1915, p. 74.
27. *Ibid.*, April 10, 1913, p. 12.
28. Zahniser to the author, in a personal interview, September 7, 1951.
29. Mrs. Sunday, in a letter to the author, December 30, 1951.

30. *The Pilot* (Boston), June 23, 1917, p. 1.
31. Personal interview with the author, September 4, 1951.
32. This list is among the Sunday papers at Winona Lake, Indiana.

CHAPTER 7

"This Great Plumed Knight Clothed in the Armor of God"

1. *New York Times,* February 15, 1915, p. 1; April 8, 1915, p. 5.
2. *Ibid.,* January 9, 1915, p. 10, and Brand Whitlock, *Forty Years of It* (New York, 1916), p. 257.
3. *Boston Herald,* January 19, 1917, p. 1.
4. *Ibid.,* January 12, 1917, p. 5.
5. *Providence News* (Providence, R.I.), October 18, 1918, p. 10. For a typical tribute to Sunday by Bryan see the *Boston Herald,* November 26, 1916, p. 5.
6. Charles Stelzle, *A Son of the Bowery* (New York, 1926), p. 169.
7. H. H. Klein, *Rockefeller or God: Who Will Rule?* (New York, 1938), p. 46.
8. *Zion's Herald* (Methodist, Boston), February 17, 1915, p. 206.
9. J. F. Newton, *River of Years* (New York, 1946), pp. 99–100.
10. Whitlock, *op. cit.,* pp. 186 and 257.
11. *Watchman-Examiner* (Baptist, Boston), August 13, 1914, p. 1072.
12. Wanamaker to Sunday, July 1, 1915, in the Sunday papers at Winona Lake, Indiana.
13. *New York Times,* April 17, 1915, p. 7.
14. This and other references to John Reed in this chapter are based on his article "Back of Billy Sunday," *Metropolitan Magazine* (May, 1915), pp. 10 ff.
15. *Boston Herald,* November 14, 1916, p. 3.
16. The quotation of Helen Keller is taken from an unidentified Boston newspaper dated November 19, 1916, in a scrapbook among the Sunday papers at Winona Lake, Indiana. See I. S. Cobb, "Sunday as Cobb Saw Him," *Literary Digest,* LXIV (June 16, 1917), 1870 ff.
17. "Billy Sunday Assailed by Leaders of Three Denominations," *Current Opinion,* LXII (May, 1917), 341–42; *New York Times,* May 20, 1916, p. 10.
18. *Zion's Herald,* July 26, 1916, p. 942.
19. See Lightner Witmer, *The Nearing Case* (New York, 1915), *passim,* for details.
20. Babson stated in a letter to the author, May 23, 1951: "I never made the statement regarding the Philadelphia Transit Strike; in fact, never heard of it before."
21. *Philadelphia Public Ledger,* July 24, 1915, p. 11.
22. Quay referred specifically to Wanamaker. See H. A. Gibbons, *John Wanamaker* (New York, 1926), I, 336.
23. *Watchman-Examiner,* November 19, 1914, p. 1522.
24. Basic sources for the discussion that follows are *Rocky Mountain*

News (Denver, Colo.); George B. West, *Report on the Colorado Strike* (Washington, D.C., 1915); B. B. Beshoar, *Out of the Depths* (Denver, Colo., 1942); and *The Final Report and Testimony Submitted to Congress by the Commission on Industrial Relations Created by the Act of August 23, 1912*, esp. Vol. IX.

25. *Facts concerning the Struggle in Coloado for Industrial Freedom*, Ser. I (issued by the Coal Mine Managers [Denver, 1914]), pp. 40–41.

26. *Rocky Mountain News*, June 27, 1914, p. 2.

27. The Colorado Fuel and Iron Company had always had saloons in its company towns. Welborn and Bowers testified that their workers were easier to handle because of the saloons. Though Colorado went "dry" in 1914, these towns had saloons until 1916. See *Final Report . . . by the Commission on Industrial Relations . . .* , IX, 8914–16.

28. See George Creel, "Salvation Circus," *Harper's Weekly*, LX (June 19, 1915), 580–82; see also Carl Sandburg, *Collected Poems* (New York, 1950), p. 29.

29. Reed, *op. cit.*, p. 12.

30. Quoted in F. C. Iglehart, *King Alcohol Dethroned* (New York, 1917), p. 95.

31. See *The Testimony of John D. Rockefeller, Jr., before the U.S. Commission on Industrial Relations for Jan. 26, 1915* (p. 172 in the "Confidential Proof").

CHAPTER 8

JUST "PLAIN BILLY SUNDAY"

1. *Rocky Mountain News* (Denver), September 6, 1914, p. 4.

2. *New York Times*, April 29, 1915, p. 22.

3. W. L. Clark, *Billy Sunday Unmasked* (Milan, Ill., 1929), p. 41.

4. *New York Times*, April 9, 1917, p. 1.

5. *Ibid.*, February 19, 1918, p. 13.

6. W. T. Ellis, *Billy Sunday: The Man and His Message* (Philadelphia, 1936), p. 507.

7. Charles Stelzle, "The Evangelist in Present Day America," *Current History*, XXXV (November, 1931), 225.

8. G. C. Lord, *Evangelized America* (New York, 1928), p. 358.

9. Letter in Sunday papers (dated July 19, 1915) at Winona Lake, Indiana.

10. Letter in Sunday papers (dated June 1, 1915) at Winona Lake, Indiana.

11. R. E. Garrett, *William E. Biederwolf* (Winona Lake, Ind., 1948), p. 44.

12. *Truth Seeker* (New York), May 8, 1915, p. 295.

13. W. E. Biederwolf, *The Evangelistic Situation* (Chicago, 1917), p. 43.

14. *Zion's Herald* (Methodist, Boston), January 19, 1916, p. 74.

15. Among the Sunday papers at Winona Lake, Indiana.

16. A. E. Kernahan, *Christian Citizenship and Visitation Evangelism* (New York, 1929), p. 88.

17. "Professional Evangelists," *Literary Digest*, LXXII (March 4, 1922), 33.

18. For annotation of these incidents see the author's doctoral dissertation, "Professional Evangelism: The Social Significance of Religious Revivals since 1865" (Harvard University, 1953), pp. 713-14.

19. John Reed, "Back of Billy Sunday," *Metropolitan Magazine* (May, 1915), p. 12.

20. See Ira D. Sankey, *My Life and the Story of the Gospel Hymns* (Philadelphia, 1906), p. 88.

21. Letter to the author, July 14, 1952.

22. *Illinois State Register*, March 5, 1909, pp. 1, 3.

23. J. M. Mecklin, *The Ku Klux Klan* (New York, 1924), p. 100.

24. Letter to the author, July 14, 1952.

25. *Sioux City Journal*, October 19, 1921, p. 4.

26. W. J. Cash, *The Mind of the South* (New York, 1941), p. 340.

27. The quotations from Sunday's sermon notes and outlines are taken from the Sunday papers at Winona Lake, Indiana.

28. Sunday took no part in the Scopes trial to help his friend Bryan. See *New York Times*, July 4, 1925, p. 2.

29. *Boston Herald*, February 22, 1931, p. 1.

30. *New York Times*, June 23, 1920, p. 2.

31. *Ibid.*, August 26, 1928, p. 3.

32. *Ibid.*, May 15, 1922, p. 36.

33. See Liston Pope, *Millhands and Preachers* (New Haven: Yale University Press, 1942), *passim*.

34. Personal interview with the author, October 28, 1950.

35. *Boston Herald*, March 2, 1931, p. 1.

36. Evidence of Sunday's connection with these men includes the fact that in 1934 he took part in a series of Summer Tent Meetings in Detroit under the auspices of E. J. Rollings' Metropolitan Tabernacle; associated with him in this were Luke Rader, J. Frank Norris, and A. P. Gouthey. In 1930 the last three named and also Clinton H. Churchill took part as speakers in a convention for Gerald B. Winrod's Defenders Movement in the Oklahoma City Defenders Tabernacle. For further information concerning the fascistic implications of Winrod's movement and his supporters see John Roy Carlson, *Under Cover* (New York, 1943), pp. 166-72; *Friends of Democracy's Battle* (Vol. VII, No. 11 [June 1, 1949]), a newspaper edited by L. M. Birkhead in New York; Stanley High, "Star-spangled Fascists," *Saturday Evening Post*, May 27, 1939, pp. 70 ff.; and Ralph Lord Roy, *Apostles of Discord* (Boston, 1953), pp. 31, 112-13, 351 ff.

37. See *Des Moines Register*, February 12, 1933, p. 1, and *Moody Church News* (Chicago), December, 1935.

38. Ellis, *op. cit.*, p. 438.

NOTE ON THE SOURCES

Since this book is a combination of biography and social history, the sources called upon range over a wide area. The exigencies of publishing will not permit a complete bibliography, but, as in the case of the notes for each chapter, those who are interested in more detailed annotation are referred to the author's doctoral dissertation, "Professional Evangelism: The Social Significance of Religious Revivalism since 1865" (Harvard University, 1953), in the archives of the Harvard College Library, which contains a full bibliography of both primary and secondary sources.

PERSONAL PAPERS

The principal source of information about Billy Sunday is the large, but uncatalogued, collection of sermon notes, letters, and other personal papers at the home of his widow, Mrs. Helen A. Sunday, at Winona Lake, Indiana. The manuscript sermons and sermon notes are of particular interest; they contain interlinear changes written in by Sunday which clearly disclose the lines of his thought and its development over the years. Sermon material from 1907 until 1935 permits analysis for the major portion of his career. No family correspondence was made available, although there is much on hand. Business correspondence reveals some aspects of the planning and aftereffects of the campaigns; but, since most of these details were left in the hands of the advance agent, business manager, and local committees, there are only occasional insights, which supplement the facts revealed in local newspapers and periodicals. Official reports of the expenses and organizational details of several campaigns are among the papers and provide valuable background. There are also some data on the Billy Sunday businessmen's and businesswomen's clubs. More than a dozen large albums of clippings from newspapers all over the country are somewhat marred for scholarly use by the omission of the names of the newspapers and often of the dates of the articles. Collections of photographs, gifts, and other souvenirs are of minor interest.

The files of the Moodyana Room at the Moody Bible Institute in Chicago contain a small number of letters written by or to D. L. Moody and a larger collection of letters to and from Reuben A. Torrey which throw some light on the institute's relation to professional evangelism and include references to Billy Sunday and other evangelists who were Torrey's contemporaries. The Moodyana Room also has some controversial pamphlets and tracts dealing with evangelism which are useful and not to be found elsewhere. A few bound periodicals relating to late-nineteenth-century evangelical activities and a small library of books about revivalism are kept in this collection, which is principally concerned with the founding and early years of the institute.

John Wanamaker's correspondence has apparently been destroyed, but

311

his biographer, Herbert A. Gibbons, made copies of a good many of his letters which are kept on file in a small room in the Wanamaker store in Philadelphia. Wanamaker played a large part in the Philadelphia revivals of Moody, Chapman, and Billy Sunday. A number of letters to and from him regarding revivals by these men are in this file.

PERSONAL INTERVIEWS

Since many persons who worked with Sunday and who took part in his campaigns (or opposed them) are still living, attempts were made to reach as many of these in person as possible, and others were contacted by mail. With due allowance for failures in memory (frequently correctible by reference to contemporary reports or by interviews with others), these were of inestimable help in forming a better understanding of the complicated inner workings of Sunday's revivalism, especially in regard to the conflicts between the local church workers and the Sunday party. They were also helpful in gaining an insight into the personalities of Sunday and his co-workers and in evaluating the more subtle effects of these campaigns upon individual churches. Of particular importance were the revelations regarding the motives behind co-operation or opposition on the part of those caught up in the fervor which was centered in Sunday. The following persons, either in interviews or by letter, provided particularly helpful information: Bentley D. Ackley, Roger W. Babson, William R. Barbour, the Rev. John E. Briggs, Harry C. Clarke, George Creel, David W. Darden, Leonard W. DeGast, Vincent H. Gaddis, Dr. Winifred Garrison, C. E. Gremmels, the Rev. Jasper A. Huffman, Henry M. Klein, Howard T. Knapp, Mrs. Theodore Madru, Dr. J. Palmer Muntz, Scott Nearing, N. C. Nelson, Dr. George Parkinson, John F. Reddick, Homer A. Rodeheaver, Harry G. Saulnier, Mrs. Albert J. Saunders, the Rev. Theodore F. Savage, George M. Sunday, Mrs. Helen A. Sunday, Robert Young, and Dr. Charles R. Zahniser.

NEWSPAPERS, PERIODICALS, AND CONTROVERSIAL TRACTS

The most copious sources of information for a book such as this are the files of contemporary newspapers and periodicals. From his earliest campaigns Billy Sunday was a newsworthy item in local newspapers wherever his campaigns were staged. After 1905, when he reached larger cities which had several daily newspapers competing for public attention, the coverage of his campaigns was so detailed in many cases as to include complete verbatim reports of his sermons. The revivals of 1912–18 received the most ample reports, for by then Sunday's actions were considered of importance nationally. It is in these years that nationally circulated periodicals provided the most colorful feature stories illuminating every aspect of his technique and personal habits, often reported by the most illustrious journalists of the day, including H. L. Mencken, George Creel, John Reed, Irvin S. Cobb, Lyman Abbott, Heywood Broun, Bruce Barton, Francis Hackett, and Arthur Brisbane. Much less material is available after 1920, but Sunday never sank into complete obscurity, and at his death numerous obituaries appeared in newspapers and journals throughout the country. (A large scrapbook of these obituaries is at the Sunday home in Winona Lake, Indiana.)

Religious periodicals of every denomination contain many articles on Sunday from 1908 to 1920; these are particularly useful for tracing the changing attitudes in various denominations toward him and toward mass evangelism. In this regard, those religious journals with the longest consecutive span and the widest circulation seemed most important—e.g., the *Watchman-Examiner* (Baptist), the *Christian Advocate* (Methodist), *Zion's Herald* (Methodist), the *Congregationalist*, the *Presbyterian*, the *Churchman* (Episcopalian), and the *Pilot* (Roman Catholic). The *American Issue* provided Anti-Saloon League views of Sunday; the *Truth Seeker* and the *Melting Pot*, the views of "freethinkers"; and the *Crisis*, the views of certain Negro leaders. Student reactions to Sunday's campus visits were obtained from undergraduate publications at several universities. Useful comparisons between the reception given to Moody, Chapman, Torrey, and other evangelists who preceded Sunday can also be made by turning to earlier issues of the religious and secular journals. The Iowa State Historical Library in Des Moines has a very complete collection of local Iowa newspapers for the years 1895–1908.

Controversial tracts concerning various aspects of Billy Sunday's revivals, from their theology and their psychology to their financial aspects and their influence on Prohibition, are available but are seldom reliable. Ample space was given in regular journals to critical accounts of his work, and those who peddled tracts outside the tabernacles were usually concerned primarily with making a quick profit by peddling highly sensational "exposés" to the crowds. Harvard's Widener Library, the New York Public Library, the Library of Congress, and the library of the Moody Bible Institute contain some of the more important of these tracts.

OFFICIAL RELIGIOUS STATISTICS

Anyone who has worked with the church statistics compiled in the United States censuses of religious bodies for the years 1890, 1906, 1916, 1926, and 1936 recognizes their limitations for any detailed purposes, but they are, nevertheless, useful for attaining a general picture of national church growth. More useful in measuring the effects of Sunday's revivals are the official annual reports of the various major denominations. As indicated in the text of this book, the only feasible system for measuring Sunday's influence on church growth is by individual churches on a year-by-year basis, provided that the details of the local situation also are carefully scrutinized. The Congregational, Baptist, Presbyterian, and Methodist Episcopal denominations have kept fairly complete statistics of their church membership during the period covered by this book, and they were duly consulted.

SERMONS, AUTOBIOGRAPHIES, PUBLISHED LETTERS, AND HYMNBOOKS

Only one collection of Billy Sunday's sermons was ever published, and this was the pirated edition edited by the Herman, Poole Co. of Decatur, Illinois, in 1908—*The Life and Labors of Rev. William A. (Billy) Sun-*

day, the Great Modern Evangelist, with Selected Sermons. It contains a brief five-page biography of Sunday, which is highly inaccurate, and 370 pages of sermons, extracted from a Decatur newspaper, which are full of typographical errors. Sunday disowned the book and later bought and destroyed its plates. About a dozen other sermons were published separately under Sunday's direction and were sold as tracts at the tabernacles during each campaign. The New York Public Library has the largest collection of these. Sunday's first authorized biography in 1914, by Elijah Brown, contains three complete sermons. His second authorized biography, by W. T. Ellis, also first published in 1914, consists largely of sermon extracts topically arranged (except for the "Booze" sermon, which is printed in full) and is of little use in trying to obtain any coherent view of Sunday's preaching technique. Sunday had at one time over 125 sermons in his repertoire, about 40 of which were apparently copyrighted. He hired shorthand reporters to take down his sermons verbatim on several occasions in the years 1914–17 and had these printed on newsprint in large quantities; in later campaigns he was able thus to give newsmen advance copies day by day. Many of these advance copies are still among the Sunday papers at Winona Lake, Indiana, but they have never been published. Sunday published under his name a collection of excerpts from his sermons entitled *Great Love Stories of the Bible* in 1917, but he evidently hired someone to add to them and to rewrite them; they are in no sense complete sermons. There are three collections of Sunday's epigrams: *Burning Truths from Billy's Bat* (Philadelphia, 1914), *Billy Sunday Speaks* (Grand Rapids, Mich., 1937), and *Wonderful* (Winona Lake, Ind., n.d.).

Sunday's "Autobiography," written originally in instalments for the *Ladies' Home Journal* in 1932–33, was reprinted in the third edition of the Ellis biography (Philadelphia, 1936). It contains about 65 pages, mostly reminiscences of the years before he became an evangelist.

A large list of the published sermons of other evangelists could be made, but again the significant volumes are mentioned in the chapter notes. They are valuable in tracing the change in tone which came into evangelistic preaching after the Civil War, a change which began with Samuel P. Jones and Milan B. Williams in the 1880's and reached its climax in cheap imitations of Billy Sunday. Even without examining the sermons of minor figures, it is possible to see a distinct trend toward the vernacular style and toward a highly simplified theology in the sermon collections from Finney to Moody to Talmage to Chapman to Sunday.

Autobiographies and published collections of letters are useful less for their direct references to Billy Sunday (which are surprisingly few) than for the light they throw upon contemporary opinions of progressivism, Prohibition, Fundamentalism, and World War I. By correlating these with Sunday's sermons, it is possible to see how closely Sunday embodied the spirit of his age. The slight mention of him as a moving force in contemporary life significantly indicates his lack of any leadership in the predominant movements of the times.

The hymns used in the Billy Sunday campaigns are readily available in editions published by the Rodeheaver Company at the time. The Rodeheaver Company is still in business at Winona Lake, Indiana. In addition, recordings of the hymns, many of them made by Rodeheaver at the height of his fame, are still to be found in secondhand-record stores.

RECORDINGS AND MOVING PICTURES OF BILLY SUNDAY

There are two records currently on the market which contain excerpts from Sunday's sermons (one made by Capitol Records and the other by Rare Records, Inc.). They are too brief to be of much value and were made at a late date in his career—probably after 1930. Mrs. Sunday has a private recording of a complete sermon made by her husband which is more useful, although it, too, was made after his voice had lost much of its power.

Pathé News Company made a sound movie of Sunday's sermon "Crooks, Corkscrews, and Bootleggers" in 1934, and excerpts from it were recently shown in a documentary film entitled "Fifty Years before Your Eyes" released by Warner Brothers. Even at this late date in his life Sunday's dynamic presentation was remarkable, and it is only with the image in mind of Sunday in action that the appeal of his sermons can be fully appreciated.

SECONDARY SOURCES

Sundays two authorized biographies, *The Real Billy Sunday*, by Elijah P. Brown (New York, 1914), and *Billy Sunday: The Man and His Message*, by William T. Ellis (Philadelphia, 1914), are the best secondary sources concerning his career but are of limited value partly because both were written at such an early date (and were virtually unrevised in later editions) and partly because they are obviously biased in their treatment. The two editions of Theodore T. Frankenberg's biography, *The Spectacular Career of Rev. Billy Sunday, the Famous Baseball Evangelist* (Columbus, Ohio, 1913), are more revealing, though they are by no means hostile and do not contain any material from Sunday's sermons; the first edition was only slightly revised when issued under a new title in 1917. A series of articles for the *Universalist Leader*, written by the Rev. Frederick W. Betts, who opposed Sunday's Syracuse revival in 1915, gives the best sustained view of a campaign by a contemporary observer, but it is somewhat one-sided. These articles were published in book form as *Billy Sunday: The Man and Method* (Boston, 1916). A recent biography by Melton Wright, *Giant for God* (Boyce, Va., 1951) contains little that is not in the authorized biographies and is evidently based on no independent research. Homer A. Rodeheaver's *Twenty Years with Billy Sunday* (Winona Lake, Ind., 1936) illuminates some aspects of Sunday's personality and technique but is more interesting for its author's views on the musical aspects of mass evangelism.

There is no adequate treatment of Sunday's life or career and no study of post–Civil War revivalism which presents the subject in anything like an intensive or scholarly fashion. Frank G. Beardsley and Grover C. Loud have presented superficial surveys of American revivalism, and William

Warren Sweet's book on this subject is concerned principally with pre-Civil War revivals. There are several biographies of D. L. Moody, George F. Pentecost, J. Wilbur Chapman, and a few other professional evangelists, but almost all of these were written by eulogistic delineators of both the men and their work. Various aspects of the religious scene in America since 1865 have been ably presented by A. I. Abell, C. H. Hopkins, and Henry F. May, but they do not touch upon revivalism directly. Several works have dealt with the Fundamentalist movement within the churches, but from a limited institutional point of view rather than from a broad historical one.

There is a vast amount of literature about evangelism and mass evangelistic techniques, written by various practitioners as well as by those who opposed the trend. These volumes, as well as those on homiletics, were drawn upon in large numbers to discover the prevailing attitudes of the clergy on this aspect of their calling. No list can be attempted here of the many secondary works on twentieth-century social, cultural, political, economic, and intellectual history and on the psychology and sociology of religion which form the basic background for such a work as this.

INDEX

aliens, and immigration, 146–48, 150, 235–36, 276–80, 296; on Franklin D. Roosevelt, 288–90; and Fundamentalism, 118, 121, 270–72, 280, 295; and Harding, 284; on Hitler, 288–91; on Japan, 289–90; on the Jews, 149–50, 291; and the Ku Klux Klan, 274–76, 285, 286; on the League of Nations and the World Court, 278, 284; for Leonard Wood for President, 284; on Mexico, xxiii; on Modernism, liberalism, and infidelity, 17, 124, 132, 137, 270, 276, 277, 281, 296; on moral reform, 37, 137–39, 145, 225–26; on Mussolini, 289–90; on the Negro, 272–74, 296; on oriental religions, 150, 296; on poverty, 134; and Prohibition, xx, 30–34, 38, 146–47, 149, 180–84, 231–35, 277, 284–85; on radicals, Socialists, Communists, IWW's, anarchists, Bolshevists, and "Reds," xxiv, 148, 258, 275–76, 277, 279, 281–84, 296; on railroad strike, 275; on Russia, xxvi, 281, 282, 288–89; on the Second Coming, 125–26, 137, 140, 283, 289, 296; on separation of church and state, 142, 148, 282, 296; on smoking, 133; on the Social Gospel, 137–39, 225–28; social views of, 118, 129–53, 225–28; and success myth, 135–36, 145, 148, 295–96, 297; theology of, 118–30, 295; on Unitarians, Universalists, Christian Scientists, Mormons, Dowieites, Russellites, spiritualists, and Blavatskyites, 150–51, 276, 296; on white slavery, 143–44; on World War I, xviii, xxi, xxii, xxvi, 255–60
Sunday, Mrs. William Ashley (Billy Sunday's wife; nee Helen A. Thompson), 46, 312; aids in revivals, 16, 45, 61, 76–78, 94, 271; on delegation system, 212; on freewill offering, 113, 114; and Gerald B. Winrod, 291; on Ku Klux Klan, 275; meets and marries Sunday, 6; on origin of term "sawdust trail," 97; on politics, 245; on racial segregation, 273; on Sunday's preaching, 161, 292; on unemployment, 252; on World War I, 256
Sunday, William Ashley, Jr., 178, 288
Sunday party, the; see Sunday, Wil-

liam Ashley (Billy) (career, methods, and results of), special assistants of
Swift, Franklin W., 261
Swift, Mrs. G. F., 115
Swift, Louis F., 39, 58, 115, 251

Tabernacle evangelism; see Revivalism
Tabernacles; see under Moody, Dwight L.; Sunday, William Ashley (Billy) (career, methods, and results of)
Taft, William H., 151
Talmage, Frank, 165
Talmage, T. DeWitt, 26, 39, 167, 168, 195
Tannenbaum, Frank, 236
Tapp, Sidney C., 269
Taylor, Charles F., 261
Taylor, George W., 261
Theiss, Lewis E., 234
Thompson, Helen A.; see Sunday, Mrs. William Ashley
Thurston, Charles, 217
Torrey, Reuben A., 18, 40–42, 43, 44, 79, 86, 104, 110, 169, 172, 193, 253
Trail-hitters and trail-hitting, 98–105, 194–222; see also under Sunday, William Ashley (Billy) (career, methods, and results of)
Tresca, Carlos, 236
Trotter, Mel, 115
Troubetzkoy, Princess, xxiv
Truett, George W., 261
Tuttle, Charles H., 285

United Mine Workers Union, 244

Van Dyke, Henry, 166
Van Valkenberg, E. A., 228, 241
Van Winkle, Joseph E., 12
Vance, Joseph, 204
Vanderbilt, Cornelius, 144
Vincent, John H., 49
Virginia Asher businesswomen's councils, 219
Visitation evangelism; see Revivalism

Walker, B. A., 58
Walker, W. M., 211
Walsh, Frank P., 250
Wanamaker, John, 39, 56, 58, 66, 79, 103, 145, 147, 210, 234, 241, 253, 297

[PRINTED IN U.S.A]

BV 3785
.58 M35

269
MCL

BILLY SUNDAY WAS HIS REAL NAME

McLoughlin, William G.

DATE DUE
